—◁ ▷—

THOMAS VARKER KEAM,
INDIAN TRADER

—◁ ▷—

—◄ ►—

THOMAS VARKER KEAM, INDIAN TRADER

—◄ ►—

By Laura Graves

Foreword by David M. Brugge

UNIVERSITY OF OKLAHOMA PRESS

NORMAN

FRONTISPIECE:

Thomas Varker Keam, 1842–1904. *Godfrey Sykes Collection,*
Courtesy of Arizona Historical Society, Tucson. AHS #22930.

Chapter ornament is from Thomas Keam's business stationery. The
image is based on a drawing by Jullian Scott, from the Washington
Matthews Collection, Wheelwright Museum of the American Indian,
Santa Fe, New Mexico. Photograph by Herbert Lotz. Courtesy the
Wheelwright Museum of the American Indian.

Graves, Laura, 1953–
    Thomas Varker Keam, Indian trader / by Laura Graves : fore-
word by David M. Brugge.
        p.   cm.
    Includes bibliographical references and index.
    ISBN 0-8061-3013-X (alk. paper)
    1. Keam, Thomas V.   2. Indian traders—Southwest, New—
Biography.   3. Navajo Indians—Government relations.   4. Hopi
Indians—Government relations.   I. Title.
E99.N3K324   1998
305.235'0973—dc21   97-40875
                                                         CIP

Text design by Cathy Carney Imboden.
Text is set in Perpetua.

1 2 3 4 5 6 7 8 9 10

—◄ ►—

Dedicated to
Liz King Black,
who for twenty-five years has been
my teacher, my mentor, and my friend

—◄ ►—

—◁ ▷—

CONTENTS

—◁ ▷—

ILLUSTRATIONS

PHOTOGRAPHS

—◄ ►—

ILLUSTRATIONS

MAPS

All maps are by Deborah Reade.

FOREWORD

By David M. Brugge

THE PUBLIC STEREOTYPES of Indian traders run to two extremes, that of a nobly romantic personage who befriended and defended the Indians and that of a scruffy rascal who cheated them with cheap goods, cheap whiskey, and firearms. After a lifetime of reading Indian history, I am not convinced that providing Indians with firearms was necessarily evil, despite that message in numerous Hollywood productions. Still, the extremes have colored people's perceptions not only of Indian traders, but of the Indians themselves.

Stereotypes, like much in peoples' beliefs, are based, of course, on some real situations, but often also on the generalities or predominant characteristics of a population, be it those of a gender, a race, an ethnic group, or a profession. Human beings are a diverse lot. Every person is a member of several identifiable groups that might be, and usually are, stereotyped in various ways. The social sciences deal largely with the generalities of these groups, while biographies bring us face to face with some of the individuals.

Biographies and autobiographies have become one of our avenues to a better understanding of ourselves. We are all ultimately one people, and the greatest appeal of any biographical account is that it provides a very human insight into the life of another, explicitly a real person rather than the product of a writer's imagination. These personalized narratives can help men better understand women and women understand men; the different races see each other in a more human perspective; and those of differing cultures, religions, and languages experience to some degree the lifeways and lives of those who might otherwise appear to be totally foreign.

There have been many accounts written of the lives of Indian traders and their families, some by traders themselves, some by wives and children, and inevitably, some by those for whom writing is an occupation, a part of their profession, or a serious recreation. The writings on or about traders among the Navajos and Hopis fill a long shelf in my library, and I know that my own holdings are not complete. Many are published books, some internal documents of our bureaucracies (the "gray literature" that has become a welcome source and an obstacle in many fields of study), some unpublished theses and dissertations, and some shorter pieces in popular magazines and professional journals.

The physical characteristics of this assortment form only one dimension by which it can be described. In terms of subject matter, it ranges from overall biographical coverage to detailed descriptions of trading posts and wide-ranging presentations of a less personal nature. A great deal of it was written by people for whom writing was a sideline, avocational in nature, or a means of supplementing income. Very little of the literature on the Navajo and Hopi traders can be considered truly professional and much that is does not deal so much with the lives of the traders as with other aspects of the business.

A notable feature of the trader literature is its uneven coverage. One family, the Wetherills, is well represented with at least five books plus treatment of their lives appearing in portions of several other works, while the Hubbells and Newcombs are prominent, but distinctly less so. Of the first generation of traders among the Navajos, and again among the Hopis, one of the most significant, Thomas V. Keam, has been included only in brief articles, in several chapters in Frank McNitt's *The Indian Traders* (1962), and in scattered pages in writings about the Hopis and Navajos.

Laura Graves has given us a book-length biography that finally does justice to Keam. It is a thoughtful and detailed account of the life of a complex man who combined a sense of right and wrong and of self-interest with an ability to relate to peoples of a different race and culture that was unusual for his time. Keam was clearly an independent thinker who could and did challenge authority when he found cause to do so. His influence on government policy, the methods of trade among both tribes, and scholarly studies in anthropology is shown to be earlier, and in some respects, greater, than that of all but a few traders of his generation. Yet even including obituaries, probably less than two hundred pages have been heretofore published on his life. This book more than doubles that page count, but more significantly, it greatly increases our depth of understanding of Keam. It presents new information, brings together old data in new contexts, corrects some errors in past writings, and like any good study, raises new questions.

I first saw the manuscript by Laura Graves in 1992 when it was sent to me for peer review. Although it was basically a Ph.D. dissertation at the time, I was struck by its importance and gave it more than the usual attention. Unavoidable delays have slowed its progress toward publication, but the author's persistence has resulted in a valuable contribution, one that can be placed alongside such classics as McNitt's (1962) general history of the Navajo trade and Adams's (1963) fine anthropological study of trading at Shonto. It will undoubtedly become a major source for future studies of trading and Navajo and Hopi history.

Keam knew, worked, disputed, or corresponded with a wide range of figures central to the histories of the two tribes, to the better understanding of them as peoples, and to their economic advancement. His influence on army officers and advocates of

Indian causes and his actions as a federal employee played a significant part in the history of these tribes, most often in ways deemed advantageous to the Indians, and in some respects these were to extend to Indian policy on a national scale. His role in scientific studies was largely that of a catalyst for those engaged more fully in anthropological research, including John G. Bourke, Stewart Culin, Frank Hamilton Cushing, Jesse Walter Fewkes, and Alexander M. Stephen. Stephen, in fact, was a longtime associate, employee, and colleague. Keam's own knowledge and collections were crucial to the success of much of the work accomplished by these men.

It was in trading that his contributions were probably most significant, for he was foremost a pioneer in this regard. It is unfortunate that contemporary documentation for his business activities is not nearly as complete as that for his accomplishments in other fields, for this leaves many interesting questions; but Laura Graves has found ways to address many of these matters.

Keam's more diversified business interests, including mining and grazing on Indian lands, are of a more dubious nature, for we know very little about them. In both cases, there is a strong presumption that he engaged in mining and ranching in cooperation with, or at least with the agreement of, local Navajos, but the nature of any such arrangement may never be known.

Of his personal life, we have even more limited knowledge. For me, one fascinating question that this study raises is that of his relationship with his two sons and their mother. Did he and Asdzáán Lipá unobtrusively remarry later in life? I can read that possibility into this account, but find no satisfying resolution.

Those who view human affairs only in political terms will probably always interpret Keam as a mere agent of colonialism and exploitation. However, those of us who like to look backward through the lens of the humanities will continue to try to perceive people who lived, loved, and competed within the context of their times, sometimes conforming to the standards of the societies in which their lives were enmeshed and sometimes rebelling against them, whether in quiet desperation or in overt confrontation. Keam seems to have experienced both and to have found a life worth living. And Laura Graves found it a life worth writing about.

ACKNOWLEDGMENTS

IN MY DREAM I am sitting in front of several packets of letters written by Thomas Keam to his family in England, describing his life in Arizona, the people he knows and works with, and the plans he has for his future. Underneath the packet is a pile of photographs, not formal portrait photographs but somewhat less formal scenes of Keam at the canyon. Below them are Keam's business records and a few bank statements. In reality, there are no personal letters, photographs, or business records. There is, as my friend wrote, no "dust-laden, yellowed foolscap on which he inscribed his most exclusive thoughts." I have often wondered what Thomas Keam would make of a book about his life. I can only claim that my work with Keam has been enjoyable and the people I have worked with along the way very gracious. Although I can hardly express my gratitude for their help over the years, it is a pleasure to acknowledge my debt to them.

While employed at the Museum of Northern Arizona, Flagstaff, I was lucky to work with Robert G. Breunig, Curator of the Museum; Donald E. Weaver, Jr., Museum Archaeologist; Edward B. (Ned) Danson, Director Emeritus; and Willie Coin, the museum's custodian and its Hopi consultant. The scholars shared with me their understanding of Hopi life and the complexity of the prehistory and history of the American Southwest. Willie Coin shared his world view. In my opinion, the most important work I did at the museum involved Willie Coin, whether we were working together in the collections or on the mesas together. He was a patient and generous teacher, and we enjoyed many good times. I think of him often, particularly when it rains.

While I was at the museum, I came to know two traders who remain an important part of my life and my work. Bill Malone, the trader at Hubbell's Trading Post, and Steve Getzwiller, an independent trader who lives near Benson, Arizona, allowed me to "hang around" and watch what they did. Their actions and conversations caused me to question my own and others' perceptions about traders. What I know about trading and the relationship between weavers and traders comes from them.

Philip Reed Rulon, Professor of History at Northern Arizona University, was a member of the museum's board of trustees when I first met him, and because of his interest in Indian traders, I entered the doctoral program in history at NAU. Dr. Rulon was joined by Drs. Andrew Wallace and William H. Lyon of the History Department and Leonard Ritt of the Political Science Department as my dissertation committee. They provided guidance and encouragement, and I am grateful to them for their help in developing and finalizing my dissertation, which is the foundation of this work.

At NAU I was also blessed by the guidance and friendship of another community of scholars: Professors Susan Deeds, George Lubick, and L. G. (George) Moses, who helped me broaden my understanding of the past and refine my ideas about Native American history and the role of traders in particular; and fellow graduate students G. Dudley Acker, William Haas Moore, and Joseph E. Shaffer III, who are not only great friends but also connections to a wonderful past. A glance at my notes attests to the value I place on Bill Moore's work on Navajo history. My work would be incomplete without George Moses's introduction to the study of federal Indian policy or his encouragement to adhere to the ideal of the story well told—the teacher opens the door; having entered, the student is forever changed.

I appreciate the help extended by the staff of the National Archives, the curatorial and archival staff at the National Museum of Natural History, Smithsonian Institution, Washington, D.C.; the Field Museum of Natural History in Chicago; the Brooklyn Museum; and the Peabody Museum in Salem, Massachusetts, for allowing me to have access to their accession and catalog records and correspondence as well as for permitting me to quote from those collections. Thanks, too, to the Arizona Historical Society, the Seaver Center for Western History Research at the Natural History Museum of Los Angeles County, Hubbell Trading Post National Historic Site, the Center for Southwest Research at the Library at the University of New Mexico, and the Smithsonian Institution for their assistance in finding Keam photographs and for permission to publish those photographs here. I am especially grateful to Les Douch, curator emeritus at the Royal Institution of Cornwall, for his responses to my queries about Thomas Keam's life in Truro.

David M. Brugge, former curator at Hubbell Trading Post National Historic Site and historian for the Southwest Region of the National Park Service, read the manuscript for the University of Oklahoma Press. His comments and suggestions improved my work beyond measure. I am honored that he agreed to write the foreword to my book. At the University of Oklahoma Press, John Drayton, Editor-in-Chief, and Sarah Nestor, Managing Editor, proved to be unusually patient and supportive. I am grateful that Keam came to print in Norman.

I would also like to take the opportunity to thank my colleagues at South Plains College, Levelland, Texas, especially my dean, Otto B. Schacht, and my department chair, Travis Spears, who had the courage to add me to his faculty. They have supported and encouraged the completion of this work, despite the rigors of my teaching full time and adjusting to life on the South Plains.

ACKNOWLEDGMENTS

My parents taught me that there was no task too great and that "no, I can't" was usually an unacceptable response. It would be fitting to dedicate this work to their memory. However, I reserve that honor for Liz King Black, to whom I owe all that I have become.

Because of these people, my life is full and meaningful, my work fun and exciting. They deserve the accolades, but I acknowledge as my own any errors of omission or commission that may be found herein.

LAURA GRAVES

Levelland, Texas

—◁ ▷—

THOMAS VARKER KEAM,
INDIAN TRADER

—◁ ▷—

INTRODUCTION

I FIRST ENCOUNTERED Thomas Keam in the spring of 1981 in the exhibit, "America's Great Lost Expedition: The Thomas Keam Collection of Hopi Pottery from the Second Hemenway Expedition, 1890–1894." Keam had amassed almost 3,000 Hopi pots, which he sold to Mary Hemenway in 1892. For almost eighty years, following her death in 1894, the collection languished in its original boxes in the basement of the Peabody Museum of Archaeology and Ethnology. Like the collection, Thomas Keam's life as an Indian trader in northeastern Arizona during the last quarter of the nineteenth century received little scholarly attention until it was described by Richard Van Valkenburg in "Tom Keam, Friend of the Moqui" in a 1946 article for *Desert Magazine*.[1] In 1961, Lynn Bailey published an article entitled "Thomas Varker Keam: Tusayan Trader."[2] These were short biographical sketches that assign dates to a handful of events in Keam's life. In 1962, Frank McNitt featured Thomas Keam as one of the central characters in his book *The Indian Traders*.[3] In this work Keam's life is more fully developed, and of the three biographers, McNitt alone examined the nature of Keam's profession, the Indian trade.

The Thomas Keam these scholars wrote about was portrayed in one-dimensional terms: he was a well-educated, refined English gentleman whose manners set him apart from other traders in the West and whose sense of duty demanded that he defend the weak, in this case the Hopis and Navajos, against the strong—the federal government. They were correct in their portrayal so far as they went. As a boy in Truro, Cornwall, England, Keam was well educated in public schools and graduated at age fifteen. Any education beyond that could only have been at the university level, but Keam did not avail himself of this opportunity. As an adult, his correspondence reveals him to be an intelligent, well-read, confident man who wrote in an elegant hand on well-designed business stationery. Like many Civil War veterans of his generation, Thomas Keam belonged to the Loyal Legion of the United States, a society of socially prominent and politically active Republicans, and to the Masonic Lodge in Santa Fé, New Mexico. His home in Keams Canyon was built in the preferred territorial architectural style of deep porches and high ceilings, and his profession was reflected in its interior decoration, as there were fine Hopi baskets on the walls and Navajo blankets on the floor. Yet the house was surrounded by orchards and formal English gardens, one of which was graced with a bubbling fountain. His home became an oasis where Old World and New World civilizations were blended and where travelers could find respite from the rude frontier surroundings.

Beyond these characterizations, Keam's biographers presented anecdotal evidence to suggest that Keam had connections to the anthropologists working in the American Southwest and irregular contacts with those in the Office of Indian Affairs. They attributed Keam's somewhat vaguely described efforts on behalf of the Hopis and Navajos to some unidentified humanitarian streak that eventually put him in opposition to the bureaucrats in the Office of Indian Affairs, who eventually succeeded in running him out of the country.

Had they examined Keam's activities more closely, they would have found evidence to support their tentative conclusion: Thomas Keam was a powerful and influential man. He was involved in the events surrounding the Navajos' readjustment and reacquisition of power following their return from Bosque Redondo. He was involved in most of the important political events at Hopi between 1880 and 1902, including the establishment of a school for the Hopis; the successful negotiations preventing the outbreak of hostilities when the Hopis declared war on the United States Army in 1891; and the exclusion of the Hopis from the allotment of land in severalty provided for in the Dawes Allotment Act of 1887. Thomas Keam also aided most of the first generation of American anthropologists working in the American Southwest after 1879, and he secured large collections of prehistoric and contemporary Indian crafts for the museums that the anthropologists represented. In this Thomas Keam not only identified a lucrative adjunct to the Indian trade business, but he also permanently and profoundly affected the nature of the production and design of Hopi pottery. Since none of Keam's biographers identified the extent of his power and prestige, they could neither identify the man's motivations nor conclude that Keam's power and prestige came to him because of his profession.

While Thomas Keam was developing his trading post business in northeastern Arizona, his occupation was already the subject of historical analysis. In his doctoral dissertation on the Indian trade in Wisconsin, Frederick Jackson Turner characterized the trader as "the farmers' pathfinder," the one who opened up the frontier to civilization.[4] Despite Turner's assertion, American cultural attitudes, western literature, and later the cinema almost universally characterized the Indian trader in terms that connote the absence of civilization. He was seen as an unshaven, unbathed, and unprincipled opportunist. The trader was, historian C. C. Rister noted, not the farmers' pathfinder, but "part of the jetsam of the turbulent sea of border life."[5] Along with his wagonloads of contraband, rot-gut whiskey, and guns, the trader drifted with his love for adventure, desire for profit, and freedom from arrest. From this perspective, the Indian trader was by his very presence an impediment to civilization.

Historians of the American Southwest came late to the study of the Indian trader, and they benefited from the earlier work of anthropologists and museum curators who were interested in the traders' influences on southwestern Indian crafts in general and Navajo weaving in particular. Although their focus was primarily native craft work, they were unfailing in their tribute to various traders, and consequently several traders' names became known beyond the craft and the region.[6] From these works, however, the image of the trader was of one who sat in his post waiting for a Navajo woman to bring in her beautifully woven rugs made to the trader's specifications. None of the studies asked how or why a trader could wield such influence, or why a weaver would respond to the trader's sense of design and construction.

The first historian to expand the definition of the trader on the Navajo Reservation was Robert Utley, who recognized that the trader had revolutionized the Navajos' material culture and claimed his influence was even broader because he performed many noncommercial services that "eased the Indian's transition to the new life." In this way the trader became a spokesman for the white world, and therefore his influence was considerable.[7] Frank McNitt's full-length study of Indian traders has become the standard history of the Indian trade on the Navajo Reservation. McNitt sought to measure the traders' worth and their contributions to the Indians, and concluded that such individuals helped to usher the Navajos into the modern world, a world where the trader was no longer necessary.[8] William Y. Adams, employed at Shonto Trading Post from 1954 to 1956, examined one trader and his effect on one community.[9]

Notwithstanding Utley, McNitt, and Adams, a large body of significant literature has been consistently overlooked by historians and anthropologists in their scholarly studies of Indian traders on the Hopi and Navajo Reservations. These works present a glimpse into the complexities of the trading business. The authors, traders themselves, define the trader's importance from their own experiences. All of them discuss the clients—Hopis, Navajos, and Americans—who visited the posts, and all of them in one way or another try to explain their experiences and their profession to the outside world. Their perspectives on their lives and professions are a valuable resource in the scholarship on the trading post, and their stories convey much of what Willow Roberts meant when she wrote that trading was more a way of life than a business. [10]

McNitt believed that traders were no more than shadowy figures "moving in a scene changing but unchanged and scarcely touched" by their own actions. [11] Thomas Keam's involvement in Indian affairs in northeastern Arizona during the last quarter of the nineteenth century calls this assertion into question. This Indian trader, for example, was a powerful and influential force in Hopi, Navajo, and American societies because of, not in spite of, his profession. As an Indian trader, Thomas Keam was a permanent resident among the Indians. He spoke their languages and he understood the nuances of their cultures. He was in a unique position to be the most knowledgeable white man in the region, because an Indian trader was required to know these things if his business was to succeed.

In 1880, Thomas Keam's canyon post was the only trading post between Ganado, forty-five miles to the east, the Atlantic and Pacific Railroad, fifty-five miles to the south, Tuba City, ninety miles to the west, and Lee's Ferry, over one-hundred miles to the northwest. This isolation benefited Keam in two ways: the lack of competition brought Indians to his post, and it meant that Thomas Keam was the only educated, reliable source of information in the region. His knowledge brought the anthropologists from the Bureau of American Ethnology and the Smithsonian Institution and bureaucrats from the Office of Indian Affairs to

Thomas Keam's trading post in Keams Canyon. The scientists needed Keam's access to Indian consultants who could be relied upon to impart their histories and lineages and who would sell their material manufactures to the anthropologists for their museums. The bureaucrats needed and wanted Keam's advice and assistance to implement their programs designed to civilize the Hopis. They needed his knowledge of the people as well as his practical knowledge: the location of roads, trails, springs, and running water. They also needed to know who among the Indians they could rely on to follow their programs, so that opposition could be either coopted or at least diminished.

On other reservations, the scientists and bureaucrats would have relied on agents of the Office of Indian Affairs who lived on the reservations to perform these duties. However, there were eight agents assigned to the Hopis between 1869 and 1882, and instead of living among the Hopis, they often chose to live at Fort Defiance, some seventy miles to the east. Between 1882 and 1897 there was no agent assigned to the Hopis. As the presence of agents from the Office of Indian Affairs on the Hopi and Navajo Reservations waxed and waned, Thomas Keam's residence among the Indians remained constant, and he filled the vacuum created by the agents' absence. At times, his presence among the Indians and his knowledge about them were all negative qualities in the eyes of the bureaucrats, as they believed traders kept the Indians uncivilized for their own pecuniary motives. At other times, the government exploited Keam's connections to the Indians because it needed his expertise and help in implementing programs. Despite the periodic changes in attitude, Thomas Keam stayed the course, battling those who opposed him and cultivating relationships with those who supported him.

His resolute defense of the Indians was fortified by a personal disdain for the Office of Indian Affairs born in the 1870s when he coveted an agent's position for himself. Behind Keam's numerous eye-witness reports and correspondence for the Indians that convey their desires to the Great Father in Washington, D.C., was his deep-seated animosity for those civil servants whose power rivaled his own and whose knowledge of the Indians and the area was impressive by its absence. Because of his "many years among them," Thomas Keam came to see himself as the Indians' agent, regardless of who carried the title. The Indians corroborated his belief by following his advice and proclaiming his representation of them to a number of commissioners of Indian affairs and presidents of the United States. Alongside the prideful and sometimes spiteful, Thomas Keam was a man whose commitment to honor and to the belief that a promise was to be fulfilled forced him to protect the Hopis and Navajos from the inconsistencies of the administration of the Office of Indian Affairs and the hegemonic attitudes of some of its agents.

Beyond Thomas Keam's involvement in Indian affairs and the development of nineteenth-century American anthropology lies his primary legacy: he pioneered the modern trading post business in northeastern Arizona by demonstrating that a successful trader did more than offer Indian customers the opportunity to buy canned tomatoes or yard goods. He proved that a successful trading post business was one that was diversified and that included creating a demand for native crafts by nonnative consumers. Before any others in northeastern Arizona, Thomas Keam demonstrated that anthropologists and museum personnel could be vital connections to a larger audience and that their penchant for collecting "museum quality" artifacts and contemporary craft work could be lucrative. He demonstrated for those who followed that the Indians' artifacts, and, indeed, Indian culture could be profitably brokered to a wider nonnative audience. He proved that the trader could influence Indian arts and crafts and that both trader and Indian artist could profit.

Heretofore, neither Thomas Keam's contributions to the Indian trade business nor his relations with the Hopis, Navajos, and bureaucrats in the Office of Indian Affairs have been accurately portrayed or evaluated. This study illustrates that Thomas Keam was a powerful and influential force in Indian affairs in north-eastern Arizona during the last quarter of the nineteenth century because of, not in spite of, his profession, the Indian trade.

—⊲ 1 ⊳—

IMMIGRANTS TO AN ANCIENT LAND

ACCORDING TO THE Hopis, when the humans emerged up into this world, they were divided into the different tribes we know today: Hopis, Navajos, Comanches, Utes, Supais, Apaches, and Bahanam, or whites. They knew that they could not all live in the same area, so they decided to split up. Mockingbird, who presided over these events, placed a pile of corn in front of all the people and described the varieties and the life-styles each ear represented. He let them choose their ears of corn. The Navajos chose first, taking a large yellow ear of corn. Mockingbird said that the yellow ear represented prosperity and enjoyment, but a short life. The Apaches decided not to take any corn, saying they preferred to live by the hunt. The Bahanam took wheat, saying that they preferred it to the corn because they could carry more grain more easily. After everyone had chosen, there was only one ear of corn left: the short blue corn. The Hopis took that one, knowing that it represented a hard life, but a peaceful life.

After everyone chose, Mockingbird made it so that each group spoke a different language and the tribes broke up, each to go its own way. When they first split up, they kept looking out for the others and kept track of the time, but as the days passed it got so that they forgot about each other, except in their memories and their stories. All the people, the Hopis, the Navajos, and the Bahanam, moved about the country, but finally they settled down.[1]

For the last 900 years, the southwestern edge of Black Mesa in northeastern Arizona has been the Hopis' home. Previously, they had traveled around the Southwest, their migrations bringing them in contact with people living in northern Mexico, the river valleys of the San Juan and Rio Grande, and the Great Basin. Just why these prehistoric people, called Hisotsinom by the Hopis, began coming together in the Hopi mesa country is not fully known. Perhaps climatic changes caused them to abandon the outlying areas in favor of a more sedentary way of life near the meager but reliable water sources on Black Mesa's southwestern edge. Perhaps warring neighbors forced them to gather together for protection. Perhaps, as the prophecies say, it was time for them to gather and begin living as Hopis.

Since then, the Hopis have developed a complex system for living successfully in this high desert region. Taking the corn offered by Mockingbird, or more likely acquiring it through trade with people living in Mexico, the Hopis added beans and squash to their diet. Sophisticated farming practices as well as hunting and gathering ensured successful adaptation.[2]

The Hopi country lies on the Colorado Plateau, an area characterized by mesas, canyons, plateaus, and valleys. The Hopis lived then, as they do now, on the southern edge of Black Mesa, at an elevation of 6,200 feet, 500 to 600 feet above the alluvial valley below. Precipitation, which falls either as rain in the summer or snow in the winter, averages about twelve inches a year. The average temperature is fifty-one degrees Fahrenheit.

Black Mesa forms a huge catchment basin. Rain falling on the northern portion of the mesa percolates through the porous sandstone layers until it meets an impervious layer of shale. Miles from its original source this water seeps out in springs that dot the southwestern edge of the mesa, as the mesa is lower in the south. The streams draining Black Mesa deposit silt and sand that eventually become sand dunes, which clog the drainages and washes and build up along the mesa edges, lessening runoff. Cot-

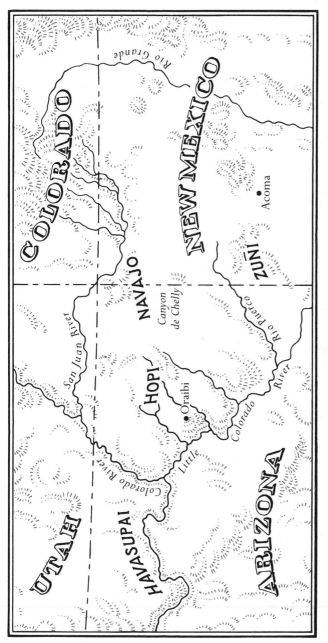

Four Corners area, showing Hopi, Navajo, Zuni, and Havasupai country, ca. 1750

tonwoods and willows grow in drainages where there is ground water. On the valley floor are sages, rabbit brush, yucca, grama grass, and in the more alkaline areas, salt bush, Mormon tea, snake weed, and sacaton grass. Along with several varieties of rats and mice, desert cottontail rabbits, black-tailed jackrabbits, rock and ground squirrels, and chipmunks are common now, and in earlier times they shared the area with deer and antelope. Among their many uses, these plants and animals supplemented the diet of the ancestral Hopis, had medicinal or ceremonial uses, and were sources of dyes for baskets and textiles or paint for pottery. [3]

The people lived in apartment-like, multistoried stone houses built in a gridlike pattern around open plazas in which daily activities and seasonal public religious ceremonies took place. Ladders protruding from rooftop entryways marked the locations of underground ceremonial chambers, or kivas, in each village. They continued to farm in the ancient methods learned through generations of experience and to influence the rain through their good behavior and prayers received by the kachinas. Oraibi, on the westernmost mesa, was a vital town by 1150 A.D.; its older neighbor, Shungopovi, was below the next mesa to the east. By the end of the fifteenth century, the number of Hopi towns had grown. Near Shungopovi was Mishongnovi, below the next mesa east were Keuchaptevela and Sikyatki, and Kawaiokuh and Awatovi were beyond on Antelope Mesa. By the middle of the sixteenth century, Awatovi, Keuchaptevela, Mishongnovi, Shungopovi, and Oraibi were relatively large towns. [4]

The cycle of life at Hopi revolved around the planting, nurturing, and harvesting of corn. Not only was corn the staple of the Hopi diet, but it symbolized the link between the the past, the present, and the future. Newborns are still protected by a perfect ear of white corn in their cribs, and blue cornmeal is fed to infants with the blessing to grow strong and live a long, happy life. Corn is used in all ceremonies, and abstract corn motifs are common designs on textiles, baskets, and pottery. To the Hopis, corn is life. [5]

A plentiful harvest signaled a time of prosperity. A mildly successful harvest ensured continued growth of the people. A meager harvest, as was most often the case according to memories, warned of difficult months to come, bringing death to the very young and the old or weak. A meager harvest caused by drought brought stepped-up raids from Navajos and Utes looking for food. The threats to a successful crop were many. Rainfall either in the wrong amounts or at the wrong time or the absence of rain could diminish the number of ears of corn harvested. Late frosts, high winds, insects, rodents, and cut worms could destroy young corn plants, and early frosts could kill plants just before the ears fully matured. Even the peoples' collective attitudes could influence the weather. Bad thoughts, especially during ceremonies, could chase the clouds away.

Village and family life had its seasonal activities, and with a few modifications, such as the adoption of sheep, goats, cows, peaches, and watermelons from the Spanish, things continued as they had for hundreds of years. In the intervening years, Hopi farmers perfected techniques that increased their chances of survival in a land that could be rather inhospitable. Survival meant that everyone worked. Men were responsible for the endless farming chores and caring for sheep, after they became common. Women were responsible for the home and tasks associated with preparing foods and raising children. Fetching water from the springs below the mesas and hauling it up to the houses in ceramic canteens was a never-ending task. Grinding corn into meal on stone metates was incessant. The tedium of everyone's daily chores was relieved by singing songs associated with specific chores and exchanging village gossip. Children led a relatively free life until they were old enough to begin learning their roles in preparation for adulthood. Girls helped their mothers with household chores and boys worked in the fields and herded sheep.[6]

Everyone participated in some way in ceremonial events. For

both boys and girls, initiation into the various religious societies and participation in ceremonies increased as they matured. Each of the ceremonies, with its complex casts of characters, ancient symbolism, and specific requirements, was an attempt to ensure that there was adequate moisture for the germination and maturation of crops. These prayers were also for the Hopi people. Their continued fertility assured the future of the group.

The prayers of the people, expressed in thought, dance, and song, were carried to the deities in the "other world" by *katsinam*. Usually appearing in groups, these benevolent visitors to the village were impersonated by initiated men who donned ceremonial garb unique to specific kachinas and danced in the village plazas. They brought with them food and gifts for the people, which were distributed during the dances. These colorful pageants were open to anyone, and Hopis would travel from one village to another, even one mesa to another, to attend.

After the katsinam returned to their homes following the summer solstice and after the harvest was over and stored for the winter, life took on a slower pace. The cold months were times for stories that contained moral lessons for everyday life and recounted clan histories. Wintertime was also a time for odd chores around the house and village. While sitting outside on one's roof in the thin winter sunlight sewing moccasins or weaving a basket, the mind recalled strains from kachina songs, remembered the past, and hoped for the future.

The Hopis did not live in the area alone. Their neighbors were the Navajos, whose history is as old and complex as that of the Hopis. (However, compared to the Hopis, the Navajos are newcomers to the Southwest.) Their migration to the Southwest was long and complicated. Based on linguistic evidence, the Navajos' ancestral homeland was located in the Lake Athabasca area of Canada. There, they hunted and fished and gathered wild plants. For some reason, perhaps environmental pressure, the Navajos left the area and their relatives about one thousand years ago.

This was not a capricious decision, even though they probably had no fixed destination in their minds. The people apparently left in organized groups or bands of related families. The culture of these immigrants is poorly known and their prehistoric homes are rarely encountered. Scanty evidence from the migration has prevented scholars from determining the exact route the Navajos took on their travels south, although the number of Plains Indian cultural traits incorporated into Navajo culture suggests that they traveled out onto the Great Plains east of the Rocky Mountains.[7]

The ancestral Navajos relied on hunting animals, often driving them over cliffs or into nets, and gathering wild plants. They used a sinew-backed bow with one-piece arrow shafts that were tipped with side-notched stone projectile points. They wore tailored skin clothes, which were dyed and decorated with colored porcupine quills. Because they were nomadic, their houses were easily moved. These houses were conical in shape and the wooden framework was probably covered with skins or brush. The people made twined, flat basket trays, knowing about weaving from their Northwest Coast relatives, but, as nomads, they made no pottery. Their religious leaders were shamans and curers. They lived in loosely organized bands of related families and reckoned their kinship through both the mother and the father.

There is little consensus among scholars on the date when the Navajos entered the American Southwest. The archaeological evidence in the area that can be definitely identified as Navajo is meager and prevents precise dates from being suggested. Some scientists argue that the Navajos were in the Southwest as early as 1000 A.D., while others say it was as late as 1450. The most compelling evidence indicates that they had moved into the San Juan and Chama River valleys of northern New Mexico and southwestern Colorado by 1300 A.D.[8]

The Navajos adopted a number of traits from their Pueblo neighbors. They began relying on farming as well as their traditional hunting and gathering strategies. Consequently, they were semisedentary. The people were organized into bands that were led by headmen and war chiefs. They traded with their Pueblo and Ute neighbors for goods they did not produce themselves. The Navajos had not been in the area too long before the Spanish arrived in 1540, searching for mineral wealth. These Europeans encountered many native peoples as they explored their northern frontier. The Spaniards often lacked precise knowledge and understanding of the various native groups they encountered, and they were often confused about them and their native names. However, they did not let their ignorance of their neighbors prevent them from accepting them as vassals of the Spanish king and converts of the Roman Catholic Church.

Don Pedro Tovar arrived at Awatovi on Antelope Mesa in 1540, and accepted what he believed to be the Hopis' pledges of allegiance to the Spanish crown and their professions of faith in the Catholic pope, and church, and the new god. As often happened when Europeans encountered native peoples, the name that was assigned to them was not always the name the people used for themselves. For the next four hundred years the Hópituh or Hópituh Shínumo (etymologically unclear, but loosely meaning "peaceful people") were referred to as Moqui, a term the Spanish may have heard from one of the Rio Grande pueblo groups or from the Zuni. Moqui, or any of the dozen or so variants of the word, is an opprobrious term meaning something like "dead people, stinking people, excrement people, or smallpox people." The Hopi were residents of the newly named district of Tusayan (possibly a Zuni term for the area).[9]

By 1600, the Spanish referred to the people they encountered west of the Rio Grande as Querechos, a generic term applied to a number of different nomadic groups. Later the Spanish referred to them as Apaches, a Spanish version of a Zuni name for non-Zuni people meaning "enemy." In 1626, Father Zaraté Salmeron called them Apaches de Nabaxu—a combination of the

Zuni term for enemy and a Tanoan Rio Grande place-name. This is the first documented use of the term Navajo. Soon, the Spanish developed a number of terms for these people based on geographic locations: Apaches de Nabajó lived north and west of the Pueblos and east of the Hopis; and Apaches de Quinía lived north and northeast of the Nabajó; Apaches de Gila lived south and west of the Rio Grande Pueblos. The Navajos did not call themselves by any of these names. They were Diné, meaning "the people, or the earth surface people."[10]

Perhaps because of their warring reputation or because they lived in small, isolated rancherias instead of towns like the Pueblo Indians, the Spanish were not as concerned with the Navajos as they were with the Pueblos. Early missions to the Navajos were quickly abandoned. For the Hopis, it was a different story. The first Franciscans arrived at Awatovi on the feast day of Saint Bernard of Clairvaux, August 20, 1629, and christened and dedicated the soon-to-be-built mission San Bernardo de Aguatubi (the Spanish variant of Awatovi). Eventually, missions were built and staffed by resident priests at Shungopovi (San Bartolomé de Xongopavi), and at Oraibi (San Miguel de Oraibi), and smaller, unstaffed *visitas* were built at Keuchaptevela and Mishongnovi.[11]

The actual successes of the Franciscans is unknown. Records of the number of converts are unclear and questionable. Archaeological evidence at Awatovi and Shungopovi indicates that the church-building programs were impressive. At Shungopovi there were Hopi houses built around the mission, indicating that the priests had enticed some Hopis to move away from their relatives in favor of the new location and the new way of life.[12]

However successful the Franciscans were initially, their programs came to an abrupt end when, in unison, the Pueblo people along the Rio Grande and at Acoma and Zuni in western New Mexico, along with the Hopis, rebelled against the Spanish priests and military and civilian population. For about ten days in the middle of August 1680, the entire region was laid to the siege as the clerical, military, and civilian population was either killed or forced to abandon the area in favor of sanctuary at El Paso del Norte. In all, about four hundred civilians were killed and twenty-one priests martyred, including Fathers José de Figueroa at Awatovi, José de Trujillo at Shungopovi, and José de Espeleta and Augustín de Santa María at Oraibi. The mission at Shungopovi was eventually dismantled. The huge, carved ponderosa pine and Douglas fir beams, obtained at great price from either the San Francisco Peaks ninety miles to the south or from further north on Black Mesa, were reused in houses at the village's new location atop the middle mesa. The mission at Oraibi met the same fate, and the beams were used as roof beams in at least one Hopi kiva. At Awatovi the church building was subdivided, interior walls were added, and Hopi families moved in, using the once consecrated church as a house. Keuchaptevela was abandoned and the people moved on top of the mesa for protection. This new village was named Walpi.[13]

Fearing Spanish reprisals, some Rio Grande Pueblo people abandoned their homes and sought refuge with their Hopi relatives. After Spain reconquered New Mexico in 1692, some Pueblo people found refuge with the Navajos and lived among them for a time. Their presence profoundly influenced the Navajos and the way they lived.

The Navajos modified their building styles and adopted painted pottery, coiled baskets, sandals, gourd dippers and canteens, and improvements in their weaving industry. The Navajos' religious practices took on some Pueblo traits, such as the reliance on masked dancers who impersonated the gods. Consequently, the Pueblos' kachinas became the Navajos' Ye'i. The Navajos adopted the use of *tablettas* and sandpainting at this time as well. Navajo rock art illustrates these changes. Certain Navajo clans reckon their origins to this period, reflecting the marriage of Pueblo women into Navajo clans. The Ma'ii deeshgiizhnii, or

Coyote Pass clan, for example, originated from Jemez Pueblo women marrying into Navajo families. Through the Pueblos living among them, a number of Spanish cultural traits were also incorporated into Navajo culture during this period. The Navajos learned to cultivate peaches and cotton, adopted improved horse gear, began to rely on sheep and goats, and learned improved animal husbandry techniques. [14]

Some Hopis eventually allowed Governor Don Diego de Vargas and his sixty-three soldiers back in Tusayan in 1692, and the area was reclaimed for the crown and the church. However, other Hopis continued to provide sanctuary to recalcitrant Pueblo people from the east. Priests returned to Hopi in the summer of 1700, when Father Garaycoechea from Zuni arrived at Awatovi. His arrival at Awatovi and his acceptance by the majority of the Awatovi people set off a series of complex events that culminated in the total destruction of the village and extermination or enslavement of all its people by Hopi warriors from Walpi and Oraibi.

The Pueblo Revolt was the only successful Native American rebellion against European powers. Even though the Spanish returned to the Southwest, the Hopis benefitted from their participation in the Pueblo Revolt and their extreme actions at Awatovi. Spain never regained control of the Hopis and the Christian god lost out to the kachinas. The Navajos benefitted as well from the Pueblo refugees who lived among them. The Navajos adopted many Pueblo traits and much knowledge, which they used to improve their lives in their new homeland.

During the 1700s, severe environmental problems strained the otherwise placid conditions between the Navajos and their Pueblo guests, and as a result, friction developed. Increased pressure from Utes to the north and their aggressive Shoshonean cousins, the Comanches, may also have contributed to the strained relations. Consequently, Navajo culture underwent a revitalization. Although many Pueblo people remained among the Navajos, certain distinctly Pueblo traits were abandoned. Painted pottery, for example, was abandoned in favor of the Navajos' older, undecorated pottery.

Ute attacks during the latter half of the eighteenth century forced the Navajos to move out of their old lands, or Dinetah, in northern New Mexico. Consequently, a general population shift occurred. The Navajos began moving south and west into the Chuska and Canyon de Chelly areas during 1753 and 1754. By the end of the eighteenth century, there were about 3,500 Navajos, according to the Spanish estimation, living in five geographical regions: San Matéo, Cebolleta, the Chuska Mountain area, Ojo del Oso, and Canyon de Chelly. They occupied a vast area from just west of the Rio Grande to Black Mesa on the west, and from above the San Juan River on the north to the Puerco River on the south, with the Canyon de Chelly region becoming the Navajos' heartland.[15]

Eighteenth-century Navajo cultural traits reflected the people's adaptability. In addition to hunting and gathering, they also maintained farm plots of corn and other vegetables and raised sheep, goats, and horses. They moved seasonally from their winter homes in the lower elevations to their homesteads in the higher elevations for summer grazing. They traded their woven blankets, made by the women and worn by men, women, and children, to the Utes to the north and to some Pueblo people.

From the time the Spanish arrived until the middle of the nineteenth century, raiding and trading were prominent components of the Navajos' economy. The Navajos stole sheep, goats, cows, and horses from their Indian and Mexican neighbors. The Indians and Mexicans stole from the Navajos. Everyone stole women and children. For the Navajos, Mexican livestock supplemented their developing herds and captives were a readily accepted medium of exchange throughout the Southwest. Trading and raiding were inseparable elements of an ancient system, and all southwestern native groups participated to some extent in this network. As a result, Mexican, Indian, and Mexican-Indian alliances, designed to recover stolen livestock and human captives, created an almost constant state of warfare in the area.[16]

For the Hopis, this was a particularly difficult time. Severe cyclic droughts, recurring smallpox epidemics, and the subsequent abandonment of the area by disillusioned people from the Rio Grande pueblos created an economically and emotionally depressed condition for the Hopis as the nineteenth century began. The Navajos' encroachment on Hopi lands and intensified demands on an already depressed environment, not to mention their stepped-up raids on Hopi villages for stored food and children, caused the Hopi to abandon their pride and ask the Spanish for protection. A Hopi delegation went to Santa Fé in 1818, but Spain was concerned with its own internal political problems and was in no position to take advantage of the Hopis' weakened condition. The Hopi delegation returned to the mesas.

For the next twenty-five years, the Mexican government carried on the same policy of military invasion and treaty-making with the Navajos, while the Hopis were left alone. Neither the Spanish nor the Mexican government was able to secure peace with the Navajos, and life in the Southwest continued as before. In 1848, after the Mexican War, the Hopis and Navajos and thousands of other native people became the responsibility of the United States. The American government took possession of the Southwest and boasted that it would do what Spain and Mexico had only promised. The Americans would bring peace to the area and raise the Indians to a civilized state. Because of their presumed peaceful disposition, the Hopis were left alone by the new government, while military expeditions were sent out to make peace with the Navajos. A few treaties were signed by the Navajos, but the Americans, like their Hispanic predecessors, failed to realize that there was no one man who would speak for all the Navajos.[17]

With the end of the Mexican War, the United States was

forced to amend its policies regarding Indians. What had once been seen as a workable policy in the eyes of the Americans, that of removing Indians and relocating them in the West beyond white occupation, was no longer practical as Americans crossed Indians' lands in their rush to California and Oregon. Now that the nation's destiny was secured between the Atlantic and Pacific Oceans, government officials were forced to develop a new policy for protecting the Indians from Americans and Americans from the Indians. The new policy, that of confining Indians to reservations, was believed to be a humanitarian alternative to extinction, and necessary for the Indians' protection and progress. As with most Indian policy designed in Washington, D.C., and implemented hundreds of miles away, the reservation policy was based more on idealism than reality, and implementation of policy was never as simple as those in Washington believed it would be.

On reservations, untainted by avaricious whites, the Indians would be educated in American cultural and industrial arts, Christianized, and prepared for citizenship. Their traditional economies would be replaced by farming, thus reducing the amount of land necessary to support the people. Each warrior, the Americans believed, would become a yeoman farmer. The humanitarians believed success was inevitable and imminent. Until that day, however, the reservation would be the Indians' home, where the government could implement its civilization programs and where it could regulate the numbers and types of Americans who had contact with the Indians.

The reservation policy was founded on the belief that the Indian tribes retained title to the lands they occupied and that the only legitimate means for extinguishing title was through treaty negotiations. This, the Americans believed, was the only legitimate and honorable vehicle available to them. The treaties defined the lands ceded to the government by the Indians and specified the amount the government would pay in annuities. These annual payments would come to the Indians in the form of goods distributed annually. With this alteration in policy came a radical administrative change. The administration of the Indians was moved from the War Department to the newly created Department of the Interior where, despite several attempts to move it back to the War Department, it remains to this day.[18]

For the Hopis and Navajos, these policy changes had little immediate effect. The Americans adopted the misnomer Moqui for the Hopi and the habit of referring to the mesas as First Mesa (the easternmost mesa), Second Mesa, and Third Mesa (the westernmost mesa), although the Hopi did not have such designations. On First Mesa the Hopis were living in two villages. Walpi, which was founded in 1692 from the old Keuchaptevela village, is on the southern end of the mesa. Its daughter village, Sichomovi, which was founded about 1750, is just to the north. The First Mesa village of Hano was not populated by Hopis, but by Tewa-speaking Pueblo people who were invited to relocate there after the Pueblo Revolt to strengthen the number of warriors in anticipation of renewed fighting with the Spanish and to protect the Hopis from Navajo and Ute raiders. They received farmlands in exchange for their protection. There are three villages on top of Second Mesa: Mishongnovi, Shipaulovi, and Shungopovi, each founded in 1692. On Third Mesa there was only one village, Oraibi. About forty miles west of Oraibi was the satellite village, Moencopi, which was built above a permanently flowing stream. The irrigated fields at Moencopi produced surplus crops to feed the Oraibi people.[19]

The Navajo population had increased over the years, and the lands they controlled expanded as well. When the Americans first came to the Southwest, they estimated there were about 7,000 Navajos living between the Rio Grande and the Colorado River. They were recognized as successful sheep herders who also had large herds of horses, but they were less well known for their abundant farms and gardens. They lived in small rancherias across this vast area and cultivated their reputation as fierce warriors and adroit traders.

Black Mesa and the surrounding plains to the east and south were the ancestral homelands of the Hopis and Navajos. Each had lived there for generations, and each group had learned to adapt to the land's peculiarities. Neither group was static—the age and viability of their lifeways was proof of their adaptability to change, for change was constant. Its causes, the environment or the movements of other native peoples into or out of the area, were usually predictable. However, the arrival of Americans into the area radically changed the Hopis' and Navajos' lives.

Although no one knew it at the time, one newcomer in particular, Thomas Varker Keam, would have a profound influence on relations among Hopis, Navajos, and Americans. The adaptation of Indians to Americans and Americans to Indians—for the changes were multidirectional—was difficult, but it was made possible by Thomas Keam. His profession, Indian trader, gave him a proximity and permanence among the Indians that was unique at the time. He became the insider in each group: he knew, understood, and oftentimes respected the Hopis and Navajos and their ways; likewise, the Americans. His knowledge of these complex groups of people and their respect of him allowed him to become a respected advisor. The practical demands of running a successful trading post required that Keam also use his influence to further his own ends, and at times he was successful in this endeavor. But at the time, Hopis, Navajos, and Americans were just becoming acquainted with one another, and Thomas Keam was a young man with many hard lessons to learn.

—◁ 2 ▷—

CAVALRYMAN

ON JANUARY 22, 1862, in the City by the Bay, Thomas Keam turned his back on the sea and what to that point had seemed his destiny. The son of a ship captain, Thomas was born and raised in the river port city of Truro in Cornwall, England. There he completed common school, which he left at age fifteen before joining the English merchant marines.[1] He arrived in San Francisco by way of Sydney and Newcastle, Australia.[2] On this day, however, Keam abandoned the sailor's life and joined a regiment in the California Volunteers of the Union Army.[3] The nineteen-year-old Cornishman intended to fight Southern rebels in a cause he could scarcely appreciate. Keam was mustered in to the California Volunteer Cavalry the same day he enlisted and sailed from the Presidio across the bay to Camp Merchant in Contra Costa County.

A few days before Keam joined up, the *Daily Alta California* carried an article praising the efforts of Colonel James Henry Carleton, commander of the California Volunteers, for his "indefatigable" efforts to prepare for the march to the battlefields in the East, and saying that the purpose of the column was "holding in perfect check the Indians of our eastern frontier, those of southern Utah and central and western New Mexico." Carleton claimed that the column's purpose was more than "the subjugation of Indians, or the guarding of our frontier against secessionists within or without the state." It was "in the opening of a mail route upon a line over which the overland mail can be transported with punctuality and expedition at any and all seasons of the year."[4] Keam's personal motivations for signing on are unknown, but like most of his companions, he probably had loftier motives than the rather pedestrian goal of a smoothly running, efficient mail route. What is certain is that Thomas Keam did not want to be a sailor any longer.

Thomas Keam had been born August 6, 1842, into a large, extended family that had lived in the Truro area for generations.[5] His father, Thomas Vercoe Keames, born November 30, 1812, was the oldest of six children born to Thomas Kemes and Elizabeth Pearce. Thomas Keam's mother, Grace Stephens, was born in Kenwyn, a parish in Truro, around 1813. Thomas Keam, who was christened Thomas James Keames, was the second child born to Thomas and Grace. His sister, Elizabeth, was born in 1840 and his younger brother, William, in 1848.[6]

There has been considerable confusion about the spelling of the family's surname, but the confusion reflects Cornish geographical preferences. In Cornwall, "between Kemes and Keam there is the usual confusion: in central Cornwall [Truro] the spelling is almost invariably KEAM. There is similar confusion between Varker and Varcoe (or Vercoe). In the western mining parishes of St Hilary and Breage . . . the name is VARKER; to the east in the "china-clay" parishes around St Austell the name is VARCOE."[7] By the middle of the nineteenth century, the family name in Truro was almost always "Keam," and that is the name that appears on the family's headstones. In Arizona Territory, where Thomas Keam spent most of his adult life, the confusion continued. Even though he spelled his surname without an *s,* Thomas Keam was almost always referred to as "Keams" or "Keames." The confusion is perpetuated by the name of the canyon where Thomas and his brother William lived. The name, Keams Canyon, is missing the apostrophe.

By 1851, the Keams were living near the West Bridge in Truro. Grace was listed in the census as a "sailor's wife." Thomas Keam Sr. was not listed in the census and was probably at sea. Elizabeth, age ten, Thomas, age eight, and William, age four, were described as "scholars." In the 1861 census the family had moved to 35 Francis Street in Truro. The elder Keam, away at sea, was again not enumerated, Grace was listed as a "master mariner's wife," Elizabeth was twenty years old, and William, age fourteen, was a "merchant's clerk." The younger Thomas Keam was also at sea, presumably realizing that his destiny was someplace else.[8]

By 1862 Thomas Keam had joined Company C of the First California Cavalry. He was the youngest soldier in the company, and the last one added to the company's ranks. He joined men whose ages ranged from nineteen to forty-two, although most of them were in their mid-thirties. Most listed as their residences various California counties noted for their mining industry. All were born in states other than California, and some were born in countries other than the United States. Along with Keam, there were three other men from England, four from Ireland, and one Scot; three men were from Germany and three from Prussia; there was one Frenchman, one Norwegian, and one Canadian. They were led by First Sergeant Christopher Woods from Maine and Sergeant Joseph Palmer from Germany.[9] As they became acquainted with each other and their new duties, they endured the hardships of a northern California winter. The winter and early spring of 1862 in California were unusually wet. "The whole country [was] flooded; hundreds of horses and cattle [were] mired down in the open plains and were lost. For weeks it was almost impossible to move a vehicle of any kind, and the movement of baggage trains was out of the question." As the men of the California Column learned how to fight Confederates, they lived in tents and undoubtedly cursed the mud.[10] Finally, on April 9, 1862, the tents at Camp Merchant were folded and Private Thomas Keam and Company C, First Cavalry California Volunteers, rode out.[11] They marched down the coast to Los Angeles and then headed east into the desert. For Keam, the sea was behind him and he rode into the anonymity of a private's life in the cavalry.

The troops were strung out across the desert: two thousand men, horses, and two hundred wagons drawn by six- and eight-mule teams, each carrying about three thousand pounds of equipment. They traveled after four or five o'clock in the afternoon and halted in the early morning, "enabling the men to sleep a part of the night." With each company traveling twenty-four hours apart, Carleton sent out advance guards to clean out and dig water wells for the men and to locate forage for the animals. "At some of the wells there was so little water that it was necessary to dip it out in a pint cup, thus consuming nearly a whole night in watering 100 animals."[12] The three hundred miles between Los Angeles and Fort Yuma were completed with little confusion, for there was no enemy closer than Tucson, Arizona. The column encountered a swollen Gila River, but nothing more broke the monotony of the journey.

When the entire column arrived in Tucson on May 20, 1862, six weeks after leaving southern California, they found it abandoned by the Confederates and almost everybody else. According to George Pettis of Company F, "the only living things found within the limits of the town were an unsuspected number of dogs and cats."[13] While in Tucson, the soldiers moved in supplies and food from Fort Yuma, rested, and made equipment repairs.[14] The wagons were in particular need of attention because "the dryness of the atmosphere and the intolerable heat had shrunk them to the point of falling apart."[15]

Waiting for the summer rains to arrive in southern Arizona, the men worked on their equipment and wondered about events of the war. Since the column had left California, there had been no word from the Rio Grande valley: No word of the Confederate invasion of New Mexico and their victory over the Union forces at the Battle of Valverde on February 16, 1862; no word of their having taken the capitol at Santa Fé; no word that the Union government had abandoned the area for Las Vegas, New Mexico. There was no news, either, that Colonel John Slough's forces from Fort Union and volunteers from Colorado had turned the Confederates out of New Mexico at the Battle of Glorieta between March 26 and 28, 1862.[16] So when Carleton gave the orders to begin the march to the Rio Grande and the companies left Tucson one by one between July 17 and 23, they left alert for renegade Confederates and Indians and with high hopes that they would have the "distinguished honor of striking a blow for the old Stars and Stripes."[17]

However, by the time Carleton and the California Volunteers arrived in New Mexico, the Confederate forces had abandoned the territory. Carleton garrisoned his men in the two southern New Mexico forts, Thorn and Craig, and the soldiers began to reestablish Union control of the area.[18] But peace was uncertain: no one knew just how far the Confederate forces had withdrawn, and rumors had them as close as Franklin, Texas. If not there, they were rumored to be just across the Rio Grande from Franklin in the Mexican town, El Paso del Norte. To determine the exact nature of the Confederate presence, Carleton ordered Captain Edmund Shirland and the 1st California Cavalry Company C, with Thomas Keam among the men, into the Trans–Pecos River area.[19]

The advance guard left Fort Craig in August and headed south along the Rio Grande into the dry rugged mountains and desert valleys of West Texas—mindful that the lack of water was just one of their enemies. For Company C, each mile they rode into West Texas was a mile over territory they did not know, and each mile put them further into enemy territory. If they did not meet Confederate resistance, then the possibility existed that they could confront Apache or Comanche raiding parties that

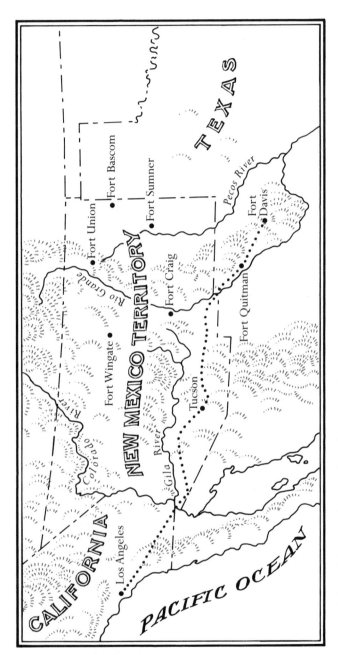

Route of the California Column and Civil War—era forts

traveled through West Texas south into Mexico in search of horses and slaves or back north to their homes. The Indians had the advantage over both the Union and Confederate soldiers. They had lived in the region for generations and knew how to live in the harsh desert environment. The soldiers, however, were confined, due to their lack of any accurate geographical knowledge or experience, to the Butterfield Overland Mail road.[20] Over this trail, coaches of the Overland Mail Company had transported mail and passengers since 1858. Along the road, which had run from Saint Louis to San Francisco during prewar times, were stage stations and military forts. The stations were now abandoned because of the war, and Company C would soon determine the status of the forts.

From Fort Craig, Company C headed out, mindful that they were the advance scouts for troops that would follow. As they rode down the Rio Grande toward their destination, Fort Davis, they passed by the town of Franklin, Texas, and Forts Bliss and Quitman, each of which would soon be reoccupied by other California Volunteers. From the river, the cavalrymen headed inland and arrived at the Overland Mail station at Eagle Springs, only to find the springs fouled by trash and carrion—proof that the Confederates had retreated further to the east.[21] Although there was water at Eagle Springs, there was not enough grass for the horses. After the men cleaned out the springs, they rode another five miles before making a dry camp for the night. The next morning they continued east toward the next mail station, Van Horn's Wells, twenty miles distant. The men encountered the same scenario of fouled water. Despite their efforts to clean up the springs, there was insufficient water for both men and horses. The situation concerned Captain Edmund Shirland, so he ordered most of the men to return to Eagle Springs. He and twenty men would continue east. Riding throughout the night, the smaller advance guard arrived at Dead Man's Hole, about thirty-five miles east of Van Horn's Wells. After watering the horses and men and resting for about four hours, the men were back in the saddle. They arrived at Barrel Springs about three o'clock the next afternoon and made camp.[22]

From El Paso the men and horses had covered just over two hundred miles in three days. They had determined that the Confederate forces had withdrawn from the region and also that Barrel Springs produced enough water to sustain a company of men. However, the situation at Fort Davis, some twenty miles to the east, was still undetermined.[23] Shirland dispatched a corporal, a private, and a Mexican guide on to the fort. After their clandestine mission was completed, the spies reported the fort unoccupied. With that good news, Shirland and the men rode into Fort Davis. They found that the Confederates had abandoned the fort but that it had been "garrisoned by the Confederate States troops since their first appearance in the country by at least a portion of one company."[24] Shirland reported that it appeared that the Confederates had also used the fort as a "rendezvous for sick soldiers" but that they, too, had left with the retreating soldiers—that is, except for one injured man whom they had left behind. He had been shot through the body by a bullet but died from arrow wounds to the head and arm. He was a grizzly reminder that only one of the California soldiers' enemies had abandoned the country. Shirland ordered the man's body buried, then they hoisted the Union flag above the fort.[25]

Although Company C had yet to encounter Confederate forces on the battlefield, what they had accomplished to this point was of the utmost strategic importance. Controlling the Trans-Pecos region of Texas, with its string of forts, stage stations, and the Butterfield Overland Mail road, meant that the Union controlled access to New Mexico, Arizona, and California. Their presence in the region would deter any Confederate attempts to reinvade the Southwest. Although Company C had yet to be tested on the battlefield, their courage had been strengthened as they had ridden through the region with fear of the unknown as their constant companion. The anticipation of meeting Confederates, Apaches, or Comanches must have been exacerbated by the very nature of the land itself. The men knew they would confront their enemy in one of two ways. They could be attacked while riding across the vast, waterless desert valleys with only creosote bushes to hide behind or by riding into an ambush at one of the springs. Either scenario—whether they were exposed in the desert or pinned down in the rugged mountains where the springs were located—benefited the attacker, not the defender. In this, both Confederate soldiers and Indian warriors held the advantage over the Union soldiers.

The men's fears were justified. After reclaiming Fort Davis, they withdrew west to a camp on the Rio Grande near Fort Quitman,[26] but not before they had fought a running battle with some Indians near Dead Man's Hole.[27] Shirland reported that they encountered a party of Indians on horseback, one of whom was carrying a white flag. Shirland said that he tried to talk with them but they seemed unwilling to do so. The captain surmised that the raiding party, which numbered about thirty men, was only trying to gain time until a much larger number of men, some on foot and many on horseback, could get closer and surround the California Volunteers. "Wishing to get rid of the footmen," Shirland said, "I made a running fight of it, expecting the mounted men to follow, which they did for a short distance; but finding it too hot for them, they returned."[28] Shirland reported that the California Volunteers killed four Indians and wounded about twenty. The Indians wounded two of Shirland's men, "one slightly and one painfully, by a pistol-ball in the shoulder."[29] Additionally, one horse was wounded.

Thomas Keam and his comrades spent the late summer of 1862 patrolling the Butterfield Overland Mail road through West Texas from their camp on the Rio Grande. They were recalled from their reconnaissance mission and stationed at Fort Craig on the west bank of the Rio Grande in southern New

Mexico. Throughout the fall, the men heard rumors about an imminent Confederate invasion. They were particularly concerned about the news, intentionally leaked by Confederate sympathizers in the El Paso del Norte area, that Colonel John R. Baylor of the Confederate States Army was in San Antonio, raising a force of six thousand volunteers to recapture New Mexico.[30] Carleton issued orders that all Southern sympathizers were to be rounded up and held at Fort Craig.[31] Although this particular invasion failed to materialize, the topic of imminent reinvasion was commonly discussed for the duration of the war.[32] However, the attention of the men in Company C was soon to be focused on another enemy.

On the September 18, 1862, Brigadier General James Henry Carleton became the commander of the Union Army in New Mexico.[33] Carleton was a deeply religious man with a stern countenance. He had neither interest in, nor compassion for, the native peoples of the Southwest. Carleton looked to a future after the war in which the American Southwest would be settled by American farmers, miners, and businessmen. But, Carleton believed, before progress could march across the American Southwest all impediments must be removed. The worst of the obstacles, in the eyes of many Americans, were the "wild" Indians: the Apaches and Navajos. These people did not live in settled communities, like the Pueblo Indians along the Rio Grande in northern New Mexico, so to make them change their habits and teach them "civilized" ways, Carleton ordered first the Apaches then the Navajos rounded up.[34] He directed his old friend and commander of a New Mexico volunteer regiment, Colonel Christopher Carson, saying,[35] "All Indian men of that tribe are to be killed whenever and wherever you can find them; the women and children will not be harmed, but you will take them prisoners and feed them at Fort Stanton until you receive other instructions about them."[36] Kit Carson's initial campaigns were successful, and by the end of the first week in November

1862 some one hundred Mescalero Apaches were camped at Fort Stanton.[37]

Meanwhile, Carleton was implementing the second phase of his long-term solution to the Southwest's "Indian problem." He ordered the establishment of a military post and Indian reservation on the Pecos River. Located a little more than one hundred miles southeast of Las Vegas in eastern New Mexico, the post was named in honor of Carleton's former commander in New Mexico, General Edwin V. Sumner. Fort Sumner was situated near a lone circular grove of cottonwood trees that gave the site its name, Bosque Redondo. Fort Sumner would protect the people of eastern New Mexico from raiding Kiowas and Comanches on the Llano Estacado and become the permanent home for the Mescaleros to the south. Unlike other camps and forts established during the Civil War to protect settlers and miners, Fort Sumner was designed to be the permanent home of the Southwest's Indians.

Carleton's plan, as it was implemented by Carson against the Mescalero Apaches, was so successful that Carson was then directed to attack the Navajos living in northeastern Arizona. The California Volunteers were sent out of their southern New Mexico forts to round up the remaining bands of Apaches.

Company C, with Captain Shirland in command and Private Thomas Keam among the soldiers, moved into the field in January 1863. They were ordered to bring in the Mimbres band of the Chiricahua Apaches under the leadership of Mangas Coloradas.[38] But before their orders could be obeyed, these cavalrymen were soon caught up in the confusion that was a factor in these Indian wars. Despite their orders and the mandate to follow them, American soldiers were often forced to contend with civilians whose involvement jeopardized the soldiers' successful completion of their duties. For Company C, the lesson was learned in the following way.

In early January 1863, Mangas Coloradas was captured by

mountain man turned prospector Joseph R. Walker. For Walker, the hostage was the insurance he needed to safely journey west across Apache country. However, Walker, his party of miners, and Mangas Coloradas were intercepted by Captain Shirland and twenty soldiers from Company C who were out on patrol. Having no other choice, Shirland moved the group to Fort McLane, where Mangas Coloradas became the prisoner and responsibility of General Joseph Rodman West, Commander of the District of Arizona.[39] According to Daniel Conner, "an honest eye witness, who had nothing to gain by distorting the facts," West's comments at the time the prisoner was turned over left no question that he wanted the Apache leader killed. That same night, January 18, 1863, as Conner watched, West's guards tormented Mangas Coloradas until he protested and then they killed him.[40]

The death of Mangas Coloradas set off a new wave of violence in the Southwest, and Captain Shirland and Company C were immediately dispatched to the field in pursuit of Apaches near Pinos Altos and the Mimbres River. The soldiers spent the spring camped along the Gila River. They traveled far into Arizona in search of Apaches, and although searching out Apaches was their objective, they spent most of the spring protecting Walker's party as it prospected for gold in southeastern Arizona.[41]

On March 22, 1863, while Company C was at Fort West, Apache raiders stole almost all of the fort's horses as they grazed just three-quarters of a mile from the fort.[42] Companies A, B, and C were back in the field again. After five days in the saddle under constant rain, the cavalrymen approached an Apache camp near Black River, Arizona, and spotted their horses. The soldiers waited until dawn the next morning before they attacked. While capturing the stock, the soldiers left twenty Apaches dead and twenty wounded. Before the men returned to Fort West, provisions gave out and "for a number of days they endured great hunger and fatigue, eating their own horses and marching over rocky country barefooted."[43] All the while they carried their comrade Private James Hall of Company B, who had been wounded during the battle and died eight days later at Fort West.[44]

This particular punitive mission yielded results; most missions did nothing more than wear out the horses and the men. During the first five months of 1863, only one scouting party in four saw any action against the Apaches. However, the campaign against the Mimbreños continued, and Company C was involved in many of these scouting missions in southern New Mexico and eastern Arizona. The lives of these soldiers were in constant danger. They were "ever being picked off, wounded, or killed, while on patrol" in extremely rough, mountainous country.[45]

Despite the danger from Apaches, Fort West was also important for protecting the miners and settlers in the Pinos Altos region. Carleton saw the importance of maintaining the peace while developing the area's mineral resources. He requested permission from Army Adjutant General Lorenzo Thomas for the California Volunteers to have time off from their other duties to prospect for gold "on their own account." This, he said, would develop the area and keep the men contented to stay in the service. Three months later, Carleton wrote General Henry Wager Halleck that he had established Fort West and had driven the Indians away from the headwaters of the Gila River, and that his men were finding gold, silver, and cinnabar there.[46]

During the next year, Company C became less familiar with the trails, haunts, and habits of their Apache foes and more familiar with life at a frontier cavalry post. From August 1863 to May 1864, they were at a place known as Camp Mimbres, which was situated on the west side of the Mimbres River just above Fort Webster and east of the mining community of Pinos Altos. Along with several other companies of California Volunteers, Keam and his fellow cavalrymen scouted for Apaches in the vicinity and protected immigrants on their way west. As more Apaches came under the government's control, escort duty became more common than Indian fighting. Camp life was spent bringing broken-down cavalry horses back to a usable condition and in incessant fatigue duties. The men were probably most concerned with getting their chores completed with the least amount of effort, staying alive, and getting back to civilization.[47]

This became increasingly important as the men of Company C were to be mustered out of the army in late 1864. Their service was completed and limited to fighting Apaches, protecting immigrants, and mining for gold. Fearful that they were to be marched back to California to be mustered out, the veterans were pleased to hear that the secretary of war had ordered the Californians to be discharged in New Mexico. This unusual decision allowed the soldiers turned miners, or miners turned soldiers, to remain close to the area's gold fields and pleased Carleton, who believed these experienced men would help develop the area's economy.[48]

Before Thomas Keam ended his service with the California Volunteers, his company was merged with Company B, stationed at Fort Sumner. Company B's service during the war was spent entirely at Fort Sumner guarding Apache and Navajo Indians incarcerated at the Bosque Redondo Reservation.[49] During the fall of 1864, the men spent their time enlarging irrigation ditches, allotting farm lands to Indian families, helping them construct villages, and planting over twelve thousand trees. Agrarian and civilization programs were occasionally replaced with missions to bring renegade Indians back to the reservation or to punish other raiding Indians.

After receiving $13 a month as a California Volunteer, Private Keam was mustered out on January 22, 1865, after three years in the service of the United States Army. He had not seen action against the Confederates, but along with his company he had endured a number of campaigns against the Apaches. Throughout Keam's service in the California Column he served without special distinction. He apparently did nothing that warranted special mention in his superiors' reports nor anything to earn him the wrath of his superiors, but seems to have showed some capacity for leadership. Keam's time as a civilian was brief as the next month he joined the New Mexico Volunteer Cavalry and was mustered in as a Second Lieutenant in Captain Saturnino Baca's Company E.[50]

Second Lieutenant Keam was assigned to Fort Stanton as post adjutant, where he spent the spring of 1865. In April he was transferred to Fort Bascom. The fort, which was only two years old, was situated on the Llano Estacado in eastern New Mexico. The soldiers offered protection to the sparse civilian population, and they rode out on occasional patrols against the Kiowa and Comanche to the east. When the soldiers were not out on patrol, they were at work improving the fort and its buildings. Water was hauled from the Canadian River, and cedar pickets and posts came from the breaks in nearby canyons.

Daily life at the fort was boring and tedious. Within five miles of Fort Bascom a town sprang up, offering some diversion from the daily grind. The soldiers' epithet for it, "Liberty," became its official name. With the boredom of routine, the atmosphere at Fort Bascom may have become more relaxed, and discipline, as well, may have become more accommodating.[51]

All of this changed drastically when, in July 1865, Lieutenant Colonel Edward H. Bergman arrived to command the post.[52] He was a tall, thin man with an erect, unbending posture. A relaxed atmosphere must not have been Bergman's notion of what army life was supposed to be, and Keam may have been singled out to demonstrate the change in policy. There remains a popular notion about the discipline at Fort Bascom at this time that claims it was common for those guilty of minor offenses to be punished by doing time at the "California Walk." Commemorating the California Column's march across the deserts to New Mexico, offenders marched around the post's parade ground pulling a huge, pine tree trunk. Those convicted of more serious offenses were punished by hanging by the thumbs for a specified period of time.[53]

As an officer, Keam would not have personally endured these peculiar forms of punishment, but subsequent events show that he was clearly upset with the form of punishment meted out to enlisted men. By July 20, 1865, Keam was under arrest and charged with seditious conduct. Bergman charged that Keam invited the officers of the fort to a meeting to decide what they should do about the commander's unjust and tyrannical behavior. He alleged that Keam had no cause or provocation to complain about Bergman's ill treatment of him. Bergman claimed that Keam was trying to raise discontent and dissatisfaction among the officers. In a second charge, Bergman said that Keam had not discussed these complaints with him or sought redress through the appropriate means.[54]

Keam may have been given the opportunity to resign his commission. However, he requested that he be allowed to be retained in the military service of the United States in his present capacity. The request was granted, and Keam was transferred from Bergman's Fort Bascom to Fort Stanton, where he remained under arrest for the next three months. By November 1865, he was present for duty at Fort Stanton and had resumed his duties. He remained at Fort Stanton, continuing to perform his duties as post adjutant and occasionally as company commander, until September 30, 1866, when he was discharged at Santa Fé.[55]

Thomas Keam had been in the service of the United States Army for four years and nine months. He had marched from San Francisco to Santa Fé, down the Rio Grande into the rugged mountain country of West Texas, out onto the Llano Estacado, and into the mountains of eastern Arizona. He had seen a large portion of the American Southwest and must have found something in the area that suited him. However, his service was not limited to sightseeing; he had endured the heat of battle against one of the nation's most formidable foes, the Apaches. He had also spent some time among the Navajos while they were at the Bosque Redondo Reservation. Although he recognized these groups as enemies, he must have seen something in them that interested him. Perhaps he had learned to speak their language, and in his conversations with the Indians he found men and women he liked.

It seems that in the years Thomas Keam was in the army he found a country that suited his disposition. Even though the Southwest is mostly high desert and Keam's homeland, Cornwall, is all but surrounded by the sea, the two are relatively similar. Cornwall is an ancient land that has withstood numerous attempts to incorporate it into English culture and politics. Like the Southwest, it has been the crossroads for several distinct cultures and yet has maintained its own unique life-style.

Cornwall, like the American Southwest, is a land of mysteries and legends. There are numerous prehistoric sites, tombs, ceremonial centers, and megaliths. These places, and the castle sites, figure prominently in the rich folklore of the land. The lure of treasure and the stories of gold and silver coins washing up on the beach after a storm have led more than one Cornishman to dig for the earth's wealth in spite of ghosts, witches, charms, spells, and curses.[56] Unlike the Southwest, however, Cornwall held no promises for its people in the mid-nineteenth century. During Thomas Keam's childhood the Cornish mines played out and the ocean's fish were all but gone, and many Cornishmen had immigrated to the United States. The American Southwest offered unlimited economic promise after the Civil War. Like other California Column Volunteers, Thomas Keam responded to the region's offerings and remained in the area. Like the others, he too must have wondered in which profession opportunity could be found. Ranching was an option, as was business, politics, or even crime. Mining was also an alternative, and Thomas Keam had acquired practical training in that field. He had been in two rich and famous gold regions before arriving in New

Mexico, and had picked up some knowledge of the business while in port in Australia and New Zealand. He certainly heard talk of California's gold fields while in San Francisco and in the company of so many former miners in the California Column. While they were at Fort West, the men had also been given time off from their duties to look for copper and silver.

For this twenty-four-year-old Cornishman, the future was bright and full of opportunity, and for the first time in his life Thomas Keam was on his own. Neither a ship captain nor an army officer could dictate his actions. Finally, he was independent of others. So equipped, Thomas Keam disappeared from all official records, and his actions for the next couple of years are unknown. His biographers have suggested that Keam headed up to southern Colorado to trade with the Utes. Although he never mentioned it himself, the suggestion is plausible because southern Colorado offered Thomas Keam two things: the absence of people who could tell him what to do, and the presence of potentially rich mine fields. If he did indeed trade with the Utes, that is where Thomas Keam learned that he could support himself as an Indian trader while he cast about for a more prestigious and lucrative career. [57]

—◁ 3 ▷—

SPECIAL AGENT FOR THE NAVAJOS

IN FEBRUARY 1869, Thomas Keam rode to Fort Defiance in northeastern Arizona Territory, where he had been hired as the Navajo agency interpreter.[1] He reported to Major James Carry French, who was himself the newly appointed agent for the Navajos and had previously served as agent for the Jicarilla Apaches and the Capote and Wiminuche Utes in southern Colorado. Even though the fort itself was old and in a poor state of repair, everyone around it had only recently arrived, including the Navajos who had returned from Bosque Redondo just six months earlier. Because it was the agency headquarters, the fort became the hub around which the Navajos and Americans adjusted to peace and to each other. Fort Defiance became Keam's home, and he remained in the vicinity for more than a decade.[2]

As the agency interpreter, Thomas Keam was involved in most of the negotiations between the agent and the Navajo leaders. Because of this and his honest, fair, and, at times, controversial support of the Indians instead of the government, Thomas Keam was respected by the Navajo headmen. His stature, influence, and knowledge of the Indians caused him to move up in the administrative ranks at the agency. However, these qualifications quickly became liabilities as far as the Office of Indian Affairs was concerned, and Thomas Keam was forced from government service. Even so, Keam continued to counsel the Navajo leaders while he tried to influence the implementation of Indian policy in the Navajos' favor.

At Fort Defiance the government, through its agency employees, attempted to implement its civilization programs to its newest wards, the Navajos. The Navajos themselves had just returned to Fort Defiance after their exile at the Bosque Redondo Reservation. They had finally come under the army's control during Colonel Christopher Carson's winter campaigns of 1863 and 1864. For the next three years, the Navajos endured the hardships at Bosque Redondo, or Hwééldi, as they called it. By early 1867, affairs at Bosque Redondo had reached an all-time low. The harvest had failed for the third year and government rations, which were always insufficient, were cut short. Disease and starvation stalked the Navajos. They were constantly beset by raiding Utes, Kiowas, and Comanches. The Comancheros, a group of New Mexican traders of mixed ethnic origin, also found Navajo livestock to be a convenient commodity for their illegal trading operations on the Texas plains.[3]

Public opinion in New Mexico was polarized over the reservation and the policy of James Henry Carleton. The commander of the New Mexico Military Department was always under fire either from his colleagues in the military, civilian reformers, or the New Mexican population. His solution for New Mexico's Indian problem, the Bosque Redondo Reservation, had proved disastrous because it lacked two essential qualities: fertile soil and good water. In January 1867, James Henry Carleton was removed as commander of the army in the Department of New Mexico.[4]

As the debates ground on in the New Mexico newspapers and the Navajos continued to suffer on the reservation, officials in Washington, D.C., attempted to solve the Indian problem in the West. An eight-member commission was organized by Congress in early 1868 to negotiate peace treaties with the hostile Indian tribes across the West. On May 28, two of the commissioners, General William Tecumseh Sherman and Samuel Tappan, arrived at Bosque Redondo committed to securing a peace treaty from the Navajos. However, the Navajos already knew they were returning home. A few days before the commissioners arrived, Barboncito and a number of Navajo headmen had gone out on the plains away from the Bosque and found a coyote. After surrounding it, Barboncito explained to the animal the Navajos' situation: they had worked hard, had lived in the proper way, and had kept their hearts pure, but they were unhappy and they wanted to go home. Blessing the coyote, Barboncito placed a shell bead in the animal's mouth and released it. The animal walked away, heading west. All that remained for the Navajos was to secure their fate from Sherman's grasp.[5]

During the council, Sherman asked Barboncito, the Navajo spokesman, to tell him the truth about their lives at Bosque Redondo. Sherman said that the Navajos had made war against the United States and that they were placed on the reservation to teach them to become farmers. He said that the government had spent money to protect them and to train them. He acknowledged that the Navajos had worked diligently, but wondered why there were no crops or herds. The Navajos, he said, had failed; they were as poor as when they arrived. Sherman wanted Barboncito to explain the failure in spite of all of their combined efforts.[6]

Even though the translation process was cumbersome, with James Sutherland translating the English into Spanish and Jesús Arviso translating the Spanish into Navajo and back again, the eloquent Barboncito explained the Navajos' experience at the Bosque. He said that when the Navajos were created, they were shown four mountains and four rivers and told to live within those boundaries. By going past them to the Bosque Redondo, they had violated their fathers' commandments and consequently reaped nothing but death and failure. He said that they had worked hard, had built buildings and irrigation ditches and planted crops, but failure was their reward. This ground, he claimed, "was not intended for us." Everything they did brought death. "Some work at the acequias, take sick and die; others die with the hoe in their hands; they go to the river [up] to their waists and suddenly disappear; others have been struck and torn to pieces by lightning."[7]

If Sherman was not convinced, Barboncito claimed that neither the Mexicans nor the other Indians wanted the Navajos living in the area because "we are a hard working tribe of Indians, and if we had the means we could support ourselves better than either Mexican or Indian." Barboncito carefully corrected Sherman's allegation that the Navajos were poor when they arrived at the Bosque Redondo Reservation by pointing out that he and many others in the room had been wealthy and had once possessed large herds of sheep and horses. He reminded Sherman that the Navajos were once successful herdsmen and farmers and that they had brought their herds and abilities with them to the reservation.[8] Barboncito concluded his impassioned speech saying that he wanted to see his birthplace once again and pledging the Navajos' cooperation with the Great Father. "If we are taken back to our own country we will call you our father and mother, if you should only tie a goat there we would all live off of it, all of the same opinion."[9]

Sherman agreed that everyone loved the country where they were born and raised, but explained that the world was big and that there were many more people to be considered than just the Navajos. He acknowledged that the Navajos were unhappy at the Bosque Redondo and suggested that a group of headmen visit the Indian Territory to the east and select a reservation there. If that was not an acceptable notion, then they could discuss returning to their homelands only after specific boundaries were established. To Sherman's suggestion of a reservation in Indian Territory, Barboncito said, "I hope to God you will not ask me to go to another country except my own." On that note, Sherman adjourned the council until the next morning.[10]

The council was reconvened with a ten-member Navajo council in attendance and Barboncito its acknowledged headman. The people gathered around to hear Sherman's pronouncement: If Barboncito would promise peace and recognize the boundaries set by the government, then the Navajos could return home. Barboncito agreed and Sherman asked the crowd if they agreed to have Barboncito speak for them. Their answer was a unanimous "*aoo'*"—yes. [11] The details were all that remained for the commission and the Navajo council. Two more headmen were added to the council, the boundaries were identified, and provisions were made for the Navajos to trade and hunt off the reservation. The treaty was drawn up and signed on June 1, 1868. [12]

Within the month, the Navajos were home again. The abstract boundary lines identified in the treaty were meaningless to the Navajos, who claimed their homesites where there was good water, good grazing and farmlands, and tradition. Some bands settled near Fort Wingate in New Mexico, others settled near Fort Defiance, and others returned to their homes across the Defiance Plateau to the west. The Navajos who escaped Carson's roundup returned from the Colorado River region. For the Navajos, however, life did not return to its pre–Bosque Redondo ways. From that day on, the American government played an increasingly larger role in the Navajos' daily lives and consequently the Navajos' and Americans' lives became intertwined. At Fort Defiance, the headquarters of the Navajos' new agency, the agent and his staff, which included Thomas Keam, began the difficult task of reestablishing the Navajos in the area.

Fort Defiance is located at the mouth of Canyon Bonito along the west side of Black Creek in eastern Arizona. The area is blessed with fertile valleys and good water, but the conditions at Fort Defiance were not so luxurious. Everyone who lived in the compound complained about the accommodations. In 1871, an agent described the situation in his annual report, saying that the adobe buildings at the agency were the remains of an old abandoned military post and that they were badly worn before the troops left them at the beginning of the Civil War. Although the adobe walls were still partially intact, the wooden door and window frames had been burned by the Indians. "The foundations of some of the buildings are giving way," he said, "and the walls of others are badly broken, while the roofs of some are only kept from falling in by propping them up. All the rooms are without floors and very poorly lighted."[13] Conditions had not improved at all by 1883 when Agent D. M. Riordan reported that he had to tie his children in chairs to keep them out of the water when it rained. He said that it was not much better when the rain quit, because snakes came out of their hiding places in the walls of his "palatial quarters."[14]

In the years preceding the Civil War a hierarchy for administering Indian affairs was developed. Policy was formulated in Washington, D.C., administered by a regional superintendent, and implemented by an agent. The agent was responsible for one tribe or band of Indians and was stationed on the reservation. He carried out treaty obligations, distributed annuity goods, implemented federal civilization programs, and attempted to maintain the peace between the Indians and their neighbors.[15] Because the agent had daily contact with "his" Indians, his temperament, sensitivity, and personality could, and did, determine the atmosphere on the reservation. If the agent respected his charges and they, in turn, trusted him, affairs on the reservation were for the most part harmonious. If, on the other hand, the agent was out of touch with the daily events at the agency or ill tempered, the atmosphere was discordant.

The agent was responsible for managing the consequences of events over which he had no control. Contingency plans to deal with the effects of drought, floods, or unseasonal frosts that destroyed the Indians' crops were either ill conceived or mismanaged, in part because the agency budget did not allow for emergency purchases to subsist entire tribes for any length of time.

The agent was also responsible for administering underfunded and understaffed programs for civilizing and educating the Indians. The agent must have felt caught between a number of forces, none of which understood his situation. The Indians did not understand that he could not miraculously circumvent purchasing procedures and thereby deliver badly needed goods, and no amount of personal charisma or good will could feed hungry Indians or entertain them as they waited for annuity goods to arrive.[16]

Off the reservation, the faceless bureaucracy in the guise of "Washington," or the "Great Father," or the commissioner, or the superintendent did not understand all that was required to keep the Indians on the reservation. The agent may have believed that the bureaucracy was concerned more with reports and receipts than with the welfare of the Indians. Further contributing to the everyone's stress was public opinion. From civilian employees on the reservation to citizens in the vicinity to reformers everywhere, all had an opinion about how well the agent was carrying out his duties or how efficiently the "Indian problem" was being solved. Public opinion carried a significant amount of power in Indian affairs because the positions in the Office of Indian Affairs were political appointments and everyone served at the pleasure of someone else.[17]

In return for fulfilling his responsibilities and balancing all the conflicting demands, the agent received an annual salary of $1,500. The salary level had been set in 1834 and remained the average until 1890. Because of poor pay, impossible demands, and frequent changes in administration in Washington, D.C., agents did not stay in their positions very long. The average length of tenure for agents on the Navajo Reservation between 1869 and 1913 was two years.[18]

At Fort Defiance, the agent, Major James Carry French, was aided by a staff that included a herder, a butcher, and an interpreter, Thomas Keam. As was the case during the treaty negotiations, conversations between the Americans at the agency and the Navajos were conducted in a combination of English, Spanish, and Navajo, with Spanish being the lingua franca. Only after Keam and other Americans became more proficient in Navajo could Navajo to English and English to Navajo translations be conducted. As the interpreter, Keam was required to be in close proximity to the agent's office at all times. By virtue of his job, Keam was privy to all business that transpired between the Indians and the agent. In this, he came to understand their opinions. He realized that the Indians' actions were not just unthinking or unreasoned reactions to the government or their enemies. Working alongside the Navajo headmen from the Fort Defiance region, learning to appreciate their reasoning and mastering the diplomacy practiced by Barboncito, Delgadito, Ganado Mucho, Narbono, Manuelito, and others, Thomas Keam became an admirer of and an advocate for the Navajos. Together, Keam and the headmen solved many different problems, and each grew to understand and appreciate the other's perspectives and motivations.

Keam did not become a "member" of the tribe nor did he forsake his Victorian culture or beliefs. He did not question the government's superiority over the Indians. He believed that assimilation, the result of Christian education, was the only reasonable goal for them. Keam, however, realized that the Navajo people possessed dignity and that their past experiences had taught them many valuable lessons. To help them solve their problems and settle their disputes, Keam worked with the Navajo headmen; he did not dictate solutions to them. As he conducted his duties as interpreter and representative of Agent French, Keam had the opportunity to visit a number of isolated regions on and near the reservation. Through the headmen, Keam became acquainted with a number of Navajo families, not just those living at or near the agency.

In 1869 there was plenty of activity to occupy the agency personnel. In March there was a smallpox epidemic, and in June a hail storm and late snow ruined the Navajos' crops. There was

constant tension between the Navajos and their Ute neighbors to
the north and their New Mexican neighbors to the east. Raiding
back and forth was common and the potential for violence was
high. Since their return from Bosque Redondo, the Navajos'
flocks of sheep and goats were slowly increasing through government annuities and raiding, an old, efficient, albeit illegal,
activity. Trade, when practical, with non-Navajo ranchers was
also an effective way of obtaining animals. As their flocks increased, Ute and New Mexican ranchers found Navajo herds
equally accessible resources. Raiding back and forth, which was
a very old habit, brought many complaints to the agent, and
French and Keam spent a good deal of time negotiating for the
return of stolen livestock and the payment of restitution to ag-
grieved families.[19]

Sometime during 1869, Thomas Keam married a young Navajo woman, Asdzáán Libá, or Gray Woman. She was Áshįįhí, a
member of the Salt People clan, and had been born about 1852
in the Moqui Buttes region south of the Hopi mesas. She had not
lived at Bosque Redondo, but "had been left on the Rio Grande
River." Thomas Keam and Asdzáán Libá were married in the traditional Navajo ceremony.[20] According to custom, Keam would
have given the parents of Asdzáán Libá a number of horses and
gifts to symbolize the engagement. The Navajo wedding ceremony traditionally occurred in the evening at the bride's parents' hogan. The couple was seated across from a medicine man
and the family and guests filled in around them. The bride first
dipped water out of a pitch-covered basket with a gourd dipper
and washed the groom's hands. Between the couple, a Navajo
ceremonial basket was set with its design break pointing to the
east. The basket contained an unflavored cornmeal mush encircled by pollen. White pollen was sprinkled across the cornmeal
from east to west and yellow pollen was sprinkled in a line from
south to north. The groom took a pinch of cornmeal from the
east side of the basket and the bride followed; they each ate in

turn from the south, the west, and then the north. Lastly, they each ate a pinch of cornmeal from the center. The basket containing the cornmeal and the pollen was then passed around to the guests, who ate from it, and then the ceremony ended. The bride's family received more gifts from the groom, and the wedding feast began. The festivities lasted all through the night, with the elders giving the newlyweds advice on proper conduct for their happiness, and the party broke up at dawn. Completing the ceremony two or three days later, the couple washed each other's hair with yucca soap. So prepared, Thomas and Asdzáán Libá set up housekeeping at Fort Defiance.[21]

In the summer of 1869, Agent French was replaced by Army Captain Frank Tracy Bennett, a jovial, rather rotund man the Navajos called "Fat Belly."[22] Bennett and Keam became fast friends and developed a harmonious working relationship. In addition to Keam's unofficial duties as interpreter, he also acted as Bennett's secretary or clerk, writing almost all of Bennett's letters in his precise and very readable hand.

In January 1870, Bennett expanded the interpreter's staff by hiring Thomas Keam's younger brother, William. William Keam was the third child of Thomas Vercoe and Grace Stephens Keames. He was born August 18, 1846, in the family home in Truro. Just how and when he arrived in the United States is unknown. William presumably left Truro and his mother and sister, Elizabeth, shortly after his father's death in October 1868. That Bennett hired young Keam as an agency interpreter may have had more to do with Thomas's skills and recommendation than with William's knowledge of Spanish and Navajo. Certainly his job skills were strengthened with "on the job" training, for within a month William and Special Indian Agent Lieutenant S. Ford left the fort in search of captive Navajo children living in the Cebolleta, Albuquerque, and Santa Fé areas.[23]

The year 1870 was not much different for the Navajos and their civilian companions than the previous years. Raids continued and the weather played its tricks, making farming uncertain. A shaky peace between the Navajo chiefs and their traditional enemies, the Zuni, was negotiated in November. As the year came to a close, Agent Bennett prepared to relinquish his control over the Navajos—a reflection of decisions made in the nation's capital during 1870.

Having succeeded in abolishing slavery, American reformers gathered around a new cause: solving the "Indian problem" through increased civilization programs. The first response had been the Peace Commission. The next was a revised Indian policy, and because it was formulated during the administration of President Ulysses S. Grant, whose campaign slogan had been "Let us have Peace," the policy became known as "Grant's peace policy." It reflected little that was new in Indian policy, save direct involvement of Protestant religious groups, but it carried with it a renewed zeal for dealing with the problems of American Indians.

While the fundamental policy remained unchanged, its administration and implementation were dramatically altered by the reformers. Failures in the past, they believed, were almost guaranteed because of the presence of corrupt or immoral agency employees and traders on the reservations. The reformers intended to replace them with men of high moral character. They would construct churches and schools for the Indians on the reservations, and missionaries and teachers would implement the civilization programs for the federal government. Together the government and the Protestant denominations would prepare the Indians to live in the white world.[24]

In July 1870, the United States Congress forbade military personnel from holding civil offices, such as being Indian agents, in an attempt to regain its power of political appointments. However, President Grant took the initiative and expanded an old policy in which the American Board of Commissioners for Foreign Missions, an interdenominational committee that provided missionary teachers to the Indians. The Navajos, Hopis, and several other tribes were assigned by this interdenominational board to the Presbyterian Board of Foreign Missions, which approved the hiring of agency personnel for the Hopis, Navajos, and others.

The Presbyterians viewed their responsibilities to the Navajos just as they did those to any other alien group they served. The missionaries first were to learn the native language, then to lead the Indians to Christ and civilization. The Presbyterian Foreign Mission Board secretary said, "our work among the Indian tribes was very much the same as among the 'other heathens of a strange tongue' such as the Hindus or Siamese." Although the agents worked for the commissioner of Indian affairs in Washington, D.C., and wrote annual reports to him, Presbyterian agents served the Presbyterian Board of Foreign Missions and reported regularly to its secretary, the Reverend John C. Lowrie, in New York City. Their correspondence with the commissioner concerned day-to-day administrative matters, such as the shipments of beef and corn, inventories, and threats to peace on the reservation. The correspondence between the agents and the missionary board covered a wide variety of topics ranging from practical matters to assessments of the success of Indian office programs. "Undercover" reports from the various Presbyterian appointees at the Navajo agency flowed regularly to the mission office. The men reported on other agency employees, military personnel, and each other. There is a distinct quality of pettiness and bickering in this correspondence, which undoubtedly reflects the difficult conditions under which the Presbyterians lived and worked, their lack of immediate success in Christianizing and "civilizing" the Navajos, and their individual personalities.[25]

James H. Miller was the Presbyterians' first agent to the Navajos. He arrived at Fort Defiance in January 1871. Regardless of his faith and blessings from the Presbyterians, Miller faced the same problems as his predecessors and the same administrative responsibilities as other Office of Indian Affairs employees.

The weather, food shortages, and raids preoccupied the agent. To other agency employees and the Navajos, Miller was just another new agent they had to get accustomed to and train.

In September, Miller dispatched Keam, another interpreter Jesús Arviso, and Navajo headman Narbono to a New Mexican town near Cebolleta. Some New Mexicans had killed two of Narbono's men and there had been the usual Navajo reprisals. Keam managed to negotiate a settlement in which the New Mexicans paid for the dead men's lives in livestock that would be given to their families, and Narbono promised to stop his raiding. Keam and the party returned to the agency, having averted another disaster. In reward for having performed his duties well, Miller raised Keam's annual salary to $700.[26]

The next month, Keam and Anson Damon, the agency butcher, arranged for the distribution of the Navajos' annuity goods. Annuity goods were not handouts but were part of the government's payment to the Navajos for the lands they relinquished when they signed their treaty in 1868. For the agent, ration time was a chance to estimate the Navajo population. Yet only the most naive or officious believed that all Navajo people came to Fort Defiance for rations. Many groups, especially those in the Monument Valley area to the northwest and the Colorado River area to the west, rarely, if ever, came in contact with the agent.

For the people who came into the agency, ration time was a social event. Women, dressed in woven black wool dresses, red woven sash belts, and buckskin leggings and moccasins, stood wrapped in striped woven shoulder blankets, or serapes, with their children and with their babies strapped snugly on cradleboards. The men were dressed in cotton duck pants with the side seams split to the knees, buckskin moccasins, cotton calico shirts, and colorful striped wearing blankets. They sat in their saddles exchanging information and comments. They gathered in the plaza of the agency, which had once been the parade grounds of the fort. Most of the families had traveled for miles and camped overnight in the area. In addition to receiving their payments, it was a time for horse racing, gossiping, and renewing friendships. Although the distribution of the goods was for the most part an orderly, organized affair, the air must have been filled with the dust of people coming and going, milling horses, and the murmur of Navajo and Spanish conversations.[27]

In the 1870s, the Navajos received such household goods as tin pans, dippers, kettles, bridle leather, sewing awls, and awl handles. For the women, the government allocated fancy calico for shirts and brown sheeting for pants so they could make Anglo-style clothes for their families. Recognizing the value of the Navajo weaving to the people's economy, the government distributed yarn, dyestuff, and thread. In 1871, 3,000 yards of bayetta were distributed, along with 4,500 pounds of scarlet yarn, 650 pounds of indigo, 250 dozen wool cards, and 200 pounds of linen thread.[28] The bayetta cloth, a long-nap, commercially prepared wool flannel, was unravelled by the weavers and the threads reused in blanket weaving. Red bayetta was the preferred color, as a good red dye was difficult to produce using natural dyes. Indigo, a dye produced from plants grown in South Carolina, produced a blue color that was also favored by the weavers.

The distribution of goods was accomplished in three days, and the Navajos' request for more sheep in the next annuity was supported enthusiastically by Miller. Life at the agency resumed its pattern, even though the payroll was eight months behind schedule and no one had any cash money to spend.[29] Thomas Keam's salary was raised to $100 per month, and his family was growing: Tómas, the first child, was born in 1870 and Billy was born in 1871.[30] William Keam, too, had married a Navajo woman, and they were also living in the area. For the Keams, life seemed settled. They had growing families and good jobs with the government. For the Navajos, still joyous over being back within the four sacred mountains, life was resuming normalcy. Miller was proving to be an effective, patient, and understanding agent.

But not everyone at the agency was pleased with Miller or his execution of the job. The complaints did not come from officials in Washington, D.C., or the agency staff or even from the Navajos. They came, instead, from one of the Presbyterian missionary-teachers at Fort Defiance, James Roberts.[31] Roberts was one of two Presbyterian teachers at Fort Defiance; the other was Charity Gaston, the first teacher assigned to the Navajos in 1869.

Roberts's complaints were not about his Navajo students, their absence from school, his schoolroom, or the lack of school supplies, but about the moral climate at the agency. His letters to Lowrie were long and complaining, and they detailed what he judged to be Miller's acceptance and approval of American men living with Navajo women. Roberts, like many of his generation, did not approve of mixed marriages, and he did not recognize the validity of the Navajo wedding ceremony. Even if he could have understood that an American man would prefer a permanent relationship with a Navajo woman to one with another American woman, a Christian wedding would be the only way to make the union legal. That a number of agency employees lived with Navajo women offended his sense of morality, and by virtue of his convictions he was forced to eliminate these unholy unions. If he could not banish the offending couples from the reservation, he could at least banish them from the agency. In his moral outrage, Roberts convinced Miller to replace several agency employees guilty of cohabiting with Navajo women. Thomas and William Keam and Anson Damon, the agency butcher, among others, were spared in this first housecleaning.[32]

Miller was caught between his personal code of morality, which was not much different from Roberts's, and his practical nature, which required that the agency be staffed with competent men. He understood that as agent he was required to fire anyone who violated the law or impeded the progress of civilization. He also understood that on the frontier many jobs would remain vacant for want of a man who never swore or took an occasional drink, for profanity, gambling, and drinking alcohol were as egregious offenses as cohabitation. That mixed marriages were common in the American Southwest was not justification enough for them to be accepted custom elsewhere. Miller was caught between doing his job on the one hand and serving a higher master on the other.

Roberts's lengthy letters to Lowrie detailing the situation and complaining about Miller's lack of support finally prompted Miller to justify his actions. While explaining his opinion to Secretary Lowrie, Miller demonstrated his practicality in dealing with the situation as well as his ability to split moral hairs, saying that "There are none of the employes [sic] living with Indian women but three and they have children and treat their families well. The Indians consider them as married." Miller told Lowrie that it would not be "proper or safe to separate them [the families] as the Indians are much attached to them [the American men]. I am afraid such a course would confuse rather than advance the cause."[33]

Dr. John Menaul, Charity Gaston's fiancé, substantiated Miller's claims in a letter to Lowrie in which he tried to explain the situation at Fort Defiance. According to Dr. Menaul, "Roberts feels that he [sic] was always right and that what he would do ought to be done, irrespective of the evils which might result." He continued saying that "Because I am on friendly relations with the men here (Employes and others) [he] takes it for granted, that it is at the sacrifice of [my] Christianity." In other words, tolerating an employee who lived with an Indian woman without the benefits of a Christian wedding was unacceptable. To tolerate such a thing was to sanction it.[34]

Roberts's problems were not limited to the morality of the agency employees, but included the Navajo students he was supposed to be teaching. Roberts complained to Lowrie that the reason his school was not successful was that he did not have an actual schoolhouse and implied that any fault to be found lay somewhere other than at his own feet. In January 1872, Miller wrote about Roberts that "The Indians are too much prejudiced against him and I am inclined to think he is so constituted as not to be able to remove the prejudice[;] at least he seems to make but little effort to do so." Miller suggested to Lowrie that if Roberts did not make a change in his attitude and demeanor for the better, Miller would ask to have him replaced. The Navajo chiefs were so displeased with Roberts that they threatened to go over Miller's head and go directly to the commissioner of Indian affairs to get Roberts removed.[35]

Roberts finally resigned his position in the spring, but his letter-writing campaign had found receptive ears in New York City and among the other Presbyterians in New Mexico. He was gone from the agency, but his legacy remained. The men discharged by Miller on Roberts's recommendation were also a source of discontent at the agency. They were mad at having been fired and had gathered together with others living just south of the reservation boundary who were equally unhappy about the changes in agency administration.[36]

With Roberts gone, peace, however tenuous, was restored at the agency and Miller was able to turn his attention to the Navajos. On June 4, 1872, Miller planned an expedition to explore potential farmlands north of Fort Defiance along the San Juan River. He had a notion that with the addition of a subagency in the area to protect the Navajos from the Utes, the Navajos would move into the area to farm. He left control of the agency to Thomas Keam and, along with B. M. Thomas, the agency farmer, John Ayres, and Jesús Arviso, Miller rode out of Fort Defiance. On June 11, the party was camped near the San Juan when they were awakened at dawn by a gunshot and the "whistling of an arrow." The men sprang up in time to see two Utes running away with some of their horses. About this time, the men realized that Miller had not moved from his bedroll. When they checked on him, they found that he had been shot through the top of his head. Burying him in a shallow grave, the men returned to the agency to tell their sorrowful tale. By the time the details were straightened out and word sent to the army at Fort Wingate, the perpetrators were long gone. The Office of Indian Affairs determined that the case was closed and that nothing could be gained from further investigation, although there was some good evidence as to who the murderers were.[37]

Miller's death left the agency in a sad state for a number of months. The civilians were not just upset about Miller's death and sorrowful for his widow and son, but acrimonious over the Office of Indian Affairs' decision to drop the case. For Keam, now in charge of the agency, the hoped for promotion came at the expense of another's life. He and Miller had made an efficient and effective team. Although Keam was not a Presbyterian, Miller apparently realized that competence, like morality, was not limited to just one Christian denomination and supported and defended Keam on a number of occasions.

With Miller's death, Keam continued to manage the affairs of the agency. He arranged for aid to Navajo farmers after a late frost killed their crops, he and Manuelito arranged for the return of some stolen livestock, and he purchased goods from nearby traders to feed some hungry Navajo families. On August 6, 1872, Keam's thirtieth birthday, he was officially appointed Special Agent for the Navajos by Special Indian Commissioner General O. O. Howard.[38] William Keam became the agency clerk.[39] The position of special agent was a parallel position to that of agent. Usually, a special agent was responsible for a specific area of interest, such as farming. Because the position was poorly defined and the special agent's powers equal to the agent's, it was a potentially confusing and unharmonious arrangement. That same month, Keam implemented one of Bennett's and Miller's ideas by organizing a police force of Navajo men. The "Navajo cavalry," as Keam called it, was headed by Manuelito and the thirteen chiefs and comprised of 130 horsemen. Their goals were to guard the reservation boundaries, arrest thieves, and return stolen livestock.[40]

Keam carried out Miller's plan for assessing the San Juan area. In September, he rode up to the area, some ninety-five miles north of Fort Defiance, surveyed the area, and marked what he thought was an excellent place for a subagency. Keam's descriptions of the area were glowing: "In this immediate vicinity[,] I found some of the best & most fertile lands in New Mexico, one strip being ten (10) miles long and averaging one and one half (1½) miles wide, containing nine thousand six hundred (9600) Acres, this and other in the vicinity, having advantages over every other part of the Navajo Reservation, in climate and water facilities." The area was perfect for the Navajos' needs and those of the agency employees. "Corn enough could be raised here, and in the immediate vicinity[,] to support the whole Navajo Nation. There is also sufficient fuel to last several years, then it could be obtained from a short distance say five (5) miles."[41]

There was just one drawback to this ideal place. Even though a number of Navajos were "willing & anxious" to move up there, Keam reported they were always in fear of raids from the Utes. "They informed me that the Ute Indians, had told them that they would not allow buildings to be erected there, or farming to be done." Keam offered his assessment of the Ute problem:

I would here state that the few Utes who visit this part of the Reservation in small numbers, (as there are not over three hundred in all who pretend to claim this country,) are a great source of trouble and dread to the Navajos; and as they never have, made an attempt to work and still persist in this mode of living, they come to the cornfields of the Navajoes in season and make them common property by helping themselves, and the Navajoes to avoid trouble bear with them patiently. These few Utes have now more land than the whole Navajo tribe, and not only refuse to work themselves, but cause trouble [to] the Navajoes, who are exerting themselves to become selfsustaining.

Keam fully favored the establishment of a subagency on the San Juan not just because it was a productive area, but also because also it would further the civilization process and solidify the Navajos' claim on the area. He encouraged Superintendent of Indian Affairs for New Mexico Nathaniel Pope to solicit an appropriation for the development of the area and to support the Navajos' efforts to support themselves.[42]

In his duties as special agent and because there was no agent at Fort Defiance, Keam filed the agency's annual report to the commissioner of Indian affairs. Keam reported on the affairs at the agency and at the Navajo school. "There has been one school at this agency, conducted by Mrs. C. A. G. Menaul but owing to the great difficulty in learning our language but little progress has been made." He suggested that "a farm should be connected with each school, conducted on the industrial and manual-labor plan, and that the children be furnished with food and clothing." Keam's suggestion of a vocational training school, like the Navajo cavalry, was one that Miller had suggested earlier. "These children, having been accustomed to a wild life, dislike too much confinement, and when school-hours are over they should have a play-ground connected with the school in which to enjoy themselves."[43] His suggestion that the schoolchildren be fed and clothed and provided a playground reflects Keam's practicality and understanding that if the children were enticed to come to school and made comfortable there, they would prevail upon their parents to let them stay in school. Although Keam understood Navajo society and culture, he fully supported the notions of the Office of Indian Affairs and the public at large in their belief that education and Christian teachings were the avenue to civilization. He never veered from his belief in the value of industrial arts education.

Although he had exercised his duties as agent by reporting to the commissioner of Indian affairs, Keam was probably not too surprised when he was not promoted from special agent to agent. On September 7, 1872, the Presbyterian mission board named W. F. Hall agent for the Navajos.[44] Hall adopted Miller's and Keam's ideas about establishing a vocational school for the Navajos. After all that had happened, it seemed that Agent Hall and Special Agent Keam had created an atmosphere in which the agency would run smoothly and the Navajos would race toward the rewards of civilization, but that was not to be—Lowrie wanted Keam fired.[45]

Lowrie respectfully requested Secretary of the Interior Columbus Delano to remove Thomas Keam as Special Agent to the Navajos. Saying that the board bore Keam no animosity, they believed, however, "that the interests of the Navajo Indians will be much benefitted by the appointment of a sub-Agent [sic] who is more in sympathy with efforts to promote educational and moral interests of the Indians, one whose example will encourage all such efforts."[46] It did not matter to Lowrie that Keam spoke Navajo and Spanish and was considered by the Navajo headmen as a friend. That Keam was held in high regard by the army officers stationed at Fort Wingate did not affect Lowrie's decision. Keam's beliefs in the salvation of education did not alter the board's opinions. To Lowrie and others, Keam lived with Asdzáán Libá without the benefits of a legal, Christian wedding. The fact that the Navajos, Asdzáán Libá, and Keam viewed their wedding as binding did not fit into the Presbyterians' definition of marriage. Consequently, Keam was an immoral man and therefore unfit to lead the Navajos, through example, to civilization.

Keam's family had been a source of concern for some time.

Just two days after naming Keam special agent in August 1872, General O. O. Howard, Superintendent of Indian Affairs for New Mexico, wrote to Keam claiming he had information from a good source that some of Keam's employees were cohabiting with Indian women, gambling, and using profanity. Howard demanded that the unidentified men be fired. Keam answered Howard's charge in a letter to Superintendent Pope, saying, "There are two Employees of this Agency living with and married to Navajo women according to the customs of the Navajoes which in no way conflicts with their morals. These men have families and naturally look to the women as their wives, and treat them as such." Keam deflected the complaints saying, "I judge this false information has been given by some party who from mercenary and office seeking motives, under the cloak of Christianity, seeks to injure these men."[47] In that Keam was not mistaken.

A number of parties had written to the Presbyterian mission secretary, John Lowrie, about the immoral atmosphere at Fort Defiance. The former missionary-teacher Roberts continued to complain to Lowrie and others long after he had left the agency. His complaints were echoed by other Presbyterians in New Mexico, among them the Presbyterian agent to the Pueblo Indians, William F. M. Arny. Arny was probably the one who alerted Howard to the goings-on at the agency. He wrote Lowrie about the allegations of cohabiting, gambling, drinking, and swearing. In his reply, Lowrie wrote that the missionary board did not want to pass on every man hired by each agent because it was the responsibility of the agent to hire decent, moral men. However, the board did want to recieve pertinent information about the moral and religious character of each person employed at each agency, and he noted that Arny should keep that in mind. Arny's and Roberts's complaints prompted Lowrie's request that Keam be fired as special agent.[48]

Keam's replacement, suggested by Lowrie in the same letter

that asked for Keam's removal, was J. L. Gould of Santa Fé, a Presbyterian who had worked in some "temporary service" at the Cimarron Agency for the newly appointed New Mexico Indian superintendent, Colonel L. E. Dudley.[49] Gould and Hall were soon continuing the programs established by Miller and Keam before them, testimony to the former officials' realistic assessment of the situation at the Navajo agency. Gould reexamined the San Juan area and judged its potential for a subagency just as Keam had done. He reported to Dudley that the location would make a fine subagency. In fact, his letter is but a duplicate of the report Keam wrote some ten months earlier.[50]

In less than a year from his appointment, agent Hall was asked by Lowrie to resign. Lowrie's request angered Hall, who tried to explain the conditions at the agency to the secretary. Hall claimed that any problems at the agency were Thomas Keam's fault. Hall said that Keam was bitter about not being named the agent and was trying to get Hall fired. Hall claimed that when Keam was the special agent he handed out annuity goods, but that when those were gone Keam told the Navajos he was powerless to do anything more and sent them to Agent Hall. This, Hall complained, made him look bad in the Navajos' eyes and made Keam look like their friend. Above all, Hall feared Thomas Keam, because if crossed he would unleash the Navajos, whom he alone controlled. Hall feared for his own safety because he claimed the Navajos had killed agent Miller, and Hall feared the same was in store for him. There were enemies everywhere, Hall claimed, and they outnumbered the Presbyterians one hundred to one. No one could have worked harder under the circumstances than Hall.[51] Lowrie was unmoved, however, and the former agent Hall was added to the list of fired agency employees, a list that included Thomas Keam.

Thomas Keam had been employed at the Navajo Agency for four years. Each year had brought positive recognition of his work in the form of promotion. Each year also brought him increasing stature and authority among the Navajos. Although Hall's complaints may be slightly exaggerated and the fear for his life brought on by an emotional state exacerbated by personal paranoia and the alien world in which he lived, he correctly identified one thing: among the Navajo headmen Thomas Keam was an influential man. However, he neither controlled them nor dictated to them. Instead he steered them on a course consistent with their abilities; he encouraged them to take advantage of the government's weaknesses and force it to make good on its promises. In time, other agents would echo similar complaints about Keam as they tried to defend their positions in the Office of Indian Affairs.

Regardless of his perceived power, Thomas Keam was powerless to do anything to save his own job. He had been judged unfit to fill the position of special agent and there was nothing he or anyone else could do to reverse the almost dictatorial power of Reverend John Lowrie and the Presbyterians. While employed at Fort Defiance, Thomas Keam had relied on his own abilities and his good relations with the agents to maintain his position. Realizing that neither was valuable where Lowrie was concerned, Thomas Keam set out to cultivate more powerful supporters. However, he did not eliminate the source of the Presbyterians' immediate concerns: he did not marry Asdzáán Libá in a Christian ceremony and he did not become a Presbyterian. Instead, he moved to a location a couple of miles south of Fort Defiance and the reservation's southern boundary, to a place he called Fair View. There he plotted to get hired as the Navajos' agent.

—◀ 4 ▶—

CONFRONTING WILLIAM F. M. ARNY

THOMAS KEAM WAS thirty-one years old in 1873. He was married and had two sons, but he had no job. By clan rights, Asdzáán Libá could have moved her sons and husband to her family's land to farm and herd sheep. This apparently was not to Keam's liking, because they stayed in the vicinity of Fort Defiance. Instead he applied for a license to trade at Fort Defiance.[1] As the post trader, Keam would have been assured a steady clientele as well as agency supply contracts. He would also have firsthand knowledge of events at the agency, which would include such things as gossip circulating prior to an agent's resignation. A trading post removed from the agency would have none of these extras that Keam seemed to believe were so necessary. Like the lame-duck agent, W. F. Hall, Thomas Keam awaited the arrival of the new agent.

The Navajos' new agent was William F. M. Arny, the choice of Presbyterian Board of Foreign Missions secretary John Lowrie.[2] When Arny arrived at Fort Defiance, he was neither inexperienced in the Indian affairs of New Mexico, nor was he a novice in the machinations of territorial and federal politics. He had worked for the Free-Soil Movement in Kansas in the 1850s and had helped elect Abraham Lincoln to the president's office in 1860. In return, Arny was named agent for the Utes and Jicarilla Apaches. Between 1862 and 1873, Arny served as secretary of the territory, Special Agent for the Indians of New Mexico, and Pueblo Agent. During the years he worked for the Republican Party, Arny accumulated substantial political power and cultivated a large number of supporters in New Mexico and in the nation's capital. His political standing was enhanced by his membership in the Presbyterian Church.

A man of such considerable experience with the Indians of New Mexico and with such impressive political connections could have been a powerful ally for the Navajos, but what seems to have been serious character flaws prevented Arny from doing anything good for them. His biographer characterized the man as twofaced, duplicitous, indiscreet, and self-righteous. His eagerness to win approval and fame caused him to tailor his beliefs and statements to the views of his audience. His tendency to believe in the correctness of his positions prevented him from compromising with those with slightly different opinions. His ability to manipulate the press often resulted in minor differences escalating into controversies involving the honor and integrity of everyone involved.[3] Arny's actions at Fort Defiance proved each characterization correct.

Arny arrived at Fort Defiance on August 12, 1873, but was prevented from taking charge by Hall. Claiming that he had not received official instructions, Hall refused to turn over the agency possessions to Arny.[4] While everyone waited for official notification, Arny fumed that his progress was being impeded. Finally, on September 1 after Hall signed over the agency property inventory, Arny became agent.

While waiting to take over the agency, Arny was convinced that the rumors he had heard and the stories related to him by James Roberts were all true. In his first week as agent, he refused Thomas Keam's application for a trading license, a prerogative of agents prior to 1876, saying that William Keam, who was to be the clerk, was not a United States citizen, and in any event neither men were "proper persons." Technically, Arny was correct in refusing the license, as neither of the Keams were United States citizens and he was well within his authority to refuse the license on moral grounds. He was mandated by the 1834 trade and intercourse laws to do so. With the Keams taken care of, Arny requested permission from the commissioner to fire a number of agency employees. Jesús Arviso, the interpreter, was unfit to serve the agency because he was Mexican. In addition, Arny claimed, he lived with two Navajo sisters at Fort Defiance even though he was married to a woman at Cubero. To make matters worse, Arny claimed, Arviso was "addicted to gambling." Consequently, Arviso's presence at the agency was a bad influence on the Indians. The chief herder, W. W. Owens, the agency butcher, Anson Damon, and Perry Williams were fired because of their improper intimacies with Navajo women, and by the end of the month Charles Hardison and William Clark were also fired because they were married to Navajo women.[5]

Arny believed he had cleansed the agency of the "squaw-men." Jesús Arviso, Anson Damon, and the others who had been fired joined the growing number of white men with Navajo families, many of them one-time agency employees, who lived just beyond the reservation's southern border—and the agent's control. If Arny believed that the former employees would abandon the area just because he had fired them, he was mistaken. Although they were no longer employed by the federal government, these men, like Thomas and William Keam, were permanent residents of the area by virtue of their Navajo families. They were resourceful and not necessarily dependent on a government salary for their only employment. They had families to provide for, livestock to manage, and business to conduct. They lived in the area by choice, not by government assignment.

Content with his quick successes, Arny turned his attention to more complicated and potentially more lucrative endeavors. Arny's scheme involved withdrawing the lush, mineral-rich San Juan River area from the Navajo Reservation so that mining districts could be developed there unencumbered by Indian claims. He had been interested in the qualities of the San Juan drainage in southwest Colorado since 1860, when he was agent for the Colorado Utes. After exploring the region and suffering a case of gold fever, Arny unsuccessfully attempted to remove the Utes from the area through treaty negotiations and later supported legislation to remove them.[6] But upon becoming the Navajos' agent, Arny approached the San Juan gold fields from a different direction with a plan certain to free the area from Navajo claim and sure to win Washington's approval.

First, he launched a series of attacks on the earlier plans to establish a subagency on the San Juan, claiming that the area had no agricultural value and that the expense of a subagency was prohibitive. Second, he increased the already high level of apprehension of the war that could result from Navajos, Utes, Mormons, and miners competing for the same land. These ploys were powerful. The genius of his plan, and the ensurance of its ultimate success, was to get the Navajos to voluntarily request a land exchange. He would convince the Navajos to trade the San Juan River and Carrizo Mountain areas for land south of the agency.[7]

The proposed land exchange required all of Arny's energies during the spring and winter of 1874. It required that he convince the commissioner that the Navajos wanted the land exchange and that he get the Navajo headmen to appear to support the exchange. To this end, he penned a letter for the headmen to the commissioner requesting a meeting in Washington, D.C., to discuss a number of issues. The Navajo headmen wanted to go to meet with the president and the commissioner, and Arny promised the trip in return for their signatures, or marks, on his plan. Whether the headmen understood exactly what Arny had written is unclear.

In this elaborate scheme, Arny had to appear to the commissioner to oppose the plan. Implying that he was caught between trying to please the headmen and honor all previous promises and doing what he knew was best for the Navajos, Arny confided to the commissioner, saying, "I have always endeavored to discourage it [the plan] and in the last council I urged that the money [for the trip] could be expended more profitably in the purchase of sheep for them but they persisted in their desire to go to Washington, and said that the agents French, Bennett, Miller, and Hall all promised that they should go and disappointed them."[8]

Arny rationalized that adding land south of Fort Defiance to the reservation would solve several problems. It would place Navajos already living there under reservation jurisdiction and agency control, and it would give him leverage to further remove the enclave of former agency employees living between the reservation border and Fort Wingate. Arny played down the agricultural qualities of the San Juan region and greatly exaggerated the potential of the lands to be added.

Commissioner Smith reluctantly gave his permission for the trip, provided the expenses were paid for by the Navajos out of their own funds. They left Fort Defiance in November, stopping en route in Santa Fé and Denver. They met with General William T. Sherman in Saint Louis and went on to Bloomington, Illinois, Arny's old home. Along the route the Navajos displayed themselves and their products, which included saddle blankets, pottery, and baskets. Alongside the display of native crafts, they exhibited gloves and neckties, presumably to demonstrate their adoption of acculturated dress styles. Of particular significance was the exhibition of two early flag pictorial blankets commemorating the nation's centennial. One had "1776–1876" woven into the design, and the other featured four small stars for the Colorado, Utah, New Mexico, and Arizona territories in addition to the thirty-six stars for the states.[9]

Arriving in Washington, D.C., with Arny were Manuelito; Juanita, Manuelito's wife; Manuelito Segundo, their son; Carnero

Mucho; Ganado Mucho; Mariana; Tinne-su-su; Cabra Negra; Cayetanito; Narbono Primero; Bueno Cinna; and Barbes Hueras. Arny employed two English-to-Spanish interpreters, "an old frontiersman for whom no one seems to know any name except `Rocky Mountain Bill' " or Kentucky Mountain Bill, and "Wild" Hank Sharp. Ironically, Arny was forced to hire Jesús Arviso to translate Navajo to Spanish.

While the entourage was waiting to meet with President Grant and the commissioner of Indian affairs, they visited many sites around the city and met several people who had lived among them. The Navajo headmen presented a colorful spectacle, as they were elegantly dressed in tanned buckskin knee-length pants decorated with silver buttons; colorful calico shirts; and elaborately striped wearing blankets. They wore red, shin-high buckskin moccasins with silver buttons. Most wore silver concho belts and strings of turquoise beads. All of them wore silk scarf headbands, except Ganado Mucho, who favored a cap, and Carnero Mucho, who sported a formal silk top hat. Juanita wore buckskin moccasins, a dark wool, woven, Navajo-style dress with red diamond borders around the hem and shoulders, and a multistrand shell necklace. [10]

For Arny, who used the Navajos' entire trip to his best advantage, the highlight was a testimonial dinner held by fifty of his Washington acquaintances. His friends spoke of Arny's work for the "cause of humanity and the elevation of black and red races." Arny's "long, semireligious response continued until almost midnight, when the group retired after singing *Home Sweet Home*."[11]

Flushed from the accolades of his supporters, Arny could see his plans about to come to fruition. All that remained was the meeting with President Grant. But while Arny was away from the Arlington House Hotel on the eve of this most important meeting, Thomas Keam prevented the meeting from taking place as scheduled. Keam was in the capital on personal business, but that night he put personal concerns aside, arrived at the hotel, and led Manuelito and several others away for a late-night tour of the district and its saloons. While together, Keam showed them Washington's bright spots and presumably explained to them the real reason Arny wanted them to meet with Grant. He must have discussed Arny's plan for taking the San Juan River region from them and explained how Arny had gotten their sanctions on the deal. When the party reeled into the hotel lobby they encountered Arny's fury. The irate agent confined the errant Navajos to their rooms because they were drunk. Keam's ruse worked. The meeting with Grant was rescheduled, and when it took place, there was no mention of the well-publicized land exchange.[12]

That the Navajo headmen did not comprehend the true nature of Arny's reason for the trip to Washington, D.C., is due more to Arny's program of disinformation than the Navajos' lack of critical thinking. Because Arny controlled the information, he was able to manipulate the headmen and the Navajo people in turn. By revealing the hidden purpose of Arny's plan, Thomas Keam broke Arny's hold over the Navajos. Consequently, the Navajos were freed from the agent's control. Arny's devious personality and fraudulent plans were revealed to the Navajo headmen, the San Juan area was saved, and any remaining questions about Arny's credibility were answered.

Thomas Keam was not in Washington, D.C., to prevent the Navajos from falling into Arny's corrupt plan. He was battling a much more elusive adversary: the faceless bureaucracy of the Office of Indian Affairs and the second comptroller of the Treasury Department. From the time he was fired as special agent for the Navajos in the spring of 1873, Keam had been trying to collect his salary for his last seven months of employment. The government owed him $691.30. In August of 1873, after two letters and a telegram to the Office of Indian Affairs, Keam was assured that his audit had passed inspection in the Office of Indian Affairs and was soon to be passed on to the Treasury Department for settlement. A year later, the Treasury Department still had Keam's unpaid claim. In October, the Treasury Department acted upon his claim by not acting on it, saying that they questioned Hall's authority to hire Keam as a special agent. In essence, they said the agency was not authorized to have a special agent because they had a clerk and did not need a special agent. Therefore, the position was unnecessary and the Treasury Department was not authorized to pay the bill. The Treasury Department sent back the claim to the Office of Indian Affairs with a request that they get the former agent Hall to prove he had authority to hire Keam as a special agent. Keam had met the second comptroller and was informed that his pay was suspended until such time as the Office of Indian Affairs could show authority for his appointment and authorize the payment of his salary. That Keam had been promoted to Special Agent for the Navajos by Superintendent of Indian Affairs for New Mexico General O. O. Howard in 1872 must not have figured into the bureaucrat's reasoning. Neither did the fact that Keam was on the payroll as special agent before Agent Hall was hired to work at the Navajo Agency, nor that the agency had hired Special Agent J.L. Gould to fill Keam's vacant position.[13]

Although Keam had not come to Washington, D.C., to prevent the success of Arny's trap, his well-developed sense of justice forced him to intercede on the Navajos' behalf. Clearly he was opposed to the Navajos being tricked out of the lush and potentially valuable San Juan area. In his years of service to the people, he had come to respect them and the progress they had made. His moral outlook demanded that he protect them from Arny's plans, but his dislike for Arny and his desire to have his job fueled his desire to derail Arny's plan. That Arny was publicly embarrassed by Keam's actions was an unexpected bonus.

The Navajos, returned to New Mexico in February 1875. The headmen complained that little had been accomplished and that the trip was made for the "glorification of Gov. Arny." They complained that they had traveled around the country as a show and that "no pains were taken to explain to them the many things they saw."[14] Arny returned a few days later to find that the weight of his intrigues had brought the agency to the verge of anarchy and his career was falling down around him. The agency supplies were depleted, its funds spent, and the Navajos starving and suffering from a severe winter. His appeals to Commissioner Smith for emergency appropriations went unfunded. Undaunted, Arny spent $7,000 to buy supplies for the Navajos. Smith and others in Washington, D.C., were tiring of Arny's disregard for established bureau procedures, his devious plans, and his promises. They were generally concerned about Arny's inability to keep his accounting books correct and current, and particularly concerned about a questionable $7,500 purchase.

In May, the Navajo headmen filed a complaint against Arny with the commissioner. They said he lied to them. They complained that Arny forged their signatures on supply vouchers and personally used property and funds appropriated for the Navajos. They said they had no faith in Arny, that he was "lying, vacillating, and unreliable," and that he was always using "high sounding and meaningless words." The headmen asked that Arny be replaced. They wanted Thomas Keam. "We believe Thomas Keams [sic] to possess all we ask for. He has lived many years among our people, he knows us, he speaks our language, we can make known our wants to him without the damages of false interpretations of wicked and selfish interpreters."[15] John Lowrie, secretary of the Presbyterian Board of Foreign Missions, joined the clamor for Arny's resignation and encouraged Commissioner Smith to ask for the same. This time, however, Lowrie made no suggestion for a replacement agent.[16]

Meanwhile, Arny gathered together his files, letters of support, and plans for another San Juan land exchange and headed for Washington, D.C., to plead his case. His defense focused on discrediting his detractors, primarily the "squaw-men." Undaunted by agency problems, Arny spent a considerable amount of time in the capital pitching a new version of his San Juan land deal. Shortly after the Navajos left Washington, D.C., Arny's original plan was scrapped because the land in the proposed southern extension had been given to the Atlantic and Pacific Railroad. Arny had drawn up a map with his new proposed land exchange. The San Juan area would be exchanged for an "equal" amount of land on the east and west of the present reservation. Arny's map grossly distorted the actual amount of land to be added. All of his plans and enthusiasm were to no avail. Washington had tired of Arny's troublemaking, and even the Presbyterians realized that Arny was not the solution to the Navajos' problems. Arny returned to New Mexico and submitted his resignation effective December 31, 1875; but his final days in the Indian service were anything but serene.

In August, the Navajo headmen took over the Fort Defiance agency and exposed the contents of Arny's personal storerooms. They found 16 bolts of calico, 4 bolts of manta, 110 pounds of yarn, denim material, 13 red blankets, packages of linen thread, 7 gross of handkerchiefs, shears, butcher knives, 75 pairs of children's shoes, tin cups, 240 tin pails, 432 tin pans, 54 spades, 3,300 pounds of flour, and 54 pounds of coffee. Mrs. Arny claimed that this was her husband's personal property. More than likely, it was what was left from the $7,500 vouched for by the chief's forged signatures. Arny submitted a letter of resignation dated August 25, effective immediately.[17]

One month later, Major William Redwood Price of the 8th Cavalry, stationed at Fort Wingate, was dispatched to inventory the supplies at Fort Defiance in order to determine what was agency property and what was Arny's personal property.[18] Arny initially wanted to inventory the goods at the agency so he could determine what he was liable for. Presumably all that was left over, therefore, would be his. Price did not accept that suggestion. Arny then proposed that, because he did not want to haul all of the supplies away from the agency, he, as agent, would issue and sign a voucher for the value of the goods.[19] In other words, Arny, the agent, would issue a pay voucher to himself as the owner. Price did not approve of this plan either. Of the inventory, Price said that the biggest problem was that the material Arny claimed was "similar to that heretofore issued to the Indians."[20]

Price was also hampered in conducting the inventory because all the employees except one had "been summoned to Albuquerque to appear before the Grand Jury" called to indict those parties who were involved in the problems at the agency.[21] The grand jury was investigating allegations filed by Arny and by W. W. Owens and F. J. Tanner, employees at the agency. Owens, who had been fired by Arny but was apparently back in his good graces, and F. J. Tanner swore that William Keam, Daniel Dubois, and Anson Damon "have by a course of systematic misrepresentation and intermeddling excited the Navajo Indians to opposition to the Agent and employees of the Agency & also to arouse in said Indians a spirit of hostility to the Government and dissatisfaction with the policy of the Government towards them."[22] In Arny's sworn statement, he claimed that neither William nor Thomas Keam were United States citizens; that Thomas Keam, Daniel Dubois, and Anson Damon had counseled the Indians to ignore the agent; and that they promised that when Thomas Keam replaced Arny as agent, the Navajos "would not have to work" and annuity goods would be given to the chiefs to be distributed by them.[23] Arny's allegations resulted in charges being filed in District Court in Albuquerque against William Keam for selling liquor to the Indians and against William Keam, Daniel Dubois, and Anson Damon for sending seditious messages to the Indians. Almost two years later, the three were found to be not guilty. There were no charges filed against Thomas Keam.[24]

Thomas Keam had not been on the reservation since the spring of 1873, when he was fired as special agent. Presumably he had not met with any Navajos until December 1874, when he met with the Navajo headmen in Washington, D.C. During this time, he made a trip to visit his mother, who was ill, in Truro. While on the East Coast, Keam visited with his friend E. R. Haight who superintended the Washington branch office of the Washington Gas, Coal, and Coke Company, and he spent time in New York City.[25] While in Washington, D.C., Keam received a license to trade with the Hopis west of Fort Defiance.[26]

During the late summer and fall of 1875, Keam applied for Arny's job as agent for the Navajos. He explained his qualifications to the secretary of the Presbyterian Board of Foreign Missions, John Lowrie, and reminded Lowrie that the Navajo headmen supported his application.[27] He supplied endorsements from Associate Justice H. S. Johnson, Clerk of the 2nd District Court of New Mexico F. W. Clancey, and thirty-three other New Mexicans.[28] Lowrie may have requested information from Presbyterians in New Mexico, because others wrote in response to Keam's application. Undoubtedly aided by Arny's and Roberts's information, George G. Smith, the Presbyterian minister in Santa Fé, added his impressions for Lowrie's consideration.[29] Smith's ethnocentrism and denominational superiority were typical of many Presbyterian missionaries and ministers to the Indians. Smith reported on the gossip surrounding Keam; he did not write from any firsthand knowledge of the situation or the man:

> All agree that he [Keam] is undoubtedly fully competent to manage those Indians but he has two children running with them [the Navajos] now, and the question is has he, as he professes, repented of his former loose life? Is he, as he now professes, now a *Christian [sic]*. If so, is he willing to *marry [sic]* the mother of those children, if she is living?[30]

Smith found Keam's marriage to Asdzáán Libá as immoral as Roberts and Arny had. Smith's comments reflect the prevalent attitude of the time that Indian women were duped into relationships with white men in which they were used by them and then abandoned, left to support themselves and their bastard children. That Keam had not married Asdzáán Libá in a Christian, legal ceremony reflected a darker side of Keam's character and called into question his own profession of Christianity. Because she was an Indian, Asdzáán Libá was not to blame in this matter because she was naive. That she had been seduced by Keam's superiority was obvious to Smith. "Mr. Crothers [agent at Hopi, 1871–1872] tells me she is, for a squaw, a superior woman, and that she has some education (Spanish) and moreover that she supposed she was really the wife of Keames [sic]. Mrs. Miller, the wife of the former agent of the Navajos asked her how long she expected to live with Keames [sic]. 'Why do you ask me that question', she replied, 'I shall live with him as long as life.'" The only way for Keam to clear up this issue, in Smith's opinion, was "to marry the squaw, if she is still alive." A Christian man would not and could not live with a woman, even an Indian woman, without the sanction of a Christian marriage.[31]

Lowrie probably wrote Keam about these allegations that, if correct, could jeopardize his application. In an uncharacteristically personal letter, Keam explained his situation to Lowrie. "Although it now causes me mental pain to refer to what I had hoped was buried in the past, it having transpired three years ago[,] it was a fact [the marriage], the experience and remorse of which has long ago taught me was a grose [sic] wrong I then committed."[32] Having confessed his mistake, Keam suggested that his future actions would be less impetuous. "This sad experience combined with my own personal feelings and standing in society, has with Gods [sic] help fully fortified me, against anything of this nature ever again transpiring." He continued, blaming his actions on "inexperience and youth." Keam did not say whether he and Asdzáán Libá were still married.[33]

Either because of his apparent qualifications or the contradictory nature of the letters reflecting on his qualifications, Keam's application gained the attention of officials in the Office of Indian Affairs. They suggested that Keam forward testimonials to Lowrie's office in New York City. This Keam did. He gathered together letters of recommendation from Colonel L. E. Dudley, Superintendent of Indian Affairs of New Mexico, and Major William Redwood Price of the 8th Cavalry.[34] These he forwarded to George Smith in Santa Fé. "I have presumed to entrust it [the application and endorsements] to your care for endorsement, and at the same time ask you to please forward it [to Lowrie] for me, with such remarks as you deem proper."[35] Keam unknowingly scuttled his own application. Smith dutifully forwarded Keam's package to Lowrie with the requested remarks. "I can not endorse his application," Smith wrote. "Of his competency I have no doubt whatever. Of his knowledge of the character and traits of the Indians there can be no question." But "*the shortness of my acquaintance with him [sic]* and the *distrust of his motives and character [sic]* shown by many good men would be sufficient to deter me."[36] Smith claimed that Keam did not have the trust of the men Smith knew and trusted; therefore, Keam ought not to be agent.[37]

Undaunted by the board's decision to name Alexander Irvine to the agent's post, Keam managed to keep the door from shutting completely on his application.[38] He thanked Lowrie for his help while his application was being considered, and he tried to deflect some of the charges against him. He said that the only reason he wanted to be the Navajo agent was that the Navajos wanted him and asked him to serve. He admitted there were personal motives behind his application, but they were among the most honest of reasons. He wanted to make certain that his son, Tómas, was educated. It was a duty he was bound to uphold, although this might be difficult to accomplish. He recognized Lowrie's advice, saying, "in your letter you stated that I should marry the mother of the child," but he claimed that that would not be possible because "the woman . . . has married one of her own people." Keam's "absence from this reservation and territory for over two years" was to blame. "Under these circumstances I shall do all in my power to educate the boy, so that he may be a good example to the tribe and in [the] future he will be a great service toward their civilization and enlightenment."[39]

Once again Keam's application for the Navajo agent's job was refused. There was no question that Keam was qualified for the job. Perhaps it was his qualifications and his relations with the Navajos that the officials, like the agents, feared most. Keam had no other alternative but to return to his trading post one mile south of Fort Defiance, where he had all the business he needed. He returned alone, however. Asdzáán Libá had decided that Keam was not returning from England and she had divorced him.[40] She had remarried and, with the boys, Tómas and Billy, had moved away from Fort Defiance and lived near Black Mountain.[41] William Keam, who was Agent Irvine's interpreter at the Hopi agency, and his wife ran the trading post near the Hopi mesas in northeastern Arizona.[42]

Thomas Keam's post, called Fair View, was close enough to Fort Defiance that he found out quickly that Agent Alexander Irvine was resigning in the summer of 1877, and Keam applied for the job. This time he must have believed that all the impediments to his appointment had been removed. He had become a citizen and he was no longer married. He systematically marshalled his support and announced his intentions to be named agent by writing to President Rutherford B. Hayes. He stressed his knowledge of the Navajo Indians and reminded the president that he had once been their special agent. He claimed, "I am satisfied of being able to control them, with the satisfaction both to the government and Indians, in carrying out the policy of the government towards them."[43]

Four days later, in a letter to John Lowrie, Keam said he fully understood and concurred with the aims of civilizing and Christianizing the Indians:

and I assure you no one would take a greater interest or work more diligently to accomplish this object than myself; being particularly interested in them, from my thorough knowledge of them all these last eight years; am satisfied I could readily carry out your desires in behalf of Missions and Schools.

Having their entire confidence (which takes a stranger years to gain) I think they will readily comply with my wishes when fully & properly explained how much it is to their interests and that of their children, that they attend school and receive a Christian education.

To accomplish this is no easy task, but will require the Agent to put his heart and energy to work in the object; and take pride in showing good work.[44]

Keam mentioned that Lowrie would be receiving letters of recommendation from the missionary-physician John Menaul, formerly at Fort Defiance and now at Laguna Pueblo; J. V. Lauderdale, surgeon at Fort Wingate; and Reverend Sheldon Jackson, Superintendent of the Presbyterian Missions for New Mexico, Arizona, and the Rocky Mountain Territories.[45]

Keam forwarded letters of recommendation to the Office of Indian Affairs from Captain Frank Tracy Bennett, former Navajo agent; Lieutenant S. B. Stafford at Fort Wingate; and Colonel Edward Hatch, who called Keam a "high minded business man, thoroughly acquainted with the Indian character."[46] A petition was sent from the citizens of New Mexico to Secretary of the Interior Carl Schurz urging Keam's appointment. They wrote to counter any derogatory statements that might be on file in the Office of Indian Affairs. They began their petition:

We the undersigned citizens of the United States residing near the Navajo country make the following statement:

That we have been personally acquainted with Thomas V. Keams [sic] for these last eight years, and know him to be an honest, industrious, strictly temperate, and every way qualified to fill any office of trust and responsibility. We further believe the statements made against him to be false, designing and malicious, as we know he is averse to the use of intoxicating liquor as a beverage, not using it himself, and does allow his power to bring to justice and furnish any party concerned in its being conveyed or sold to said Indians.

We also know the Navajo Indians have confidence in and request Mr. Keams *[sic]*, and for our protection, the safety of our property, and the proper government of the Indians, we ask for his appointment as Navajo Agent, as it is the very best that can be made.[47]

The petition was signed by ninety-six individuals.

Even Alexander Irvine, the outgoing agent, wrote in support of Keam's application. Writing from Fort Defiance on September 20, 1877, the agent, claimed that

I have been acquainted with Thomas V. Keams *[sic]* for these last six years and intimately acquainted with him for these last two years he was living near Fort Defiance.

And to the best of my knowledge he has never lived with a Navajo squaw as his wife[.] [H]e neither uses himself nor believes in the use of intoxicating liquors as a beverage[.] And I am satisfied that he has never issued or disposed of intoxicating liquor to the Indians and all statements accusing of such I believe to be false and malicious.[48]

To the officials in Washington, D.C., the letters were of no count. Neither the army, the citizens of New Mexico, nor the agent himself carried enough weight to counter the gossip.

Keam's Presbyterian support was withdrawn by J. V. Lauderdale, the surgeon at Fort Wingate. He rescinded his letter of support, saying he had learned from Agent Irvine that Keam was not a "suitable person for the position."[49] Since first writing, Lauderdale had learned that Keam was living with an Indian woman to whom he was not married. Lauderdale continued, saying that he had learned of "other practices which do not make him a pattern of the higher civilization which it is desirable that the Indian should copy."[50] Lauderdale went on to cast doubt on Sheldon

Jackson's recommendation of Keam, saying that if Jackson knew what Lauderdale knew, Jackson would withdraw his support. Either Lauderdale was mistaken about when Keam was living with his Navajo wife, or Keam was living with another Navajo woman.[51] In either event, Keam's support from the Presbyterians in the area, vital to his success, was withdrawn.

Colonel Hatch's letter of recommendation was forwarded to the secretary of the interior by Commissioner Smith. With it Smith attached Arny's two-year-old affidavit, made when he charged William Keam and others with selling liquor and sending seditious messages to the Indians. Smith reasoned that Arny's allegations reflected on Keam's moral fitness for the position. A week later Keam found out that John E. Pyle was named agent for the Navajos.[52] He was supported by Lowrie because of his knowledge of Indians.

However disappointed, frustrated, and angry Thomas Keam may have been, he was soon aiding Colonel Edward Hatch and the army with the Mimbres Apaches. On September 2, 1877, Victorio and about three hundred Apache men, women, and children abandoned the strife of the San Carlos Reservation and headed for their home near Ojo Caliente. Hatch ordered everyone into the field to find the escapees. On September 29, Keam, two Ojo Caliente headmen, and five Navajo scouts left Fort Wingate, heading south across the lava beds to the vicinity of Mangas Mountains, about ninety miles away.[53] Keam had been hired by the army as the interpreter.[54] He also served as the temporary superintendent for the Apaches who had surrendered. For Keam, this service must have provided some diversion from his troubles with the Office of Indian Affairs and the Navajo Agency. It also gave him the opportunity to further prove his value to the army, which did not question his abilities as the civilian bureaucrats did. The job gave Keam the opportunity to revisit an area that he probably had not seen since his army days, fighting the same Apache groups some twelve years earlier.

On October 3, Keam reported that his party "arrived in the vicinity of their [the Apaches] camp due south of Ojo del Gallo, finding them scattered over the mountains."[55] By noon he had induced 179 men, women, and children to surrender:

> I then held a council with and informed them my purpose was to take them all to Fort Wingate. The Chiefs told me some of them intended to [go] back into the mountains. These I requested to step aside and separate themselves from the others at once, as I would be responsible only for those who went with me and conducted themselves right, and would have troops sent after those that left. The dissatisfied then came to me individually and said they were tired of running over the mountains and being bad men, that they would also go with me and remain with their chiefs. I then issued them what rations were furnished me, and instructed them not to leave the trail without first obtaining permission, which I found they complied with.[56]

During the trip to Fort Wingate, Keam had several opportunities to discuss their problems and future with the Apaches. As he had done numerous times before with the Navajo headmen, Keam probably counseled the headmen to try to cooperate with the Americans, explaining that they were not going to go away and leave the Apaches to determine their destinies alone. He likely explained that cooperation was the only way they could hope to keep their families together. Keam probably used the Navajos' improving conditions to show how cooperation would benefit the Apaches. They apparently listened, because they asked Keam to help them convince the army that San Carlos was not where they wanted to live. They told him that they would cooperate if the army would let them return to their homes near Ojo Caliente.[57]

Keam continued to oversee the Apache prisoners, escorting them on hunting expeditions and giving them permission to be away from his daily supervision only for such occasions as to hunt and to gather piñon nuts. On October 11 Colonel Hatch ordered them to Ojo Caliente, where they arrived on the November 9,

1877.[58] As the Apaches settled in for the winter, Keam was making good on his promise to the Apaches who wanted their family members at San Carlos returned to them. Keam wrote Colonel Edward Hatch:

> Since my return here, these Indians have been making constant enquiries and [are] very anxious to know whether their relatives at San Carlos will be restored to them again. I would state that it is almost a daily occur[ence] of one or two coming to me, and begging in tears, to have either a father, mother, or children, restored to them here, who are still retained at San Carlos. I have already made an official report on this matter, and stated I thought it but an act of humanity, that their desire in this should at once be complied with; as it would satisfy them the intention of the Government, was to treat them kindly as long as their conduct merited it. . . . I would much like to see it done as soon as possible, as I am confident it will have a good effect on the whole tribe; and it would be great satisfaction for me to show what had been accomplished for them.[59]

Colonel Hatch reminded Keam that this request had been "referred to higher authorities some time ago" and said that an answer was anticipated. He told Keam that "it was recommended that their families be brought from San Carlos."[60]

Two weeks later Keam sent out the same plea to Captain A. E. Hooker of the 9th Cavalry, who was commanding the troops at Ojo Caliente, saying that the chiefs were anxious to hear when their families would be reunited. He reported that the chiefs were looking forward to the spring planting season and were only waiting for their families to help—and for the promised spades and hoes. Keam also told Hooker that his business required him to be near Fort Defiance soon, and he asked to be relieved of his duties on March 10. Keam was officially dismissed as interpreter and acting superintendent of the Apache Indians five days later, when he returned to Fair View, his trading post just south of Fort Defiance.[61]

However preoccupied Keam was while he was with the Apaches prisoners, he did not let the issue of his appointment to the Navajo Agency slip so easily from the attention of the commissioner of Indian affairs. In a letter to the secretary of the interior, Keam said that he had it on good authority, that of New Mexico Congressman S. B. Elkins, that he could not get the "appointment or any other under the Govt. as long as the charges now filed against you stand."[62] Keam implored the secretary to inform him in writing what the charges were, as it was only just that he know. Keam's answer arrived January 4, 1878: "there is at present no vacancy to fill at the Navajo Agency."[63] Because there was no vacancy, there was no need to itemize the allegations against Keam.

However, the issue was not dead. After General Sherman toured the area in September 1878, Thomas Keam was again suggested to replace Pyle as agent for the Navajos. Sherman said that Pyle should be transferred and Keam appointed "simply because he is *asked for [sic]* by the Indians themselves."[64] Sherman said that Keam had been a soldier in the Civil War and the officers of the army considered him to be honest, true, devoted to the Navajos, and able to talk to them in their language. He was, in Sherman's opinion, far better qualified to assist the commissioner in carrying out his "professed desire to Christianize and Civilize this interesting group of aboriginies."[65]

But the secretary of the interior was in no humor to listen to Sherman's advice about Thomas Keam's application for the agent's job or about anything else, because the Department of the Interior, of which the Office of Indian Affairs was a part, and the War Department were locked in a bitter dispute over who should control Indian affairs.[66] Following the Civil War and renewed hostilities between the United States Army and various Indian tribes on the northern Great Plains, in the Northwest Coast, and in Arizona, the transfer issue had gained public attention. General Sherman was a particularly vocal advocate for transfer, claiming that the army, with its fort system and quartermaster and commissary staffs in place, could effectively and efficiently issue annuity goods, and that the commanding officer could implement policy. That the army could either prevent or put down uprisings was another obvious benefit of the transfer. Although the measure passed the House of Representatives several times, it failed in the Senate each time, due in large part to the efforts of the Christian reformers who fought to maintain control of the formation and implementation of Indian policy and the hiring and firing of Indian agents.[67]

That Thomas Keam had worked for and was supported by the United States Army and had Sherman's recommendation was, to the secretary of the interior, the commissioner of Indian affairs, and Reverend John Lowrie a clear indication of his unfitness to serve. George Smith, the Presbyterian preacher in Santa Fé, reported to Lowrie on his most recent actions to prevent the Navajo Agency from falling into Keam's hands.[68] He had just finished a letter to the commissioner about the "mischief-makers" who were trying to get Pyle removed and Keam named as agent. Smith claimed that Frank Tracy Bennett and other army officers had tried to give Sherman a bad impression of Pyle. They planned for Sherman to write the secretary of war, who would in turn write the commissioner of Indian affairs, who would then appoint Keam. Smith gloated: "My letter to the Comm. exposed the plot & remonstrated against the appt [sic] of the unworthy man."[69] He told Lowrie that "unscrupulous men like Keames [sic] annoy those whose places they covet" and that the powerful chiefs were willing to sell their friendships and influences in exchange for gifts to which they were not entitled.[70]

This time, Keam was caught on the wrong side in the battle between the civilians and the military for control of the Indians, and by the time Sherman wrote suggesting that Keam be named in Pyle's place, the Office of Indian Affairs was in no humor to take seriously any recommendation coming from the army. Additionally, the commissioner was not about to nominate a specific man to an agency just because the Indians wanted him for their agent.

From the time that Thomas Keam rode into the Fort Defiance agency in the winter of 1869 to 1878, he had acquired unique experience. He knew the Navajo people as well as any non-Navajo at the time. He knew their culture and spoke their language. He was respected by the headmen and by many other Navajo people. His experience, sensitivity, and acumen enhanced his qualifications. Personally, he believed in the inevitability of the Americans' domination of the Indians, and he believed it appropriate. His personal philosophies were compatible with those of the nation's humanitarians. Keam had cultivated what he thought were the right supporters: politicians, local ranchers, and army officers. But for one reason or another, their recommendations were tainted in the eyes of the Office of Indian Affairs. Keam's qualifications were ultimately of no interest to the Presbyterian Board of Foreign Missions. The board's repeated denial of Keam's application for the position of Navajo Agent was justified by the board's questions about Keam's morality and even his Christianity. The focus of their concern was Keam's family. In Asdzáán Libá the board saw the sin of cohabitation; in Tomás and Billy they saw the result of that sin. However reprehensible these problems were, the board's denial of Thomas Keam's application masked what they believed were more dangerous tendencies. That the Navajo headmen wanted Keam as their agent suggested either that Keam had duped the Navajos or that he and the headmen were working in collusion in some nefarious scheme to defraud the government. Beyond this was the question of Keam's loyalty. In a dispute between the Navajos and the Office of Indian Affairs, could Keam be trusted to support, defend, and implement the bureaucrats' programs?

—◁ 5 ▷—

CONFRONTING GALEN EASTMAN

Thomas Varker Keam was a hardheaded man where the Navajo agent's job was concerned. Other men may have accepted repeated denial and found another career, but as 1878 ended word had it that Agent Pyle was resigning his position, and Thomas Keam was again hopeful that this time he would be hired for the vacancy. In January 1879, Keam renewed his application for the agent's position "in the event of there being a vacancy." He restated his belief that there were claims prejudicial to his appointment and begged Secretary of the Interior Carl Schurz for the opportunity to prove them wrong.[1]

Keam's application was again discredited and his morality questioned in yet another letter written by George Smith, the Presbyterian minister in Santa Fé. He wrote John Lowrie, secretary of the Presbyterian Board of Foreign Missions, saying that Agent James Miller's death in 1872 should be investigated more closely. Although he did not name Keam specifically, he said that even though the "squaw-men" and the Navajos claimed Miller was killed by some Utes, "This is a lie. The Navajos killed Miller." He claimed they had been encouraged by those living south of Fort Defiance. Smith saw Miller's murder as an example of the lawlessness on the reservation caused by the presence of immoral white men, or "Canaanites" as he called them, and vowed that "No Indian Agent shall be murdered by a tribe under Presbyterian care and the matter hushed while I am in the region."[2] Writing to the commissioner of Indian affairs, Lowrie validated Smith's character, saying he was reliable and informed. He said that any problems former Agent William F. M. Arny had at the Navajo Agency were problems caused by the "squaw-men." In the end, Keam's application was for naught; Pyle resigned and was replaced on April 4, 1879, by Galen Eastman, John Lowrie's nominee.[3]

Keam probably heard about the nomination through the grapevine long before he received any official notification. From his Fair View trading post, one mile south of Fort Defiance, Keam was familiar with the goings on at Fort Defiance, as Navajos and agency personnel frequented the popular location. Since 1875 Thomas Keam had owned and operated two trading posts: the Fair View post and another thirteen miles east of First Mesa in a canyon known locally as Keam's Canyon. Keam's brother, William, ran the canyon post and William Leonard and Walter Fales ran Fair View, while Thomas Keam traveled to England and Washington, D.C., and plotted his strategy to win the coveted agent's position. Fair View was situated at the northern end of the valley, known as the Cienega Amarilla, or the "Sinagee." The valley is broad, well watered, and grassy. On the west side are the pine-covered mountains of the Defiance Plateau and on the east are red sandstone bluffs. Thomas Keam's neighbor was Anson Damon, the agency's former butcher, who also ranched in the valley. He and Keam were the first Anglo settlers in the area. They were joined in 1882 by another Anglo rancher, Sam Day Sr.[4]

Initially Galen Eastman's actions and suggestions about reservation issues were positively received. He and Keam maintained civil relations with one another, even though Eastman had the position Keam coveted. William Keam had minor duties at the Hopi agency, for which Eastman was also responsible, as that of "acting surgeon" filing the December 1879 sanitary report.[5]

Agent Eastman got along well with the Navajos. He listened

to their requests for more land to the east and south of the present reservation, and acted on their complaints that the agency physician, Walter Whitney, be replaced. Eastman, in turn, pressured Whitney to resign. Eastman recommended a doctor from Grand Haven, Michigan, Eastman's hometown, as Whitney's replacement. Eastman also hired his son, Edward F. Eastman, as agency carpenter and storekeeper, fired the agency clerk, Harry Simpson, and replaced him with James R. Sutherland, another hometown acquaintance. According to A. C. Webber, a clerk at George Williams's trading post, Eastman offered to make Webber an agency clerk and agency trader if Webber would make Eastman's son a partner in the business. Others claimed that Eastman was selling goods to the Navajos through middlemen on the West Coast.[6]

During 1879 Galen Eastman had other problems to contend with, and although these were things he could not control, he was directly responsible for their consequences. The summer had been particularly dry, crops were threatened, and Navajos had been forced to find water for their sheep in areas claimed by non-Navajos. Navajos competed with Anglos and Mormons along the San Juan and Little Colorado Rivers for water that the Indians were accustomed to using as needed. The Zunis also complained to Eastman about Navajos grazing their animals on Zuni land. The settlers complained to the agent and to the commissioner of Indian affairs about the Navajos, and the Navajos complained to the agent about whites living on their land.

These were troublesome times for the agent. Competition between Anglos and Indians for land and water was common in the Southwest. However mild, panic was beginning to set in in the Anglo communities near Fort Defiance as Navajo renegades were found among Victorio's Apache warriors in southwestern Arizona. In September 1879, the panic grew following an uprising at the Ute Agency in southwestern Colorado in which the agent, Nathan Meeker, and eight of his employees as well as three women and two children at the agency were captured. The uprising was put down only after a week-long standoff between three hundred Ute warriors and the army. Popular opinion, however unfounded, claimed that the Navajos and Utes, and perhaps the Apaches, had joined together to drive all Anglos from the region.

The military, which had responsibility for all Indians off the reservation, was certain that Agent Galen Eastman was incompetent to handle the problems facing him: keeping the Navajos on the reservation and dealing with hysterical Anglos in the area to prevent war from erupting. The military would be called in to deal with the consequences of Eastman's actions. While Galen Eastman's abilities and his honesty were in question, Thomas Keam regularly called these ineptitudes to the attention of the Navajo headmen. He did not allow officials in Washington, D.C., to forget that he was still interested in the agent's job.[7]

Eastman did follow through on his promise to the headmen that the reservation be expanded. On January 6, 1880, President Rutherford B. Hayes signed an executive order expanding the Navajo Reservation fifteen miles to the east and six miles to the south. This expansion in effect reduced the numbers of Navajos living beyond the reservation boundary and increased the number of Indians under Eastman's responsibility. The expansion also brought the "nest of cunning, malicious, corrupting white men," Thomas Keam among them, living south of Fort Defiance under the agent's control. These former agency employees, Anson Damon, Thomas Keam, and others, now lived on Navajo land and did so at the pleasure of the agent, Galen Eastman. Thomas Keam's Fair View Trading post and his cattle ranch were threatened. Eastman urged the commissioner to allow Damon to stay, in part because he agreed to cooperate with and support the agent. Eastman urged the government to compensate the others for their improvements, but force them to move out, because he believed they were bad influences on the Indians.

Eastman told Keam that he was going to have to move from Fair View. He was well aware of Keam's interest in his job and of the allegations about Keam's past. To prevent any trouble from Keam, Eastman reminded the commissioner that Keam had tried to cheat the government into paying $150 for a horse that Keam claimed was stolen. As Keam learned later, the horse was killed by his own herder, but Eastman claimed that Keam had never withdrawn the claim—an obvious ploy to steal from the government.[8]

Keam's bid for the agent's position was supported by a number of military men who saw in Eastman's mismanagement the potential for a war waiting to erupt with the Navajos. To the military, Keam seemed much more qualified to administer the Navajos and keep the peace.[9] In June, Eastman was removed from the agent's position and Captain Frank Tracy Bennett ordered to oversee the agency at Fort Defiance and at Hopi.[10] Immediately, Keam was proposed as the Navajos' agent. Even the Presbyterian teacher at Hopi suggested Keam. Charles Taylor's justification for suggesting Keam reflected the cold reality of the situation at the Navajo agency. "I am convinced," he wrote, "that we [the Presbyterians] had better not run the risk of another failure in this agency as I feel that we are almost sure to if we bring a stranger to this post [Defiance]." He said that things were going to get worse on and near the reservation because of the Utes and Apaches in the area, the expanding railroad, "and worst of all the Mormons are doing all they can to gain the Indian influence which they will turn against us. At such a time," he cautioned, "it is decidedly important that we have an agent who understands these circumstances and the people and their language as well." Taylor contradicted all his Presbyterian predecessors and suggested Thomas Keam for the job. He said, "He cannot be recommended as a Christian but as the most suitable man under the present condition of affairs."[11]

While the officials in Washington, D.C., gathered information and suggestions, Keam's old friend and one-time Navajo agent Frank Bennett took control of the Navajo and Hopi agencies. In the meantime, Thomas Keam had moved from Fair View, which was still in operation, to his canyon post near the Hopis, presumably to oversee the post while William Keam regained his health. Since he was there, Bennett asked Thomas Keam to supervise the Hopi agency inventory, a technicality required when an agency was transferred from one agent to another, because Bennett could not get away from Fort Defiance to handle it himself.[12] Bennett's trust in Keam is reflected in this request. The two men were old friends who had undoubtedly spent many hours discussing agency events from the positions both of insiders and of outsiders, looking on in mixed horror, indignation, and bemusement.

Ironically, the former agent Galen Eastman was ordered to turn over the Hopi agency property to his enemy, Thomas Keam, who was standing in for the new agent, Frank Bennett. Eastman was escorted by his son, Edward, who was no stranger to controversy himself. He had been ordered from the Hopi agency in June as much for his own safety as for peace at the agency. Edward Eastman had apparently upset E. S. Merritt, the Hopi agency teacher, because Merritt threatened "to blow E. F. Eastman's brains out." Merritt had pointed a loaded revolver at Eastman's head and would have killed him if a third party had not intervened.[13] The inventory revealed that many items were missing from the agency, including hardware, dye, cloth, and 1,500 pounds of food. Eastman blamed the discrepancy in the inventory on Merritt, who, according to Eastman, took the goods and used them "to pay his squaw concubines with."[14]

In the late summer Bennett invited Keam to visit the Fort Defiance Agency, saying, "I shall be glad to see you here at anytime," and then he added some personal news. "Hope you can come soon. I go to Ft. Wingate tomorrow morning [and] take your brother with me. He is very sick and I shall try and have him comfortably [arranged] for medical attendance there."[15] Bennett's letter was dated August 15, 1880. Three months later, William Keam was dead. There is no indication of the cause of William Keam's death; presumably, because of the length of his illness and the commonness of the disease, it was tuberculosis.

But Thomas Keam's desire to be the Navajos' agent would not die, and Keam continued to apply for the job from his now-permanent home in Keams Canyon. In 1881, he had more reasons than before to be hopeful that his application would be accepted by the Office of Indian Affairs. In Washington, D.C., there was talk of reforming the process by which civilians were appointed to government jobs, and Keam hoped that his experience would count for more than it had when the missionary boards controlled appointments to the Office of Indian Affairs. Locally, there was talk of war on the Navajo Reservation, and the local army officers were publicly crediting Agent Galen Eastman's inept administration for the situation. The army and the Navajos wanted Eastman out and Thomas Keam in the position. Keam consequently must have believed that his chances for becoming the Navajo agent had improved. However, his application was again turned down. Keam was still "not a fit person to receive an appointment as an Indian agent" according to the commissioner of Indian affairs.[16]

In early 1882 Keam went to Washington, D.C., where he met with Samuel Kirkwood, the new secretary of the interior, to talk about affairs at the Navajo agency and his application for the agent's position.[17] Keam was hopeful that the new administration in Washington would see his application for the agent's position in a more favorable light than the previous administration had. He returned to his canyon trading post convinced that the secretary was interested in the Navajos' affairs, but without an answer to his application.

In early May, Ganado Mucho rode over to Keam's trading post. He was not interested in buying food or selling wool. Instead he wanted Keam to help him run off the Navajos' agent, Galen Eastman, who had been reinstated. Ganado Mucho spoke for the old Navajo headmen. They wanted Keam to write the secretary of the interior. They wanted the secretary to send his answer to Keam, who would then read the letter to the Navajos. They said they did not trust Eastman to do this for them. The Navajos wanted Eastman removed, and if the government was powerless to do this, they threatened to run Eastman off the agency and take him to the railroad so he could leave the country.[18] E. S. Stevens, acting commissioner, answered their letter. He spoke to Keam, not the headmen who initiated the correspondence, telling him to inform the Navajos that the Office of Indian Affairs was convinced there were "villainous white men" giving the Navajos bad advice. The Navajos' plan to get rid of Eastman was just what these white men wanted to bring about a war so they could take over the Navajos' land. He told Keam that if the Navajos removed the agent, "they will be put down if it takes the whole Army of the United States to do it." To Keam specifically, Stevens said that his influence should be used to induce the Navajos to cooperate with the agent.[19] The Navajos had their answer. The Office of Indian Affairs stood behind their man and believed any problems at the agency or on the reservation were the result of white men who were using the Indians. The Indians' complaints were generated by these duplicitous men. In other words, the Indians had no valid complaints or opinions about their own welfare.

The atmosphere on and near the Navajo Reservation was tense and war hysteria was common: several non-Navajo communities had sprung up on the periphery of the reservation, miners were constantly violating the boundaries and the law, whiskey sellers were doing a booming business southeast of the reservation, and the agent, Galen Eastman, was proving inept. The military insisted that Eastman be removed because he was the cause of all of the trouble. The military and the Navajo headmen agreed on the solution to their problems: Thomas Keam could settle the disputes if only the Office of Indian Affairs would allow him to be the Navajos' agent.[20] The Department of Justice sent an investigator to the reservation to ascertain the facts of the situation, and he called for Eastman's removal and Keam's appointment. However, no one in the nation's capital was listening.[21]

At the agency at Fort Defiance, Eastman was trying to hold on to his position while campaigning for another less stressful and more lucrative one someplace else. Like the former agent William F. M. Arny, Eastman lashed out at his detractors in order to defend himself. Eastman's attacks fell on everyone in the area, even the postmaster at Fort Wingate. Thomas Keam in particular was singled out by Eastman, because he symbolized everything evil in the area and represented the greatest threat to Eastman's job. Eastman wrote his brother-in-law, Michigan senator Thomas W. Ferry, restating some of the charges against Keam in case they might be "overlooked." He reminded Ferry of Keam's fraudulent claim for a horse that Keam believed was stolen. Eastman said he had proved the horse was killed by Keam's herder and claimed that Keam had not rescinded his claim.[22] Eastman conveniently did not remember that Keam had asked that the claim be returned to him, and he forgot the way he had found out the horse had been killed: Keam had told him.

Eastman also wrote to the commissioner reminding him of the charges against Keam and replying to the charges levied against him personally by the Department of Justice investigator and others. Eastman was not going to let anyone remove him from his job if he could help it. About Keam, he mentioned his marriage to Asdzáán Libá, "that he was more or less mixed up in the case of the killing of a Navajo by his brother William [and] that he was identified with the traders here," suggesting that Keam was part of Eastman's infamous "Santa Fé Ring," a group of New Mexican businessmen who allegedly tried to cheat the government in fraudulent contracting schemes.[23]

In the early summer Eastman discovered a way to completely discredit his detractors and secure his own position. He wrote the commissioner of Indian affairs, "I have the honor to state that yesterday [June 19, 1882] Mr. Philip Zoeller an entire stranger to me, arrived at this Agency direct from the Moqui Pueblo Agency or 'Keam's Canon' being the same locality and voluntarily made the statement contained in the following affidavit[.]"[24] It corroborated allegations that Eastman had heard from other miners in the vicinity. Although Eastman had not reported these rumors, he forwarded Zoeller's affidavit to the commissioner and said that he would forward others if and when they became available.

About Keam, Zoeller said: "I firmly and conscientiously believe that said Keam has guilty knowledge (if not the instigator) of the murder of one Myrick [sic] and one Mitchell prospecting miners in the vicinity of Navajo Mountain. Keam had full knowledge of their whereabouts as they came to his place for supplies, they were murdered during the winter of 1879–1880."[25] Zoeller's charges against Keam were serious: the murders of Merrick and Mitchell had exacerbated the war hysteria sweeping the reservation.

Merrick and Mitchell were two miners killed between Navajo Mountain and Monument Valley in December 1879 or January 1880. Their deaths and the mine they were looking for have become part of the folklore of the region and their names immortalized by two buttes in Monument Valley. Little factual information is known about the two. Ernest Mitchell was the son of Henry L. Mitchell, part-time rancher and trader at McElmo Canyon near Bluff, Utah. Merrick's identity, and even his full name, is unknown. Henry Mitchell wrote Eastman in February 1880 that he had just returned from burying the bones of his son and Mr. Merritt, as he called him, and that they had been killed "30 miles off the Reservation" by some Navajos and Utes. In addition to his son and Merritt, Mitchell claimed there were five other missing men whose bodies had not been found.[26]

Mitchell's letter was not the first news that Eastman had heard of a possible murder in the Monument Valley area. Earlier in the month Eshke-beschinny (Boy with Many Horses), Ganado Mucho's son, and another Navajo headman had told Eastman that they had heard from another Navajo that some Paiutes had murdered two men for their animals and supplies.[27]

Nothing came of any of the investigations, and the matter was dropped because the men were believed to have been murdered off the reservation; that is, until Zoeller came into the agency, two years and six months later, with his story of Thomas Keam's involvement in the whole matter. That Zoeller's implication of Keam in the murder of Merrick and Mitchell was not investigated by the Office of Indian Affairs or given much credence by Eastman is indicative of the lack of evidence substantiating his claims. However, his other allegations fit quite nicely into Eastman's preconceived notions about Keam's influence over the Indians and his desire to have Eastman's job. Zoeller blamed Keam for all of the troubles at the agency and on the reservation.

> [Keam] frequently told the Indians that he acts under the authority of the General Government and endeavors to make them believe that he has special authority over this whole section of the country and more particularly over all the Navajos and their Agent.
>
> I also know and state that he had full knowledge of the alleged intention of taking Agent Eastman to the Railroad, [I] believe he was the cause or instigator of the idea, and firmly believe were it not for said Keam such talk would never have originated. . . . That said Keam went to Washington, and told the Navajos he would come back as their Agent.[28]

Zoeller's motives for appearing at Fort Defiance and taking the trouble to seek out Eastman to state his knowledge of an event several years old are unknown. His claims pose several problems. Philip Zoeller said he had lived at Keams Canyon for two years, meaning that he arrived at Keams Canyon about 1880, which suggests that he would not have been at Keams at any time to hear Thomas Keam planning the murder of Merrick and Mitchell. They would have been dead by the time that Zoeller arrived at the canyon. Also, Zoeller claimed that Keam knew about the miners' plans because they had gotten supplies from Keam's post and told him about them. It is unlikely that Merrick and Mitchell would have outfitted or resupplied at Keam's, because Mitchell's father was a trader and goods bought from him by his son would presumably have been much cheaper than Keam's. Also, the distance from Keam's post to the Navajo Mountain–Monument Valley area is more than one hundred rugged miles across Black Mesa; from the same region to Bluff, Utah, is about seventy-five miles of easy travel. The proximity of Bluff, cheaper goods, and Mitchell's family would lead one to assume that the logical decision to go to Bluff would have been made. More than likely the miners did not buy goods at Keam's trading post or anywhere else, since they left Mitchell's ranch with a "well stocked larder," more than enough supplies to support themselves for the sixty days they planned on being away.[29]

The source of Zoeller's complaints against Keam are evident: he believed that Keam was preventing him, and probably others, from going up into the Navajo Mountain–Monument Valley region to look for the mine because, according to Zoeller, Keam had Indian guards preventing any white men but himself from prospecting in the vicinity. Zoeller clearly believed that Keam was preventing him from venturing into the area to find the wealth that was undoubtedly awaiting anyone who managed to get past Keam's Indian guards.[30]

Zoeller's allegations of murder and extortion were never given any credence by the commissioner or even by Eastman. The charges that Keam had told the Navajos he was going to be their agent and that he exerted unusual influence over the Indians were obviously of more concern to Eastman. If Eastman could "get" Keam on some kind of technicality like influencing the Navajos to disobey their agent or for sending seditious messages to the Indians, he might have grounds to have Keam arrested under violations of the trade and intercourse laws.

In August, Zoeller's claims were substantiated by two other miners, Jonathan P. Williams and William Ross, who had been prospecting on the Colorado River and near Navajo Mountain. They were escorted to the agency by Edward Eastman, the agent's son. Williams and Ross filed their affidavits with Agent Eastman. They said Keam had told the Navajos that he was in charge of all the Navajos and the agent. Williams said he had been told that Keam had said when he returned from Washington, D.C., and was named agent he was "going to drive away all the American families and employees from the Reservation as he did not want any white women [sic] to be there at their Agency."[31] Williams and Ross added that they had met "Chief Hoskay na ne" [Hoskaninni] and he had showed them "*the gun belonging to the murdered Mitchell and Myrick [sic]—saying that Thos Keams [sic] gave it to him [sic]* and Said chief further Stated that when Said Mitchell and Myrrick [sic] were killed (/79/80) the Indians took all their goods to Keams Store, except one mule, which Said Keams told them not to give up until the friends of the dead men paid them fifty dollars Ransom."[32]

Nothing came from Galen Eastman's collection of affidavits, and as 1882 drew to a close he was replaced by D. M. Riordan.[33] Thomas Keam's application was not considered, nor was he contacted about the allegations. Like the agents who had preceded him, Galen Eastman failed to realize that policy formulated in the nation's capital could not be administered unilaterally on the reservation without the full cooperation and participation of the people and their leaders. Like the others, Eastman blamed his lack of success on the unscrupulous white men living near the reservation who counseled the Indians to disobey the agent. As in the past, Thomas Keam was believed to be the group's leader.

Eastman and the other agents were correct in one sense:

Thomas Keam encouraged the Navajo headmen to demand that an inept agent be replaced. He encouraged the Indians to exercise control over their lives and determine their own course of events. Why would Keam do this? There is no indication that Keam and the headmen were in collusion to defraud the government in some sort of contracting scheme. Nor is there any proof that the Navajos controlled any precious commodity that they were willing to share exclusively with Thomas Keam. Instead, it seems that each group was using the other for its own ends: Thomas Keam wanted the agent's job, and the headmen wanted an agent who would deliver annuity goods directly to them for their distribution, for this would have solidified the leaders' power and positions in the eyes of the people.[34]

Zoeller's allegation that Thomas Keam was somehow responsible for the murders of Merrick and Mitchell is far fetched. However, his allegations and those of Williams and Ross that Keam tried to restrict other miners' access to the area is intriguing in light of subsequent events. Their allegations that Keam told the Navajos he was in charge of all the Navajos and the agent is the earliest indication that Thomas Keam himself realized his power in the region was in some ways exclusive.

Thomas Keam had spent the better part of a decade trying to get rehired by the Office of Indian Affairs. Even though each of his applications for the agent's position was carefully calculated and each letter of recommendation glowed with the applicant's capabilities and dedication to the Navajos, there remained "serious charges" against him. The allegations were vague and unsubstantiated and their sources never disclosed.

In retrospect, it appears that Keam was haunted by ghosts from his past. They were so powerful—and they fell on such receptive ears—that neither Keam nor his supporters could exorcise the gossip, innuendos, and lies. Those who believed the allegations—government bureaucrats, missionaries, and Indian agents—were guilty of at least two misconceptions. To them

Keam's reputation was consistent with their prejudices about Indian traders and other opportunists on the western frontier, and they believed that Keam, like his ilk, was somehow cheating the government and the government's wards, the Navajos.

That Keam was the choice of the Navajo headmen did not improve his standing in the government's eyes or his chances of being named agent. It simply supported the allegations of Keam's detractors that he and the chiefs were in partnership in some evil scheme. In retrospect, Keam's relationship with the Navajos was his greatest liability. An alliance between Keam, as agent, and the Navajos against the federal government could have been a powerful and a potentially destructive one. Keam's influence with the Navajos was the one quality that the Office of Indian Affairs did not want in an agent. An agent was to keep the government's wishes and policies above all else, whereas Keam could not be counted on to keep the Navajos' wishes in perspective.

Keam's perceived power over the Navajos was also seen as dangerous, and it was the one quality that each of the agents feared or of which they were jealous. The letters from the various agents complaining about "squaw-men" were in essence complaints about those men who had more influence over the Navajos than they did. The "squaw-men," in general, and Thomas Keam, in particular, became convenient scapegoats for the agents' failures. For many, Keam's mere presence on or near the reservation suggested that the Navajos would comply with the government's wishes only if Thomas Keam told them to cooperate.

That the government saw the Navajos as Keam's dupes is an example of the Great Father's myopic view of his children's power over their own destiny. The Navajos used Keam and the perception of his power to their own ends. Their complaints about the numerous agents following their return from Bosque Redondo echoed more than petulance or dissatisfaction. While reservations across the West were shrinking, the Navajos successfully manipulated the government into doubling their reservation between 1868 and 1882. Following Bosque Redondo, the Navajo headmen created an environment in which their power was solidified and the people's power expanded, and they used Thomas Keam to bolster their position. Each time the Navajos wanted to rid themselves of an agent, they threatened some sort of disturbance and suggested they would cooperate with the government if the agent was replaced by Thomas Keam. The Navajos used Keam as a foil in their battles with the Office of Indian Affairs.

Just how Thomas Keam saw all of this is unknown. He had been living with the Navajos long enough to have a fairly sophisticated understanding of their lifeways and attitudes. His facility in the Navajo language allowed him to understand the subtleties and nuances of most conversations. He probably understood that the Navajos were using him, but he was using their recommendations to further his own cause as well. Their recommendations of him and his personal prestige among the people were powerful endorsements in the world of the American Southwest in the 1880s. Certainly his stature in the vicinity did not hurt his trading post businesses. That the Navajos wanted him as their agent undoubtedly brought more letters of support from the local citizens and the army than there would have been if the Navajos had had ambivalent feelings about him.

Keam's desire to be the Navajos' agent appears to have been sincere. He had spent a considerable amount of time, energy, and money trying to get the job. His personal beliefs about the inevitability of assimilation and the benefits of an industrial arts education placed him well within the mainstream of Americans' beliefs at the time. Keam was responding to a deep-seated belief that he could help the Navajos progress to the desired goal: civilization and citizenship. Keam's familiarity with the Navajos either allowed or demanded that his judgments about them be more practical than those of the Presbyterians who tried to push

the Navajos to civilization. Certainly Keam's humanitarian attitudes were not clouded with the zealot's blindness, but that does
not mean that he did not see the need for the Indians to adapt to
the "civilized" world around them.

Keam's numerous applications for the agent's position also reflect several personal qualities: Keam responded to the Navajos'
flattery by seemingly making a career of applying for the agent's
job, but because of repeated rejection he became a spiteful man.
That he was consistently turned down caused Keam to question
the competence of the Office of Indian Affairs, and repeated rejection caused him to become bitter where it was concerned.
Keam obviously believed that he alone was qualified to lead the
Navajos. This belief grew over the years as he witnessed one
inept agent after another force-fit flawed policies while his own
qualifications and suggestions were disparaged. Because he was
clearly qualified for the position but never chosen to serve,
Keam developed a tendency to criticize the actions, attitudes,
and motivations of all the agents and missionary-teachers with
whom he came in contact. Keam's attitude manifested itself in a
belief that no agent was as knowledgeable, as experienced, or as
powerful as he, and Thomas Keam spent the remainder of his life
proving just that to the bureaucrats in the Office of Indian Affairs.

—◄ 6 ►—

INDIAN TRADER

THOMAS KEAM MAY have had his sights set on the agent's job at Fort Defiance and may have spent a considerable amount of time promoting his application, but he had not neglected the operation of his two trading posts. The Fair View post, located several miles south of Fort Defiance, had been in operation since 1873, and the operation at Keams Canyon, thirteen miles east of First Mesa, since 1875. Keam owned these posts, but the day-to-day business fell to his clerks, Walter Fales and William Leonard at Fair View and William Keam at Keams Canyon.[1] Thomas Keam lived at Fair View, that is when he was not in Washington, D.C., visiting bureaucrats or in Truro visiting family. When William's health failed in the late summer of 1880, Thomas Keam moved to Keams Canyon. Keam may have seen his move to the canyon as temporary—filling in during his brother's absence—and the post as a convenient repository for the inventory from the Fair View post. That post was closing because the expansion of the Navajo Reservation had placed it under the jurisdiction of the Navajo agent. With William's death, Thomas Keam's family consisted solely of his mother, who lived in Truro. Elizabeth, Keam's sister, had been dead since November 1865; Keam's father had been dead since October 1868; William had died in November 1880. Thomas Keam's former wife, Asdzáán Libá and their sons, Tomás and Billy, lived south of Keams Canyon in a new family.

William Keam's death changed Thomas Keam's future. Instead of phasing out the Keams Canyon post or relying on clerks and managers, he permanently moved to the canyon and began expanding his holdings. Ironically, the Indian trade eventually provided Thomas Keam with the power and prestige he thought he would get as the Navajos' agent. But he could not have known that in 1880. All he knew was that the canyon post was located on public domain land and that he could run the post and raise cattle far removed from any Indian agent's control.

By this time, a well-established method of regulating trade with the Indians was in place. The nation's founding fathers believed that regulated trade with the Indians was vital to maintaining the peace on the frontier. Since then, and by virtue of the Constitution, trade with the Indians has been regulated by the federal government. After decades of piecemeal legislation, the requirements for trade with the Indians were firmly in place by the early nineteenth century. To trade on a reservation a man had to possess a license that after 1876 was approved by the commissioner of Indian affairs. In addition to a security bond, the individual had to supply references, prove his moral fitness to be among the Indians, and be a citizen of the United States. Clerks who worked for a trader were also subject to approval. The trader and his clerks had to obey all laws, regulations, and directives from the commissioner, who controlled almost all aspects of the trade and specified the kind and quantity of goods sold as well as the trader's profit margin. To trade on the reservation without a license meant forfeiture of all goods and payment of a fine. Trading posts established off the reservation, like Keam's canyon post, were not regulated by the Office of Indian Affairs, and traders at these locations were not required to have a license.[2]

American traders in northeastern Arizona neither invented nor introduced the concept of trading to the native peoples of the Southwest. By the mid-1800s trade was an ancient and complex way of life there. Prehistoric groups in the American Southwest and Mesoamerica had elaborate trade networks that incorporated areas bounded by the Pacific Ocean, the Gulf of Mexico, and the Mississippi River valley. The Pueblos, the early Navajos, Apaches, Comanches, and Utes were integral members of this network. Each group manufactured goods from its own environment and region and exchanged them for exotic goods it could not produce itself. When the Spanish, Mexican, and American colonists moved to the Southwest in historic times, they too were incorporated into the trade network.[3]

The Navajos produced woven blankets and sashes, some buckskins, and baskets. The Hopis produced incense, cotton twine, cane, reeds, and gourds as well as foodstuffs such as corn, piki bread, flour, melons, chiles, and dried fruit. The Utes produced buffalo robes; buckskin and elkskin for clothing, saddle bags, and bandoliers; and furs. The Rio Grande Pueblos produced, turquoise and shell beads, and foodstuffs.[4]

Trade was such an important component of the natives' lives in protohistoric and historic times that a well-developed standard of exchange existed. For example, a Navajo wearing blanket could buy a string of turquoise. A smaller blanket could be exchanged for a turquoise pendant; a large blanket and a saddle blanket could bring the Navajo trader two turquoise ear pendants, three strands of abalone shell beads, or two turquoise ear beads. In trading with the Hopi, a Navajo trader could receive a forty-eight-pound sack of unhusked corn for one dressed sheep. A dressed sheep could also purchase a smaller sack of corn and a bowl of ground cornmeal or a small bag of dried peaches and a tray of piki bread. House rafters made of dressed pine poles would bring ten sacks of unhusked corn; juniper firewood bought one sack of corn per length of wood; a goat brought eighty to one hundred pounds of corn. An elaborately striped wearing blanket, known in the vernacular as a "chief blanket," could buy five buckskins, a dressed buffalo robe, or a good mare from Ute and Apache traders.[5] Among the Navajos, trade was such an important aspect of their economy that it had become ritualized in prayers, songs, and ceremonies to ensure success and protect the traders from harm when they left Dinetah. "Even at the present time [1948] it is customary for a Navajo to sing a song or say a prayer, for good luck, while on the way to the reservation trading post."[6]

The Hispanic and Anglo settlers in the Southwest raised horses, mules, and other forms of livestock such as sheep and goats. These exotic animals soon figured prominently in the ever-increasing economic sphere, along with other "Anglo-controlled" items such as bridles, packs, saddles, guns, ammunition, iron, iron tools, alcohol, and brass, copper, and silver jewelry. An active trade in Hopi, Zuni, and Rio Grande Pueblo slaves for use as domestics in Hispanic New Mexicans' homes seems to have also kept Hispanic, American, and Indian traders busy.[7]

The establishment of reservations in the American Southwest and the influx of American settlers made it difficult for Indians to travel about the region as they had done for centuries. Consequently, it became more common for the Indians to trade with Anglo traders who were set up at more or less permanent locations in the area. There, at seemingly more convenient distances than in the past, the Navajos, Utes, Hopis, and Paiutes had an alternative to traveling a week or more to find those goods they could not produce for themselves. At the posts the Navajos, for example, could bring in their manufactures—blankets, piñon nuts, and wool—and trade them for coffee, sugar, salt, flour, and commercially woven fabrics. Later, traders even carried those exotic, Indian-made goods, such as turquoise and shell beads, buckskins, and baskets, that the people needed for their ceremonies.

The early Anglo traders, following the pattern set by earlier fur-trapping and trading mountain men, traveled among the Navajos on a regular basis, trading out of tents and wagons and staying in a specific location for just one season before heading back to Taos or Santa Fé. One of the earliest known of these traders was Frederick Smith, ancestor to a long line of twentieth-century traders, who traded around the Navajo Mountain area in the late 1850s. Smith, whom the Navajos called "the man who moves camp after dark," traded gunpowder, flints, lead, bullet molds, cloth, dye, robes, Green River knives, iron bridle bits, and manufactured silver jewelry to the Navajos in return for "some money," furs, livestock, and "valuables taken in raids."[8]

After the Navajos returned from Bosque Redondo to their newly established reservation in 1868, a few traders such as Romulo Martinez, who opened a post in Washington Pass in 1873, set up business on the reservation near the Navajo Agency at Fort Defiance. However, the majority of early traders set up their businesses beyond the boundaries of the reservation and the regulatory control of the Office of Indian Affairs and its agents. Hermann Wolf, who had trapped all over the American Southwest during the middle decades of the nineteenth century, established a permanent trading post on the Little Colorado River in 1868 near present-day Leupp. Keam's Fair View post was opened in 1873 several miles south of Fort Defiance and the Navajo Reservation border. "Old Man" William Leonard moved from Fort Defiance to a location near present-day Ganado on the Pueblo Colorado Wash about 1874. There was a post at Horse Head Crossing (near present-day Winslow, Arizona) on the Little Colorado in the 1870s run by a man named Berrando, and Thomas and William Keam bought out a trader in 1875 who had been trading for some time in a canyon thirteen miles east of the Hopis. Further west from what was soon known as Keams Canyon at Moencopi, Thomas S. Hubbell (no relation to John Lorenzo Hubbell, who later traded at Ganado) opened a post in 1871 or so, and another trader opened a business nearby at Willow Springs in 1876. Three miles beyond Hubbell's store at Moencopi, George McAdams, Frederick Smith's nephew, opened a post on Rabbit Mesa at Sheep Dip Wash in 1879. The Mormons operated at least two posts in the area: Jacob Hamblin's post at Lee's Ferry on the Colorado River in 1874, and a post and woolen mill at Tuba City operated between 1878 and the early 1880s by John W. Young, the son of Brigham Young.[9]

The number of trading posts built along the Mormon Wagon Road (or the route south from Lee's Ferry to Tuba City to the Little Colorado River) expanded as a result of the construction of the Atlantic and Pacific Railroad and the growth of wholesale businesses in Holbrook, Winslow, and Flagstaff. Near The Gap, a notch in the Vermillion Cliffs, Joe Lee and J. C. Brown built a post on the east side of Hamblin Wash in 1880, and C. H. Algert built a post at Bodeway Mesa near Cedar Ridge in 1881. George McAdams built a post at Powderhouse Canyon in 1885 in partnership with the Babbitt brothers, who ran a wholesale business in Flagstaff. At Echo Cliffs, McAdams and C. H. Algert built a post in 1891. At Musha Springs, C. H. Algert had a post from 1880 to 1882 and, after trading at several other locations, he opened another in Tuba City in 1886. Near Tonalea, or Red Lake as it is sometimes called, McAdams operated a post in 1881; Sam Smith had a post there in 1890, as did Samuel Scott Preston in 1891. At Cow Springs, Fred Voltz and Joe Lee ran competing posts across the road from one another from 1894 to 1896, and Benjamin and Bill Williams operated a post there in 1895. Joseph Hyrum Sr. operated a post at Tokesjhay Wash in 1881 and 1882, and Bill Williams ran a post at Blue Canyon from 1882 to about 1897, when Algert opened his business there.[10]

Trading posts began small and were constructed using naturally available materials. In the more forested areas of the Navajo Reservation, trading posts were made of logs set upright in a trench, stockade style. Hermann Wolf's first post on the Little Colorado River was a one-room, twenty-by-forty-foot building constructed of cottonwood and willow logs. Other than a door, there were no openings except for rifle ports. The roof was flat and covered with red clay. Along the Mormon Wagon Road,

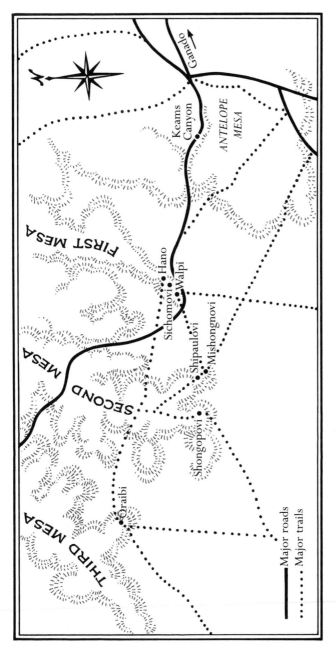

Hopi country, showing Hopi villages and Keams Canyon

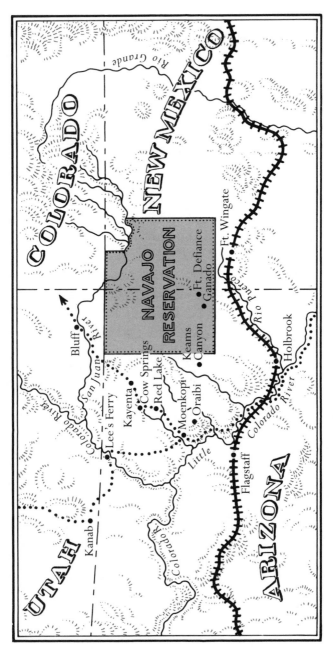

Four Corners area, showing towns, roads, and railroad

stone construction was more common. The posts at Black Falls, Willow Springs, Blue Canyon, and Moencopi, for example, were all built of stone with mud roofs. C. H. Algert's store at Musha Spring was a hogan, but it was abandoned after two years when it was covered up by blowing sand. In addition to using what was available naturally or "mining" prehistoric sites for rock building materials, traders also adapted other materials to their construction repertoire. For example, the stone trading post at the Rainbow Lodge had an attached wooden shed constructed of Arbuckle Coffee crate slats. Only after the business was on firm footing would a log and mud roof be replaced by a corrugated tin roof, or porches, window screens, or flower beds added.[11]

There were various motivations for a man to become an Indian trader. For some, trade with the Indians must have been seen as an easy way to riches. For others, like Anson Damon, the trading business was a way to support a growing Navajo family while living on the reservation near relatives. For yet others, like Jonathan Williams, a trading post provided the necessary entree—and permit—to stay on the reservation while investigating the country's mineral resources.

Before a trading post was constructed, the location might be tested for the suitability of the vicinity, the productivity of customers, and the competition. The temporary post set up by Charles Hubbell and Elias S. Clark in Washington Pass, high in the Chuska Mountains, in 1884 was nothing more than a large one-room tent. Although this post was made of canvas, it contained all the necessities for the traders and their customers:

> The undivided compartment of the great tent served as a place of business, a kitchen, and a sleeping-room. Across the front part of the tent a rough counter had been erected, backed by a high line of shelves, on which were piled rolls of red flannel, calico, cans of preserved vegetables and fruits, bags of coffee, sugar, and all heterogeneous collection of goods suited to attract the eye and supply the wants

of a semi-savage people. In front and behind the tent, huge bags stuffed with the wool of Navajo sheep, that had been received in trade from the Indians, lay waiting departure for the East.[12]

As soon as the trading season was completed, Hubbell and Clark packed up their tent, trade goods, and wool sacks and headed back to Gallup to sell their wool and count their profits.

Before a permanent location was decided upon, several considerations had to be taken into account: the people in the region had to have enough raw materials with which to barter, and the location had to be accessible both to the Indian customers and to the trader's freight wagons. The physical requirements for any trading post location were few: a steady supply of good water, people to trade with, and accessibility. Consequently, many posts were built near springs, old traces, and trails, and as the trader's business increased improvements to the roads soon became a priority, especially as the number and regularity of freight wagons to and from the post increased.[13]

For most of the early traders in northeastern Arizona, though, trading was of secondary importance. These men, among them "Old Man" William Leonard, Thomas Keam, Lorenzo Hubbell, and Sam Day Sr., originally settled outside of the reservation boundary and established cattle ranches with trading posts at the ranch headquarters.[14] The expansion of the Navajo Reservation forced some traders to either abandon the area entirely or take up trading exclusively. In this sense, politics and the good fortune of the Navajo people played some part in determining these men's choices for becoming Indian traders. For all of them, however, there must have been intangible reasons for their remaining in the trade business. The absence of an alternative career or training for any other job off the reservation or the lack of will to sell out, pick up, and move after years among the Navajos must have influenced some. The realization that the post location had become home, regardless of who owned title to the land, must have kept some men in the trade business long after it was profitable or practical.

The canyon where Keam's post and ranch were located is thirteen miles east of the Hopi villages on First Mesa. It is a northeast-southwest tending canyon formed by an intermittent stream that drains Antelope Mesa. The canyon is relatively short, three miles or so from its wide mouth to its narrow head, where it is several hundred feet deep. Like the surrounding countryside, the canyon supports cottonwoods and willows along the creek and sages, rabbit brush, yucca, and grama grasses elsewhere. On top of the mesa there are junipers, and further north, pine trees. The canyon is exceptional because it is blessed with several springs that provide a steady supply of good water.

The Hopis called it Poongo-sikia, after a plant that grew there that they used for greens, or Masíptanga, Moth Canyon. The Navajos referred to it as Lók'a'deeshjin, which means "reeds extend along black." Christopher Carson's New Mexico Volunteers camped there on their Navajo campaign on August 13, 1863; they called it Volunteer Canyon.[15] By 1882 it was known as Keams Canyon. Although William and Thomas Keams' early facilities were simple, when Thomas Keam moved to the canyon in 1880 he began an active program of building and remodeling. H. W. Dodd had operated a short-lived post in the canyon before 1875,[16] and the Keams may have bought out Dodd's buildings and improvements, as Thomas Keam did those of an unidentified builder in late 1882.[17] These buildings eventually became the nucleus of Keam's trading post. Thomas Keam had created a well-designed and organized trading post complex that looked like a small town instead of a styleless collection of oddly assembled buildings.

To protect his investment from future reservation expansions, Keam proclaimed that he had staked a claim to 160 acres in the canyon under provisions of the Desert Lands Act, which allowed any citizen to file a declaration to not more than one section of land at 25¢ per acre.[18] After three years the claimant was issued a patent, provided water had been conducted to the land. As the canyon was blessed with plenty of spring water, the latter stipulation was of no concern to Keam, who had the land surveyed and mapped.

Thomas Keam's trading post was nestled in a nook of the north wall of the canyon. It was made up of a ∪-shaped building that contained an office, dining room, and kitchen on one side, a large warehouse, thirty-two feet by twenty-four, in the middle, and a smaller warehouse and the store on the other side. The warehouse, complete with large doors, was nothing more than a storage facility for the post. In it were stored bulk groceries and merchandise as well as the wool and pelts the Navajos brought in for trade.[19] The store consisted of one large room, seventeen by fourteen feet. Around the inside walls were shelves for groceries, clothing, and yard goods. Bulky goods, like pots and pans, tin buckets, pails, and galvanized tubs, were hung from the rafters along with such goods as slickers, saddles and harnesses, lengths of rope, tanned buckskins, whips, and quirts. Everything for sale was on display as much for the customer's convenience for as an accommodation to the lack of storage space. A counter of unusual height and width encircled the shelves. The trader, or his clerks, stood behind the counter, handing things down to the customer for inspection. Navajo customers had preferred brands. Arbuckles "Ariosa" coffee was the most popular brand, and both whole beans and ground coffee were sold at the post. The availability of whole-bean coffee meant that the trader had to stock coffee grinders for sale as well as providing one in the store. "Star" and "Horseshoe" chewing tobacco and "Bull Durham" smoking tobacco were also popular. Stetson hats, Levi Strauss pants and overalls, and woolen blankets from the Pendleton mills were on hand. Navajo customers favored saddles that were small and "double-rigged" (having two cinches), with leather-covered saddle horns. It seems that each trader had a story about buying and stocking some brand of seemingly equal quality, in the trader's estimation, only to have it sit on the shelves while the shoppers requested the "standard" brand. In addition of manufactured and processed goods, traders also provided butchering facilities and butchered local meat.[20] Keam's trading post had two presumably unique features. Most traders kept a box of loose tobacco on the counter for the convenience of the customers. Keam provided a "little iron figure representing a wrinkled old man smoking a lighted taper" that customers could use to light their hand-rolled cigarettes. He also kept a pet snake that inhabited the shelves of the store and darker recesses of the warehouse and lived on rodents that also inhabited the post.[21]

On the back of the smaller storeroom was the carpenter shop, and behind that a cellar and a two-room house with a fenced yard and shade trees. Behind the post and abutting the canyon wall were a horse corral and stable, a cow lot and stable, a hay corral, and pig sty. The corral contained the livestock brought in to the post for trade. The entire facility was enclosed with a stone fence on the east and west. Across the road were a chicken house and duck house, complete with a pond.[22]

The dozen or so buildings were all built of dressed sandstone laid in adobe mortar, with walls averaging two feet in thickness. The roofs of all the buildings were made of dressed pine poles, rafters, and joists covered with boards overlaid with clay, which Keam said was "an improved modification of the Mexican earth roof." The roofs projected over the walls about eighteen inches in order to protect the walls. The eaves were made of wide boards, and there were numerous runoff spouts. The carpenter and blacksmith shops were not floored, although all of the other rooms were substantially floored with pine boards. The ceilings of all rooms were eight to eight and one-half feet high, and interior walls were plastered and whitewashed. Keam used the plentiful and economical, locally occurring gypsum to keep all his "buildings with white, glossy coats, both inside and out."[23]

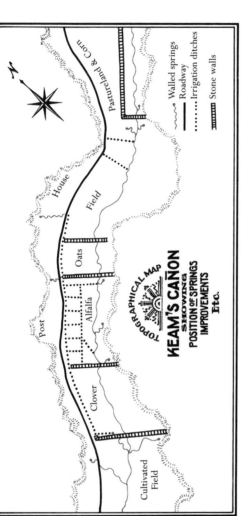

Keams Canyon, showing springs, fields, and improvements. Alexander McGregor Stephen drew this and the following two maps to accompany Keam's offers to sell the facilities for the Hopi school. Field number one was made up of twelve acres of pastureland and corn; field number two, two acres of oats; field number three, five acres of irrigated garden lands and alfalfa; field number four, four acres of clover; and field number five, five acres of cultivated land. All of the fields were separated by stone walls, and all fields but number five were irrigated. The six springs were improved and also walled. Spring number one produced seven and one-half gallons; spring number two, six gallons; spring number three, six gallons; spring number four, three gallons; spring number five, six gallons; and spring number six, three and one-half gallons. Stephen noted that the combined flow was twelve gallons but did not indicate the rate of flow. (From map, Office of Indian Affairs, number 1265, Record Group 75)

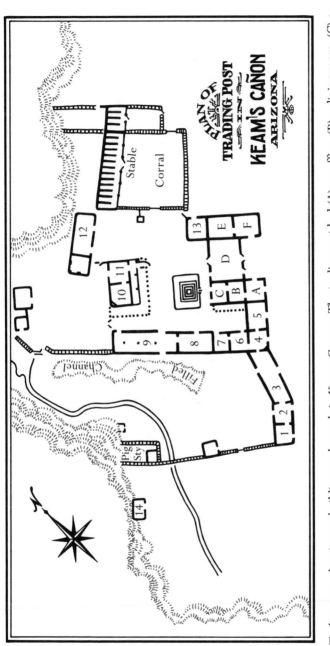

Trading post, showing outbuildings and corrals in Keams Canyon. The trading post had (A) an office, (B) a dining room, (C) a kitchen, (D and E) two warehouses, and (F) the store. Outbuildings included (1 and 2) employees' quarters, (3) a proposed school room, (4, 6, 7, 10, and 11) dwelling rooms, (8 and 9) a wood house and proposed dormitories, (12) a carpenter shop and shed, (13) a blacksmith shop, and (14) Indian quarters. (From map, Office of Indian Affairs, number 1265, Record Group 75)

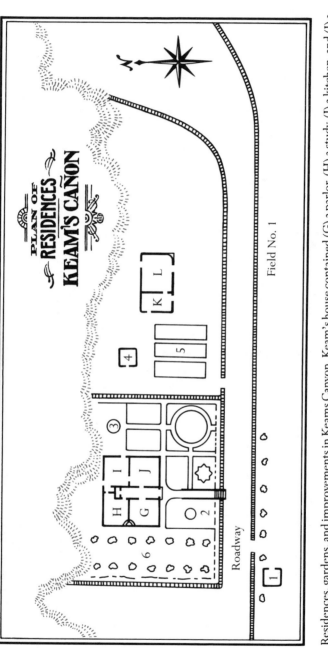

Residences, gardens, and improvements in Keams Canyon. Keam's house contained (G) a parlor, (H) a dining room; the house just east of Keam's house (K and L) had two dwelling rooms. Outside Keam's house were (1) a poultry house, (2) a fountain, (3) a cistern, (4) an outhouse, (5) a garden, and (6) an orchard. (From map, Office of Indian Affairs, number 1265, Record Group 75)

Keam's house, which was up the canyon some one hundred yards from the trading post itself, was also constructed of dressed sandstone. There were four large rooms measuring fifteen by fifteen feet each. A study and a parlor were on one side of a long, wide hall, with a dining room and a kitchen on the other. The ceilings in his home were ten feet high, and the walls were "carefully finished and handsomely papered, and the floors carpeted."[24] The deep windows were decorated with potted flowers, and the house was decorated with fine Navajo blankets, sheepskin rugs, Hopi pottery, and photographs from the Smithsonian Institution and A. C. Vroman of Pasadena, California. On the shelves in the living room were books by Shakespeare, Thackeray, Dickens, Taine, and other authors as well as an "unusually good representation of standard American and English magazines and newspapers."[25] The house was enclosed by a stone fence surrounding a fine, terraced yard with a formal garden of mignonette, candy-tuft, and asters in front, with a fountain "supplied with excellent spring water brought through iron pipes and forced up by a hydraulic ram." On the west of the house was an orchard.[26] The kitchen (under the supervision of a cook) was supplied with water from a cistern twelve feet deep and ten feet in diameter. A bunkhouse for the cook and a laborer were up from the house about fifty yards.[27]

The post and house were located under the eave of the canyon's north wall. The lee of the canyon was protection from winter and spring winds, and the southern exposure ensured warm, bright sunshine during most of the year. In front of the trading post and house complex were a road and a natural drainage as well as an irrigation ditch fed by the springs. Across the road, Keam planted hundreds of trees. Several miles of rock fences enclosed the farmlands, with five walled fields and pastures ranging from two to twelve acres in size. From the twenty-seven acres under cultivation, Keam harvested corn, oats, alfalfa, and clover for hay. Two irrigated fields produced

Keam's original trading post in Keams Canyon in the mid-1880s. This photograph, which conforms to maps drawn of the post by Alexander Stephen, is attributed to James Mooney, the Smithsonian Institution anthropologist who visited Keam and Stephen while doing fieldwork among the Hopis in February and March 1893. Smithsonian Institution, photograph number Ariz 366A.

garden vegetables, including potatoes. The springs, of which there were six, produced enough water for household use and for farming.[28]

Without the trading post component to Keam's operation, there would have been little reason for the rancher to become familiar with his native neighbors. His speaking ability in Navajo would have degenerated and his acquisition of the Hopi language would have been limited to rudimentary greetings and simple conversations without much substance. His trading operation prevented that from happening and prevented Keam from becoming the isolated rancher surrounded by unfamiliar natives.

The post brought Hopis and Navajos to Keam's ranch everyday, and each day saw much the same kinds of activity. The trader's day was taken up in fulfilling the needs of his customers. They arrived on horseback and in wagons and stayed most of the day, or overnight in some instances, to complete their business. Because going to the post was not a daily or weekly event, the list of business to be taken care of was long and the visiting savored. No one was in any particular hurry, nor was anyone rushed through the trading process.[29]

The operation required that Keam be on hand to supervise his clerks, interpret idiomatic expressions for both clerk and client, and visit with his customers. The most important quality for any Indian trader among the Hopi and Navajo was his ability to sit and pass the time of day in unhurried conversation. Exchanging tidbits of local gossip, weather information, and jokes placed the trader and his customer in equal positions. Each had something to give to the conversation, something to gain from the business transactions, and reasons to protect his own integrity as well as that of the other.

Trading was an occupation to which no other compared. It was "more of a way of life than a regular business."[30] A successful trader knew his clients individually; he knew their families, clans, and relatives, their idiosyncracies, their preferences and dislikes, and their financial situation almost as well as his own. Lorenzo Hubbell explained it like this: "Out here in this country, the trader is everything from merchant to father confessor, justice of the peace, judge, jury, court of appeals, chief medicine man and de facto czar of the domain over which he presides."[31]

Keam's experience had taught him that an Indian trader, un-

In front of Keam's original trading post in Keams Canyon, Ca. 1884–1889. Like other traders, Keam bought wool, hides, and animal skins. Cobb Collection, Center for Southwest Research, General Library, University of New Mexico, negative number 000-119-0509.

like a country or company store manager in rural America, did much more for his clients than provide them the opportunity to purchase canned tomatoes and yard goods. The trader extended credit to his customers from one wool season to the next. He also extended credit secured by jewelry and baskets—collateral unrecognized by shopkeepers in other parts of the country— and he loaned the collateral back to its owners if it was needed in a ceremony before the loan was paid. The trader also served as the Indians' banker, holding cash in his safe.[32] The trader was often called away from his post to perform the duties of a doctor, duties for which only his experience had trained him. The trader's immunity to the dangers associated with Navajo deaths ensured that he was called to perform burials for his Navajo customers. As an interested and appreciative outsider and a friend, the trader was often invited to various ceremonies and celebrations. In fulfilling these social obligations, he donated food and delicacies (such as soda pop in a later generation), for the celebrants. Consequently he became a part of his customers' world and gained an understanding of it rivaled by only a few outsiders.

Keam and the other traders possessed one skill that the Indians did not have—the ability to read and write English. In later years, after Navajo and Hopi children went off the reservation to attend school, traders wrote letters for the parents and translated their children's letters to them. Also, traders served the railroads and government agencies by supplying men for jobs and arranging for their pay and its proper distribution to the men's families while they were away. Traders arranged with the postal service officials to establish an office at the post, as Keam did at the Keams Canyon post in 1882.[33] Consequently, the trading post became the center around which information was exchanged, government programs introduced and explained, and social events announced. As a result, the post became the center of community life for the natives and the trader became the link to the outside world.

In many instances, the trader was the only American that the natives knew very well. Certainly, by the late nineteenth century, Americans were no longer rare visitors on the reservation, but the trader, because of his permanence, proximity, knowledge, and familiarity, was in a unique position to explain Americans to the Hopi and Navajo customers. Because there was an element of trust between the trader and his native customers, his explanations often carried more weight than those of the agents, who never stayed in office very long, or the missionary-teachers, who rarely took the opportunity to get to know the people they came to teach. In many instances, the trading post was located some distance away from the agency headquarters, and the trader was the most familiar American to the Indians. This was particularly true for the Navajos, whose agency was at Fort Defiance. The Hopis' agency headquarters was at Keams Canyon, but because of the vagaries of congressional funding, their agency was often closed, and when it was open, the agent preferred to stay at Fort Defiance or Fort Wingate. The agency buildings were rarely places where the Hopis or Navajos lingered. As one trader put it some years later, "the government doesn't want a bunch of Indians hanging around over there [at the agency buildings], the way they do at the trading post."[34] The trading post was familiar ground; the trader a part of their lives. The agency headquarters represented everything alien and uncertain.

The trader consequently filled in the gap between the Indians and the federal government. In negotiations, he was often called upon to help translate for the Indians and the government. He quite naturally became an advocate for the Indians, looking out for their best interests, protecting them from the government, and sometimes protecting them from themselves as they acquired the sophistication to negotiate.

Not everyone who entered the business was successful. Insensitive, unintelligent, or dishonest traders did not stay in business long. The trader Mitchell, who ran a post north of the reservation on the San Juan River in the 1880s, was known to be particularly irascible and ugly tempered. A Navajo man who suffered the trader's wrath in the form of a paralyzed finger, the result of a blow received from the trader, said he was "no good whatsoever."[35] All trading with him seemed to result in an argument and one particularly delicate situation resulted in the trader's shooting and killing one Navajo man and seriously wounding another.

An apocryphal story has it that a trader, usually a young novice from the East, had been exploring the ruins in his area and, in one, found a burial and recovered the skull from it. In his excitement, and in ignorance of Navajos' fear of the dangers associated with the dead, the trader displayed the skull on the counter of his post. He eventually left the country bankrupt and uncertain what had driven his customers away.[36]

As in any business, Keam and the other traders were motivated by one goal: they were in business to make a profit. But there were several factors that affected the trader's profit margin. His prices had to be competitive so that customers came to his post to sell their goods and buy his merchandise. However, he could not afford to give away his merchandise, or even some of it, to get customers.[37] To keep customers, many traders extended credit to them. Although Keam claimed he did not do so, credit was another factor that could tip the balance between profit and loss.[38] If the customer's credit was extended beyond his ability to pay, the trader's prosperity was threatened. But in the long run, the trader could not afford to bleed his customers dry either by extending too much credit or by demanding unreasonable payments for fear that the customer would abandon the post, and his debt, in favor of another more lenient or reasonable trader.[39]

The trader had his own credit problems, as his purchases were also on credit. He bought his goods from wholesale companies in Albuquerque, Gallup, Holbrook, Winslow, or Flagstaff, and when the trader received money he passed it on to the wholesalers. The trader's goods were freighted from the wholesaler to the post, with the freight cost added onto the sales price of each object. For example, it cost between 50¢ and 75¢ per hundred pounds to haul goods by wagons from Manuelito to Fort Defiance, a distance of thirty miles. Railroad freight from Albuquerque to Manuelito was about $1.04 per hundred pounds.[40] Keam owned several freight wagons to haul his goods back and forth between the canyon and Holbrook to cut down on his freight costs. The trader's profits fluctuated with the prosperity of his clients. If the people's economy suffered because of disease or drought and they could not pay their debts at the post, the trader had no choice but to extend more credit, hopeful, if not secure, in the knowledge that better times would bring everything back into balance so that he could pay his bills at the wholesalers. In essence, if the people prospered, so did the trader; if they did not, everyone suffered.[41]

Wool, pelts, Navajo blankets, piñon nuts, pots, baskets, and kachina dolls were all "money" at Keam's post. All were readily accepted items for barter, but not all trading episodes were even exchanges, and some method had to be devised, acceptable to both parties, for compensating for the change due the customer in a cash-poor environment. In addition to offering credit, traders modified an old trade custom and offered tokens in lieu of hard money. Tokens were metal and usually stamped with the trader's name and the token's value. Keam was no exception to the practice and occasionally issued some sort of token.[42]

Tokens were, on the one hand, a way of ensuring that the seller would return to the issuing post to redeem the value of the tokens, as they were not usually redeemable anywhere other than the issuing post. On the other hand, traders were more generous with tokens than they would have been with "real" money.

Although there were traders who abused the use of tokens, and the Office of Indian Affairs opposed the system, it was another way in which the dignity of both the buyer and the seller could be respected and maintained. The trader could afford to give more value to his customers' manufactures when he was allowed to use tokens in lieu of hard cash. The sellers often received more total value when they accepted tokens. If, at the end of a deal, the trader threw in a few dollars more in tokens than was due the seller, the seller profited because those tokens would be accepted at face value in the next trading encounter. As complicated as trading appeared to the outsider, it was an old system and it worked for both the buyer and seller.

Thomas Keam's post catered to two kinds of clients: Navajos to the north, east, and south and Hopis to the west. Each group had specific needs, and likes and dislikes, and each had specific items with which to trade. Keam's popularity as a trader came from his understanding of the peoples' natures, his ability to cater to their needs, and his willingness to help them develop their individual economies. If he had not worked to help the people in the region, they would have gone to another trading post where the trader was not so stubborn or lazy, even if it meant riding past Keam's front door to get to the other post.

The Navajos' economy was based primarily on sheep and the wool they produced, and secondarily on goats. As their flocks increased, the Navajo economy flourished and the Indian trader prospered. In the first years after the Navajos' return from Bosque Redondo, the number of sheep and goats was low, estimated to be about 125,000 animals. By 1880, the number had risen to 700,000 sheep and 300,000 goats. From the sheep, the Navajos sheared 800,000 pounds of wool. Three years later, after a very severe winter that claimed at least 50 percent of the herd, the wool clip was low and the fleeces light, weighing about one pound each. But by 1886, the number of sheep had risen again, to about 800,000, and the number of goats had risen to about 300,000. In 1886 the wool clip was a 1,500,000 pounds and sold for 6¢ per pound at the reservation and off-reservation posts. In 1887, the wool clip "fell about 300,000 pounds below that of last year." The price was, 2¢ to 3¢ per pound higher, which created "a lively competition among dealers." In 1888, the wool clip was 1,200,000 pounds, the fleeces a bit heavier, one and a half pounds each, and traders paid 8¢ to 10¢ per pound for the wool. By 1891, the fleeces averaged three pounds each, reflecting an improvement in weather and range conditions.[43] The dollar value of wool bought by the trader gave the Navajos impressive spending power at the post. In 1890, for example, the price per pound for flour was 2.8¢ and the Navajo wool price per pound was 9¢. In 1900, the price per pound of flour dropped to 2.4¢, while the price per pound of wool was up to 10¢.[44]

Wool and mohair were the most important by-products of the sheep and goat business, but these little animals also provided meat for the people. A dressed sheep provided more meat than a single family could eat before the meat spoiled, but to consume a sheep meant the loss of lambs and needed wool. Goats, on the other hand, were smaller and the meat could be consumed before it spoiled. Goats commonly produced multiple births so that butchering a goat was not as detrimental to the family's economy as butchering a sheep. Even though goats seemed to be a better investment and mohair brought more money per pound, the Navajos raised more sheep than goats because they preferred sheep. Even the pelts that came from the butchered sheep and goats figured prominently in the Navajos' economy, and traders readily purchased them. In 1886, sheep pelts, of which there were 240,000, sold for 10¢ each and the 80,000 goat pelts sold for 15¢ each. In 1888 300,000 sheep pelts brought 10¢ each and 100,000 goat pelts brought between 25¢ and 50¢ each.[45]

Throughout the years, the Navajos kept back about 25 percent of the wool clip for their own use in blanket weaving. The sale of Navajo blankets had become very important to their economy. Reflecting this importance, the sales of Navajo blankets became regularly mentioned in the agents' annual reports to the commissioner of Indian affairs. In 1887, for example, the agent reported that there were about 2,700 blankets produced, which sold for between $1 and $100 each. Of the 2,700, about 25 percent were "fancy" and sold for as much as $4 to $100 each. Cheap blankets, bringing from $1 to $5, were also produced. In 1891, the agent estimated that the Navajos sold about $24,000 in blankets.[46]

Sheep, whether providing lambs, sheared wool, or wool woven into blankets, supported the Navajos' economy. Sheep brought the people wealth, and sheep in some form brought them to the trading posts. Sheep herding, as it developed after 1880, as well as the trading posts, changed Navajo subsistence, since they depended on trading posts to buy their livestock and supply a reliable source of food. The trading post replaced the traditional subsistence-based strategies: hunting, gathering, and raiding.[47] At the trading post, sheep—either in the form of wool or woolen blankets and rugs—were turned into food. Both the people's and the traders' economic success depended on sheep. The Navajos required the trader to buy the lambs, the wool clip, or rugs because the trader could transport the commodities to the wholesale buyers located off the reservation. The trader, in turn, relied on the Navajos' sheep, wool, wool by-products because their sale paid the people's bills, which meant he could pay his own creditors.

The Hopis raised just a few sheep and retained almost all of the wool for their own use. Their agrarian production resulted in only an occasional surplus. If the standards of the typical nineteenth-century Navajo trading post were applied to the Hopis, there was no reason to build a post near the Hopis, because the people were too poor to trade for or buy the trader's goods. By the standards of the time, the Hopi had nothing the trader wanted or could in turn sell himself. Thomas Keam realized that if his trading post was to be successful, he must rely on both Navajo and Hopi customers, and in order for the cash-poor Hopis to have the ability to shop in his store, he would have to help them find something of value. Consequently, Hopi pottery and baskets made by the women and kachina dolls carved by the men became readily accepted items for trade at Keam's post. Just as other traders developed markets for Navajo blankets and later for rugs, Thomas Keam developed markets for Hopi pots, baskets, kachina dolls, and numerous other minor crafts. Keam bought the Hopis' artwork, which brought the people into his trading post.

The Hopi trade was never as well known as the Navajo trade. Navajo wool became part of a well-established and well-regulated worldwide economy that included American traders and wool buyers, but Hopi craftwork did not become part of a worldwide economy. Hopi pottery, for example, sold for much less than Navajo weaving and consequently was less profitable. Even as late as the 1920s and 1930s, Hopi pots sold for between $1.25 and $5, and it was not until the mid-1970s that prices jumped into the several-hundred-dollar range. A trader had to sell a lot of Hopi pots to make the same profit he made on the sale of one Navajo rug.[48]

As the Navajo rug business grew and became more widely known, so too did a number of traders whose names were linked to a particular style of rug. No Anglo trader to the Hopis ever had his name attached to a style of pottery. However, the most significant reason the Hopi trade never gained the fame of the Navajo trade lies in the fact that traders at Hopi were usually Hopis, not Anglos. In the early twentieth century, all but two of the traders at Hopi were Hopis, and most villages had at least one part-time entrepreneur who ran a store in his home. The most well-known of the Hopi traders was Thomas Keam's protégé and one-time sheep herder Thomas Pavatea, who lived below First Mesa where the town of Polacca is today. His business, like Keam's, was primarily in wholesaling Hopi arts and crafts to other traders and to middlemen in Holbrook.[49] Pavatea's store competed with stores owned by Sam Pawkis, Thomas Tawaquaptewa, and Naquiestewa, all at Oraibi; Taylor Tabo, at First Mesa; and the James brothers, who had a post-freighting business at Moencopi. Sekakaku had a store below Shipaulovi and began a dynasty of sorts, as his descendants were involved in the Sekakaku trading center below Shipaulovi on the highway.[50]

In encouraging both Navajos and Hopis to trade at his post, Keam demonstrated his good business sense: more customers equal more money. However, Keam demonstrated an even more sophisticated business acumen in encouraging Navajos to bring in wool and weaving while he encouraging Hopis to bring in pots, baskets, and kachina dolls. Each group had its own specialty; Keam did not encourage his customers to compete against each other in order to get buying power at his post. Keam developed his clients' economies, and in turn his trading post prospered.

At the post Keam offered the necessities—coffee, sugar, salt, and canned fruits and vegetables—to his customers, and he offered the extras as well: kerosene lanterns, galvanized tubs and buckets, sheep shears, wool cards, silk scarves, shoes, and velveteen, calico, and muslin fabrics. Given the unique needs of the native customers, traders stocked things that their urban counterparts did not keep on hand. Among these kinds of items, Keam kept some turkeys at the post and sold them or their feathers to the Hopis for their ceremonial prayer sticks. In one instance, Keam fired a clerk who sold a turkey to a Hopi man for what Keam felt was an extremely inflated price. The turkey, he reasoned, had a much more important function to the Hopi man than it had strutting around Keam's barnyard.[51] Certain Navajo ceremonies required a specific items; weddings, for example, required a specific type of basket whose manufacture by Navajo women was strictly regulated by numerous taboos. To circumvent the taboos but not the basket's ceremonial value, Navajos bought these baskets from Paiutes living to the west. To accommodate Navajo customers, traders carried these baskets in stock, as well as tanned buckskin and, occasionally, medicinal or ceremonial herbs. Traders also carried for sale, and accepted in pawn, turquoise beads, necklaces, and other jewelry. These items reflected the unique needs of Navajo and Hopi customers and the trader's understanding of his clients' needs.

When Thomas Keam opened the door to his trading post in 1875 and invited Hopi and Navajo customers in to shop, Navajo women had not begun to weave wool floor rugs. Hopi potters and basketmakers had not begun to make their wares for anyone's use other than their own, and rarely did these have any commercial value. Kachina dolls were carved only for ceremonial gift-giving, and the sale of these special items was of questionable morality. The only native commodity with any economic value to American traders was Navajo wool. However, by the time Thomas Keam closed the door of his trading post in 1902, all of these things, and many others besides, had become valuable and sought-after commodities at the trading posts across the Hopi and Navajo Reservations, as well as across the United States and Europe.

7

ADVISING THE ANTHROPOLOGISTS

In 1880, Thomas Keam's canyon post was the only trading post between Ganado, forty-five miles to the east; the Atlantic and Pacific Railroad, fifty-five miles to the south; Tuba City, ninety miles to the west; and Lee's Ferry, over one hundred miles to the northwest. This isolation benefited Keam in two ways: the lack of competition brought Indians to his post, and it meant that Thomas Keam, the only educated, reliable source of information on the region, became an influential and prestigious individual. In 1880 the Black Mesa region, and the native people who lived there, were the focus of much of the early anthropological work conducted in the United States. As a man familiar with the region, the location and condition of trails and water, as well as the Indians, Thomas Keam's knowledge was a marketable commodity. Because he was an astute businessman, he capitalized on the prestige that his regional knowledge and familiarity with the Indians brought him.

Keam's relationship with the scientists began in 1879, when the first anthropological expedition arrived at Keams Canyon, and continued throughout Keam's life. Keam's canyon post was the catalyst for the relationship. Because of its location, his post became the "port of entry" to all of the Black Mesa country and its inhabitants. Consequently, the post became the stopping place for the growing number of scientists and others exploring the area. There they could outfit their exploration parties and communicate with the outside world, as the post had one of the few post offices in a vast area.[1] By 1890, Thomas Keam regularly entertained some of the most influential American scientists at his canyon post, and he was, in turn, entertained by them and their friends in their homes in Washington, D.C., New York City, Boston, and Philadelphia. He also advised high-ranking government officials in the Office of Indian Affairs about the needs of the Hopis and Navajos.[2]

On many reservations, the agent would have served as the intermediary between the Indians and the outside world, and agents had wide-ranging powers to regulate the number and nature of nonresident Indian visitors. At Hopi, however, there was no agent between 1882 and 1897, so Thomas Keam filled the vacuum. As the resident trader, he was the only man who could arrange for local guides and establish contact with the various Hopi and Navajo headmen. Thomas Keam thus became the vehicle through which the outside world made contact with the Hopis and Navajos living in the area. As the number of Americans gaining access to the Black Mesa area increased, so too did Keam's position as the local authority become more widely acknowledged. The scientists' needs, and especially their desires for native crafts, caused Thomas Keam to expand the nature of his trading post; that, in turn, effecively changed the trading-post business in northeastern Arizona in the last decades of the nineteenth century.

The first anthropological expedition arrived at Keams Canyon in 1879 under the auspices of the Smithsonian Institution and the newly created Bureau of Ethnology. The bureau was created in 1879 under the directorship of Major John Wesley Powell, the Grand Canyon explorer, geologist, and ethnologist who had visited the Hopis at Oraibi in 1869.[3] Colonel James Stevenson headed the expedition. He was accompanied by his wife, Matilda Coxe Stevenson, as well as Frank Hamilton Cushing and the photographer John K. Hillers. They were charged with studying the Hopis' and Zunis' architecture and "domestic arrangements" and with making collections of their pottery and other arts for the Smithsonian Institution.[4]

Powell and those who worked under the auspices of the bureau were influenced philosophically by the eighteenth-century Enlightenment thinkers as well as by their own contemporaries, Herbert Spencer, Louis Henry Morgan, and Sir John S. Lubbock. Morgan's theories of society and its evolution most shaped the thinking of these first ethnologists.[5] To account for the differences between the societies around the world that were becoming so apparent in the nineteenth century, Morgan suggested that all societies on the earth at all times progressed in the same manner from a rude, or savage, level through various refining stages to a civilized state. He and his learned followers saw man's evolution from savage to civilized as a linear progression, a pathway that was the same for all societies at all times. To view native Americans, or Africans, or Chinese was to view a stage from western Europeans' own past. Morgan's followers, which included almost all of the anthropologists in America at the time, did not use racial or biological explanations for the differences in peoples' cultures and behavior. Instead they used an ethnocentric ruler calibrated with definitions based on their own culture to measure the degree of civilization for all peoples of the world.[6]

As zealous as any reform-minded group, the anthropologists believed that their work would provide the directions necessary for the nation's leaders to draw up a humane, practical policy for the Indians. Their research, Powell claimed, would produce more effective and more efficient policy because it was based on science.[7] For the anthropologists, the notion of progress and civilization was not only an intellectual belief—it was a practical certainty. Civilization was an inescapable product of any group's existence, and through scientific research the route from savage to civilized would become identifiable. Because of this, it did not matter if, with the scientists' help, the Indians passed over several rungs on their journey to the top of civilization's ladder. The ethnologists believed that their work was of vital importance and that it must be conducted with haste.

The bureau scientists working at Hopi were guided by these beliefs as well as by their own individual interests and areas of expertise, which determined as much as anything what they collected and how they perceived what they saw. Because of the pressure to collect anything and everything in a hurry, these first ethnologists literally stormed the mesas in an attempt to fulfill their duties. In 1879, the Stevensons collected over 3,000 Hopi pots, baskets, and other crafts.[8] For Keam, the anthropologists' penchant for collecting Indian-made crafts encouraged his hopes that a market for them could be created.

Thomas Keam and his trading post became the hub around which all of this scientific activity turned. Any other trader could have provided the same accommodations and equipment, and in time many others did, but Keam provided more. His personal knowledge of and familiarity with the Indians expedited the anthropologists' work. As a willing participant in their research, Keam created an environment in which the scientists could study the Indians unencumbered by the many problems encountered during fieldwork, such as language barriers and uncooperative informants. There is no indication that Keam was widely read in anthropological theory, but his personal philosophy about the Indians and their future was consistent with the social theories directing the anthropologists' work. He, too, believed that the only future left to the Indians was one in which they accepted the gifts of civilization and adapted to it.

The bureau's work at Hopi in the early years of the 1880s brought Keam two things. First, it introduced Keam to men of similar tastes and beliefs, and these men in turn accepted him into their world. He visited with them at his canyon home and at their Washington homes, where they introduced Keam to a Washington elite who eagerly listened to his stories about the Hopis. Second, these scientists, working under the auspices of the nation's museums, proved to Keam that there was a lucrative market for Hopi manufactured goods. They wanted authentic Hopi goods for their research, and Keam was in the best position to provide them. Because of his location and expertise and his growing inventory of Hopi- and Navajo-made crafts, Keam was involved in virtually every scientific expedition to the area. By the end of the century, he had worked with the most important American anthropologists and had sold collections to the most prestigious American and European museums.

The relationship between Keam and the anthropologists, which began in 1879, became even more important to both when, in August 1881, Thomas Keam traveled to Fort Wingate to meet Captain John Gregory Bourke, who wanted to see the Hopis' biennial Snake Dance.[9] Bourke was no stranger to the American Southwest nor to the study of the West's native peoples. In 1869, while on the staff of General George Crook, he had fought against the western Apaches and developed a keen interest in their culture. In 1881, Captain Bourke was again in the Southwest to study its native peoples.[10]

Keam met Bourke and the artist Peter Moran at Fort Wingate, and they headed for Keams Canyon. Although strangers initially, Keam and Bourke had several mutual friends—among them William Leonard, the trader at Fort Defiance, and the Navajos' former agent and friend, Captain Frank Bennett. From Fort Defiance to Keams Canyon, the party accumulated more guests who wanted to enjoy the outing to the Snake Dance. Eventually the entourage included Keam; Bourke; Moran; Leonard; George "Barney" Williams, who traded on the Pueblo Colorado Wash; Williams's partner, Mr. Webber; the Fort Defiance physician, Dr. Elbert; and Bourke's orderlies, Sinclair, Gordon, and Smallwood. Ganado Mucho, the old headman, also rode along with the party, and they were all guided by a Navajo man, Hi-daltchattli, or "The Wrestler," who also went by the name of George. Bourke expressed his concern that Keam's hospitality would be taxed with so many guests, but as Bourke said, "the matter seemed not to give him the slightest concern. 'If you fellows'll take what I've got, without growling, why, you're welcome, and that's all there is about it;' and he added: 'I've got lots of grub and dishes, and a pretty fair cook, and plenty of blankets. What more do you want? You don't expect to find a Crystal Palace down at my place, do you?'"[11]

What Bourke found along the way to the Snake Dance was a friend. He and Keam were remarkably similiar in many ways. Bourke has been described as "intelligent and witty" and a rather handsome man with a lively sense of humor. He, like Keam, was "quick to judge or prejudge others," and each had a finely tuned notion of duty. Both had learned the hard way that experience and expertise could, at times, lose out to political patronage and the well-placed public-relations article. As soldiers during the Civil War, they had fought the Apaches, and each had been forced to replace any feelings of enmity with respect for the natives. Because of their experiences, they shared rather critical opinions about the administration of Indian affairs. Bourke had seen Galen Eastman's disastrous administration in action at Fort Defiance and fully agreed with Keam that he should be removed. Because of their compatability, Keam and Bourke became fast friends and the friendship lasted until Bourke's death in 1896.[12]

Through John Gregory Bourke, Keam learned more about the formal study of Indian cultures, and he was incorporated into a small group of scientists who were at the time pioneering the anthropological study of the native peoples of the Southwest. The group included Bourke, Washington Matthews, and Frank Hamilton Cushing. At the time each member of the group was systematically studying the life-styles of the Hopi, Navajo, and Zuni. Eventually each member would leave his mark on this new field of study and on the people he investigated. Matthews, the physician at Fort Wingate, had lived among the Hidatsa during the 1870s.[13] Like Keam, Matthews had married a Hidatsa woman with whom he had one son. Matthews's work there was covered in two of his books, *Grammar and Dictionary of the Language of the Hidatsa with an Introductory Sketch of the Tribe,* published in 1873, and *Ethnology and Philology of the Hidatsa Indians,* published in 1877. He was a dedicated ethnographer and was interested in Navajo culture in general and healing ceremonies in particular. In 1880, the army stationed Matthews among the Navajos at the request of John Wesley Powell. Matthews and Keam were friends until Keam's death in 1904.

Frank Hamilton Cushing worked for the Bureau of Ethnology. Cushing had been at Zuni since 1879 and was rapidly becoming a part of their society. Instead of watching the Indians from afar, he lived with them, participated in their ceremonies, and eventually "entered so far into the life of the pueblo that he not only was formally initiated into the tribe but became a member of the tribal council and of the Bow Priesthood."[14] Like the others, Cushing had also had a number of run-ins with the local agent and missionaries at Zuni and had exchanged harsh words with the Navajo agent Galen Eastman over the shooting of some Navajo horses trespassing on Zuni land.[15]

At Keam's house, awaiting the party's return, was Keam's housemate and eventual member of the group Alexander McGregor Stephen, a man whose studies of the Hopi would equal any of the ethnographies by Bourke, Matthews, or Cushing and whose knowledge of the Hopi would be unrivaled. Stephen had lived at Keams Canyon for the better part of 1881. He was born in Edinburgh, Scotland, about 1845 and graduated from the University of Edinburgh. In 1862, he enlisted as a private in Company A of the 92nd New York Infantry. Upon completion of his first tour of duty, he reenlisted and was transfered to the 96th New York Infantry, Company G, as a first lieutenant. He was mustered out along with his regiment on February 6, 1866, at City Point, Virginia.[16] Before arriving at Keams Canyon, Stephen had spent the previous twelve years as a "metalurgist and mining prospector in Nevada and Utah."[17]

These men, Bourke, Matthews, Cushing, Stephen, and Keam, formed a network through which they encouraged, protected, and promoted each other. Each extended his connections to the others and, when possible, they all funneled work to one another.[18]

From his experience at the Oglala Sun Dance, Bourke knew that recording complex ceremonies was too much for one person, and he planned to enlist the help of Stephen; Dr. Sullivan, the agency physician; and the others to watch the dance. "To get the best information obtainable," Bourke wrote, "our party concluded to split into squads of two and three each, wandering about at will in every direction in Suchongnewy [Sichomivi], Hualpi [Walpi] and Hano, and occassionally re-uniting for comparison of notes." For Keam and Stephen, this was undoubtedly their introduction to ethnographic fieldwork.[19]

While waiting for the Snake Dance, Bourke's party amused themselves around Keam's trading post. They accompanied Dr. Sullivan, himself something of a Hopiphile, to the ruins at Awatovi, where they collected pottery sherds and other artifacts. While exploring Antelope Mesa, they met Lorenzo Hubbell, who joined their Snake Dance party. The next day the group explored the canyon around the trading post and examined the rock ledge where Kit Carson's men had commemorated their 1863 stay in the canyon.[20]

The party finally left Keams Canyon for First Mesa and the Snake Dance, securing sleeping quarters and food at the house of Tochi in Sichomovi. That evening Bourke visited a kiva at Walpi, and Mr. Whitney watched a dance at Hano. Before turning in for the evening, the men, obviously in high spirits, "assembled on the flat roof of our house, and made witching air of night musical with the stirring words of old army songs and choruses. It was almost dawn," Bourke wrote, "before Sherman got through 'Marching through Georgia,' and we had thrown ourselves down upon our blankets to catch a short nap before morning."[21]

That morning Bourke and his friends watched the Hopis prepare for the Snake Dance. Bourke examined a number of kivas, measuring them and noting their architectural details. He made extensive notes on the kinds of snakes the Hopis had collected and how they were handled, and purchased a number of items related to the ceremony. Keam, who had been detained at the ranch on business, arrived at the village and found Bourke busy taking notes and Moran sketching scenes in the kiva.[22]

As the ceremony got underway they found seats on the second story of a house near the "sacred rock," a large sandstone column in the plaza at Walpi. From their vantage point the men could easily view the plaza and all of the ceremonial doings. Moran was seated just below Bourke on the plaza, where his sketching was "watched by a coterie of four naked boys, three mongrel pups, two full-grown Navajoes, and six Moquis." Bourke estimated that there were about 750 people in attendance. There were "a half-dozen tall, lithe, square-shouldered Navajoes, and as many keen, dyspeptic-looking Americans," an American lady, and representatives from the other pueblos.[23]

The Snake Dance is an ancient and very complex ceremony performed by members of the Snake Society every other year after the summer solstice. Its purpose is to bring rain. Since it was first documented by Americans in 1879, it has been widely described and viewed by thousands of people. It's popularity by the late nineteenth century is partly due to Bourke's study. His *Snake-Dance of the Moquis* was originally published in 1884, three years after this visit, and was at that time already the fourth published report on this particular ceremony.[24] Keam is also partly responsible for the popularity of the Snake Dance, because after this dance he routinely arranged for accommodations at the canyon and at First Mesa and for Hopi "interpreters" or guides to accompany American scientists, photographers, and tourists.

After this particular dance, the party left First Mesa and headed back to Keam's ranch, but their swift progress was interrupted by a late evening thunderstorm. The rain fell so quickly that normally dry washes were suddenly boiling rivers, and the anthropologist-tourists were forced to seek shelter underneath their wagons until the storm dissipated. As the stars twinkled above they waited for the raging water to run itself out. Eventually the party gathered at Keam's house, where Stephen prepared them a hearty meal, and they prepared to go back to their homes. Bourke and his entourage headed west again, where they visited several other Hopi villages before going back to Zuni. Williams and the others returned to their homes on the Pueblo Colorado Wash and at Fort Defiance.[25]

For Keam and Stephen, the first of what would become many "tours" of the Hopi and the Snake Dance was successfully concluded. Keam and Stephen had been introduced to a new world, not the world of the Hopis, which they knew, but the world of American science with its growing interest in the native peoples of America. Both Keam and Stephen discovered that they had particular talents that placed them in the forefront of this new world. Both had received training in the methodology of ethnography as it was practiced in the nineteenth century, and Keam had inadvertently stumbled upon another aspect of the trade business that he would expand upon over the years. Keam recognized that the Hopis and their exotic Snake Dance had the power to entice American spectators to this remote region, and he never let another Snake Dance pass without capitalizing on the tourist business it brought to his trading post.

The Snake Dance very quickly became a biennial event for Anglos in northeastern Arizona. There, local tourists and travelers from afar gathered to marvel at the dancers. In 1895 the photographer Adam Clark Vroman saw his first Snake Dance and noted there were about forty tourists—newspaper correspondents, scientists, and artists—camped below First Mesa; in 1897, he recorded over two hundred tourists at the Snake Dance.[26]

For the Hopis, Bourke's visit was also an important event. No other man, Hopi or otherwise, had ever been allowed to see and record what Bourke had, unless of course the man was initiated into the Snake Society. Bourke's actions undoubtedly caused much comment in the village, and that fall at Zuni, Nanahe, a member of the Snake order, berated Bourke for his actions during the Snake Dance. The men of the society were particularly unhappy with Bourke's appearance in the kivas and with his notetaking. "We didn't like to have you down there," he said. "No other man has ever shown so little regard for what we thought, but we knew that you had come there under orders, and that you were only doing what you thought you ought to do to learn all about our ceremonies. So we concluded to let you stay." He said that the only reason they allowed him to witness so much was that Cushing had told Nanahe that Bourke represented the Great Father in Washington and that the Great Father wanted to know what his children believed. But Nanahe said that Bourke would be the last white man allowed to see those things.[27]

With Bourke gone, Stephen began his work at First Mesa by learning the Hopis' and Tewas' languages and recording their songs and ceremonies. Keam began collecting more Hopi crafts and started work on his own manuscript on the Snake Dance. In late 1882, he wrote his only ethnographic report. Entitled "An Indian Snake-Dance," it was based on the Snake Dance that Keam and Bourke and the others viewed together. It was published in *Chambers's Journal of Popular Literature, Science, and Art*.[28] The editors William and Robert Chambers introduced the author, saying: "Lieutenant T. V. Keam, who for many years has acted officially under the United States' [sic] government among the Indians, gives the following account of a curious ceremonial which he and others witnessed some time ago at a Moqui village

Thomas Keam's arrangements for tourists to the Hopi Snake Dance included quarters at Sichomovi, the village just east of Walpi. Shown here are Mrs. Lowe of Pasadena, California; Mr. Crandall; Mr. H. N. Rust of South Pasadena; A. C. Vroman, the photographer; and Sheldon Montoya, the driver. The painted sign nailed to the ladder next to Crandall reads "T. V. Keams *[sic]*. A. C. Vroman, photographer, 1895. Vroman Collection, Seaver Center for Western History Research, Los Angeles County Museum of Natural History, catalog number V-516 (626).

in the north-east of Arizona." Keam related the history of the Snake Society as it was told to him by "an ancient chieftan of that tribe."[29]

According to this chieftan, a Hopi "chief" floated down the San Juan River to its mouth, where he left his raft or canoe. He climbed the rocky shore to a summit where a family of Indians lived. They took him in and even allowed him to take "the wisest and most beautiful maiden for his bride." Before long, the chief forgot about the Hopis because he was so happy, but eventually the spirits of his fathers called him and he and his bride returned to his home. At Hopi, the bride was not received with warmth or friendship, and to spite her hateful neighbors she gave birth to "a brood of serpents" who were invincible to arrows or clubs and who slew the Hopis' children. "The people, pursued by this terrible foe, fled from the land of their fathers, til, on reaching the country in which they now dwell, a mighty serpent lashed their pursuers to atoms, and commanded the Moquis to possess his hills and valleys, and to live at peace with all his kind." In gratitude for saving them the Snake Dance was established, and for centuries, "no snake has been killed by that tribe, nor Moqui bitten who follows the teaching of the snake-priests."[30]

Keam's description of the dance is straightforward. He gives the number of days involved in preparation for the public ceremony, describes the methods used in capturing the snakes, and precisely describes the dress of the snake priests and dancers. Of the dance, he wrote:

> The dancers first advanced towards the grotto [a cotton-wood tent containing the snakes] wands in hand. Then wheeling around, they separated twelve a side, and formed in line, representing the two sides of a triangle, of which the grotto was the apex. The eighteen followed, dividing equally, and facing the dancers, while all joined in a wild chant, accompanied by a continuous sounding of the above-mentioned rattles. . . . [After about a ten-minute chant] [a]nother dance and chant followed; upon the conclusion of which the nearest priest on the right entered the grotto on hands and knees among the writhing and hideous mass, soon reappearing with a large snake in his mouth, its head and tail twisting about his face. Being taken by the left arm by a fellow-priest next him, he was led around the mystic circle. The snake was then dropped on some sacred corn-meal which the squaws had scattered within its bounds. . . . The ceremony was then repeated by the other dancers . . . until the whole had been taken from the grotto and placed in the hands of the attendant priests. The snakes were then thrown, a writhing mass, into a pile of corn-meal, upon which the whole priesthood rushed pell-mell to the pile, and seizing them in their hands, divided into

four bands, tore wildly down the rocky slopes of the *mesa* [sic], and liberated their captives in the sands on the north, south, east, and west sides of the village.[31]

Two articles on the Snake Dance had been published by 1882; however, his was the first to be written by an eyewitness of the ceremony.[32] Keam's account is dispassionate and, with the exception the value-laden term "hideous mass," Keam demonstrated his ability to displace his own cultural values and report on the actual events of the ceremony. Unlike many of his contempoparies, including Bourke, Keam's detatchment is remarkable. However, this was his only venture into ethnographic reporting and study. Perhaps ethnographic work did not suit Keam personally. More than likely, the work was too time consuming and the rewards were too elusive.

Instead, Alexander Stephen became the ethnographer and Thomas Keam ran the trading post, and Keam hoped he could sell the Hopi crafts he was collecting to his anthropologist friends. Stephen worked in the field, rarely leaving his house at First Mesa or his quarters at Keams Canyon, while Keam, on the other hand, personally made frequent trips East to expedite his various plans. He visited old friends such as James and Matilda Coxe Stevenson, Victor and Cosmos Mindeleff of the Bureau of Ethnology as well as new acquaintances like Spencer Baird of the Smithsonian Institution, to whom he had been introduced by Frank Cushing.[33]

By the mid-1880s Keams Canyon had become the nominal field headquarters for the Bureau of Ethnology scientists working in northeastern Arizona. James and Matilda Coxe Stevenson had worked in the area since 1879. They had studied the Hopis and Zunis and their lifeways and had collected thousands of artifacts from them.[34] In 1882 the bureau stationed the brothers Cosmos and Victor Mindeleff at Hopi to conduct Hopi ethnographic studies.[35] In 1883 and 1884 the scientists were exploring and mapping Anasazi ruins in Chaco Canyon, Canyon de

Chelly, and Walnut Canyon, as well as visiting the Hopis and Zunis. Thomas Keam and Alexander Stephen aided the scientists with their work. They served as or arranged for interpreters, lined up cooperative informants, and solved the myriad problems encountered during the ethnographic field sessions. Keam even packed and hauled their collections to the railroad at Holbrook.[36]

By the mid-1880s the scientists had amassed a substantial collection of Hopi material. In 1879 they procured 3,000 Hopi pieces, in 1881 5,000 artifacts from the Hopis and Zunis, and in 1882 2,000 Hopi artifacts.[37] To give the scientists credit for collecting all of the material in the field directly from the Hopi makers is to misunderstand the seasonal nature of anthropological fieldwork, the seasonal nature of Hopi craft production, and the importance of Thomas Keam and his trading post in this situation. The Stevensons did their fieldwork during the summer for two reasons: the region's sublime weather and the timing of the Hopi kachina dances. As summertime is the season for kachina dances, it is not a time of very active craft production; neither is spring, with its planting requirements, nor fall, with its harvest demands. Craft production, specifically the manufacture of pottery or baskets, was confined mostly to the postharvest and preplanting winter months. Because craftwork was done in the months when the anthropologists were away, they needed someone to purchase artifacts as they became available. Thomas Keam and his trading post filled the needs of both the anthropologists and the Hopi artisans. Consequently, Keam's trading post became the primary source for the Stevenson's collection. In this manner, Keam not only strengthened his relationship with the Hopi artisans; he also solidified his role as purveyor of Hopi craft work and culture to the scientists. Clearly the Stevensons did not document their arrangements with Thomas Keam, for this could have devalued their fieldwork, but for the bulk of their Hopi collections this is a very plausible circumstance.[38]

In late 1884 Keam's and Stephen's relationship with the bureau scientists and the Smithsonian's curatorial staff became more complex. The Smithsonian wanted to borrow a number of prehistoric artifacts and ethnographic specimens for its exhibit at the New Orleans World's Industrial and Cotton Exposition to be held in 1885. Keam's response to their request was typically positive and his offerings typically expansive. Writing to Spencer Baird, Keam outlined what he could provide the museum. In addition to the more common pots and baskets, Keam offered two complete male and female Hopi and Navajo costumes. To display the costumes accurately, Keam suggested that Mindeleff make sketches of the costumes and people so that the museum's model-makers could produce appropriate Navajo and Hopi mannequins.[39] In addition, Keam wanted the Smithsonian to pay the passages for several of the best Hopi and Navajo weavers to demonstrate at the fair. Presuming that the Smithsonian would see the desirability of this living exhibit, Keam had already talked with the weavers about this plan, and he assured Baird "they have agreed to accompany me, take with them their looms and show their methods of weaving."[40]

Keam's letter drew attention in the museum. On it George Brown Goode, assistant secretary of the Smithsonian, wrote, "Who is Keam and what [are] his relations to the work[?]"[41] Baird responded: "McChesney[42] can tell you all about him[,] an Indian trader who spends much time in the Ethnol.*[sic]* Bureau with Stevensons. He sent a very large collection to Maj. Powell on approval[.] Very old and valuable according to Stevenson."[43] Clearly this was not the first time Keam had offered his services or his collections to the Smithsonian.

As fall progressed, negotiations for the New Orleans exhibit materials became more concrete. Writing to William Henry Holmes, now in charge of the exhibition, Keam detailed his plans to ship the collection. He said that it would be accompanied by Alexander Stephen, who would be on hand to answer questions and "explain the details of dress."[44] In a postscript Keam added "am satisfied when you see all the collection together, with the information we have, you will not say I ask a high price for it."[45] The loan, at least in Keam's eyes, was really a sale pending the museum's approval.

Stephen's presence in Washington, D.C., served two purposes: it ensured the collection's safe arrival at the museum, and Stephen, with his notebooks of native terms and inventories, demonstrated to the Smithsonian anthropologists just how valuable and complete the collection was as an ethnographic research collection. Keam clearly recognized that the real value of the collection to the scientists lay in the ethnographic information that he and Stephen had collected, and he marketed the collection based on this knowledge.[46] In the end, the Smithsonian exhibited Keam's Hopi baskets, pottery, and dance paraphernalia, prehistoric pottery and baskets, and mummified human bodies.[47] However, the Hopi and Navajo weavers and their looms presumably did not go to New Orleans and the Smithsonian did not buy Keam's collection.

Back home in northeastern Arizona, Keam and Stephen resumed their respective duties. Cosmos and Victor Mindeleff of the Bureau of Ethnology were conducting research at Hopi, and although they were camped below Mishongnovi at Second Mesa, they occassionally stayed at Keam's trading post to visit with the Navajos who lived in the area and traded at the post. In August they watched the Snake Dance at Mishongnovi on the seventeenth and at Walpi on the eighteenth. Stephen and Keam also helped Dr. Harry C. Yarrow, acting assistant surgeon of the United States Army and an early physical anthropologist, who was interested in Navajo medical practices and Navajo and Hopi burial customs.[48]

Keam's and Stephen's assistance was regularly acknowledged in the Stevensons', Mindeleffs', and others' reports for the Bureau of Ethnology.[49] Stephen's work was moving beyond mere assistance, however. In the eighth *Annual Report for the Bureau of*

Ethnology he contributed to the introductory chapter "Traditional History of the Tusayan" and provided the ethnographic documentation of rites associated with house-building as well as native descriptions and nomenclature for architectural details.[50] Because of his working relationship with the Mindeleffs and his acknowledged research skills, Stephen was hired during the 1887–1888 fiscal year to collect "traditions and other matter" from the Hopi and Navajo. He submitted a number of short papers on these topics and on Hopi houselore, and presented descriptions and drawings of Hopi and Navajo temporary shelters.[51] Stephen continued to work on comparative architectural studies under Victor Mindeleff's direction during the next year.[52] He was particularly interested in collecting native terms and establishing etymologies of the various terms associated with building and building styles, but his interests ranged far beyond architecture. According to the summary of his work for 1888 and 1889, "he gathered typical collections of baskets and other textile fabrics illustrative of the successive stages of their manufacture including specimens of raw materials and detailed descriptions of dyes used."[53] These collections documented the principal patterns in use at the time, and Stephen collected the Indians' explanations of the objects' uses and cultural significance.

Stephen's work for the bureau was innovative in a number of ways. His comparative linguistic studies and ethnographic collections were as current as work being conducted anywhere in the world. Unlike many of the scientists who worked at Hopi for a few months at a time, Stephen lived with the Indians permanently. He was able to view and participate in daily village, clan, and family activities. Unlike some of his peers who came to watch one season's kachina dances, Stephen was there to see all events during the Hopi ceremonial and secular calendar.

Much of Stephen's early ethnographic work was conducted at Keam's trading post. The number of Indian patrons who came to the post enabled Stephen to perfect his Navajo and Hopi language skills and also his interviewing techniques. When a Hopi woman brought in a pot or basket to sell at the post, it was an easy and natural situation in which to ask seemingly unimportant questions related to the pot or basket: what is the material, where do you get it, how do you prepare it, does this design have a name, does the design have a symbolic meaning, and so on. The trading post facilitated Stephen's work for the bureau. Not only were patrons potential ethnographic contacts, but also the post was a culturally neutral setting in which clan histories, architectural terminologies, and craft manufacturing details could be collected and discussed away from village gossip, which may have made otherwise helpful consultants uncooperative. Certainly the trading post facilitated Stephen's collecting of finished and partially finished baskets, textiles, and other manufactures. There Stephen or Keam would purchase or barter for the partially finished goods. The word that Keam was buying partially finished crafts undoubtedly circulated quickly, and others would have volunteered to have such goods purchased and thereby participate in the ethnographic experiment. Collecting and documenting ethnographic details on the manufacture of craftwork was at that time an innovative research method; one hundred years later it is still a standard component of material culture studies.

The ethnographers made Keam's post their headquarters because it was only 13 miles from First Mesa, where most of them preferred to work. However, the post's importance was due to more than its proximity. There the scientists could withdraw from the Hopis' world and enjoy the companionship of men like themselves. At Keam's table they could discuss their work, analyze and revise their initial conclusions, and refresh their commitment to their work. There, too, the scientists had access to two men, Keam and Stephen, who comprehended the nuances of their questions and could answer their questions from nearly an insider's perspective. At Keams Canyon the ethnographers had English interpreters of the Hopis' culture.

While Keam was involved in the development of Hopi ethnography, he was at the same time single-handedly expanding the job description of the Indian trader in northeastern Arizona. Thomas Keam's involvement in the sale of prehistoric Indian artifacts and contemporary arts and crafts predates that of other traders in the area who were heretofore believed to have begun this aspect of the trade business. For example, Lorenzo Hubbell began his post at Ganado in 1878. Between 1882 and 1886, he abandoned the trade business and served instead as sheriff for Apache County, Arizona Territory. Hubbell's direct influence on the design of Navajo rugs, such as Ganado Red rugs, did not begin any earlier than 1891. The Wetherills did not "discover" the ruins at Mesa Verde, Colorado, until 1888 and did not move to Chaco Canyon and Pueblo Bonito until 1895. They supported their excavations there by running a trading post and by associating with the Hyde Exploring Expedition. Sam Day and his sons established a trading post near Canyon de Chelly in 1902, where they aided a variety of scientist excavating ruins in the canyon. John Wetherill established the Oljato post in 1906. From his post he aided Byron Cummings of the University of Utah in his archaeological explorations of the area, and together they located Rainbow Bridge in 1909.[54] Keam's success in identifying ancillary investment opportunities demonstrated to his peers and those traders who followed that the sale of Indian crafts, and indeed Indian culture, was extremely lucrative.

In 1886 Keam demonstrated just how lucrative these aspects of the trade business could be when he became involved with the Second Hemenway Expedition. The Hemenway Expedition began in 1886 with Frank Cushing as director. Cushing's ethnographic work at Zuni caused him to become interested in Pueblo prehistory, and he proposed to excavate several significant ruins in central and southern Arizona. To fund his project, he enlisted the support of Mary Tileston Hemenway, a Boston philanthropist. In 1886 the First Hemenway Expedition was organized. It comprised a staff of scientists; Dr. H. F. C. ten Kate, a physician and physical anthropologist; Professor Adolph Bandelier, a historian; F. W. Hodge, the expedition's secretary; and Charles A. Garlick of the United States Geological Survey, who was a topographer and engineer. The expedition was under the direction of Cushing and a board of directors headed by Mrs. Hemenway's son, Augustus. He was aided by William T. Harris, commissioner of education, and the journalist Sylvester Baxter, a Cushing devotee who had written widely about Cushing's work at Zuni.[55]

Cushing's health, which had always been poor, sabotaged the expedition's future. Initially Cushing sought respite from the rigors of the field in a vacation to southern California. Thinking that a change of scenery was all that was necessary, the expedition continued in Cushing's absence with Washington Matthews as acting director. Matthews had been suggested to the Hemenway Expedition board by John Gregory Bourke, and the recommendation presumably carried with it Cushing's and Baxter's approval. Cushing's illness, however, did not respond to the California sunshine, and that plus his complete lack of administrative capabilities finally forced him to abandon his position as head of the expedition.[56]

In 1888 a new director was named to head the expedition. The board chose Dr. Jesse Walter Fewkes, a man with no anthropological training or experience but who was a former Harvard classmate of Augustus Hemenway.[57] Presumably Bourke, Matthews, Cushing, and Baxter opposed the nomination, but they must have realized that the Ivy League network was more formidable than the network of pioneer anthropologists working in the remote deserts of the American Southwest. Before resurrecting the Hemenway Expedition, Fewkes availed himself of some anthropological training. He worked for a few weeks collecting stories from the Wabanakis in Maine and spent a short field season at Zuni. At Zuni, Fewkes's methodology failed to impress Matthews, Cushing, or the others who had worked in the region for so many years. His activities were widely circulated among the network of friends, and Matthews cynically reported to Cushing that Fewkes had become an instant expert on Zuni even though he did not speak Zuni or Spanish or employ either of the two Zuni men who spoke English.[58]

Believing himself to be adequately trained as an anthropologist, Jesse Walter Fewkes assumed the directorship of the Second Hemenway Expedition. He did not continue Cushing's excavations in southern Arizona but instead headed for easier fields and more easily attainable goals. He proposed that the expedition collect Hopi crafts and clan histories. To assure his success, Fewkes relied exclusively and completely on Thomas Keam and Alexander Stephen. Fewkes attained the one goal instantly when the expedition paid Keam $10,000 for a collection of Hopi artifacts.[59] The other goal, that of recording Hopi clan histories, required more of Fewkes's time and energy, but it was eventually attained when the expedition hired Stephen to compile the clan histories and describe the Hopis' ceremonies. He was paid a monthly salary from 1892 to early 1894.[60]

The collection was made up of the 2,000 or so artifacts Keam had at the Smithsonian and the 2,500 or so pieces he had in his "Indian room" at the trading post.[61] The entire collection included a number of pots and baskets from prehistoric sites in the region, a small number of nineteenth-century textiles and baskets, and almost 3,000 pots made during the eighteenth and nineteenth centuries.[62] A small collection of kachina dolls and a variety of ceremonial objects completed the collection. According to Stephen's chronological analysis of the collection, the prehistoric pieces were acquired by Keam, who had "been collecting relics of the Ancient Builders throughout the region of the Southern confines of Colorado and Utah. These have been exhumed from burial places, sacrificial caverns, ruins, and from sand dunes in the locality of ancient gardens."[63]

In addition to his own excavations, Keam acquired some of the older pieces from Indians who brought them into the post to trade. The historic pieces, Stephen claimed, came from the Hopi women themselves who had preserved them as heirlooms. The bulk of the collection, especially the contemporary pottery, came to Keam through the normal operation of his trading post. Acquiring the kachina dolls probably required more sophisticated negotiations, as they had no prior commercial value and were not widely sold until the mid-twentieth century. Undoubtedly the purchase of the ceremonial objects such as dance costumes and accoutrements required clandestine negotiations.

The collection of Hopi artifacts, especially the pottery, purchased from Thomas Keam illustrates the complex relationship between Keam and the First Mesa potters and the economic power his post wielded in the region. It also illustrates how efficiently he responded to the increasing demands of museum scientists for authentic Hopi crafts and the new demands of American tourists who were just "discovering" the American Southwest and wanted small mementos of their journey.

When Thomas Keam established his canyon post in 1875, Hopi women in all the villages on each mesa made decorated and plain utilitarian pottery, including bowls, ladles, cups, storage jars, and canteens, as well as a variety of specialized pieces for ceremonial use. Most of the designs on the painted pieces at that time reflected a strong Zuni-Spanish influence.[64] Off and on during the eighteenth and nineteenth centuries a number of First Mesa Hopis had abandoned their drought-stricken homelands for refuge with the Zunis. There, Hopi potters adopted many Zuni pottery designs, and in 1875 the First Mesa potters were still painting arabesques, filigrees, and other curvilinear designs on their bowls, jars, and canteens. By 1880 or 1881, however, Hopi potters began abandoning the old motifs in favor of stylized birds and bird parts such as feathers, wings, and parrot beaks. The women also began painting dragonflies and tadpoles on their pots. These are ceremonially significant elements

because of their association with rain, water, and other wet places. Potters also began to paint kachina faces, such as Palhik-mana and Hahaiwu'uti, on the insides of bowls and the outsides of jars. By 1890, First Mesa potters had completely stopped making pottery with the old Zuni-Spanish designs in favor of these new designs.[65]

Hopi potters also experimented with new vessel shapes and sizes, and they produced a number of exotic pieces such as ladles with Koyemsi effigy handles and triangular and rectangular tiles.

Keam's Indian Room, as photographed in 1900. In December 1899, Keam wrote Professor Franklin Hooper, director of the Brooklyn Museum, that his collection of prehistoric and contemporary Hopi and Navajo materials, including a number of fossils, could be had for $2500. The complexity of Keam's collection is seen in the variety of Hopi kachina dolls, dance paraphernalia, pottery bowls, jars, tiles, Hopi coiled and wicker baskets, Apache baskets, and Navajo and Hopi wearing blankets used as floor rugs. Note the number of Vroman photographs on the walls. The oil painting of the Indian woman is now in the Hubbell Collections at Hubbell's Trading Post, Ganado, Arizona. A. C. Vroman, photographer, 1900. Vroman Collection, Seaver Center for Western History Research, Los Angeles County Museum of Natural History, Los Angeles, California, catalog number V-1011.

None of these forms—ladles, tiles, salt-and-pepper cellars, candlestick holders, miniature versions of Hopi bowls and jars—had a utilitarian function in the Hopi household. Their only function was economic, and the only place where their economic value could be realized at the time was Thomas Keam's canyon trading post. The abandonment of the old Zuni designs, the adoption of new ones, and the production of exotic and miniature forms are all reflections of Keam's influence.

The new designs, the stylized birds, feathers, wings, and parrot beaks, are actually prehistoric design elements. Potters who lived at Awatovi and Sikyatki and other sixteenth- and seventeenth-century prehistoric villages in the Jeddito Valley east of First Mesa used them on their pottery. The designs the nineteenth-century Hopi women were painting on their pots were very similar to those their ancestors had used 300 or 400 years earlier.

How did this revival, now referred to as the Sikyatki Revival, come about, and what was Thomas Keam's role in it? In the collection of pots Keam sold the Hemenway Expedition, there are seven reproductions of prehistoric Hopi pots.[66] Keam more than likely commissioned them to supplement his prehistoric pottery collection or to provide whole specimens for broken or incomplete originals. In either case, he commissioned the pieces and the women involved in the experiment successfully completed the replicas.[67] Apparently the experiment caught on, for there are a number of Revival-style pots in the collection showing strong Sikyatki influence that were not commissioned by Keam.[68] These pots cannot be mistaken for original prehistoric pieces, because they were not used (they were sold new) and an analysis of their clay would reveal differences in clay source. Keam's experiment was highly successful. By 1890 the transformation of Hopi pottery was complete, and by the mid-1890s Hopi potters had discovered the clay beds of their ancestors and were painting the Sikyatki Revival designs on unslipped yellow clay just as their ancestors had done.

It is clear that Keam's desire for reproductions of prehistoric pots influenced the group of potters living at First Mesa. That he was commissioning prehistoric reproductions would have encouraged other women to duplicate the styles, as those were what the trader was buying. This same scenario has played over and over again throughout the history of the commercialization of southwestern native crafts.[69] However, this does not mean that the Hopi women slavishly reproduced pots with Sikyatki designs simply because Keam demanded them. Had the revival not reflected a Hopi aesthetic, it would probably not have been adopted so completely and it would not define what we know Hopi pottery to be today. No amount of economic incentive or control could have perpetuated a style that was essentially non-Hopi or that the potters did not like. The exotic forms, such as ceramic Hopi girls with maiden whorls, were adopted by the potters because the essence of the design was Hopi. Just how Keam directed the potters is unclear. He could have simply announced that he was buying only those pots with the revivalist designs (as at least two traders of Navajo weaving did during the twentieth century). However, more than likely—and his collection reflects this—Keam continued to buy pots with the Zuni designs while encouraging, perhaps through higher prices, the manufacture of revivalist styles. As has been demonstrated throughout the twentieth-century southwestern Indian art market, artisans are quick to respond to the slightest stylistic innovation, from any source, when the incentive is strong.[70]

Had Keam not created an Anglo market for Hopi pottery, he would not have bought pottery from the makers and Hopi ceramic manufacture would have declined. As it was, his newer, better, and cheaper cast-iron alternatives quickly replaced many Hopi utilitarian pots. Potters too poor to buy these goods made their own imitation ceramic tea kettles and pots with bottoms designed to fit into the burner ring of a wood stove.[71] If there had been no Hopi need for decorated bowls and jars, these too would no longer have been made. Instead, Keam encouraged Hopi women to bring him their decorated wares and he created a market for them.

The sale of almost 5,000 artifacts to the Hemenway Expedition apparently did not make a dent in Keam's existing collection, nor did it curb his collecting. Between 1893 and 1901 Keam loaned prehistoric and ethnographic material for the World's Columbian Exposition in Chicago in 1893,[72] the Trans-

Mississippi and International Exposition in Omaha in 1898,[73] and the Pan-American Exposition in Buffalo in 1901.[74] He also sent material to an exhibition in Paris in 1899.[75] He sold a significant collection to the Field Museum of Natural History in 1894 and lesser collections to the museum over the years until 1904.[76] He also sold small collections to the Smithsonian Institution,[77] the Museum für Völkerkunde in Berlin,[78] and the Rijsmuseum voor Volkenkunde in Leiden.[79]

Keam's initial connection with the Field Museum came through his participation in the Chicago World's Fair. After the close of the fair, with its extensive ethnographic displays, and an international anthropological congress where Bourke, Cushing, and Matthews presented reports on their research and Fewkes read a paper entitled "The Walpi Flute Observance" that was based on Stephen's fieldwork, a group of concerned Chicago businessmen, including Marshall Field and Edward Ayer,[80] met with the chief of the fair's Ethnology Department, Frederick Ward Putnam. Together they established a museum to house the fair's most significant anthropological collections.[81] In late 1894, Keam shipped the Field Museum about 1,000 prehistoric and contemporary Hopi specimens valued at $2,000.[82] This purchase, among the museum's first, consisted of 216 pieces of prehistoric pottery; 150 Hopi, Navajo, Paiute, and Cohonino baskets; 50 kachina dolls; a wide variety of textiles; and a number of miscellaneous hunting tools and weapons such as rabbit sticks, clubs, arrowpoints, and spears. Keam also sold a "small lot of turquoise amulets, bone awls, and shells from a cave [a shrine] at Awatabi [sic],"[83] as well as some ceremonial costumes, headdresses, and tabletas.[84] The money for the purchase of this collection came from Edward Ayer,[85] a friend of Keam's and a California Column veteran who was also the first president of the board of the Field Museum.[86] Keam's subsequent sales to the museum included 2 Navajo dresses,[87] a collection of Hopi potter's tools (clay, pigments, polishing stones), several unfired pots, a woven Hopi rabbit-skin blanket, several Navajo blankets, a Navajo loom with a partially finished blanket on it, a medicine man's kit,[88] and 4 Navajo games.[89] Keam also sold the museum a number of paleontological specimens.[90] Keam's proximity and ethnological expertise led the Curator of Anthropology at the Field Museum, George A. Dorsey, to enlist Keam's help with the construction of a number of Hopi ceremonial altars for exhibit.[91] Dorsey's instructions were explicit, and he used Hopi names for certain items to make sure that Keam got exactly what the anthropologist wanted.

By the turn of the century there was no question about the salability of Hopi material culture. Between 1880 and 1900, Keam collected and sold in excess of 8,000 prehistoric and contemporary pots; hundreds of coil and wicker baskets, textiles, and games; and hundreds of Hopi tools, weapons, and miscellaneous household items.[92] He also collected and sold hundreds of kachina dolls, which had never had a commercial value, and he collected and sold many different types of Hopi ceremonial objects, such as dance paraphernalia and costumes including kachina masks.[93] By the turn of the century, Keam had proved that the Hopis' prehistoric cultural remains and their contemporary manufactures had commercial value in the United States and Europe.

Keam's work for and with the anthropologists was not without its drawbacks. As early as Nanahe's complaints about John Gregory Bourke's notetaking at the 1881 Snake Dance, much of the anthropologists' work was opposed by many of the natives on moral grounds. The relationships among the anthropologists, Keam, and the Indians were often complicated by these clandestine research topics. Keam's acquisition of ceremonial artifacts and dance paraphernalia had to be conducted in secret. These items were not owned in the American sense of the term by the Hopi caretakers, and their sale was morally incorrect. Likewise, some of the research carried on by Cushing and Matthews, for example, was questionable. Cushing's explorations for shrines in the Zuni area had to be carried out in secret, because their continuation was against the wishes of the Zunis.[94] Matthews cautioned Keam not to let the publication of his *Navajo Legends* or its pictures be seen by Navajos at Keam's post for fear that they would be upset by seeing the information in print. Alexander Stephen constantly complained that his informants withheld information from him because he was not qualified to know it.[95]

Jesse Walter Fewkes, in particular, was also not pleased about Keam's work with the Hopi potters. He complained in print that the contemporary Sikyatki revival pieces that were sold by "unscrupulous traders as ancient" were so good that they would eventually become accepted by less-adept archaeologists and museum curators than himself as "ancient Hopi ware." Keam's and Fewkes's relationship was superficially cordial, but it was not without its personal jealousies. The network enjoyed by Keam, Bourke, Cushing, and Matthews never included Fewkes, and Fewkes went so far as to discredit the value of the Keam collection that he had purchased for the Hemenway Expedition, saying that it was useless and had no scientific merit.[96] Further complicating the situation was the tendency of the anthropologists to collect material for their host museums in addition to other museums. Both Cushing and Adolph Bandelier collected material for German museums while they were employed by the Hemenway Expedition,[97] and Keam more than likely acted as a middleman in several similar deals.[98]

In the early 1880s, Thomas Keam and Alexander Stephen were the only avenues to the Hopis' world, and they controlled who had access to the Hopis, but their work brought the Hopis to the attention of a larger group of anthropologists and tourists. The Snake Dance drew hundreds of tourists, soldiers, and cowboys to the mesas. The hundreds of turn-of-the-century Snake Dance photographs by Vroman and others attest to the bazaar-like atmosphere that developed around this ancient ceremonial.[99] By the late 1890s, other anthropologists arrived at Hopi to stay. H. R. Voth, a Mennonite missionary, settled at Oraibi in 1893. His ethnographic studies of Third Mesa ceremonies were designed to enable him to discuss and discredit Hopi religion,[100] and his numerous publications with the Field Museum[101] on many aspects of Hopi religion and his detailed reproductions of Hopi kiva altars for the Field Museum, Hopi House at the Grand Canyon, and the Alvarado Hotel in Albuquerque demonstrate just how far others traveled on the trail blazed by Thomas Keam. By the turn of the century, the flood of American anthropologists and tourists at Hopi was so great that Keam was only one of a number of traders selling Hopi arts and crafts and conducting tours of the Snake Dance and the region. He had lost his position as the only avenue through which Americans saw the Hopis.[102]

Thomas Keam pioneered the modern trading-post business in northeastern Arizona. When he first opened his post he operated like other traders in the area: he sold groceries and American manufactured goods to his Indian customers in exchange for their wool, the occassional surplus food crop, and the rare silver coin. But Thomas Keam identified and proved that a profitable trading post was one that was diversified. In this, Thomas Keam capitalized on his clients' unique manufactures and created a market for them so that they could be converted into cash in the trader's till. Keam also recognized the value of connections to the world of anthropologists and museum curators and the need for an active tourist market. He was the first trader in northeastern Arizona to identify and cultivate these aspects of the nineteenth-century Indian trade business in northeastern Arizona and this, in turn, made him a wealthy man.

By the turn of the century Keam could look back to his first encounters with Bureau of Ethnology anthropologists James and Matilda Coxe Stevenson, the Mindeleff brothers, John Gregory Bourke, Washington Matthews, and Alexander Stephen and count among his friends the most influential of the first generation of American anthropologists. Together they introduced the scientific community to the Hopis. Through them Keam worked with the most prestigious American museums and museum curators: Spencer Baird and George Brown Goode at the Smithsonian; Frederick Ward Putnam, William Henry Holmes, and George A. Dorsey at the Field Museum; and Stewart Culin at the Brooklyn Museum. Keam's location, his trading post, and his penchant for collecting were encouraged by these scientists, and through his friendship with them Keam augmented his trading business with the sale of Indian artifacts.

While Thomas Keam was exploring all the possibilities of the nineteenth-century Indian trade in northeastern Arizona, he was never far removed from the day-to-day affairs of his Indian neighbors and clients. During the period in which Keam's trading post was growing, the effects of policies formulated in Washington, D.C., reached him at Keams Canyon and reached the Hopis to the west. This time, however, Keam was more powerful than before, and his connections and supporters more influential. Consequently, his power was impossible for the bureaucrats to ignore.

—◁ 8 ▷—

ADVISING THE INDIAN OFFICE

THE THINGS THAT brought the anthropologists to Thomas
Keam—the location of his trading post thirteen miles east of
First Mesa and his familiarity with and knowledge of the region
and the Hopis and Navajos who lived there—also brought bureaucrats from the Office of Indian Affairs to Keams Canyon.
This time the bureacrats sought out Thomas Keam for his advice
and assistance. Such a radical change in their attitude toward
Keam and his knowledge came about because of a change in who
influenced the formulation and implementation of programs
designed to Americanize the American Indian. The new reformers and the Indian office bureaucrats, like the scientists,
needed and wanted Keam's advice and assistance in implementing programs to "civilize" the Hopis. Traditionally, the Office of
Indian Affairs relied on its agents to perform these duties, but
there was no agent at Hopi between 1882 and 1897. Also, the
Navajo agent who was administratively responsible for the Hopis
was more than seventy miles away at Fort Defiance and generally preoccupied with the Navajos and their problems. As he had
for the scientists, Thomas Keam readily filled the vacuum created by the agent's absence.

During this time, Thomas Keam performed many of the duties of an Indian agent. He met with and wrote reports to the
secretary of the interior and the commissioner of Indian affairs;

led a delegation of Hopi elders to Washington, D.C., to meet with Commissioner Thomas Jefferson Morgan; and negotiated between the two governments when the Oraibis declared war on the United States Army.[1] That the officials in the Office of Indian Affairs met with Keam, solicited his opinions on certain matters, and followed his advice on some occasions validated Keam's belief regarding his position in the region. Keam may not have had the title "Indian agent," but he had the prestige that he attached to the position.

However, Thomas Keam had several things that agents did not normally have: he was unencumbered by the personnel policies of the Office of Indian Affairs and called on his colleagues in the Washington scientific community and Indian reformers in Philadelphia to encourage the government to follow through on his advice and the government's promises and responsibilities to the Hopis. Keam was also an influential presence among the Hopis, a luxury no agent in the region could claim. The Indians sought Keam's counsel and recognized him as the government's representative to them. Keam's influence resulted in a more peaceful environment in the region. Keam also capitalized on his unofficial role as government agent. He used his influence and that of his friends, Anglo and Hopi alike, to compel the government to buy his canyon trading post and ranch buildings to open a school for Hopi children. He also convinced some Hopi parents to send their children to the school.

Even before 1875, when Thomas Keam and his brother, William, opened their post in the canyon, and in 1879, when the Bureau of American Ethnology sent its first anthropological expedition to study the Hopis, the American government had been aware of the Hopis' distinctive culture. Dr. P. G. S. ten Broeck, an army surgeon, visited the mesas in the spring of 1852; Lieutenant J. C. Ives of the Army Topographical Engineers passed through in 1858;[2] and Colonel Christopher Carson and the New Mexico Volunteers camped in Keams Canyon in 1863 as they

rounded up renegade Navajos.[3] After exploring the Grand Canyon, the one-armed soldier-scientist Major John Wesley Powell
resided at Oraibi for about a month, collecting pottery and baskets and studying the Hopi language.[4] Jacob Hamblin, the ex-
plorer-saint, led Mormon missionaries to the Hopis at Oraibi
in 1858.[5] The federal government, however, did not establish
an agency for the Hopis until 1869, when the Moquis Pueblo
Agency, as it was called, was established at Keams Canyon.[6]
A. D. Palmer was the first agent. He was followed by W. D.
Crothers (1871–1872), W. S. Defrees (1873–1874), and W. B.
Truax (1875–1876).[7] None of these men lived at the agency in
Keams Canyon or issued any goods to the Hopis, although Defrees built a few structures there. The agency, such as it was, was
discontinued in 1876 because of limited congressional funding,
and the Hopis were administered to from the Navajo Agency at
Fort Defiance.[8] In 1878, when the Hopi agency was officially
reopened, W. R. Mateer was assigned as agent. He was replaced
in the spring of 1880 by a Mr. Boynton, who, with his family, arrived at Fort Defiance at the height of Galen Eastman's Navajo
war hysteria. Fearing for their safety, they immediately returned
east, leaving the newly established Hopi agency without an
agent.[9]

John H. Sullivan of Madison, Indiana, who was eventually
hired to fill the position, arrived at Keams Canyon October 14,
1880.[10] Two weeks later, Charles A. Taylor, the missionary-
teacher hired by the Presbyterian Board of Home Missions, arrived with his extended family. Sullivan and Taylor immediately
disagreed about almost every aspect of the administration of the
Hopi agency. Although they were both Presbyterians, Sullivan
looked to Washington, D.C., and the Office of Indian Affairs for
leadership, while Taylor looked to the Presbyterian Board of
Home Missions. They disagreed about the allocation of agency
buildings and about the Hopis themselves. Sullivan found the
people to be industrious and well behaved, while Taylor saw

them as dirty and half-civilized. They also disagreed about who should fill the local agency positions. Taylor wanted his brother, his sister-in-law, and his wife to fill the various posts, while agent Sullivan had his own family and friends to take care of.[11]

In January 1881, Sullivan hired his son, Jeremiah Sullivan, as agency physician. Dr. Sullivan had a scholar's interest in the Hopis and their culture, and his actions enraged Taylor, who, like James Roberts at Fort Defiance almost a decade earlier, saw Sullivan's interest in Hopi culture as potentially damaging to his education programs. Taylor immediately began a successful campaign to have Agent Sullivan removed. Jesse Fleming, Taylor's candidate, arrived on February 4, 1882, and proved to be just what Taylor wanted: he hired Taylor's brother and sister-in-law and accepted Dr. Sullivan's resignation.[12]

Subsequent events, however, proved how powerless the Hopi agent was. Dr. Sullivan left the agency at Keams Canyon, but he did not leave the area. He moved to a house at Sichomovi on First Mesa, where he practiced medicine and studied the Hopis and their culture. Agent Fleming had the right to fire Sullivan as an agency employee, but he had no power to run him out of the country because there was no reservation over which this agent presided. The only things he controlled in the area were the agency buildings and its employees. Visitors to the Hopis could come and go at their leisure, miners could explore the region, and traders like Thomas Keam could trade without a license.[13] Even the Navajos living on Hopi ancestral lands were free of the Hopi agent's control. No one, except the agency employees, had to answer to the agent, and everyone in the vicinity recognized his lack of power.

To remedy the situation, the government ordered Fleming to create a reservation for the Hopis.[14] This, the government reckoned, would give the agent the necessary power to evict the offender and regulate the growing number of Americans visiting the Hopi people. However, on the same day that President

Arthur signed the executive order creating the reservation, Agent Fleming resigned his job, the Presbyterian Board of Home Missions recalled Charles Taylor, and in a fit of fiscal conservatism the Congress closed the Hopi Agency and combined it, once again, with the Navajo Agency. [15]

It is inconceivable that Thomas Keam was unaware of the discussions preceding the establishment of the reservation, given the proximity of his trading post to the agency headquarters and his propensity for making the agency's daily business his own. However, he did nothing to prevent the creation of the reservation, even though a reservation jeopardized his cattle ranch and presented bureaucratic obstacles for his trading post business. Instead of limiting his holdings or looking for a potential buyer, he expanded his operations. He bought two stone buildings from an unidentified owner, bought a building constructed by the Presbyterian Board of Home Missions for the missionary-teacher Taylor, and, in an attempt to protect his hold on the canyon, filed on 160 acres in the canyon under provisions of the Desert Lands Act. [16] Keam's actions alarmed Fleming, who was all but packed up and ready to move back to Michigan. In one of his last reports to the commissioner of Indian affairs, he expressed concern that the Hopis were losing land just as the ink was drying on the executive order reservation designed to protect their land claims. According to Fleming, who had seen Keam's map and the claim,

> [it] include[s] lands that have been cultivated by the Moquis for years prior to said T. V. Keam's residence here; that said claim includes the lands that are enclosed by a substantial stone fence; which was erected for and on behalf of the Moquis, by one of your agents—Mateer, I think—some years ago; and that these lands are some of the very few upon which wheat can be grown successfully, and the Moquis use it for this express purpose. [17]

Even though a reservation had been set aside for the Hopis, it was a reservation on paper only. Its boundaries were nothing more than arbitrary points on a map connected by straight lines without consideration of natural features, water, or conflicting land claims. Before the region could be surveyed and official boundary lines established, there would be time for Thomas Keam to protect his investment and somehow withhold it from inclusion, despite the Hopis' prior use. If this proved impossible, then the government would have to compensate Thomas Keam for his improvements on the land.[18]

However, Fleming did not call for any departmental retaliation to prevent Keam from taking ownership of the buildings or the land. Instead, he urged the commissioner to respect Keam's land claims: "Mr. Keam is a perfect gentlemen [sic] in his manners, and has ever treated me in my presence courteously & gentlemanly, and I have no desire to see him deprived of his rights. Should the Reservation lately established invalidate his claim in any way, I think he should be made secure of his property or be paid for improvements he has made, but I protest against this people being deprived of their lands."[19] Before this problem could be addressed, however, Fleming faced potentially more serious charges, and he dropped all mention of Keam's claims while defending himself and the missionary-teacher Taylor. Fleming was accused of the mismanagement and misappropriation of agency funds, the charges focusing on Keam's purchase of the Presbyterian Board of Home Missions building.

Henry T. Martin of Holbrook, Arizona Territory, wrote to Congressional Delegate Granville H. Oury that

> on or about the *first of January, 1883* [the agent did] *permit one Taylor a missionary teacher, to sell to one Keam, an Indian trader, a certain house erected by the United States upon public domain [sic]* and adjacent to said Agency, and did give to said Keam a title thereto; said house being valued at ($250.00) Two hundred and fifty dollars (more or less) and did permit said Keam to remove said house to his *trading post [sic]* near said Agency.[20]

George Blake of Williams, Arizona Territory, and James P. Langdon, an Albuquerque physician, substantiated Martin's allegations. Blake claimed that the house referred to was constructed by agent John Sullivan and paid for in government goods, and Langdon said Keam was "a London thief and deserter from an English frigate."[21]

Fleming explained to the commissioner that the building in question was built by Taylor with materials supplied by the Presbyterian Board of Home Missions.[22] It was not government property, and since the house was no longer needed by the mission board, it had the right to divest itself of its property. Keam, with cash in hand, was a ready and willing buyer. The allegations of mismanagement and misappropriation of funds were dropped, and Thomas Keam was not contacted to explain his actions or intentions. While the Christian mission boards had directed the formulation of Indian policy as implemented by the Office of Indian Affairs following the Civil War, the 1880s ushered in a new group of humanitarian reformers who were influenced by the social Darwinistic theories of the time. They maintianed their influence for the remainder of the nineteenth century and were zealous in their beliefs in the superiority of American culture and Protestant Christian morality. These reformers were self-described as "friends of the Indians." Equipped with their eye-witness investigations, written reports, and suggestions, they lobbied the United States Congress for reform. They saw no value in Indian cultures or the future of the reservation system and the segregation it represented. Instead, they looked to a future when all vestiges of Indianness would be eradicated. It was, as Francis Paul Prucha wrote, "an ethnocentrism of frightening intensity."[23]

Even though the demands of his trading post and the requirements of the bureau anthropologists, James and Matilda Coxe Stevenson and Victor and Cosmos Mindeleff, kept Keam busy during 1882 and 1883, he had other demands on his time as well. In the spring of 1884, he made one of his biennial trips to Washington, D.C., and on this particular trip he met with the Secretary of the Interior Henry M. Teller. Among the business they discussed, Keam relayed the details surrounding the deaths near Monument Valley on the Navajo Reservation of two American miners, Samuel Walcott and James McNally. After he returned to the canyon, Keam reported on new developments in the case and other events of interest to Secretary Teller. He wrote to say that Clee-e-cheen-beaz-be-ny, a Navajo man, had been at the trading post and had told Keam what he had learned about the murders from the Indians themselves. Keam explained that the Indians had apparently killed one man with an axe. The other man, he reported, had been shot at repeatedly with his own rifle and finally ambushed and killed a day later.[24] Keam said he sent Clee-e-cheen-beaz-be-ny to Fort Defiance to file a report with Acting Agent S. E. Marshall, and Keam told Teller that the murderers ought to be captured and punished, because these Indians were "a set of villains and murderers" and one of them had even shot his own brother some time ago.[25] He continued that "these wretches should not go unpunished or no ones [sic] life will be safe travelling through that country," and that if they were to go unpunished it would have "a demoralizing effect on those disposed to be good."[26] The secretary of the interior referred Keam's letter to the commissioner of Indian affairs for his "especial attention" and told him that "these men ought to be arrested and punished."[27]

Keam also evaluated a sheep-breeding project that the Navajo agency personnel had proposed be carried out at Washington Pass. He reminded the secretary of his own familiarity with the area—and the agent's lack of familiarity—saying that any plans would be compromised because of the area's weather: "undoubtedly whoever recommended this never visited the place in winter, when it is often covered with two feet of snow." Keam claimed that a recent late snow in the area, which the agent should have known about, would have caused a more prudent man to abandon the project. According to Keam, the agent should have figured it out for himself.[28] Keam's letter to the secretary of the interior was nothing short of an official report on current events on the Hopi and Navajo Reservations complete with suggestions for the government's official actions.

Henry Moore Teller was neither an uninformed political appointee nor a zealous ideologue like so many of his predecessors.[29] He had a sincere interest in Indian affairs, and as a westerner he brought a practical perspective to the Department of the Interior. While a senator (1876–1882, 1885–1907) and as secretary of the interior (1882–1885), Teller opposed the removal of the Nez Perce from Idaho to Indian Territory and the plan to reduce the land claims of the Colorado Utes. He advocated decreased funding for off-reservation schools, such as Carlisle Indian Industrial School in Pennsylvania, and increased appropriations for reservation industrial arts schools. Teller accepted Keam's reports and recommendations because they substantiated his own perceptions about the management of Indian affairs.

Keam also reported to Teller about a meeting of Navajo headmen and Hopi elders at the post at which he told them about Teller's concerns for their future, of his plans for the development of water resources on the reservation, and the creation of an industrial school and farm.[30] Both Teller and Keam were advocates of industrial arts schools, and the one proposed for the Hopis and Navajos that Teller and Keam dreamed of and planned for was to be built at Keams Canyon—that is, if Keam's property could be purchased by the federal government.[31] This was clearly the main topic of conversation between Keam and Secretary Teller in the spring of 1884. Indeed, Teller had attached an amendment to the 1884 Indian appropriation bill that, if passed, would have authorized the secretary to spend up to $25,000 for the purchase of "the buildings and other improvements" in

Keams Canyon for an Indian industrial school, provided the owner would relinquish all rights, title, and interest to the government. [32]

Although the amendment did not pass, Thomas Keam had put his plan in motion. Keam had long been an advocate of schools on the reservation, and this and subsequent events prove his humanitarian concern for the Hopis' and Navajos' future and well being. However, Keam's offer to sell his holdings to the government illustrates another constant element in Keam's makeup. To this point in his life, Thomas Keam's actions were well thought out and methodical. He was neither quixotic, irrational, nor generous to the point of bankrupting himself. In every business decision, Keam's actions were calculated to benefit himself in some way. For reasons that remain unclear, Keam wanted to divest himself of his property in the canyon and the only buyer for it was the United States government. Perhaps the $25,000 Teller represented was enough for Keam to abandon this particular claim in the face of what the school represented: reopening of the agency and bureaucratic control over his trading post. Perhaps he realized that he could open another post at another location without losing either his Indian customers or his anthropologist clients. Perhaps a government school and government contracts would compensate for his apparent loss. In any event, Thomas Keam campaigned to get the government to buy his canyon. He enlisted the support of the agent at Fort Defiance, his anthropologist friends James and Matilda Coxe Stevenson and Dr. Harry C. Yarrow, and Herbert Welsh and his powerful Indian Rights Association. To these advocates, Keam added the most powerful and persuasive voices of all: the Hopi village elders from First and Second Mesas.

In the fall of 1884, the agent at Fort Defiance filed his annual report for the "Maquis Agency" and the "Makis." However linguistically confused the agent was, John Bowman was an advocate for a school for the people. The Hopis "manifest an earnest desire to educate their children," he wrote, and after talking with "the most thoughtful of their headmen," Bowman figured that of the 1920 Hopis, "they will furnish at least two hundred and fifty scholars of suitable age."[33] Bowman claimed that "with proper encouragement they would maintain a school and keep it well filled with their children," that is, if buildings could be found for a school. "It is true," he wrote, that "the Government has no building which could be used for that purpose, nor are there any in the vicinity of their villages, but Mr. Thomas V. Keams [sic] of Keams Cañon has kindly offered to place at my disposal a comfortable building adjoining his trading post." Bowman described the facilities and farmlands, even though "the attention of the proper authorities [the secretary of the interior and the commissioner of Indian affairs] has already been drawn to the adaptability of Mr. Keams's [sic] property as an industrial school."[34]

Later that fall, in a letter to the commissioner, Bowman transmitted Keam's offer of three rooms at the trading post for a school and urged the commissioner to take advantage of Keam's generous offer.[35] But, Keam's offer did not receive a response from the Office of Indian Affairs until May 1885. The commissioner wanted to know if Keam was still willing to rent his facilities to the government and to do all the necessary improvements to place them in a "suitable fix" for a boarding school.[36] Keam wrote back saying he would make ten rooms suitable for an Indian school available to the government for $60 per month. He said the rooms would be ready the July 1, 1885, or earlier if necessary.[37] But by August it was clear that there would be no school that year for the Hopis.[38]

Thomas Keam was not deterred. Instead of relying on the agent to get the school established, Keam wrote directly to the new Commissioner of Indian Affairs, J. D. C. Atkins. "Dear Friend," he wrote, "I have just heard through my friend Colonel Stevenson [James Stevenson of the Bureau of American Ethnology] that you are in the Indian Department. As your short stay here some years ago gave you some knowledge of the Navajos and Moquis in this part of the country I trust you will use what influence you may possess with the Dept [sic] for the benefit of the Indians."[39] Keam restated his offer to rent the government ten renovated rooms for a school. He complained that "for some reason the school has not been started and I learn the Dept [sic] has decided against it as it is remote from the Agency . . . [but] as schools have been strongly advocated, and the civilization of the Indians the aim of the Dept [sic]; it is a great pity that these Indians should be deprived of a school on such trivial grounds."[40]

Atkins wrote two months later that "after consultation with the Superintendent of Indian Schools, it has been decided that it would not be advisable to go to the expense of organizing a boarding school whose accommodations could not be provided for more than 24 pupils." He continued, "Can you arrange your buildings for the accommodation of 50 pupils—say 30 boys and 20 girls?"[41]

Keam's response signaled a change in his tactics, and his old and almost bitter attitude toward the Office of Indian Affairs surfaced. He told Atkins, whom he no longer addressed as "Dear Friend," that his initial offer of ten rooms for twenty-four students was based on projections made by a special agent from the Office of Indian Affairs who had been at the canyon in May 1885 to assess the potential school site.[42] He, not Keam, had determined the school "experimental" and he, not Keam, thought that twenty-four students would be an advisable number.[43] Keam, who was an old hand at dealing with the inconsistencies of the Office of Indian Affairs, made certain that Commissioner Atkins understood exactly what Keam had to offer. He sent Atkins detailed maps of the canyon and drawings of his facilities, and arranged for James and Matilda Coxe Stevenson to call on the commissioner to explain Keam's plans.[44] Keam also wrote a brief account of the cultures and personalities of the Hopis and Navajos and judged their potential for civilization.[45] "Having lived among them so long I take some interest in them and have often explained the necessity of their improving their water supply [by improving springs;] they fully understand it, and are willing to work, but like children require assistance in management." An industrial arts school would teach the Hopi students how to manage water resources, build modern houses, and repair farm implements and wagons. "If encouragement in this way could be given them it would wonderfully increase what is most needed by them, and also teach them it's to their interest to be industrious."[46]

With the maps and descriptions of the people, Thomas Keam added the one thing certain to warm the coldest heart or at least loosen the tightest purse strings: a petition for a school signed by twenty village elders from First and Second Mesas. They wrote:

We live in stone houses upon the mesa top high above the valley. In bygone time we were forced to live here to be safe from our foes. But we have been living in peace for many years and we have been thinking.

We would always like to observe the precepts which our fathers taught, because they are true. But there are better ways of getting a living from the earth than our fathers knew, and we would like to learn them. . . .

We have seen a little of the Americans' ways and some of us would like to build homes similar to theirs, and live as they do, in the valleys.

We can build good houses, with stone walls and clay roofs, but doors, and windows, and board floors were unknown to our fathers, yet they are beautiful, and we would like to have them. But we are poor and unable to buy them, and we ask you to help us.

We are also greatly concerned for our children. We pray that they may follow in their fathers' footsteps and grow up—good of heart and pure of breath—Yet we can see that things are changing around us, and many Americans are coming to the region. We would like our children to learn the Americans' tongue and their ways of work.

We pray you to cause a school to be opened in our country, and we will gladly send our children.[47]

What more could a commissioner want? The Hopis had requested a school for their children justifying their request in the same language used by the Office of Indian Affairs to describe its own goals.

Commissioner Atkins finally responded to Keam's offer. The Office of Indian Affairs wanted to rent all of Keam's buildings and fields for a school for the Hopi children. Even though this request included Keam's trading post building, he reluctantly agreed to rent his entire complex of buildings and fields to the government for $1,800 a year.[48] However, the deal was not finalized for fourteen more months, and Keam was forced to reduce his price to $1,200 because he could not perfect the title to the canyon.[49] The rental negotiations were finally concluded in May 1887, and the Keams Canyon school opened October 3, 1887, with nineteen girls and thirty-one boys in attendance.

The tenacity required to bring about the establishment of the Hopi school was similar to that which kept Keam's application for the Navajo agent's job active for so many years. In both situations, Thomas Keam seemed to be motivated by honest humanitarian emotions, but as in all of his actions, he stood to profit from the Hopi school. Indeed, the culmination of two of his business schemes, the sale of his holdings in the canyon to the federal government and the eventual success of his cattle ranch, depended on a successful school.

With the school open and off to a shaky start, Keam garnered the support of his influential friends in Washington, D.C., to keep his offer before Congress while working to keep the Hopi children in class.[50] In a letter to John B. Riley in the Office of the Superintendent of the Indian School Service, Keam reported on the students: "They are the best behaved and finest looking lot of Indian school children I have ever seen together in civilized

View of the first Keams Canyon school, showing the former trading-post buildings and newer school buildings. This location was abandoned in the mid-1890s, and a new facility was built further down canyon. Courtesy of Arizona Historical Society/Tucson. AHS #336.

clothing. So far they are perfectly happy and contented and everything looks promising for one of the most successful Indian schools ever started."[51] He continued, "As this promises to be one of the largest schools established, the question of the Government owning this property and erecting sufficient buildings to accommodate two or three hundred children presents itself more forcibly than ever."[52]

In the sale of the canyon, Keam's most influential support came from his old friends, former Secretary of the Interior Henry M. Teller and Herbert K. Welsh of the Indian Rights Association. The association Welsh headed sought to solve the "Indian problem" through legislation. It kept the reformers' issues and proposed solutions before Congress and the American public by means of lectures, newsletters, and pamphlets and maintained a full-time lobbyist in Washington, D.C. The Indian

Rights Association was only one of several reform groups that were broadly united in their Christian beliefs. They believed the salvation of the Indians—their Christianization and civilization—would only come about after they were educated, made legally responsible for their actions under United States civil laws, and motivated to work because they had title to their own piece of land.[53]

Their motivations and beliefs complemented Thomas Keam's personal beliefs. He had been an advocate for law and order and industrial arts schools on the reservation since 1872, when he created the Navajo police and urged the Office of Indian Affairs to support a Navajo school at Fort Defiance. Due to of his conformity to the reformers' beliefs and his knowledge of the Hopis and Navajos, Thomas Keam was a welcome participant in the reformers' group. Because they supported him and publicly acknowledged his status and authority, Keam cultivated their support for his plans for a Hopi school and the eventual sale of his land to the government.

Herbert Welsh had visited Keam at the canyon in 1884 and again in 1888 to visit the school at Keams Canyon and investigate affairs on both the Hopi and Navajo Reservations.[54] Keam made the arrangements for Welsh's visit and guided him around the area. When he returned, Welsh championed Keam's offer to sell his holdings for a school. He lobbied Commissioner of Indian Affairs John Oberly[55] and took the issue to the reform community, enlisting their support.[56] He also introduced Keam's offer to Senator Henry Dawes.[57] James Stevenson also spoke on Keam's behalf on several occasions with the commissioner, and Matilda Coxe Stevenson wrote an editorial entitled "An Arizona School Site" for *Lend a Hand,* a reformer publication.[58] Keam did not rely solely on his friends to see his offer through to completion, however. In the spring of 1889, he went to Washington to shepherd his proposal through the Senate.[59]

Keam's offer was quite simple. For $18,500 the government

could buy the existing buildings—the house, the trading post, school rooms, dormitories, staff quarters, and other miscellaneous buildings—valued at $10,700; the corrals, stables, and outbuildings valued at $2,150; and the trees (of which there were about four hundred), ditches, dams, fences, and roads valued at $5,650.[60] Because the school was open and staffed and children were in attendance, and because so many advocates were in favor of it, the government finally accepted Keam's offer. He deeded his property to the federal government on July 13, 1889,[61] and received $10,000 for his improvements, though the price was "far below the estimated value of the property."[62]

Although the government bought Keam's improvements, it did not validate or acknowledge his claim to the land itself. In the records of the offer to sell, Keam placed no valuation on the land, only on his improvements. Keam's attempts to get title to the land under the Desert Lands Act never came to pass because of a technicality: the land was not surveyed, and therefore it was exempt from inclusion under the act. However, the procedure of buying out improvements had precedent. Anson Damon, Samuel Day Sr., and others were compensated for their improvements when the Navajo Reservation was extended in 1880.[63] The alternative, getting the government to acknowledge an owner's rights to the land, was difficult, expensive, and time consuming. It took J. L. Hubbell almost twenty years to get the government to recognize his right to 640 acres at Ganado.[64] Thomas Keam could have taken this route as well. He also could have pressed the technicality under the Desert Lands Act that the land need not be surveyed even though a number of territorial and federal agents assumed otherwise.[65] Keam did not pursue this either. Instead he accepted the $10,000 offer from the government.

With the deal closed and the quitclaim signed, Thomas Keam was forced to rearrange his facilities to accommodate his trading post business. He had initially moved the post up to his house when the post was rented to the government in 1887 for the school, but when the sale was completed, he moved all of his operations down to the mouth of Keams Canyon and acquired a license to trade with the Hopis.[66] Keam solicited and received permission from the First Mesa village elders to use the location for fifteen years. They wrote the commissioner of their arrangements with Keam and their support of his application, saying;

> For many years we have known Thomas V. Keam as our friend, he holds our full confidence, and we have every trust in his intentions. He has assisted us in many ways upon numberless occasions, he is always our helper.
>
> We are desirous to have him live close beside us, and for and in consideration of his many good deeds to us, we do hereby grant him permission to erect buildings, and make such other improvements, within the space of five acres, as he may deem necessary, at the Spring known as *Nü-nü-pa* and traditionally claimed by us. To have and to hold the same for his exclusive use and benefit for a period of fifteen years, at the end of said period, the houses and other improvements shall revert to us.
>
> It is further understood, that after the improvement of the water supply at said Spring, such water as may not be needed by Thomas V. Keam, may freely be used by any Moqui Indians desiring to move down from the mesa and establish farms at that place.
>
> We respectfully and urgently request the Father at Washington to appoint Thomas V. Keam as the Sole Indian Trader *[sic]* for the Moqui people, because we know him to be honest, and we hold him close to us as our dear friend.[67]

Recommendations were submitted by Jonathan McChesney, chief disbursing officer at the United States Geological Survey; Victor Mindeleff of the Bureau of Ethnology; and I. Heylen MacDonald, who was a patent lawyer. Mindeleff and MacDonald signed Keam's bond. Of Keam's character, MacDonald said he knew Keam "to be well educated and of [the] highest attainments." Mindeleff said he knew him "to be a gentleman and a scholar of the first water," and McChesney knew "him to be a gentleman in all respects and reliable in every particular." All agreed that Keam did not drink alcohol and he was a man of high moral character. Mindeleff characterized Keam as "an A #1 Indian trader." Keam's license was approved July 29, 1889.[68]

Even though Keam incurred the expense of relocating his trading post to the mouth of Keams Canyon and was forced to comply with government regulations to be a licensed trader, he capitalized on the proximity of his trading post to the Keams Canyon school. He provided the agency with oats, hay, and corn, as well as two hundred grape vines; one hundred blackberry, one hundred raspberry, and five hundred strawberry plants; and three hundred asparagus roots for the Hopi school gardens. In 1890 he also sold thirty *Moody and Sankey Gospel Hymns* hymnals and five other music books to the school.[69] As the only rancher in the immediate vicinity, he became the primary contractor to supply the school with beef and mutton.[70] In 1889 he contracted to supply the agency with 20,000 pounds of beef for $10.00 per hundred weight. During the next eleven years, Keam supplied over 280,000 pounds of beef to the agency. After eleven years of contracting with the government, he had more than compensated for the $8,000 difference between the asking price and sale price of his improvements in the canyon.

Thomas Keam's contracting with the government was hardly unique. Texas cattlemen had long contracted for beef for various Indian agencies. In spite of falling beef prices on the national and international markets, beef contracts for the Rosebud and Pine Ridge Indian agencies in the Dakotas were let at $2.73 and $2.83 per hundred weight for over twelve million pounds of beef in 1880. The next year beef was contracted for $3.87 at Rosebud and $3.91 at Pine Ridge. The figures had risen to $3.73 and $4.09 in 1883.[71] Prices for beef sold to the Indian agencies in New Mexico and Arizona were similar. Contracting for beef at the Indian agencies was a rather lucrative business. Cattle trailed from Texas to the Dakotas, for example, could be fattened up while awaiting slaughter on reservation lands at no expense to the owner. Thomas Keam was in an even better position to minimize his costs and maximize his profits, because he did not have to trail his cattle very far from his ranch near Dilkon to the Hopi school, nor did he have to pay taxes on the land, because he grazed cattle either on free range or on reservation land.[72]

With the demands of a cattle ranch and his new trading post in operation, one might conclude that Thomas Keam's interest in the daily affairs of the Hopis and their school might have waned. If anything, however, Keam increased the time he spent minding the school's business and the Hopis' affairs. Keam and Welsh discussed and evaluated the educational progress at the Keams Canyon school and kept up a lively evaluation of the teachers and agents. Together they kept the activities on the Hopi and Navajo Reservations before the various commissioners.[73]

They were concerned about the problems between the Hopis and Navajos and their disputes over land and springs claimed by the Hopis but used by the Navajos.[74] To defuse the situation, Keam suggested and Welsh agreed that the secretary of the interior appoint three people as commissioners to mitigate the situation.[75] All agreed that "an army officer, the agent for the Navajos, and a citizen known to both tribes having knowledge of the country" should meet with the Indians.[76] Keam even suggested that troops be used to drive off the Navajos. He believed that this would not only impress the Navajos, but it would absolve the Hopis of any blame in the matter.[77] A month after Keam suggested this, Captain Wallace of the 6th Cavalry and a company of men arrived at Keams Canyon.[78] Together Captain Wallace and Keam visited the villages, and Keam claimed the Hopi were "moderate in their demands and complaints[,] only mentioning such springs as are within a radius of twelve or fifteen miles from their villages."[79] Keam asserted that the removal of Navajos could not cause too much hardship as "there are only a few families living within the described lines."[80] Two years later, Keam reported to Welsh that the problems between the Hopis and Navajos continued.[81]

Keam was in a unique position to know what was going on in the region because of the Hopis and Navajos who traded at his post, his frequent travels in the region, and his knowledge of and familiarity with the Indians. He was asked by the commissioner of Indian affairs to assess the feasibility of building an industrial school for the Navajos on the San Juan River.[82] A year later he pleaded with the commissioner for assistance to Navajos who were suffering from the winter and from inadequate food supplies.[83] His correspondence with the commissioner was designed to inform as well as influence, and his correspondence with Herbert Welsh was designed to keep the reformer apprised of what he and the Indian Rights Association could do to help the Indians, or how they could pressure the Congress or the commissioner to make decisions favorable to the Indians. But as he used his knowledge to advise the commissioner and Welsh and influence their actions, Thomas Keam was not above pointing out the civilian agents' inabilities.

The Hopis valued Keam's assets—his knowledge of and familiarity with Americans and his abilities to move within their powerful circles in the nation's capital—and they, too, considered his advice. More than any other issue, the school at Keams Canyon challenged Keam's skills as an advisor and his role as intermediary between the government and the Hopis. From the government's perspective, the Keams Canyon school symbolized all that was positive and promising from its civilization programs. From Keam's perspective it symbolized the practicality of the Hopis' cooperation with the government. Not surprisingly, however, the school symbolized many other things to the Hopi people. It became the object that represented their concern about the future, social and cultural change, political factionalization within the villages, and the question whether or not to rely on tradition for guidance in dealing with the issues.[84] The problems had existed among the Hopis before the school was built, but the school, especially for many Second and Third Mesa people, soon objectified or symbolized these deeper problems.

The proximity of First Mesa to Keam's post and the on-again-off-again agency meant that those Hopis and Tewas had regular contact with Keam and the other white men. Second Mesa, some twenty-five miles from Keams Canyon, was more removed from their influence, and Oraibi, fifteen miles beyond Second Mesa, was outside the Anglos' influence. But the Great Father did not recognize this. It was assumed in Washington, D.C., that one village and one mesa were pretty much like the others and that support at First Mesa for something like a school reflected a pan-Hopi attitude. The government believed that the First Mesa Hopis' prosperity would cause the other Hopis to follow, envious of their more advanced and sophisticated relatives. The bureaucrats also wanted the Hopis to move down from their mesa-top villages to the plains below. The Great Father's agents saw the villages as enclaves of traditionalism and pagan rituals, and believed the move would destroy these negative forces. The government reasoned that the move would do two things for the people: a dispersed population would check the Navajos' encroachment on Hopi land, and it would facilitate allotment of land in severalty.

The Hopis, on the other hand, were not united in agreement on what they wanted from the government. There were those at Oraibi, Shungopovi, Mishongnovi, and Shipaulovi who would have preferred that the Great Father abandon the vicinity entirely. Others at Hano, the Tewa village, Sichomovi, and Walpi at First Mesa were interested in acquiring many of the things the government offered. Still others, from all mesas, were interested but wary.

To convey the government's wishes to the Hopi *kikmongwi,* or village elders, the federal government relied on Thomas Keam. Even though Keam recognized that not all Hopis supported the school and what it represented, and he knew that support diminished with each village to the west, Keam nonetheless cooperated with the government. He was also a product of his own culture and a captive of his belief that the power of civilization and progress would inevitably encompass all of the Hopis. Thomas Keam relied on his power and prestige among the people to get them to recognize this, but he also used that same power and prestige to maneuver the federal officials into making decisions that would benefit and protect the Hopis while they were adjusting to the changes.

In the summer of 1890, Thomas Keam accompanied Agent C. E. Vandever and five Hopis, Simo of Walpi, Polaccaca and Anawita of Sichomovi, Honani of Shungopovi, and Loololma of Oraibi, to Washington, D.C., to meet with Commissioner of Indian Affairs Thomas Jefferson Morgan.[85] During the meeting, the commissioner stated his beliefs to the Hopi leaders that they should change their lives to accommodate the new world in which they lived. He told them that they should pattern themselves after white people who work hard all of the time; that they should educate their children in schools so that they, too, would be hard workers. He wanted the Hopi leaders to visit Carlisle Indian School in Pennsylvania after they left Washington, D.C., to see "Indian girls and boys doing just as white boys and girls do."[86] He told them to send their children to school at Keams Canyon and to join and encourage others to join those who had moved down from the mesa top onto the plain below.[87]

The Hopis were concerned with the practical matters that Morgan's desires would create for them if they did as he wanted. The elders said their people needed protection from the Navajos in the area who stole Hopis' horses and tried to control the springs. This would have to be done before the Hopis would feel safe down below. They claimed that they needed more water and irrigation capabilities, so that they, too, could have greener crops. They also believed that if they had more sheep, they could produce wool like the Navajos. The men agreed with Morgan that moving down from the mesas could be a good thing, but to do this they needed certain amenities from the Great Father such as windows, doors, stoves, and wagons. If the commissioner could give them these things, they would try to get their people to move.[88]

After they returned home, Thomas Keam visited the villages at the Hopis' request "for the purpose of counciling [sic] with all of them, regarding the school and their moving from the mesa top to the valleys below near their farms and water."[89] In a report to the commissioner, he wrote that the trip had impressed the Hopis and that it had been the only topic of discussion in the villages since their return. He reported that Agent Vandever "informed me that there would undoubtedly be sufficient funds" to furnish each family with about twenty sheep, chairs, windows, and doors and that the lumber would be provided from the government sawmill. Keam said that when he explained these things to the people, they were pleased. He suggested to Commissioner Morgan that the government ought to help the Hopis with these things, as it had promised, as "such assistance rendered them now will place them in such position to be self reliant and independent in the near future."[90]

That fall, Commissioner Morgan led an entourage to Hopi that included, among others, Morgan's wife, a chaplain, a general, two lieutenants, and a "small escort of cavalry."[91] Morgan was there to inspect the pupils' progress in school and to explain in person why each village must increase the number of children it sent to the school. On November 1, 1891, Thomas Keam, the teacher Ralph Collins, and the entire party headed for First Mesa.[92] Keam was in his element. Not only was he the generous host providing accommodations for the delegation from the nation's capital, but he was the tour guide, introducing the delegates to the Hopis' world. Keam was never far from the center of attention as he translated the conversations and the wishes and needs of one party to the other. According to Julian Scott, special agent for the eleventh census who was also along on the visit, the Hopis were very shy upon meeting the Americans, but as Keam had vouched for their "characters and good intentions" the Hopis were reassured, paid them "every kindly attention," and even allowed them into a kiva at Walpi.[93] The next day elders from all the villages met with Commissioner Morgan and General A. D. McCook, commander of the Department of Arizona, at Keam's house. There, where chairs had been placed "on the piazza," they discussed the problem of Navajo encroachment on Hopi land, and Morgan presented his demand for an attendance quota for each mesa.[94] Morgan gave the Hopis ten days to fill the school with seventy-five boys and girls, an increase of forty more students than were attending.

Commissioner Morgan, former commander of a regiment of black soldiers during the Civil War and a Baptist pastor, made Indian education the central concern of his administration. Morgan, like many of his peers, believed that education had the power to replace "uncivilized" habits of dressing, living, and working with those that would make the educated Indian a respectable American. He advocated mandatory school attendance and day schools in every Indian village, boarding schools at agency headquarters, and integrated public schools near reservations.[95] Morgan told the Hopis that the government wanted them to send their children to the school at Keams Canyon not because of any ulterior motives but because, through education, the Indians and their descendants would be able to meet "the great, unavoidable problems of the future" such as the preservation of their race, as well as the chance to improve their condition and "rise in the scale of intelligence and importance among other people of this great country."[96] The Hopis were more concerned about Navajo encroachment than about school attendance.

The meeting ended, with each group certain that their points had been understood as reasonable and therefore accepted. Two weeks later, because the children had not arrived, Thomas Keam, Ralph Collins, the Keams Canyon schoolteacher, Julian Scott from the census party, and six men from First Mesa (Tom Polaccaca, Shaquana, Nahji, Adam, Eona, and Petsci) went out to secure the truant children.[97] They began their chore at Oraibi, where they talked with the kikmongwi Loololma. Loololma had traveled to Washington, D.C., to meet with the commissioner and had also spoken with him at Keams Canyon. Both times Loololma had complained about a "bad element" at Oraibi who were opposed to both Loololma and the school.[98] Loololma, who was not necessarily opposed to the notion of education, took Keam and the others to a kiva in Oraibi where one of his detractors was sewing moccasins. Keam asked the man to come out so they could talk. Despite repeated requests, he did not do so, and Keam eventually went into the kiva and forced the man out.[99] He admitted that he opposed Loololma, whereupon Ralph Collins, apparently tiring of Keam's diplomacy, demanded, "We are here for children and we want them right now."[100]

Keam interrupted Collins, saying, "We have come on behalf of the commissioner in Washington, who desires that this opposition [to Loololma and the school] should cease and that you and your relatives act as La-lo-la-my [Loololma] has done, throw away your old ideas about injury of education and send your children to the school in the cajon. We have come prepared to take them, and want you to get them ready."[101] The people were given one hour to get their children ready to leave, and in the meantime the First Mesa men talked with the Oraibis about the benefits of education. The Hopi guides, the Americans, the children, and the recalcitrant Oraibi left Third Mesa and headed east to Second Mesa and the village of Shungopovi. At Shungopovi, after a long discussion between the village elders, the Shungopovi people "pledged her full quota of pupils."[102]

At Mishongnovi and Shipaulovi councils were held to remind the people of their promise to send their children to school, in spite the parents' concerns that their children would miss out on their religious instructions as well as household and agrarian duties if they went to a boarding school. At Shipaulovi Scott said patience ceased to be a virtue, and the Americans forcibly removed several school-age boys from a kiva where they were undergoing religious training.[103] Scott continued:

> Here a scene occurred which I shall long remember. The women, who were the worst among the objectionists [to the schools], set up howls and lamentations which would put the coyote of the desert to shame. There was very little use for the salutation "lo-la-mi" [an all purpose greeting] on this occasion, for we were beset on every side by expressions of scorn and condemnation; but it took only a few moments to hustle away the scions of the ancient Moqui civilization from their now thoroughly aroused and protesting mothers.[104]

At Mishongnovi, the kikmongwi said they had already discussed the situation and had come to agree to send their children to the school, but that they would come on their own in a few days.[105] Finally, the party arrived back at the canyon and the children were enrolled in the school. The recalcitrant Oraibi man was detained until he saw the benefits of the school. However, the children from Mishongnovi failed to arrive, and the men returned to the village to enforce the attendance quota. They conducted a house-to-house search for hidden children.[106]

That winter, discussions in the villages, especially Oraibi, must have centered on nothing but the school and what it represented. One faction at Oraibi was so unhappy with Loololma's actions that they locked him in a kiva, and in December soldiers were dispatched to release him and arrest the offender.[107]

To make matters worse, land surveyors had begun surveying the land around Third Mesa in preparation for allotment of the land in severalty. Not only had the government failed to explain the concept, but also the Hopis could not understand why, after so many generations of successful land management, they should change their farming practices. Near Third Mesa, the surveyors' stakes were pulled out of the ground. For want of a better excuse, troops from Fort Wingate were sent to Oraibi on June 21, 1891, to arrest the guilty parties. When the soldiers entered the village they were confronted by armed Hopis and impersonators of Maasaw, an Earth Deity and God of the Underworld; Kookyangsowuuti, Spider Grandmother; and Pöökong and Palengawhoya, the Warrior Twins. The appearance of the deities was a formal declaration of war.[108] Maasaw told the soldiers to leave the village or hostilities would commence, but the threat was not carried through to the beginning of actual hostilities because Lieutenant L. M. Brett withdrew with his men to Keams Canyon, where he awaited additional forces with more powerful weapons.[109]

Keam reported on these events to Herbert Welsh. He said that the trouble had begun at Oraibi because of a "fanatical priesthood," which was opposed to Loololma and "any advance toward civilization." They had destroyed the allotment surveyors' stakes and had "horsewhipped an Indian in their service."[110]

A few days later, Colonel H. C. Corbin, Assistant Adjutant General, arrived at Keams Canyon with four troops of cavalry and two Hotchkiss guns.[111] They prevailed upon Thomas Keam to accompany them to Oraibi. In a report on the events, Keam wrote:

> they called down to see me, and asked me to accompany them to Oraibi, which I could not refuse. Of course, all kinds of questions were then asked in regard to the resistance the Oraibis would make, and my idea of the whole matter, and last, but not least, their dependence on my knowledge of the water supply for the whole command. . . . After consultation we decided to get an early start on July 1.

. . . We met a courier from Oraibi, who informed us that the Oraibis had threatened to kill La-lo-la-my [Loololma] on sight of the troops and were prepared to fight. [That morning] with Eone [a Hopi guide] and I leading, we moved up the sides of the Shimopavi [sic] mesa, over it, and into the Oraibi valley, and on and to within 3 miles of the village. Here a halt was made, and after consultation with those in command I volunteered to go to the mesa, send for the hostiles, and, if possible, get them to come back with me to where the troops were halted. I rode up close to the village and sent "Honani" of Shimopavi [sic] to inform the leaders I desired to see them. He returned saying they would not come. I again sent him back to tell them that serious trouble would result if they did not meet me at once. This brought 6 of the leaders down. . . . After saying a few words to them, I escorted them to the troops, where they were made prisoners and heard some good advice from Colonel Corbin. . . . The order was now given to mount, and we rode up to the village, taking the whole command, with 2 Hotchkiss guns. Here we took the war chief and his son prisoner. . . . The son, being asked what he had to say, replied: 'I was prepared to fight the few soldiers that were here some days ago, because I thought we could kill them and drive them away; now, however, it would be useless. I never saw so many Americans before. You have my friends prisoners and I am not able to fight all these soldiers; take me, as I am in your power.' The troops were then arranged in front of the village, and after Colonel Corbin had explained to the people what was to be done with the prisoners, and impressed them with obedience to their chief La-lo-la-my [Loololma], he said he would show them what would have been done with the Hotchkiss guns if they offered resistance. [112]

After the guns were fired over the heads of the villagers, Keam and the troops withdrew and headed back to the canyon with nine prisoners who were headed for Fort Wingate. [113] Those hostile to their leader, Loololma, and to the school had been removed from the village and, true to form, the Americans believed that all impediments to the government's programs had been removed. Keam and the soldiers withdrew from Oraibi, relieved that the impasse had been resolved without bloodshed but certain that the hostile Oraibis had been impressed by the power of the government. Keam returned to the canyon, and the soldiers returned with their prisoners to Fort Wingate.[114] Two days later Keam and Alexander Stephen rode over to Walpi, where they celebrated the nation's birthday with a "pyrotechnic display on top of the highest house in Walpi."[115]

Standing on a rooftop at Walpi on a summer's night with the San Francisco Peaks appearing close enough to touch but in reality over one hundred miles to the south, Thomas Keam had more than the nation's birthday to celebrate. In 1891 he was at the height of his career. His trading post was popular among Hopi and Navajo customers as well as anthropologists, museum curators in the United States and western Europe, and the increasingly common tourist. As far as the Indians, scientists, and bureaucrats in the Office of Indian Affairs were concerned, Keam was an ally and friend whose advocacy and advice served them well. Not only was he financially secure, but he also possessed a large measure of prestige and authority.[116] Because of his location, knowledge, and experiences this Indian trader was more influential than any Indian agent, and his authority was unrivaled.

CONFRONTING CHARLES BURTON

ALTHOUGH AMERICANS WERE making inroads into northeastern Arizona in 1891, Thomas Keam still presided over the area in his unofficial role as Indian agent. He filled the void created by the government when it closed the Hopi agency in 1882, and for a decade his opinions were solicited and sometimes followed by Commissioner of Indian Affairs Thomas Jefferson Morgan and Herbert Welsh of the Indian Rights Association. His influence in the region was exclusive and unrivaled, and the fifty-year-old Cornishman had no reason to believe in 1891 that his future work for the Hopis would be compromised or that his power would be challenged. However, Keam's business success brought changes to the region, and these changes ultimately affected the nature of his influence. His work with American anthropologists, the collections he sold to American and European museum curators, and those he exhibited in international fairs made the Hopis' life-styles, history, and craft work known to a larger population outside the region. Hopi scholarship became popular. Over 250 books and articles were written in English, German, and French about the Hopis between 1870 and 1900. By 1903 there were at least two children's books featuring Hopi stories, and in 1907 the University of Leipzig granted the Ph.D. for one of the earliest doctoral dissertations on Rio Grande Pueblo and Hopi history.[1] American tourists were common at

Hopi, especially during the Snake Dance, because Keam initially provided Hopi guides and accommodations and these tourists found his Hopi pottery, basketry, and kachina dolls to be satisfactory mementos of their trip to "Hopiland." Keam's success as an Indian trader caused others to believe that they, too, could run profitable businesses in the area. Frederick and William Voltz opened a trading post below Third Mesa in 1891.[2] Ten years later there were five posts owned by Hopis and two others owned by Americans.[3] The Mennonites, mindful of the Hopis' unmet spiritual needs, began a mission below Third Mesa in 1893.[4] But more than anything else, Keam's success in establishing a boarding school at Keams Canyon changed the demography of the region. Teachers, seamstresses, and cooks were necessary for the school, and they lived at Keams Canyon. A day school was opened for the Oraibi children in 1893.[5] Another was opened below First Mesa in 1894,[6] and a third at Toreva Springs below Mishongnovi and Shipaulovi in 1897.[7] The day schools brought even more employees to the region, and their activities were coordinated by the superintendent of schools who worked at the Keams Canyon school and answered to the agent at Fort Defiance.

The consequence of all this was that many more Americans lived in the region than before, and they soon questioned Keam's unrivaled stature in the region as well as his unchallenged access to those in the Office of Indian Affairs. Those encountering Keam during the last years of his life who had no reason to object to or fear his power described him as the "baronial entertainer of the country side," a cultured and "sweet gentleman" who was a friend of the Indians.[8] Godfrey Sykes, a friend of Keam's and Alexander Stephen's who clerked at Keam's post whenever Keam went to Washington, D.C., or England, claimed that both Hopis and Navajos "trusted and admired" him.[9] Writing a generation later, Albert Yava said the Hopis and Tewas trusted Keam, that he really had their interests in mind, and that "he was always working for them."[10] Sykes likened the atmosphere around the post to that which "may have existed around patriarchal or feudal establishments," and although he was writing metaphorically, Keam's position in the region did in some ways resemble the feudal estate.[11] Thomas Keam served both the Office of Indian Affairs and the Hopis. If the Hopis viewed Keam's activities positively, however, others saw them in a different light. Instead of viewing him as an avuncular feudal lord, Thomas Keam was, to them, the despot whose power had become corrupt and self-serving. They tended to view traders in general, and this one in particular, as predators of unsuspecting and ignorant Indians—impediments to progress.

The intrusion of the outside world into Thomas Keam's domain began slowly. Keam believed that he could weather the complaints as he had those in the past, but the new intruders were also powerful. Their actions and Keam's failing health combined to undermine his influence and prestige, so that shortly after the turn of the century there was little evidence that Thomas Keam had ever lived in the region or influenced the relationship between the Great Father and the Hopis.

In 1894, Thomas Keam used his influence in the reform community to halt the government's program of allotting land in severalty to the Hopis. This plan, devised by Senator Henry Dawes and others, passed the Congress in 1887 as the Dawes Allotment Act.[12] It was the culmination of the Indian reformers' beliefs that the ownership of private property would speed the Indians' adoption of "civilized" ways and break up the reservations. Without reservations, the reformers believed, there would be no need for an Office of Indian Affairs and the government's operation would be streamlined.[13] That the Hopis were exempted from the allotment program is testament to Keam's remarkable abilities to influence Indian policy where the Hopis were concerned.

At Hopi, an allotment agent had been in the area since 1892.

Of the several million acres within the Hopi Reservation only 120,000 acres of land had been determined to be "usable" from an American agricultural perspective, and land had been allotted to those Hopis who would accept it.[14] Despite the reformers' high hopes, the implementation of the allotment of land in severalty at Hopi was ill conceived, not just because it contradicted the Hopis' concept of land ownership but also because the ever-changing physical landscape at Hopi precluded the creation of fixed boundaries.[15] Both Thomas Keam and the Hopis knew this, and together they forced the government to abandon the program at Hopi. To do this Keam contacted his friends, among them the anthropologists James Mooney,[16] Frank Cushing, and John Wesley Powell as well as the Mennonite missionary at Third Mesa, Frederick Voth, and General A. D. McCook, former commander of the army for the Department of Arizona and now commander of the Department of Colorado.[17] Keam called on his friend and lawyer, W. Hallett Phillips of Washington, D.C., to state the legal case against the allotment of Hopi land. In a letter to Commissioner of Indian Affairs Daniel M. Browning, Phillips cited the 1876 United States Supreme Court decision, *United States v. Joseph,* which denied the applicability of the 1834 Trade and Intercourse Act to the Pueblos of New Mexico because they had been determined to own title to their land due to provisions in the Treaty of Guadalupe Hidalgo. Phillips claimed that because the Hopis were Pueblos, allotment was unnecessary; the land belonged to them and not the federal government.[18]

The Hopis did as they had done to get the school at Keams Canyon and building materials for their houses: they wrote to the "Washington Chiefs," saying:

> During the last two years strangers have looked over our land with spyglasses and made marks upon it, and we know but little of what it means. As we believe that you have no wish to disturb our Possessions, we want to tell you something about the Hopi land.

None of us wer[e] asked that it should be measured into separate lots, and given to individuals for they would cause confusion.

The family, the dwelling house and the field are inseparable. . . .

A man plants the fields of his wife, and the fields assigned to the children she bears, and informally he calls them his, although in fact they are not. . . .

According to the number of children a woman has, fields for them are assigned to her, from some of the lands of her family group, and her husband takes care of them. Hence our fields are numerous but small, and several belonging to the same family may be close together, or they may be miles apart, because arable localities are not continuous. There are other reasons for the irregularity in size and situation [and they explained the details of Hopi land use]. . . .

These limited changes [as explained above] in land holding are effected by mutual discussion and concession among the elders, and among all the thinking men and women of the family groups interested.

The American is our elder brother, and in everything he can teach us, except in the method of growing corn in these waterless sand valleys, and in that we are sure we can teach him. We believe that you have no desire to change our system of small holdings, nor do we think that you wish to remove any of our ancient landmarks, and it seems to us that the conditions we have mentioned afford sufficient grounds for this requesting to be left undisturbed.[19]

Keam also enlisted the support of Herbert Welsh and the Indian Rights Association. Even though the reformers were ardent advocates of the Dawes Act and its provisions, in the Hopis' case they opposed the allotment of land in severalty because of Welsh's long association with Keam and Welsh's firsthand knowledge of the Hopis. Both Keam and Welsh believed that if the Hopis' reservation was broken up through allotment, Navajos living in the vicinity would encroach even more on Hopi land and the result would be disastrous.

Keam told Welsh that the Hopis had asked Keam to enlist Welsh's support for their petition "so that they may continue to live unmolested, happy, and prosperous."[20] Welsh promised his help, saying he would forward Keam's letter to the Indian Rights Association's lobbyist in Washington, D.C., and instruct him to help the Hopis.[21] Keam continued to keep the Hopis' plight in Welsh's mind. He related events surrounding the difficulties that had arisen between two Hopi families who had built houses on lands claimed by a third family. Keam wrote that this

> caused constant quarreling and dread of each other. The rightful owners of the land believed the whites kept them off on account of a Land Agent having been here with the object of allotting land, when the houses were built. The interested parties with their relatives were on hand with the expressed desire to have the matter settled by me. After an hours talk we decided the question to the satisfaction of all concerned, so that they departed for their homes friendly and happy.[22]

Welsh wrote the secretary of the interior about the inadvisability of allotting land to the Hopis.[23] By the end of 1894, the implementation of the program at Hopi was abandoned. In the annual report issued by the commissioner of Indian affairs, Daniel M. Browning announced the abandonment of allotment at Hopi, saying, "The work of the allotting lands in severalty to the Moquis Indians has been discontinued. All but a few of the Indians had made their selections . . . but a small number continued their objections to the allotting work. This opposition, together with formal objections to the approval of the allotment presented to this office by Friends of the Indians, led to a discontinuance of the work in February last."[24]

Commissioner Browning's decision was supported by the acting agent at Fort Defiance, Lieutenant E. H. Plummer, who wrote, "It has been the custom for years for these people to cultivate their lands in common. Owing to the shifting nature of their planting grounds, it would be almost impossible to maintain any allotment to individuals. It is believed that the best interests of the tribe would be promoted by granting the [Hopis'] petition."[25] Their opinions were also supported by the allotment agent, John Mayhugh.[26]

Keam continued to look out for the Indians' well being. After having met with the commissioner in Washington, D.C., in November,[27] Keam and Captain Constant Williams, the new acting agent at the Navajo Agency, and two troops of cavalry rode over to Oraibi "for the purpose of arresting the leaders of the hostile faction, who had taken forcible possession of the farms of other [nonhostile] Oraibis at Moen Kopi *[sic]*." They arrested nineteen "of the bad element that have been leaders in every measure of hostility toward the Agents of the Govt *[sic]* or such reforms as they may advocate."[28] Keam suggested that the men be "deported" and kept away for two years. If this were done, their influence would be diminished and they would learn a lesson. A month later the men were imprisoned at the military prison on Alcatraz Island, California, for eight months.[29]

Keam also wrote the commissioner about the plight of many Navajo families due to the severe weather. "In my many years of residence among these people," he wrote, "I have not known such a large number of them in the extremity of want that exists among them at present. Some assistance should be rendered them before the winter is over, or numbers of them will starve as a great many are now living on the charity of others whose supply of food is limited to a few sheep and goats, the corn crop being an entire failure."[30] Writing on the same topic to Herbert Welsh, Keam said that he planned to "ask my friends in Washington to use their influence to secure an appropriation for the assistance of those who will suffer from hunger and want if some help is not forthcoming."[31]

In February 1895, Keam wrote Captain Constant Williams, acting agent at Fort Defiance, that the Blue Canyon Trading Post was for sale by its owner. Jonathan Williams, the owner, estimated the post's value at $10,000 but was willing to sell out for $2,500 or rent the buildings to the government if necessary. He authorized Keam to "act for him in this matter." Keam believed that the facilities and location, although remote from the agency, would be ideal for a school for the Navajos. Captain Williams forwarded Keam's letter to the commissioner with his endorsement, and a school was opened there in 1899.[32]

But it was the outbreak of smallpox, one of the oldest consequences of the "discovery" of the New World by the Old, that stirred Keam to action and rekindled the bitterness he felt about the Office of Indian Affair's ineptitude. Although there had been previous epidemics in the area, the outbreak in December 1898 was particularly severe, due in part to the fact that the poorly provisioned physician at the Keams Canyon school was immediately overwhelmed and the agent was a safe distance away at Fort Defiance. Although they closed the schools[33] and attempted to quarantine the Oraibis in their village on Third Mesa,[34] the disease went unchecked, and the government's seeming indifference infuriated Thomas Keam. In an attempt to force the government into action, Keam called on his friends in Washington, D.C., to pressure the Congress to pressure, in turn, the secretary of the interior and the commissioner of Indian affairs, who would pressure the agent, whose only orders were to keep the Office of Indian Affairs apprized of the death count.

Keam wrote Jesse Walter Fewkes, an anthropologist in the Bureau of American Ethnology, to tell him to postpone his visit to First Mesa and to ask for his influence in solving the problem. Keam described a grim situation:

> The last message we had five days ago [February 17, 1899] there had been up to that time twenty-five deaths at East Mesa and fifty-four at Middle Mesa. And on that day, five

days ago, a number of Oraibis had come over from their village to a ceremony at the Middle Mesa, so you can see what an awful condition of affairs things are in, as no effort has been made to quarantine the villages where the dreadful disease is carrying them off daily. I expect to hear next the disease has broken out at Oraibi. Its now over two months and not one effort made by the Agent to supply the convalescent with new clothing or fumigate their houses. A physician from the Railway came here to see me and get the situation of affairs; he told me they could learn nothing from the Agent. He was sent from Albuquerque by the Santa Fe Pacific Hospital Association. We gave him all the data. . . . The day after his arrival he telegraphed for a physician and nurse for Middle Mesa. He stayed with me two days, and promised on leaving to telegraph Washington and try to get something done at once. . . . I also sent five hundred pounds of sulphur to fumigate all the houses at East Mesa. . . .

I never heard of such a shameful thing, these poor people being allowed to suffer and die without proper efforts being made by the Government (who would claim them as wards under any other circumstances to save them).[35]

In the end, the agent at Fort Defiance did as he was ordered and gathered statistics. Of the estimated 2,500 Hopis, 187 people died in this outbreak of smallpox.[36]

As the nineteenth century drew to close, life at Hopi was changing. In 1880 the people lived in villages atop the mesas in houses without stoves, tables, chairs, or lamps. A ladder through the roof provided entryway to many of the houses. The people's diet consisted mostly of squash, bean, and corn dishes prepared in a hundred different ways. Occasionally, these were supplemented by mutton and goat meat and the occasional rabbit, ground squirrel, or deer. Thomas Keam's trading post offered exotic goods: coffee, sugar, galvanized pots and pans, and manufactured cloth.[37]

After Americans from the Office of Indian Affairs arrived, they encouraged the Hopis to abandon their homes and adopt a civilized way of life.[38] These people wanted the Hopis to wear American-style clothes: men should wear pants, shirts, jackets, and hats and cut their hair short; women should wear cotton dresses instead of their black wool dresses and mantas; children should be clothed like their adult counterparts, and they should attend school. The Americans wanted the Hopis to abandon their religious ceremonies, especially the dances with which the Americans were most familiar because they were conducted in public. They wanted the Hopis to move down to the valleys below the mesas, where they could cultivate the soil like other American farmers. Commissioner Morgan explained this to them in 1890, and since that time he and his successors had made building materials available to those who would move. The government provided wood for floors, roof beams, doors, and windows and made stoves and household furniture available to them. By the turn of the century almost one hundred houses, known to the Hopis as *palakiki,* or red houses, because of the rust color of their tin roofs, had been constructed. The government also sunk several water wells, improved springs, constructed several dams, and opened a model farm to teach the Hopis how to cultivate crops.[39]

These improvements, however, failed to change the Hopis in the fundamental ways the government hoped for. Americans had viewed the villages as enclaves of traditionalism and believed that houses below the mesas would break the hold of "uncivilized" and unprogressive habits. However, the plan was not popular with the Hopis, and as early as 1893 the agent reported that of the two dozen houses completed, none were lived in permanently.[40] In 1894, the agent reported: "The plan for building houses in the valleys for these Indians . . . does not seem to be as successful as desired. . . . Their habits, customs, and general mode of living are so intimately connected with the conditions of life on the mesas that it is doubtful whether anything less than compulsion will cause them to abandon their pueblo dwellings."[41]

The Hopis were no longer able to isolate themselves from the Americans as they had done, and they were soon caught up in changes occurring thousands of miles away; however, they managed to maintain their independence. Like the allotment of land in severalty, the Hopis declined some of the Great Father's gifts outright and accepted others, like the furnished houses, on their own terms. Even the smallpox epidemic failed to force complete compliance with the vaccination and fumigation programs that followed, despite the use of troops.[42] The schools were also supported by some Hopis and denounced by others. In 1899, for example, only 120 students were enrolled at the boarding school at Keams Canyon or the day schools at Polacca, Second Mesa, or Oraibi.[43] Factionalism over the schools, among other things, had become so severe that troops were commonly dispatched to remove troublemakers from the villages or to keep hostilities from commencing.[44]

The interdependent and mutually beneficial relationship that had existed between Thomas Keam and those in the Office of Indian Affairs came to an end in 1897, when William A. Jones was appointed commissioner of Indian affairs by the newly elected Republican President William McKinley.[45] Although Thomas Keam was a Republican, like his fellow Loyal Legion members, he was representative of an older generation, and Jones of a younger one.[46] Jones did not look to the past for direction, because of its demonstrated inabilities to deal with society's problems. Like the other progressives of his generation, Jones looked to statistics and efficiency to demonstrate progress and direct policy.[47] He relied on educated professionals like himself, not people like Keam whose advice was designed to perpetuate the status quo. Jones believed that the government had created a population of people totally dependent on it for all decisions affecting their lives and for all supplies. He thought that the only way to bring the American Indians into mainstream American life, to make them feel at home in America, was for the government to cut off all rations and support. Only when the Indians were forced to rely on themselves, Jones believed, could they stand on their own feet.[48] These attitudes determined the way Jones and his agents would solve the "Indian problem." He believed that one of the impediments to progress for Indian children was traditionalism among older Indians.[49] He advocated a school curriculum that was efficient and designed to inculcate the principles of work.[50] Jones believed that once the "Indian problem" was solved, the reservations eliminated through the allotment of land, and the Indians became full participants in the American dream, the federal government could terminate its relationship with the Indians.

These philosophical changes and attitudes toward the past administrations, as well as the progressives' perceptions regarding the exclusivity of Keam's influence in the Office of Indian Affairs, brought renewed complaints about the old way of doing business. The complaints represented a dissatisfaction with the informal relationships between the government and influential civilians in general and Thomas Keam's relationship with government officials in particular. The progressives questioned Keam's connections with government officials because they opposed the buying and selling of influence in government. To them, Thomas Keam was nothing less than a political "boss," who symbolized all that was wrong with the status quo.

Dr. E. Snyder, "a lady from Philadelphia," forwarded her complaints about Keam to Arizona congressman Nathan O. Murphy. She said he had the "meanest and bad face of anyone I have met for years . . . it 'dishes' about the eyes and nose." According to Dr. Snyder, Keam's business practices were questionable and he "has had a monopoly of this country for years [and] he tries to run everything to suit himself." She complained that Keam needed to "learn his place."[51]

Dr. Snyder's real intent was to support Frederick and William Voltz's application for a license to trade below Oraibi. To do this, she deprecated the competition—Thomas Keam. She summarized the quality that newcomers despised about Thomas Keam. His business operated without competition, and his opinions were the only ones to which the Hopis had access. The progressives disapproved of the laissez-faire government of their fathers and were determined to eliminate these informal relationships.

Their judgements were correct. Keam had powerful allies in the government and the reform community. It was to his advantage to control the Indian trade business in the region. His profit margin at the post was such that he could afford a little competition selling groceries, but his craft business excelled because of his exclusive control of that particular market. He also benefited from the agents' location in Fort Defiance instead of Keams Canyon. Had he wanted an agent to take care of the Hopis business, he certainly had the connections to make it happen. Instead, Thomas Keam acted as the agent and, to many, "ran everything to suit himself."

However, that suggests a simplicity of motive that Keam's actions do not always support. There is no question that Keam was concerned with running a profitable trading post and ranch, but like many American businessmen of his generation he saw nothing wrong with bringing others along with him on the road to financial gain. His successes in the craft business, for example, improved the Hopis' economy as well. The boarding school needed beef to feed its students and staff, and Keam had beef cattle to sell. Even though Keam's businesses were contrived to fill a need, the newcomers could not get beyond the image of the conniving, exploitative Indian trader to see that many of Keam's actions were determined by very real humanitarian feelings. He could have exploited Hopi craftspeople and schoolchildren alike, but his actions do not support that image. He, like many of his generation, ran a profitable business while keeping the community's good at heart. But the progressives did not see Keam in that way. As they viewed the situation, Keam's actions reinforced their beliefs that Keam had operated unchecked in the past. Now that they were on the scene, Keam had to "learn his place," because his time, and that of his generation, had passed.

In 1899, the Office of Indian Affairs reopened the Hopi Agency and sent out a new superintendent of schools, Charles Burton, who also filled the agent's position.[52] Burton was a young man, only twenty-seven years old, and determined to perform his duties efficiently and effectively. He was the kind of employee whose actions were calculated to draw the attention of his superiors, and he seemed to keep his eye on the possibility of promotion. He was as intractable in his opinions about how the Hopis should be educated and "civilized" as Keam was. Both men were certain that their views were correct, and they did not get along.

However, enmity between the two was not immediate. There had been talk about relocating the Keams Canyon boarding school. The Office of Indian Affairs had sent out an investigator, Mr. Butler, to assess the old site and the proposed new site, which was down canyon about a mile and a half. Agent Burton gave Keam a copy of the report, and Keam wrote to A. C. Tonner, assistant commissioner, about the report's "many inaccuracies" and "misleading" details. In Keam's six-page rebuttal he repeatedly pointed out the inspector's lack of familiarity with the region and its climate, discounting the inspector's perceptions about the availability of spring water, the problem from flood runoff, and the cost of building materials. Keam wrote that his "dealings with the Indian Office for many years have always been most pleasant, and I am actuated only by a desire to see an important measure of this kind carried through successfully; unbiased by any erroneous statements. Eighteen years residence and experience in this cajon, has given me an opportunity to know whereof I wrote."[53] That spring, Keam discussed these matters in a meeting with Commissioner Jones in Washington, D.C.[54]

Meanwhile, Keam's meeting with the commissioner to refute Inspector Butler's proposal and support Agent Burton's plan was seen in an entirely different light by the teachers at the Hopi day schools. They believed Thomas Keam was in Washington, D.C., to get Agent Burton fired. In the spring of 1900 they appealed to the commissioner, believing that "undue influences" might cause the removal of their "esteemed, honest, and highly Honourable" superintendent, Charles Burton. "In the past," they claimed, "influences have been brought to bear at the Capital for the removal of no less than three pure and good men at this place."[55]

There is no indication from Keam's early letters to the commissioner of a problem between Burton and him. In fact, Keam's comments are uncharacteristically generous where Burton is concerned and there are no complaints about Burton in his 1899 letters to Herbert Welsh, Keam's personal "sounding board" where agents were concerned. In a letter to Commissioner Jones, Keam proclaimed his support for Agent Burton's decision to move the school down canyon and said that Inspector Butler had "ignored Mr. Burton's ideas, and acted most discourteously toward him."[56] Keam had never been reticent in speaking plainly about his lack of confidence in a number of agents, and there is no reason to believe he would have spared Burton if there had been a problem. However, by 1901 the teachers were correct in their belief that Keam was trying to get Burton fired. The reason for the ill feelings that developed between Thomas Keam and Charles Burton had two components: Keam claimed that Burton employed dictatorial tactics to enforce school attendance, and Burton claimed that Thomas Keam would not relinquish "control" of the Hopis to Burton.

Keam wrote the commissioner of Indian affairs about a meeting he was invited to at First Mesa. He said the chiefs of the three villages told him that Mr. Barnes, the teacher at the Polacca Day School, went to Walpi in search of truant children and, suspecting that they were in the kiva, went in. Upon entering he drew "a pistol, cocked it, and placed it at the side of an Indian named Luman-a-qua-sy, and told him he had come to kill him for preventing his boy from going to school." Keam said the Indians dared Barnes to shoot, saying that if he did so "he would not leave the place alive." Other Indians in the kiva told Barnes to put down the gun, as "Washington did not send him there to kill them but to educate their children," and they threatened him, saying that he had "done a great wrong and Washington should hear of it." They said that Barnes left the kiva and went to the Keams Canyon school, where he enlisted the help of an agency policeman who helped to him to arrest Luman-a-qua-sy. Keam reported, "All the Moquis are incensed over this, and say that Mr. Burton upholds the teachers of both the East and Middle Mesas in their actions of overawing them with pistols for the purpose of securing their children to attend the day schools to make a showing of a large attendance." Keam continued, relying on a ploy that had worked for the Navajos whenever they had an agent they did not like, saying that the Hopis ask for a "Superintendent who is in sympathy with them, and will protect them . . . one who has proper control over his teachers," and they want "teachers who do not resort to the use of pistols to carry out their desire among the Indians. Granted this, they will feel happy and not be in fear of those who are sent here, and paid by the Government, to help and protect them."[57]

A week later Burton forwarded his own version of the event in the form of testimony from the Hopi day school teachers to the commissioner. Richard Barnes admitted he had gone up to Walpi looking for a student and had entered the kiva. He said he had eventually taken two policemen up to the village but said nothing of a pistol. "There is a restless, rebellious spirit abroad among the Hopis at this mesa lately," he said, that "has of course communicated itself to the school children much to the detriment of my work."[58] The other teachers reported similar feelings of unrest and discontent, and they blamed Keam's meeting with the First Mesa men.[59] Frank Voorhies, the teacher at the Toreva school at Second Mesa, said he had heard that Keam had counseled the Indians to disregard the government employees. Voorhies complained that "civilization and progress among these people is an impossibility so long as this man Keam remains among them. That the only way to enlightenment among them lies in his ejectment from the Reserve."[60]

Voorhies took it upon himself to "ask around" about Keam. He asked Benjamin Williams of Gallup, New Mexico, about Keam's morals, his previous interference in the government's work among the Indians, and his trading practices.[61] Keam intercepted the letter "from a former clerk of mine" and forwarded it on to the commissioner, saying that Voorhies "appears to combine the office of detective with that of teacher, in behalf of Supt [sic] Burton, who he styles 'a certain party.' "[62]

Voorhies received a response to his inquiry from Ben Williams's brother, William, saying that he had clerked for Keam for seven years and that during that time Keam "always had Mokie girls around him and he would let them sleep at his house." Williams claimed that Keam opened his post on Sunday and that his usual profit on merchandise sold to the Indians was between 30 and 40 percent. Williams corroborated Voorhies's belief that Keam had Ralph Collins removed from his teaching post and that he "made the Indians believe that he was the rising sun and that they should look to him for light."[63]

The schoolteachers must have been very busy that early spring at Hopi, what with teaching school and writing and signing petitions about Keam. They sent petitions to the commissioner, their senators, and Vice President Theodore Roosevelt.[64] In the letters they pleaded to have Keam's trading license revoked, saying that he charged white residents fully 25 percent more for goods at his store than at stores along the railroad and that his post was open on Sundays. They claimed that he had incited the

Indians to unrest and rebellion and encouraged them to refuse to send their children to school; that he had "shown great discourtesey [sic] toward the constituted U.S. authority"; and that his influence on the Indians was reprehensible. They claimed he had joined some of the Indian clans and was a priest in at least one. It was clear to them that Thomas Keam was "an enemy to all progress among the Indians," that he was an immoral man because he spent the night in the Hopi villages, and that he had fathered "two mixed blood boys."[65]

Burton pleaded with the commissioner:

> I respectfully request that the matter contained therein be given special consideration for on the removal of this man from the reservation hangs the future welfare of the Moqui people. I do not hesitate to say, Mr. Commissioner, that his presence here has been the serious drawback to the progress of these people. If he would attend strictly to his business of a trader and let the management of the Indians and their troubles to the ones appointed for such matters it would be a different thing; but he takes it upon himself to inquire into and many times to settle disputes among them as if he were agent himself. He goes often to the villages and remains over night in their squalid homes and I am sure that it is unnecessary and unbecoming a gentleman of the culture and refinement that he claims to have. He opposes the children going away to school as I showed you . . . thereby largely defeating the policy laid down by your office and rendering my work in many cases ineffective; he opposes the building of Indian houses down in the valley; he encourages the people in their heathenish dances and tells that it is good; he . . . holds councils with the Indians on matters foreign to his business thereby assuming authority that does not belong to him; and in fact he opposes any and all plans that will render the Indians different to what they are today or what they have been for hundreds of years before.
>
> Therefore . . . I respectfully renew my recommendation . . .

that Mr. Keam be removed from the reservation just as quickly as will not cause him too much financial loss.[66]

If the commissioner would not respond by supporting Keam's eviction, Burton had other matters that could not be ignored, and he cast a wide net to catch Thomas Keam in some violation of the trade regulations that could result in the revocation of his trading license. Sunday openings were a violation of the trade regulations, and Keam's refusal to submit to Burton, as agent, a list of his prices and mark-ups was also a violation of regulations. That Keam was alleged to have had sexual relations with Indian women could, alone, be cause to revoke his license on the grounds that he was an immoral influence on the natives. That fall Burton obtained affidavits from two Hopi women who claimed that Keam had tried to seduce them.[67] The alleged events had happened two years previously, and both women "refused to say if he actually did have criminal relations with them," but Burton claimed that "there is no doubt whatever in my opinion." There must have been some doubt in the mind of Miss Abbott, an agency employee, because she refused to sign the affidavits even though she witnessed the depositions.[68]

For some reason the teachers at the Second Mesa day school at Toreva Springs were especially motivated to protect Burton's job and complain about Keam. The teachers at the Polacca day school, where the incident with Barnes and the gun occurred, and at the Keams Canyon boarding school were strangely quiet throughout all of this letter writing. A. O. Wright, a teacher at Keams Canyon school, did submit to the commissioner a confidential analysis of the situation and the personalities involved. His letter is without the histrionics that characterized all of the others.[69]

Wright told the commissioner that the strained relations between Thomas Keam and Charles Burton were understandable because both parties had reasons to distrust each other. He said that many in the vicinity believed Keam had influence in Washington, D.C., and that he had used it on several occasions to get teachers fired. Wright said that he had heard this from Ralph Collins and the superintendent at Chilocco before he had ever thought about moving to Keams Canyon. He had also heard from the Mennonite missionary that Keam had "opposed all the good superintendents and favored all the weak or bad officers here." Wright claimed the real reason Burton was opposed to Keam was that Keam told parents not to let their children be taken off to the Phoenix Indian School. Keam disliked Burton, Wright claimed, because his teachers brutalized and terrorized the Hopis into compliance with his wishes.[70]

Wright offered his advice for mediating the disagreements between Keam and Burton:

> Supt [sic] Burton is the first superintendent who has had full powers as an agent here, and I think he has justified your choice of him for this difficult and important work. . . . [but given the difficulties] it is not remarkable if he has sometimes been incautious or unwise in his actions. . . .
>
> [Both men] are contrary in disposition and have different standards of morals and religion, and the further fact that Mr Keam for many years has been accustomed to rule this country, so that the Indians believe he speaks for Washington, and that he cannot endure an officer here who does not follow his advice and defer to his opinions. As his opinions are generally those of the Indians, like all traders, a good officer cannot entirely follow his advice. This is the irrepressible conflict, which makes it impossible to have harmony here till traders and Indians all understand that the Superintendent is the only authorized representative of the government here, and that the trader is a trader only.
>
> A change in the superintendent at this time would be at once interpreted as a victory for Mr Keam and for the non-progressiveness which he represents, and a rebuke to an ef-

ficient officer. The result would be that no superintendent afterwards could do his work so well.[71]

Wright did not think Keam's license ought to be revoked, as Burton had requested, but thought that if it was renewed, "he should distinctly understand that he is not agent, but trader, and that he must at once and forever cease his opposition to schools, and especially his opposition to non-reservation schools."[72]

Burton was not getting anywhere with his allegations, but the teachers' petitions drew a response from the commissioner's office. It was not the response for which they hoped. The Accounts Division of the Office of Indian Affairs sent out a circular or memorandum that forbid agents, inspectors, superintendents, and others from corresponding with other branches of the government, with congressmen, or with their committees. Burton complained to the commissioner that his office would comply, "but I beg suggest for the good of the service that the same provisions be made relating to Indian traders. Why," he asked, "should a superintendent be compelled to keep quiet with an Indian trader of his reservation being allowed to lobby against him unrestrained with the highest offices of the government, to the great detriment of the service as every person on this reservation knows has been done in the past?"[73]

From the spring of 1900, when the teachers wrote the commissioner in fear that Thomas Keam had used his influence to get Burton fired, until the fall of 1901, Thomas Keam was uncharacteristically silent, writing only several letters to the commissioner. Instead of responding to the allegations about him, he petitioned Commissioner Jones on behalf of the Navajos who wanted to send their children to the Keams Canyon boarding school and to complain about the establishment of a trading post at Jeddito, three miles from Keam's trading post.[74] He claimed that Burton had some "pecuniary" interest in the post and that

Hopi and Navajo agency laborers were paid in scrip redeemable only at the Jeddito post.[75] These were dispassionate complaints, lacking Keam's enthusiasm for pressing the Indians' or his own needs or any requests for others' influence over the commissioner. Rather they were pro forma letters, reflecting the fact that Keam's health was rapidly declining. In the spring of 1901 a doctor from Albuquerque had gone to Keams Canyon to treat Keam for a case of pneumonia, which he had developed after spending several weeks at his mine.[76] Even though the pneumonia had been abated, Keam's health remained poor, and he was sick again during the spring of 1902.[77] He was so dispirited that Jones's most recent directive to the agents failed to rouse him for the battle he had delighted in so often in the past, despite the Hopis' and Navajos' pleas for his help.

Commissioner Jones had sent out a directive to the Indian agents across the nation in which he claimed that long hair and face painting were impediments to civilization, and these customs "should be modified or discontinued."[78] The Commissioner claimed that the agents should encourage Indian men to wear their hair short and that "with your Indian employees and those Indians who draw rations and supplies, it should be an easy matter, as a noncompliance with this order may be made a reason for discharge or for withholding rations and supplies."[79] Returned students, who had been trained properly, should be made to wear their hair short instead of being allowed to revert to the "uncivilized" style.[80] Jones also asked his agents to encourage the Indians to adopt "the wearing of citizens' clothing instead of the Indian costume and blanket" and said that "Indian dances and so-called Indian feasts should be prohibited." He claimed that "in many cases these dances and feasts are simply subterfuges to cover degrading acts and to disguise immoral purposes."[81]

Jones wanted the agents to report their progress in carrying out the orders and instructions.[82] Charles Burton, eager to comply and mindful that merit would determine his keeping his job, broadly interpreted Jones's order. He had asked the commissioner for the authority to destroy the Hopis' kivas, believing it was necessary to eliminate the "evil" Hopi ceremonies. He also wanted authority to bar scientists, or "pottery diggers" as he called them, from the reservation for at least one year.[83] His enthusiasm for the intent of the hair-cutting order caused him to resort to force with those who would not voluntarily submit to the barber's shears. The missionaries at Second and Third Mesa protested Burton's actions, and Charles Lummis, editor of *Out West,* took up the cause.[84] The outcries forced Commissioner Jones to justify his original orders. "Although comparatively trivial in my estimation it seems the entire press of the country considered it otherwise, for it has thought it important enough to give it extended notice and make it the subject of unfavorable comment on the one hand, and some wit and much good-natured badinage on the other."[85] Jones claimed that the "the impression seemed to prevail that the Government intended to accomplish its desires by main strength and awkwardness, and there was some silly talk about 'revolt' and 'uprising.' "To counteract any misunderstanding, either by the press or by the agents, Jones refined his order. It was, he claimed, "a declaration of policy of this office," but warned that the order should be implemented using "tact, judgement, and perseverance."[86] However, Jones encouraged the agents that "they should begin gradually and work steadily and tactfully til the end view should be accomplished." Lest anyone believe that the commissioner was withdrawing or softening his order, he wrote, "Let it be distinctly understood that this is not a withdrawal or revocation of the circular letter referred to, but an authoritative interpretation of its meaning."[87] Jones defended his policy, saying that the "Government has a right to expect a proper observance of rules established for their [the Indians'] good."[88] Long hair, ceremonial dances and feasts, the reliance on medicine men, and a reverence for the past were all inimical to the progress the Office of Indian Affairs was stressing. The Indians, Jones and his employees believed, must learn to work and manage their own affairs and must blend into the dominant society. Those traditions that prevented assimilation and those non-Indians who encouraged traditional life-styles were impediments to a successful, progressive life-style.

Keam wrote the commissioner protesting Burton's actions, saying that the Navajos considered short hair "a great disgrace, that criminals and poor Navajos alone were distinguished from good men by such a mark and they all protested against such measures being used on them."[89] Keam said that the Hopis feared Burton not only because of the hair-cutting order but also because he had promised to destroy their houses and kivas. Keam's letter to the commissioner of Indian Affairs about the hair-cutting episodes, however, lacks Keam's usual zeal for pressing the Indians' causes with the commissioner. It also reflects his realization that Jones's attitudes were never going to change, either through education or an appeal to his humanitarian attitudes.[90] Even more than that, however, Keam realized that he was not going to be able to deflect this agent, this commissioner, or the unilateral implementation of a culturally flawed policy. Keam's health prevented him from taking up the Indians' cause and traveling to Washington, D.C., to persuade this commissioner of the negative effects of his policy. Instead he withdrew from the fight and relied on others to carry it on.

The battle between Thomas Keam and Charles Burton was not just an argument over how best to implement government policy, it was, in reality, a fight between young and old, between change and the status quo. It was exacerbated because neither could understand the attitudes of the other. To Charles Burton, Thomas Keam personified the ineffectual policies of the past that perpetuated the Indians' dependence on the government. The government had been duped by unscrupulous, self-serving white men like Thomas Keam into allowing the Indians to languish in an environment controlled by traditionalism, the elderly, and medicine men practicing some form of witchcraft. Burton and his superiors in the Office of Indian Affairs saw men like Keam as impediments to their programs to civilize the Indians and believed that such obstacles could not be tolerated or worked around. They had to be removed. To Thomas Keam, on the other hand, Charles Burton was just the latest in a long line of Indian agents who did not know the Indians or the region. His lack of practical knowledge, which could be gained only from years of experience, prevented him from formulating and implementing workable policies. Keam believed that Burton's zeal for performing his duties efficiently blinded him to the needs of the people.

Ironically, Charles Burton and Thomas Keam were united in their belief that education was essential if the Hopis were to adapt to the larger world in which they lived. They were divided over the methods by which that education should be delivered. Thomas Keam was not an early advocate for Indian self-determination. He, like many of his generation, adhered to the Spenserian notion that progress and "civilization" were inevitable and laudable goals. The fact that he opposed sending Hopi children away for years at a time to the Phoenix Indian School does not mean that Keam was opposed to education in general, but that he was opposed to one particular policy—the forced removal of school-age children from the reservation. He was also opposed to the kind of authoritarian behavior some men, such as William F. M. Arny, Galen Eastman, and Charles Burton, found so appealing.

But that is not to suggest that Thomas Keam was above displaying force to get the Indians to comply with policies that he had determined were in their best interests. He and Ralph Collins had enforced Commissioner Morgan's mandatory attendance policy by conducting a house-to-house search for truant children, and he had ridden at the head of the United States Army to arrest those Oraibis hostile to the Keams Canyon school.

Because he had lived among them for two decades, Keam knew the Hopis as well as any American did at the time. He came to believe that his knowledge, coupled with the work he had done for them over the years, made him more knowledgeable than anyone else—including the Hopis. At worst, Thomas Keam's most egregious sin was that of pride complicated by paternalism. The fact that the Hopis were reluctant, at times, to fully adopt certain programs such as the mandatory attendance policy meant to Keam that they required the kind of gentle, but firm, treatment a father might mete out to a disobedient child. On other issues, such as the land allotment program or the short-hair order, Keam supported the Hopis' refusals to comply.

Ultimately, Charles Burton and Thomas Keam were separated from each other because they served two distinct masters: Burton served the Office of Indian Affairs and Keam believed he served the Hopis. Keam's actions and attitudes became intractable because neither Burton nor Commissioner Jones recognized or respected Keam's authority. Keam, accustomed to the old laissez-faire relationship with the Office of Indian Affairs, could not muster the energy to develop strategies to cope with, coopt, or outlast the changes. In the end, Thomas Keam was unable to battle the hegemony of the Office of Indian Affairs. His stamina had given out, and he was forced to rely on those who followed in his path to carry on the fight. When the charges against Burton were investigated, it was because the Hopis' defiance of this maniacal agent had become a celebrated cause among the Indian advocacy groups.[91] In the end, many joined the battle because of all that Keam had done to acquaint the outside world with the beauty and dignity of Hopi society.

Keam's health continued to deteriorate. The pneumonia, the life he had led, and the stress he had undergone combined to weaken his heart. Writing Washington Matthews, himself a physician, Keam said, "I, like all individuals who have lived in the West, and away from civilization generally; we take but little care of our health, but rough it, and exert all of our energies to the utmost; which eventually develops into some trouble or breakdown from overtaxing some of the organs. I am not an exception to the rule, and while I had arranged to sell all my interests in Keam's [sic] Cañon, I was compelled to leave there hurredly on account of heart trouble."[92]

Keam's doctors may have already diagnosed the ailment, angina pectoris, and realized that his health was not going to improve if he stayed at the canyon.[93] Angina pectoris is a symptom of an underlying condition, usually obstruction of the coronary arteries. The pain, which is localized on the left side of the chest, has been described as a feeling of "tightness, strangling, heaviness, or suffocation" and is most often brought on by strenuous outdoor exercise taken in cold weather or after eating a heavy meal. It can also be brought on by emotional excitement.[94] His doctors must have counseled not only a change in location and altitude, as Albuquerque was the highest elevation at which Keam was allowed to spend time, but the abandonment of the stressful environment, Keams Canyon. With this in mind, Keam sold his trading post to J. L. Hubbell in May 1902.[95] Before leaving Albuquerque for a prolonged visit to Philadelphia and Atlantic City, New Jersey, he wrote Lorenzo Hubbell "for 'Auld Lang Syne,'" and to express his appreciation for the manner in which the sale was conducted. "I realize of course that it was a matter which may have caused some little hitch somewhere, especially in my absences and [I] take it as somewhat of a favor on your part that everything passed off so pleasantly."[96]

Keam's health was so fragile that making the arrangements for the sale of his own trading post and home had to be done from afar. The man who had taken care of his own and others' business for so many years relied on a proxy to finalize the sale of the trading post that had been his home for more than two decades. When Thomas Keam left the canyon that bears his surname for the last time in 1902, almost all physical proof that he had ever lived in the canyon was gone. The Keams Canyon school that had been Keam's original trading post was abandoned in 1896, and a new brick school was built further down the canyon.[97] The building materials were removed from the old site and used to build new agency buildings near the new school. The fields of oats and clover and the avenue with over four hundred trees were swept away in a flood, which left in its wake a forty-foot gorge through the canyon.[98] All that was left was Keam's second trading post at the mouth of the canyon, and Lorenzo Hubbell Jr. stood behind the counter.

— 10 ⊷

RETREAT TO CORNWALL

IN THE FALL of 1902, as if it were still angry for his abandonment forty years earlier, the sea tried to reclaim Thomas Keam. He wrote to Stewart Culin that he "was out boating with a couple of friends, when we collided with another boat through the carelessness of our Captain; a rope from the mainsail of the other boat in passing, caught me by the neck and pulled me to the stern of our boat, and very near overboard; it cut my neck badly, and very nearly dislocated it."[1] At the time, Thomas Keam was living at the Hotel Dennis in Atlantic City, New Jersey.[2] After leaving Keams Canyon some six months earlier, Keam had been hospitalized in Albuquerque, New Mexico.[3] Following his release he lived in rooms at the Commercial Club for several months while he gained strength for the journey to Atlantic City, where the oceanside atmosphere was believed to have restorative powers.[4] Despite his ailments, Keam attempted to conduct business as usual. He maintained an interest in a mining operation in the Carrizo Mountains on the Navajo Reservation,[5] and he had a large collection of ethnographic materials for sale.[6] He and the anthropologist and curator at the University of Pennsylvania Museum, Stewart Culin, negotiated for the sale of Alexander Stephen's journals, and Keam provided an ethnographic commentary on Culin's manuscript on Indian games.[7] Even though Thomas Keam tried to operate as usual—encouraging Culin to call on the secretary of the interior and commissioner of Indian affairs on behalf of the Hopis and writing Lorenzo Hubbell to tell the Hopis and Navajos he would go to Washington, D.C.,[8] himself to press their case against Charles Burton—Keam was often too ill to do much for anyone.[9]

Following the boating accident that fall, on advice from his physician, the sixty year old sailed on the steamer *SS Lucania* for England.[10] While abroad he toured in France, Italy, and Switzerland, and while in Truro, his hometown, he maintained rooms at the Red Lion Hotel.[11] According to the curatorial staff, when the Rashleigh mineral exhibit was installed at the Royal Institution of Cornwall Museum, Keam visited there almost daily and advised the staff on how he thought the minerals should be displayed.[12] From his rooms, Keam sent Christmas wishes to Stewart Culin and reported, "I shall remain here over a month as this mild (although damp) climate agrees with me. My friends here are numerous[.] I have had a very delightful Xmas in this old fashioned but picturesque little city. As it is also the place of my birth there are many pleasant associations concerned with it."[13]

Believing that his health had recovered sufficiently for another trip across the Atlantic, Keam returned to the United States. Before embarking for his destination, Albuquerque, Keam finalized his will in Philadelphia. The executors of his estate were Nathaniel Battershill Bullen, an accountant and childhood friend in Truro, and Thomas R. McElmel of Philadelphia, one of Keam's oldest American friends and business associates.[14] He left 120 shares of stock in the First National Bank of Albuquerque and $25,000 in trust for his wife, Asdzáán Libá, for her life. He left two-thirds of his estate to the Royal Institution of Cornwall and one-third to the Central Technical School in Truro. He left $5,000 each to Thomas McElmel, Nathaniel B. Bullen, and his cousins Frederick W. Wing of London and James Stevens of Truro. The residue of his estate went to Miss Beatrice B. Bullen. When the estate went to probate it was estimated to be worth more than £11,700.[15]

"Sincerely yours, Thomas V. Keam." This portrait was a gift to
Godfrey and Emma Sykes, who, during the summer of 1895,
spent their honeymoon working at Keam's post while Keam was
in England. The photograph was taken by Prince, Pennsylvania
Avenue and 11th Street, Washington, D.C. Godfrey Sykes Collection, Courtesy of Arizona Historical Society/Tucson.

Keam returned to Albuquerque, where he stayed at the Commercial Club for the next seven months supervising his mining operations[16] and exchanging gossip with Culin about the other anthropologists working in the region.[17] They continued to negotiate the price of Stephen's manuscript, and Keam, true to form, continued to offer for sale a number of curious and odd ethnographic objects, if Culin could find buyers for them.[18] About the Hopis and Charles Burton as well as Charles Lummis's efforts to have Burton fired, Keam had very little to say other than that Burton was getting what he deserved.[19]

After another decline in his health, Keam left Albuquerque and the region that had been his home for forty years. In May 1904 he was in Philadelphia, preparing to embark on the SS *Campania* for England—for the last time.[20] Before leaving, he wrote Washington Matthews to thank him for the offer of Matthews's publication on the Navajo Nightway Ceremony. Matthews and Keam were the sole survivors of the network of friends whose mutual interests and complimentary attitudes had been discovered and nurtured at Keam's house in the canyon so many years earlier.[21] Alexander Stephen had died in 1894,[22] John Gregory Bourke two years later,[23] and Frank Hamilton Cushing in 1899.[24] To Keam, Matthews's publication was more than just a thoughtful acknowledgement of his assistance; it was a physical symbol of Keam's life spent among the Indians. "I shall prize it highly," he wrote, "and esteem it a favour, if you will write your name in it as presenting it to me[.] I shall take it to England to show my relatives and friends there."[25]

With that, the frail Cornishman returned to the country of his birth. After having spent his entire adult life among the Indians of the American Southwest, Thomas Keam entered a world in which the distinctions between Hopis and Navajos were blurred into the generic term "red Indians" and where Arizona Territory was as exotic and abstract as the Hindu Kush. All the events and people who had established and validated Thomas

Keam's prestige and power were no longer a part of his life. His heart must have ached for the old days when he could ride up to a hogan certain the welcome would be warm and the meeting toasted with a weak cup of Arbuckle coffee, or his appearance at Walpi greeted by the delight of children searching his pockets for candy. Beyond these pleasant memories were the powerful images of meetings between himself and Hopi elders, commissioners of Indian affairs, and the presidents of the United States. For his friends and family, Thomas Keam's life in America had no connection to their lives in Truro, the "old fashioned but picturesque little city" of his birth. He resided in a country that was physically and figuratively a world away. From his rooms above 21 Lemon Street in Truro, Thomas Keam could look out on a world virtually untouched by his life. There in Truro, on November 30, 1904, Thomas Varker Keam died from angina pectoris, an ailment of the heart. He was sixty-two years old.[26]

In addition to a brief obituary in the *Royal Cornwall Gazette*[27] and the *Philadelphia Times,*[28] Thomas Keam's passing was marked by an obituary in *American Anthropologist.*[29] Stewart Culin wrote, "Mr. Keam was widely known to the Indians of the southwest as 'Tomas' and was respected and loved by them. He spoke both Hopi and Navajo fluently. Mr. Keam was a man of the highest integrity, a keen observer, a wide reader, cultivated and accomplished. He maintained an open house at Keam's Cañon for every wayfarer and his hospitality was shared alike by the scientific explorer and the wandering Indian." Culin claimed, "Mr. Keam's death will be deplored by every student and explorer of the Southwest, to most of whom he was known and beloved."[30]

The Loyal Legion of the United States, Headquarters Commandery of the State of Pennsylvania, published a circular, as was its tradition, to mark the passing of one of its companions. In addition to citing Keam's military career, it remembered his anthropological contributions and collections and his occasional visits to Philadelphia. "Here, at the United Service Club, of which he was a member, his well told stories of his life among the Indians, their usages and ceremonies, never failed to draw and keep about him a spellbound audience. Companion Keam's life was marked by simplicity, earnestness, and a quick fine sense of the meaning of duty."[31]

The Royal Institution of Cornwall published a tribute to Thomas Varker Keam in 1907, and although it was a compilation of Culin's obituary and the Loyal Legion's circular, it characterized Thomas Keam as "one of the greatest benefactors to the Royal Institution of Cornwall since its foundation."[32]

Far removed from his home in the ancient American Southwest, Thomas Keam's body was laid to rest near the remains of those of his family in the cemetery at the Kenwyn Parish Church. His grave looks out on green pastures, fields, and hedgerows. It is shadowed by the church tower, which was built about A.D. 1259, the same time the Hopis were gathering on Black Mesa.

CONCLUSION

THOMAS KEAM HAS been dead almost a century, but his name is still known in the region. This is due in part to the fact that Keams Canyon bears his surname; as well, many Navajo people have Keam as their family name; and Thomas Keam, the Indian trader, is still recognized as a good and decent man. He may be the well-known exception to the stereotyped image of the Indian trader. To my knowledge, Thomas Keam never explained how or why he ended up an Indian trader. He never justified his actions on behalf of his Indian clients and friends except for using the phrase, "because of my many years among them."

By the end of his life at Keams Canyon, Thomas Keam had lived among the Hopis and Navajos for the better part of forty years. His residence among the Indians was not occasional like that of some Anglos; it was permanent, and it was full time. His experiences, his ability to converse in the Navajo and Hopi languages, and his intimate knowledge of their cultures brought Keam prestige and influence. Thomas Keam corresponded with or met almost every commissioner of Indian affairs and president of the United States between the end of the Civil War and the turn of the century. He counted among his friends most of the first generation of anthropologists studying in the American Southwest and was an active correspondent with the Indian Rights Association.

Keam also met with and counseled the first generation of Navajo headmen to hold authority over their tribe following their return from Bosque Redondo. These men—Barboncito, Delgadito, Ganado Mucho, Manuelito, and Narbonno—benefited from their friendship with Thomas Keam and he with them. At a time when other tribes were losing land, Thomas Keam and the Navajo headmen used their influence with the Office of Indian Affairs to double the size of the Navajo Reservation between 1868 and 1882. Keam received their verbal and written support as he campaigned for the Navajo agent's job.

For the Hopis, Thomas Keam and the kikmongwi of the First Mesa Villages forced the government to build a school at Keams Canyon. Keam facilitated a meeting in Washington, D.C., between Simo of Walpi, Polaccaca and Anawita of Sichomovi, Honani of Shungopovi, and Loololma of Oraibi; the Hopi Agent C. E. Vandever; and the Commissioner of Indian Affairs Thomas Jefferson Morgan. Keam's most important contribution to the Hopis' political development was probably his work with the Indian Rights Association to exempt the Hopis from the provisions of the Dawes Allotment Act of 1887, which was designed to break up Indian reservations and allot land in severalty to the Indians. The results of the Dawes Act for tribes whose land was allotted have been disastrous; for the Hopis, the exemption has meant that they are a cohesive and politically influential tribe whose land is still intact. In 1891, riding out in front of the calvary, Keam also prevented the outbreak of hostilities when the Hopis declared war on the United States Army in 1891.

Thomas Keam's prestige and his ability to influence Anglos and Indians alike came to him because of his intimate knowledge of each of the cultures. He used that knowledge to represent each group's opinions to the other, to mitigate their differences, and to protect each group from the others and from their own poorly formulated opinions and actions. That each group, Anglos, Navajos, and Hopis, relied on Keam demonstrates that they looked to him for these services; that they sometimes took his advice means that they respected his opinions and followed the ones that made sense to them. Some, no doubt, will want to return to the stereotype of Indian traders and to condemn Keam and his actions by suggesting that Keam duped the Indians into doing what he wanted—that they only tangentially benefited from his plans and schemes. There is no evidence that Keam manipulated the Indians or the Anglos into carrying out his plans when they held contrary opinions.

In death, however, Thomas Keam should not be seen as a selfless individual motivated by an early version of Indian self-determination. To do so would not only be an incorrect characterization; it would also strip Keam of the complexities that make his life so interesting. Many of Keam's actions on behalf of the Indians were calculated to benefit both them and himself. When the Hopis got a school at Keams Canyon, Thomas Keam benefited from the sale of his property for the school and from the sale of commodities to the school for the subsistence of the students and faculty. That both Indians and trader benefited from the plan was all the better, and was a practice that kept successful traders in business: both buyer and seller had to come out ahead. Keam created a market for Hopi arts and crafts when none existed. This new market saved Hopi pottery from oblivion by converting a utilitarian product into a commercial one. Keam also facilitated the change from Zuni-Spanish pottery designs by encouraging the production of the style we now call Sikyatki Revival. And he created a market for kachina dolls, which had never been made for anything other than ceremonial gift-giving. In marketing Sikyatki-style pottery and kachina dolls for sale, Keam made some Hopi men and women wealthy and famous. These crafts became profitable aspects of the Indian trade, and they helped make Keam wealthy and known beyond both the region and his profession.

Keam acquired his visa into the high-powered political circles of his world and his intimate knowledge of the Navajos' and Hopis' lifeways because of his business: he was an Indian trader. In northeastern Arizona following the Civil War, there were very few options for an Anglo man who wanted to live and work near the Navajos or Hopis. Government service was a possibility, but Keam was unsuccessful in this endeavor. There was the possibility of marriage to a woman in either tribe, whose membership would guarantee the husband the limited right to herd cattle or sheep. Although Keam was married to Asdzáán Libá, he did not take up either the life of a herder or of an adopted member of the tribe. Other employment could have been found in the towns along the railroad—Holbrook, Winslow, or Flagstaff—but these options would have taken Keam away from the Hopis and Navajos. If he was to live among the Indians, his only option was to become an Indian trader.

The business Keam entered in 1873 was very different from the business he left in 1902. Early on, trade in northeastern Arizona was sporadic and limited to the exchange of Navajo wool for canned goods, yard goods, and the occasional galvanized bucket. Thomas Keam pioneered the modern trading-post business in northeastern Arizona by demonstrating that these standard trade commodities could be expanded to include both Navajo and Hopi arts and crafts and both Indian and Anglo customers. Those who followed Keam's model also discovered that a successful trading post was one that was diversified in all respects. Keam never marketed himself as an Indian trader, as Lorenzo Hubbell and others did. There is no evidence that he wore buckskins or "Indian dress." There have been no photographs found of Keam presiding over his store or waiting on his Indian customers; there are, however, engravings of him with Indians while conducting government officials and tourists around the villages, and there are the portraits. All show Thomas Keam as a formal, self-possessed man. In his correspondence he never stressed his profession as the source of his influence and knowledge. It is as if he was uncomfortable with the stereotypes associated with the profession and wanted to set himself apart from them. It was because of the Indian trade that Keam lived among the Hopis and Navajos, and his proximity to them enabled him to possess knowledge that few others had at the time. He became an important man in the Anglo, Navajo, and Hopi worlds because of his location and his knowledge. Consequently, the Indian trade brought him the influence and prestige he seemed to want from life. Ironically, Keam may have felt these things came to him in spite of his profession.

NOTES

INTRODUCTION

1. Richard Van Valkenburg, "Tom Keam, Friend of the Moqui," *Desert Magazine* 9 (July 1946):9–12 (hereafter cited as Van Valkenburg, "Tom Keam").

2. Lynn R. Bailey, "Thomas Varker Keam: Tusayan Trader," *Arizoniana* 2 (winter 1961):15–19 (hereafter cited as Bailey, "Thomas Varker Keam").

3. Frank McNitt, *The Indian Traders* (Norman: University of Oklahoma Press, 1962) (hereafter cited as McNitt, *Indian Traders*).

4. Frederick Jackson Turner, *The Character and Influence of the Indian Trade in Wisconsin: A Study of the Trading Post as an Institution.* (Norman: University of Oklahoma Press, 1977), 79.

5. C. C. Rister, "Harmful Practices of Indian Traders of the Southwest, 1865–1876," *New Mexico Historical Review* 6 (July 1931):232. See also Howard Lamar, *The Trader on the American Frontier: Myth's Victim* (College Station: Texas A & M University Press, 1977); Ray Allen Billington, *Land of Savagery Land of Promise: The European Image of the American Frontier in the Nineteenth Century* (Norman: University of Oklahoma Press, 1981).

6. The body of literature on the history of Navajo weaving and the traders' effects on it is very large and complex. For example, see Charles Avery Amsden, *Navaho Weaving: Its Technic and History* (Santa Ana, Calif.: Fine Arts Press, 1934, and Glorieta, N. Mex.: Rio Grande Press, 1974) (hereafter cited as Amsden, *Navaho Weaving*); Kate Peck Kent, *Navajo Weaving: Three Centuries of Change* (Santa Fe, N. Mex.:

School of American Research, 1985); Joe Ben Wheat, *Patterns and Sources of Navajo Weaving: Harmsen's Western Americana Collection* (Denver, Colo.: The Printing Establishment, 1977); Dennis Boyd, "Trading and Weaving: An American-Navajo Symbiosis," (master's thesis, University of Colorado, Boulder, 1979) (hereafter cited as Boyd, "Trading and Weaving"); Alice Kaufman and Christopher Selser, *The Navajo Weaving Tradition: 1650 to Present* (New York, N.Y.: E. P. Dutton, 1985); Steve Getzwiller, *The Fine Art of Navajo Weaving* (Tucson, Ariz.: Ray Manley, 1984).

7. Robert M. Utley, "The Reservation Trader on the Navajo Reservation," *El Palacio* 68 (spring 1961):5 (hereafter cited as Utley, "Reservation Trader").

8. McNitt, *Indian Traders.*

9. William Y. Adams, *Shonto: A Study of the Role of the Trader in a Modern Navaho Community.* Bureau of Ethnology Bulletin 188 (Washington, D.C., 1963).

10. These include Hilda Faunce, *Desert Wife* (Lincoln: University of Nebraska Press, 1981) (hereafter cited as Faunce, *Desert Wife*); Maurine S. Fletcher, *The Wetherills of Mesa Verde: Autobiography of Benjamin Alfred Wetherill* (London: Associated University Presses, 1977) (hereafter cited as Fletcher, *Wetherills*); Frances Gillmor and Louisa Wade Wetherill, *Traders to the Navajos: The Study of the Wetherills of Kayenta* (Albuquerque: University of New Mexico Press, 1953) (hereafter cited as Gillmor and Wetherill, *Traders to the Navajos*); Alberta Hannum, *Paint the Wind* (New York, N.Y.: Viking, 1958) (hereafter cited as Hannum, *Paint the Wind*); Alberta Hannum, *Spin a Silver Dollar* (New York, N.Y.: Ballantine, 1944) (hereafter cited as Hannum, *Spin a Silver Dollar*); Elizabeth Compton Hegeman, *Navaho Trading Days* (Albuquerque: University of New Mexico Press, 1963) (hereafter cited as Hegeman, *Navaho Trading Days*); Mary Jeanette Kennedy, *Tales of a Trader's Wife: Life on the Navajo Reservation, 1913–1938* (Albuquerque, N. Mex.: Valiant, 1965) (hereafter cited as Kennedy, *Tales of a Trader's Wife*), and *The Wind Blows Free* (Albuquerque, N. Mex.: Valiant, 1970) (hereafter cited as Kennedy, *Wind Blows Free*); Gladwell "Toney" Richardson, "Pioneer Trader to the Navajo," *Desert Magazine* (December 1948):26–29 (hereafter cited as Richardson, "Pioneer Trader"); Gladwell Richardson, *Navajo Trader* (Tucson: University of Arizona Press, 1986) (hereafter cited as Richardson, *Navajo Trader)*; Joseph Schmedding, *Cowboy and Indian Trader* (Albuquerque: University of New Mexico Press, 1974) (hereafter cited as Schmedding, *Cowboy and Indian Trader*); Franc Johnson Newcomb, *Navaho Neighbors* (Norman: University of Oklahoma Press, 1966) (hereafter cited as Newcomb, *Navajo Neighbors*); Bille Williams Yost, *Bread upon the Sands* (Caldwell, Idaho: Caxton Printers, 1958) (hereafter cited as Yost, *Bread upon the Sands*); Billie Williams Yost, *Diamonds in the Desert: The Family History of Bill and Gertie Williams* (Flagstaff, Ariz.: Silver Spruce, 1987) (hereafter cited as Yost, *Diamonds in the Desert*); Willow Roberts, *Stokes Carson: Twentieth Century Trading on the Navajo Reservation* (Albuquerque: University of New Mexico Press, 1987), 100 (hereafter cited as Roberts, *Stokes Carson*).

11. McNitt, *Indian Traders,* vii.

CHAPTER ONE

1. After Albert Yava, *Big Falling Snow: A Tewa-Hopi Indian's Life and Times and the History and Traditions of His People* (Albuquerque: University of New Mexico Press, 1978), 5 (hereafter cited as Yava, *Big Falling Snow*), and Edmund Nequatewa, *Truth of a Hopi* (Flagstaff, Ariz.: Northland Press, 1967), 30–31 (hereafter cited as Nequatewa, *Truth of a Hopi*).

2. The following synthesis is based on numerous published accounts and a decade of work with Hopi museum collections (prehistoric, protohistoric, and contemporary), visits to many Anasazi sites, and fieldwork among the Hopi. In the last 450 years the Hopi have been discussed and described in government reports, church documents, popular accounts, and scholarly works of varying quality. For published sources, see W. David Laird, *Hopi Bibliography: Comprehensive and Annotated* (Tucson: University of Arizona Press, 1977) (hereafter called Laird, *Hopi Bibliography*). See also Albert H. Schroeder, "History of Archaeological Research," 5–13; Keith H. Basso, "History of Ethnological Research," 14–21; J. O. Brew, "Hopi Prehistory and History to 1850," 514–23; and Frederick J. Dockstader, "Hopi History, 1850–1940," 524–32 in *Southwest,* vol. 9 of *The Handbook of North American Indians* (Washington D.C.: Government Printing Office, 1979) (hereafter cited as *Handbook,* vol. 9). See also Fred Eggan, *Social Organization of the Western Pueblos* (Chicago: University of Chicago Press, 1950).

3. After John T. Hack, *The Changing Physical Environment of the Hopi Indians of Arizona,* Papers of the Peabody Museum of American Archaeology and Ethnology 35, (New Haven: Yale University Press, 1942). See also Alfred W. Whiting, "Hopi Indian Agriculture: I, Background," *Museum of Northern Arizona Notes* 8 (April 1936):51–53; Richard Maitland Bradfield, *The Changing Pattern of Hopi Agriculture,* Royal Anthropological Institute Occassional Paper, no. 30 (London: Royal Anthropological Institute, 1971); and for Hopi agricultural practices, see Ernest Beaglehole, *Notes on Hopi Economic Life,* Yale University Publications in Anthropology, no. 15 (New Haven: Yale University Press, 1937).

4. After E. Charles Adams and Deborah Hull, "Prehistoric and Historic Occupation of the Hopi Mesas," in *Hopi Kachinas: Spirit of Life* (San Francisco: California Academy of Sciences, 1980), 11–27. The study of the prehistoric Southwest is complex. For a synthesis, minus theory, see John C. McGregor, *Southwestern Archaeology* (Urbana: University of Illinois Press, 1965).

5. Juanita Tiger Kavena, *Hopi Cookery* (Tucson: University of Arizona, 1980), 13. See also "Hopi: Songs of the Fourth World," Pat Ferrero, producer/director; Pat Burke, assistant director, 1983; and "Corn is Life," Therese Burson and Donald Coughlin, producers, 1982.

6. Robert Breunig and Michael Lomatuway'ma, "Hopi: Scenes from Everyday Life," *Plateau* 55 (1983):3–32.

7. Navajo literature is as complex as that on the Hopis. It is equally uneven in quality. Bibliographies include Peter Iverson, *The Navajos: A Critical Bibliography,* The Newberry Library Center for American Indian Bibliographic Services (Bloomington: Indiana University Press, 1976); and J. Lee Correll, Editha L. Wilson, and David M. Brugge, *Navajo Bibliography with Subject Index,* rev. ed., 2 vols., Research Report 2. (Window Rock, Ariz.: Navajo Tribe, 1969), and *Navajo Bibliography with Subject Index,* Research Report 2, supplement (Window Rock, Ariz.: Navajo Tribe, 1973). See also David M. Brugge, "Navajo Prehistory and History to 1850," 489–501, and Robert Roessel, "Navajo History, 1850–1923," 506–23 in *Southwest,* vol. 10 of *The Handbook of North American Indians* (Washington, D.C.: Government Printing Office, 1983) (hereafter cited as *Handbook,* vol. 10); Richard J. Perry, *Western Apache Heritage: People of the Mountain Corridor* (Austin: University of Texas Press, 1991). Although they deal with more recent times, Peter Iverson, *The Navajo Nation* (Albuquerque: University of New Mexico Press, 1983); Lawrence C. Kelly, *The Navajo Indians and Federal Indian Policy, 1900–1935* (Tucson: University of Arizona, 1968); and Donald C. Parman, *The Navajos and the New Deal* (New Haven: Yale University Press, 1976) have proven to be very instructive.

8. June Helm, "Bilaterality in the Socio-territorial Organization of the Arctic Drainage Dene," *Ethnohistory* 4 (1965):361–85, describes the early cultural and ecological influences that may have caused the Navajos to abandon the Lake Athabaska region. The Navajos' route to the Southwest is vague due to the scarcity of prehistoric sites that can be accurately attributed to Navajo occupation. See David M. Brugge, "Navajo Prehistory and History to 1850," in *Handbook,* vol. 10, 489–501, for a discussion of Navajo prehistory. Betty H. Huscher and Harold H. Huscher, "Athabaskan Migration via the Intermontane Region," *American Antiquity* 8 (1942):80–88, argue that the Navajo moved down the Rocky Mountains. It is also difficult to pinpoint when the Navajos entered the Southwest. Clyde Kluckhohn and Dorothea Leighton, *The Navajo,* rev. ed., (Garden City, N.Y.: Natural History Library, 1962), 33, argue that they arrived about 1000 A.D., although Dolores A. Gunnerson, "The Southern Athabascans: Their Arrival in the Southwest," *El Palacio* 63 (1956):346–65, argues that the date is closer to 1525 A.D.

9. The term "Hopi" is used throughout unless "Moqui" is used in an official title, such as Moqui Pueblo Agency, or in a quote. I recognize that I may be continuing an old but fallacious tradition of writing about a seemingly unified and monolithic "Hopi" culture, when it would be more correct to discuss the people in terms of clan, village, or mesa. However, due to the generalized nature of this chapter, I continue the tradition. In subsequent chapters, when it is pertinent, distinctions will be made.

10. Edward H. Spicer, *Cycles of Conquest: The Impact of Spain, Mexico, and the United States on the Indians of the Southwest, 1553–1960* (Tucson: University of Arizona Press, 1962), 211 (hereafter cited as Spicer, *Cycles of Conquest*). For a detailed discussion of the derivation of the word *Navajo* see Brugge, "Navajo Prehistory and History to 1850," in *Handbook,* vol. 10, 496–98; and Frank McNitt, *Navajo Wars: Military Campaigns, Slave Raids, and Reprisals* (Albuquerque: University of New Mexico Press, 1972), 4–5. For the use of and reasons for the spelling of

Navajo with an "h" (Navaho) instead of a "j" (Navajo), see Frederick W. Hodge, "The Name 'Navajo'," *Masterkey* 23 (1949):78.

11. Jack Holterman, "San Bartolome de Xongopavi," *Plateau* 28 (October 1955):29; Jack Holterman, "The Mission of San Miguel de Oraibi," *Plateau* 32 (October 1959):44; and Katharine Bartlett, "Spanish Contacts with the Hopi, 1540–1823," *Museum of Northern Arizona Notes* 6 (June 1934):55–59.

12. Lyndon Lane Hargrave, "Shungopovi," *Museum of Northern Arizona Notes* 2 (April 1930):2.

13. Ibid.; Lyndon Lane Hargrave, "Oraibi: A Brief History of the Oldest Inhabited Town in the United States," *Museum of Northern Arizona Notes* 4 (January 1932):1–8; and Ross Gordon Montgomery, Watson Smith, and John Otis Brew, *Franciscan Awatovi: The Excavation and Conjectural Reconstruction of a 17th-Century Spanish Mission Established at a Hopi Indian Town in Northeastern Arizona,* Papers of the Peabody Museum of Archaeology and Ethnology 36 (1949):8–10, 22. See also Marc Simmons, "History of Pueblo-Spanish Relations to 1821," 178–93; Joe S. Sando, "The Pueblo Revolt," in *Handbook,* vol. 9, 194–97; and Frank D. Reeve, "Federal Indian Policy in New Mexico, 1858–1880," *New Mexico Historical Review* 13 (1938):146–58; "Seventeenth Century Navaho-Spanish Relations," *New Mexico Historical Review* 32 (1957): 36–52; "Navaho-Spanish Wars, 1680–1720," *New Mexico Historical Review* 33 (1959):204–31, "The Navaho-Spanish Peace: 1720s–1770s." *New Mexico Historical Review* 34 (1959):9–40, and "Navaho-Spanish Diplomacy," *New Mexico Historical Review* 35 (1960):200–235.

14. See James Seavey Griffith, "Kachinas and Masking," 764–77, and David M. Brugge, "Navajo Prehistory and History to 1850," in *Handbook,* vol. 10, 496–98.

15. Campbell Grant, *Canyon de Chelly: Its People and Rock Art* (Tucson: University of Arizona Press, 1978), 81–82.

16. For the most recent and innovative explanation for Navajo-Spanish raiding and the subsequent wars, see Thomas D. Hall, *Social Change in the Southwest, 1350–1880* (Lawrence: University of Kansas Press, 1989). (hereafter cited as Hall, *Social Change*) Willard William Hill, *Navaho Warfare,* Yale University Publications in Anthropology, no. 5 (New Haven: Yale University Press, 1936), is also good for the ritualization of Navajo warfare and warfare against other native groups. Lynn

R. Bailey, *Indian Slave Trade in the Southwest: A Study of Slave-taking and the Traffic in Indian Captives* (Los Angeles, Calif.: Westernlore Press, 1966), 71–137; and Jack Forbes, *Apache, Navaho, and Spaniard* (Norman: University of Oklahoma Press, 1960) provide additional, if somewhat different, perspectives.

17. For Pueblo-Spanish political relations, see Marc Simmons, "History of Pueblo-Spanish Relations to 1821," 178–93, and "History of Pueblos since 1821," 206–23 in *Handbook,* vol. 9; Elizabeth A. H. Johns, *Storms Brewed in Other Men's Worlds: The Confrontation of Indians, Spanish, and French in the Southwest, 1540–1795* (College Station: Texas A & M University Press, 1975); Edward H. Spicer, *Cycles of Conquest;* and Marc Simmons, *Spanish Government in New Mexico* (Albuquerque: University of New Mexico Press, 1968).

18. For the development of Indian policy, see Francis Paul Prucha, *The Great Father: The United States Government and the American Indians,* 2 vols. (Lincoln: University of Nebraska Press, 1984) (hereafter cited as Prucha, *Great Father*); for examples of the treaties, see J. Lee Correll, *Through White Men's Eyes: A Contribution to Navajo History, A Chronological Record of the Navajo People from Earliest Times to the Treaty of June 1, 1868,* 6 vols. (Window Rock, Ariz: Navajo Heritage Center, 1979), (vi): 51–100 (hereafter cited as Correll, *Through White Men's Eyes*); Charles J. Kappler, comp., *Indian Affairs: Laws and Treaties,* 5 vols. (New York, N.Y.: AMS Press, 1971) (hereafter cited as Kappler, *Indian Affairs*); and David M. Brugge and J. Lee Correll, *The Story of the Navajo Treaties* (Window Rock, Ariz.: Navajo Parks and Recreation, 1971).

19. The Third Mesa villages, Hotevilla and Bacabi, were founded following the split at Oraibi in 1906.

CHAPTER TWO

1. Thomas Keam license to trade, United States National Archives, Office of Indian Affairs, Letter Received #19540.

2. Stewart V. Culin, "Thomas Varker Keam," *American Anthropolgist* 7 (January 1905):171–72 (hereafter cited as Culin, "Thomas Varker Keam).

3. The record of Keam's enlistment is from *Muster Roll of Captain Edmund D. Shirland, Company C Regiment of the California Cavalry Volunteers, June 25, 1863* in the California Volunteers collection, California State

Archives (hereafter cited as *Company C Muster Roll*); and Richard H. Orton, *Records of the California Men in the War of the Rebellion, 1861–1867* (Sacramento, Calif.: State Printing, 1890), p. 104 lists "Thomas Kearnes" as in Company B, and p. 114 lists "Thomas V. Kearns" in Company C (hereafter cited as Orton, *Records of the California Men*). Both individuals have the same muster-out information. This discrepency is understandable, as Company B and Company C were merged. Orton, who was adjutant general of California, used names compiled from all existing muster rolls at the California State Archives. See also George Henry Pettis, *The California Column,* Historical Society of New Mexico, no. 11 (Santa Fe: New Mexican Printing, 1908) (hereafter cited as Pettis, *The California Column*).

4. *The Daily Alta California* is quoted in William A. Keleher, *Turmoil in New Mexico, 1846–1868* (Santa Fe, N. Mex.: Rydal Press, 1952), 229 (hereafter cited as Keleher, *Turmoil in New Mexico*).

5. Thomas Varker Keam's birthdate is from A. S. Peason, Superintendent Registrar, Truro, Cornwall, England, to Carl Hayden, February 26, March 5, March 7, 1940, in Carl Hayden Biographical Files, Thomas Keam Collection, Arizona Historical Society, Tempe, Arizona (hereafter Hayden Files, Keam Collection). He was baptised Thomas James Keam.

6. Les Douch, Curator Emeritus, Royal Institution of Cornwall, to author, January 24, 1986.

7. Ibid.

8. Ibid.

9. *Company C Muster Roll.*

10. War Department, *The War of the Rebellion: A Compilation of the Official Records of the Union and Confederate Armies, 1861–1865.* (Washington, D.C.: Government Printing Office 1880–1901), vol. 1, ser. 9, 596 (hereafter cited as *Official Records*). Van Valkenburg, "Tom Keam," 9, has Keam fighting with Kit Carson against the Navajos. This is an error.

11. Camp Merchant was located near Lake Merritt in Oakland, California.

12. *Official Records,* vol. 1, ser. 9, 596–97.

13. Pettis, *California Column,* 10–11.

14. Henry P. Walker, ed., "Soldier in the California Column: The Diary of John Teal," *Arizona and the West* 13 (spring 1971):38.

15. *Official Records,* vol. 1, ser. 9, 599.

16. For the Civil War in the West, see Alvin M. Josephy Jr., *The Civil War in the West* (New York, N.Y.: Alfred A. Knopf, 1991), 3–92; 269–92; Keleher, *Turmoil in New Mexico;* Ray C. Colton, *The Civil War in the Western Territories* (Norman: University of Oklahoma Press, 1959) (hereafter cited as Colton, *Civil War in the West*); and Leo P. Kirby, "A Civil War Episode in California-Arizona History," *Arizoniana* 2 (spring 1961), 20–23. I have also relied on Robert M. Utley, *Frontier Regulars: The United States Army and the Indian: 1866–1891* (New York, N.Y.: McMillan, 1973) and *Frontiersmen in Blue: The United States Army and the Indian, 1848–1865* (New York, N.Y.: McMillan, 1967).

17. Quoted in Keleher, *Turmoil in New Mexico,* 253.

18. Fort Thorn was established December 24, 1853. It was located on the Rio Grande near present-day Hatch, New Mexico. It was regarrisoned by Union forces on July 5, 1862, although it was never fully garrisoned. Fort Craig, established in 1854, was located just north of Thorn on the Rio Grande, some thirty miles south of Socorro, New Mexico.

19. General Orders, no. 16, August 22, 1862, *Official Records* ser. I, vol. 9, 577.

20. The Butterfield Overland Mail is covered in Roscoe P. Conkling and Margaret B. Conkling, *The Overland Butterfield Mail, 1857–1869,* 3 vols. (Glendale, Calif.: Arthur H. Clark Co., 1947), for a mile-by-mile discussion of the Butterfield route through western Texas. Their maps in volume 3 are especially helpful (hereafter cited as Conklings, *Butterfield Overland Mail*).

21. E. D. Shirland to Lt. Ben C. Cutler, *Official Records* ser. I, vol. 9, 577–79.

22. Ibid.

23. According to Francis Paul Prucha, *A Guide to Military Posts of the United States, 1789–1895* (Madison: University of Wisconsin Press, 1964); and Robert W. Frazer, *Forts of the West: Military Forts and Presidios and Posts Commonly Called Forts West of the Mississippi River to 1898* (Norman: University of Oklahoma Press, 1965) (hereafter cited as Prucha, *Military Posts,* and Frazer, *Forts of the West*), Fort Davis (1854–1891) was located near the sources of the Limpia River, between present-day Alpine and Marfa, Texas. Prucha, *Military Posts,* 70; and Frazer, *Forts of the West,* 148. See also Robert M. Utley, *Fort Davis National Historic Site,*

Texas, National Park Service Historical Handbook Series, no. 38 (Washington, D.C.: National Park Service 1965).

24. E. D. Shirland to Lt. Ben C. Cutler, *Official Records* ser. I, vol. 9, 577–79.

25. Ibid.

26. Ibid.; Fort Quitman was established in 1858 and abandoned in 1877. It was located on the east bank of the Rio Grande, seventy miles southeast of El Paso, between present-day Alpine and Marfa, Texas. Prucha, *Military Posts,* 100; and Frazer, *Forts of the West,* 157–58.

27. Ibid.

28. Ibid.

29. Ibid.

30. Roy L. Swift, *Three Roads to Chihuahua: The Great Wagon Roads That Opened the Southwest, 1823–1883* (Austin, Tex.: Eakin Press, 1988), 199; and L. Boyd Finch, "Arizona in Exile: Confederate Schemes to Recapture the Southwest," *Journal of Arizona History* (spring 1992):59–60 (hereafter cited as Finch, "Arizona in Exile").

31. Darlis A. Miller, *The California Column in New Mexico* (Albuquerque: University of New Mexico Press, 1982), 13–14 (hereafter cited as Miller, *California Column in New Mexico*).

32. Finch, "Arizona in Exile," 57–84.

33. General Orders, nos. 83 and 84, *Official Records,* vol. 1 ser. 9, 582. Carleton's biographer is Aurora Hunt, *Major General James Henry Carleton, 1814–1873: Western Frontier Dragoon* (Glendale, Calif.: Arthur Clark, 1958).

34. Lawrence C. Kelly, *Navajo Roundup: Selected Correspondence of Kit Carson's Expedition against the Navajo, 1863–1865* (Boulder, Colo.: Pruett, 1970), 1–5 (hereafter cited as Kelly, *Navajo Roundup*), asserts that E. R. S. Canby, Commander of the Department of New Mexico, devised the plan for controlling the "wild" Indians on reservations in 1861. When Carleton replaced Canby in September 1862, he continued Canby's removal policy and also continued to rely on Canby's original choice, Christopher Carson. The most comprehensive synthesis of the history of federal Indian policy is Prucha, *The Great Father,* which I have relied on for the generalized discussion of federal Indian policy. However, I have found these other publications helpful: Edmund Jefferson Danziger Jr., *Indians and Bureaucrats: Administering the Reservation*

Policy During the Civil War (Urbana: University of Illinois Press, 1974); Henry E. Fritz, *The Movement for Indian Civilization, 1860–1890* (Philadelphia: University of Pennsylvania Press, 1963) (hereafter cited as Fritz, *Movement for Indian Civilization).* Alban W. Hoopes, *Indian Affairs and Their Administration, with Special Reference to the Far West, 1849–1860* (New York, N.Y.: Kraus Reprint, 1972); Reginald Horsman, *Expansion and American Indian Policy, 1783–1812* (East Lansing: Michigan State Press, 1967); Robert Winston Mardock, *The Reformers and the American Indian* (Columbia: University of Missouri Press, 1971) (hereafter cited as Mardock, *Reformers*); Roy Harvey Pearce, *The Savages of America: A Study of the Indian and the Idea of Civilization* (Baltimore, Md.: The Johns Hopkins University Press, 1953); Loring B. Priest, *Uncle Sam's Step-Children: The Reformation of United States Indian Policy, 1865–1887* (New York, N.Y.: Octagon Books, 1969); Francis Paul Prucha, *American Indian Policy in the Formative Years: The Indian Trade and Intercourse Acts, 1790–1834* (Cambridge, Mass.: Harvard University Press, 1962); Francis Paul Prucha, *American Indian Policy in Crisis: Christian Reformers, 1865–1900* (Norman: University of Oklahoma Press, 1976) (hereafter cited as Prucha, *Indian Policy*); Francis Paul Prucha, *The Churches and the Indian Schools, 1888–1912* (Lincoln: University of Nebraska Press, 1979); Francis Paul Prucha, *Americanizing the American Indians: Writings by the "Friends of the Indian" 1880–1900* (Cambridge, Mass.: Harvard University Press, 1973); Robert A. Trennert Jr., *Alternative to Extinction: Federal Indian Policy and the Beginnings of the Reservation System, 1846–1851* (Philadelphia, Pa.: Temple University Press, 1975); Bernard W. Sheehan, *Seeds of Extinction: Jeffersonian Philanthropy and the American Indian* (Chapel Hill: University of North Carolina Press, 1973); and Wilcomb E. Washburn, *Red Man's Land/White Man's Law: A Study of the Past and Present Status of the American Indian* (New York, N.Y.: Charles Scribner's Sons, 1971).

35. The most recent biography of Christopher Carson is Thelma S. Guild and Harvey L. Carter, *Kit Carson: A Pattern for Heroes* (Lincoln: University of Nebraska Press, 1984). However, Edwin Sabin, *Kit Carson Days, 1809–1869,* 2 vols. (New York, N.Y.: Press of the Pioneers, 1935) is the seminal work. See also Raymond E. Lindgren, "A Diary of Kit Carson's Navaho Campaign, 1863–1864," *New Mexico Historical Review,* 21 (July 1946):226–46; and Milo Milton Quaife, ed., *Kit Carson's Autobiography,* (Lincoln: University of Nebraska Press, 1966).

36. Carleton to Carson, October 12, 1862, *Official Records,* ser. I, vol. 15, 579–81.

37. Fort Stanton (1855–present), is located in southcentral New Mexico on the Rio Bonita about twenty miles east of Sierra Blanca River, New Mexico. Prucha, *Military Posts,* 109; and Frazer, *Forts of the West,* 103–104.

38. Colton, *Civil War,* 128; and Lee Myers, "The Enigma of Mangas Coloradas' Death," *New Mexico Historical Review* 41 (October 1966): 295 (hereafter cited as Myers, "Enigma of Mangas Coloradas' Death").

39. According to Francis B. Heitman, *Historical Register and Dictionary of the United States Army, from Its Organization, September 29, 1789, to March 2, 1903,* 2 vols. (Urbana: University of Illinois Press, 1965), 21, 1002, General Joseph Rodman West was the Commander of the District of Arizona.

40. Myers, "Enigma of Mangas Coloradas' Death," 295.

41. Lee Myers, "Military Establishments in Southwestern New Mexico: Stepping Stones to Settlement," *New Mexico Historical Review* 43 (January 1968):22–23 (hereafter cited as Myers, "Military Establishments").

42. Fort West (1863–1864) was located on the east side of the Gila river in the Piños Altos Range North of Silver City, New Mexico. Prucha, *Military Posts,* 108; and Frazer, *Forts of the West,* 116.

43. Dan L. Thrapp, *Victorio and the Mimbres Apaches* (Norman: University of Oklahoma Press, 1974), 82 (hereafter cited as Thrapp, *Victorio*).

44. *Official Records,* vol. 15, ser. 21, 227–31.

45. Thrapp, *Victorio,* 82.

46. *Official Records,* vol. 15, ser. 21, 670, 723; and Miller, *California Column in New Mexico,* 32–33, 43–62, establishes the effect of the California veterans on New Mexico's economy. See also Robert W. Frazer, *Forts and Supplies: The Role of the Army in the Economy of the Southwest, 1846–1861* (Albuquerque: University of New Mexico Press, 1983), 189 (hereafter cited as Frazer, *Forts and Supplies*).

47. Myers, "Military Establishments," 25–26.

48. Miller, *California Column in New Mexico,* 32; see also Myers, "Military Establishments"; and Frazer, *Forts and Supplies.*

49. For Carson's Navajo campaign see Kelly, *Navajo Roundup;* Clifford E. Trafzer, *The Kit Carson Campaign: The Last Great Navajo War* (Norman:

University of Oklahoma Press, 1982) offers nothing that is not already in Kelly. For Bosque Redondo, see Gerald Thompson, *The Army and the Navajo* (Tucson: University of Arizona Press, 1976) (hereafter Thompson, *Army and Navajo*); Maurice Frink, *Fort Defiance and the Navajos* (Boulder, Colo.: Pruett Publishing, 1968); (hereafter cited as Frink, *Fort Defiance*); and John P. Wilson, *Fort Sumner, New Mexico,* Museum of New Mexico Monuments Division (Santa Fe: Museum of New Mexico, 1974) (hereafter cited as Wilson, *Fort Sumner*). For a different perspective see Lynn R. Bailey, *Bosque Redondo: An American Concentration Camp* (Pasedena, Calif.: Socio-Technical Books, 1970) (hereafter cited as Bailey, *Bosque Redondo*). Van Valkenburg, "Tom Keam," 9, and Bailey, "Thomas Varker Keam," 16, have Keam with the Navajos' Long Walk to Bosque Redondo.

50. *Muster-In Roll of Captain Saternino Baca's Company E, 1st Cavalry, New Mexico Volunteers,* 2nd Lt. Thomas V. Keam, #475 in Records of the Adjutant General's Office in McNitt Collection, New Mexico State Records Center and Archives, Santa Fe, New Mexico (hereafter cited as Adjutant, General, *McNitt Collection*).

51. James Monroe Foster Jr., "Fort Bascom, New Mexico," *New Mexico Historical Review* 35 (January 1960):32–33 (hereafter cited as Foster, "Fort Bascom").

52. According to Kelly, *Navajo Roundup,* 75, n. 100, Edward H. Bergman was "twenty nine years old when he joined the [New Mexico] volunteers at Santa Fe on July 3, 1861. He was initially commissioned 1st Lieutenant, was promoted to Captain on February 15, 1862, and to Major on September 3, 1864. He was discharged on April 18, 1867."

53. Foster, "Fort Bascom," 33–34.

54. United States National Archives, War Department, *Compiled Service Records of Volunteer Union Soldiers Who Served in Organizations from the Territory* (hereafter cited as *Compiled Service Records*); see also McNitt, *Indian Traders,* 125.

55. *Compiled Service Records.*

56. Information on Cornwall and its people is based on Ian Soulsby, *A History of Cornwall* (Chichester, Sussex: Phillimore, 1986), 72; Claude Berry, *Cornwall* (London: Robert Hale Ltd., 1949); John Betjeman and A. L. Rouse, *Victorian and Edwardian Cornwall—from Old Photographs* (London: B. T. Batsford Ltd., 1974); Asa Briggs, *A Social History of England* (New York, N.Y.: Viking, 1983); Denys Kay-Robinson, *Devon* *and Cornwall* (New York, N.Y.: Arco Publishing, 1977); Daphne Du Maurier, *Vanishing Cornwall* (New York: Penguin Books, 1967), 11; Shelia Bird, *Bygone Truro* (Chichester, Sussex: Phillimore, 1981); and A. K. Hamilton Jenkin, *Cornwall and Its People* (London: J. M. Dent & Sons, 1945), 42–62.

57. Van Valkenburg, "Tom Keam," 10. The Van Valkenburg reference is uncited. Bailey, "Thomas Varker Keam," 17, says Keam's license to trade with the Utes was dated February 4, 1868. He cites the Van Valkenburg article. McNitt, *Indian Traders,* does not repeat this story. It seems that McNitt was unaware of either the Van Valkenburg or the Bailey article, for if he had been aware of it, he would have known about Keam's California Column service.

CHAPTER THREE

1. McNitt, *Indian Traders,* 125.

2. According to Frazer, *Forts of the West,* 8; and Prucha, *Military Posts,* 71. Fort Defiance (1851–1861), located at the mouth of Canyon Bonito in northeastern Arizona, was the first U.S. Army fort in Arizona Territory. It was abandoned in 1861 because of the Civil War, and reopened as headquarters of the Navajo Agency in 1868. It remains the agency headquarters today. This aspect of Keam's career is covered in McNitt, *Indian Traders,* 125–28, 132–40.

3. From the Navajos' perspective, the Bosque Redondo experience and the walk to and from it are covered best in Ruth Roessel, ed., *Navajo Stories of the Long Walk Period* (Tsaile, Ariz.: Navajo Community College, 1973) (hereafter cited as Roessel, *Long Walk Stories*); and Correll, *Through White Men's Eyes.*

4. For the American perspective on Bosque Redondo, see Gerald Thompson, *The Army and the Navajo* (Tucson: University of Arizona Press, 1976); Maurice Frink, *Fort Defiance and the Navajos* (Boulder, Colo.: Pruett Publishing, 1968); Bailey, *Bosque Redondo;* and John P. Wilson, *Fort Sumner, New Mexico,* Museum of New Mexico Monuments Division (Santa Fe: Museum of New Mexico, 1974).

5. Roessel, *Long Walk Stories,* 244–45.

6. This is after Correll, *Through White Men's Eyes,* vol. 6, 129–39.

7. Ibid.

8. Ibid.

9. Ibid.

10. Ibid.

11. Ibid.

12. Ibid., 91–100; and Kappler, *Indian Affairs.*

13. United States National Archives, Office of Indian Affairs, Commissioner of Indian Affairs, *Annual Report,* 1871, 377 (hereafter cited as Commissioner of Indian Affairs, *Annual Report*).

14. Commissioner of Indian Affairs, *Annual Report,* 1883, 120.

15. Paul Stuart, *The Indian Office: Growth and Development of an American Institution, 1865–1900* (Ann Arbor, Mich.: UMI Research Press, 1978), 27–54 (hereafter cited as Stuart, *Indian Office*).

16. The history of the administration of Indian affairs is covered in Robert M. Kvasnika and Herman J. Viola, *The Commissioners of Indian Affairs, 1824–1977* (Lincoln: University of Nebraska Press, 1979); Laurence F. Schmeckbier, *The Office of Indian Affairs: Its History, Activities, and Organization* (Baltimore, Md.: The Johns Hopkins University Press, 1927); Stuart, *Indian Office;* and Theodore W. Taylor, *American Indian Policy* (Mt. Airy, Md.: Lomond Publications, 1983), and *The Bureau of Indian Affairs* (Boulder, Colo.: Westview Press, 1984). For the influences on the administration of Indian Affairs, see Robert H. Keller, *American Protestantism and United States Indian Policy, 1869–1882* (Lincoln: University of Nebraska Press, 1983) (hereafter cited as Keller, *American Protestantism*); Mardock, *The Reformers and the American Indian;* Henry E. Fritz, *The Movement for Indian Civilization, 1860–1890* (Philadelphia: University of Pennsylvania Press, 1963); and Francis Paul Prucha, *American Indian Policy in Crisis: Christian Reformers, 1865–1900* (Norman: University of Oklahoma Press, 1976).

17. Keller, *American Protestantism,* 135.

18. William Haas Moore, "Chiefs, Agents, and Soldiers: Conflict on the Navajo Frontier, 1868–1880," (Ph.D. diss., Northern Arizona University, 1988), 91 (herafter cited as Moore, "Chiefs, Agents, and Soldiers"). Moore's dissertation has since been published; however, my research was completed before the published version. Consequently, all of my references are to the dissertation. See William Haas Moore, *Chiefs, Agents, and Soldiers: Conflict on the Navajo Frontier, 1868–1882* (Albuquerque: University of New Mexico Press, 1994).

19. Moore, "Chiefs, Agents, and Soldiers," 91–107, 116; Commissioner of Indian Affairs, *Annual Report,* 1869, 215.

20. Interview, Richard Van Valkenburg and Tom Keam Jr., August 1, 1940, Carl Hayden Biographical Files, Van Valkenburg Collection, Arizona Historical Society, Tempe, Arizona (hereafter cited as Van Valkenburg, "Interview").

21. Gladys A. Reichard, *Social Life of the Navajo Indians with Some Attention to Minor Ceremonies,* Columbia University Contributions to Anthropology, no. 7 (New York: Columbia University Press, 1928), 139–141.

22. Moore, "Chiefs, Agents, and Soldiers," 114.

23. Bennett to Clinton, February 1, 1870, U. S. National Archives, Office of Indian Affairs, Letters Received, 1849–1880, New Mexico Superintendency, (hereafter cited as *LR, NM Supt.*); Moore, "Chiefs, Agents, and Soldiers," 129.

24. Fritz, *The Movement for Indian Civilization,* 56, 76.

25. Michael C. Coleman, *Presbyterian Missionary Attitudes toward American Indians, 1837–1893* (Jackson: University Press of Mississippi, 1985), 15 (hereafter cited as Coleman, *Presbyterian Missionary Attitudes*). The atmosphere at the agency is synthesized from the correspondence of the agency employees to John Lowrie in the collection American Indian Correspondence: The Presbyterian Historical Society Collection of Missionaries' Letters, 1833–1893 (hereafter cited as *AIC-PHS*); see also Norman J. Bender, *New Hope for the Indians: The Grant Peace Policy and the Navajos in the 1870s* (Albuquerque: University of New Mexico Press, 1989) (hereafter cited as Bender, *New Hope for the Indians*). Bender perpetuates the error of referring to Thomas Keam as "Keams," even though he acknowledges the family's preferred spelling. He claims that Keam was commonly called Keams in the region and that, according to Bender, justifies continuing the error. See Bender, *New Hope for the Indians,* 213 n. 26.

26. McNitt, *Indian Traders,* 129.

27. Amsden, *Navajo Weaving,* 169, pl. 80. See also Robert A. Roessel, *Pictorial History of the Navajo from 1860 to 1910* (Rough Rock, Ariz.: Rough Rock Demonstration School, 1980), 76–79 (hereafter cited as Roessel, *Pictorial History*). See also Martin A. Link, ed., *Navajo: A Century of Progress, 1868–1968* (Window Rock, Ariz: Navajo Tribe, 1968), 14–15.

28. McNitt, *Indian Traders,* 129–130.

29. The request for sheep is in McNitt, *Indian Traders,* 130, n. 11; Miller complained to Pope about the payroll in Miller to Pope, March 2, 1872, *LR, NM Supt.*; Keam's promotion is in Quarterly Report, July 1872, *LR, NM Supt.*

30. Keam's sons' birthdates are from Van Valkenburg, "Interview," and Van Valkenburg, "Tom Keam," 10.

31. Roberts's correspondence is in *AIC-PHS*. See also Bender, *New Hope for the Indians,* 30–32, 47–48.

32. Miller to Lowrie, January 18, and February 7, 1872, *AIC-PHS*.

33. Ibid., February 7, 1872, *AIC-PHS*.

34. Menaul to Lowrie, April 10, 1872, *AIC-PHS*.

35. Miller to Lowrie, January 18, and March 4, 1872, *AIC-PHS*.

36. Ibid., January 18, March 4, and April 10, 1872, *AIC-PHS*.

37. Miller's death is covered in Keam to Pope, June 13, 1872, *LR, NM Supt;* J. H. Beadle, *Western Wilds* (Cincinnati, Ohio: Jones Brothers, 1877), 252; and Menaul to Lowrie, May 13, 1872, *AIC-PHS*. McNitt, *Indian Traders,* 132–34. Van Valkenburg, "Tom Keam," 9, has Keam at the scene of Miller's murder; this seems to have been "literary license" on Van Valkenburg's part.

38. Brigadier General Oliver O. Howard was named by President Grant as a special Indian commissioner in 1872 and charged with settling the Indians permanently on reservations. His humanitarian attitudes are covered in Richard N. Ellis, "The Humanitarian Soldiers," *Journal of Arizona History* (summer 1969): 53–66. Howard wrote of his experiences in Oliver O. Howard, *My Life and Experiences among our Hostile Indians* (New York, N.Y.: DaCapo, 1972). Thomas Keam's appointment as special agent was approved in acting secretary of the interior to the commissioner of Indian affairs, September 16, 1872, United States National Archives, Department of the Interior, Appointment Papers: New Mexico, Navajo Agency, K-Z, 1872–1903 (hereafter cited as *AP*).

39. William Keam's promotion is in Quarterly Report, July 1872, *LR, NM Supt.*

40. Commissioner of Indian Affairs, *Annual Report,* 1872, 302–3; and McNitt, *Indian Traders,* 135–37.

41. Keam to Pope, October 13, 1872, *LR, NM Supt.*

42. Ibid. See also Richard N. Ellis, *General Pope and United States Indian Policy* (Albuquerque: University of New Mexico Press, 1970).

43. Commissioner of Indian Affairs, *Annual Report,* 1872, 302–3.

44. Bender, *New Hope for the Indians,* 82.

45. Lowrie to Commissioner of Indian Affairs, April 22, 1873, *AP.*

46. Ibid. That Keam was fired by W. F. M. Arny is incorrect as cited in McNitt, *Indian Traders,* 145; Van Valkenburg, "Tom Keam," 10; and Bailey, "Thomas Varker Keam," 4.

47. Quoted in McNitt, *Indian Traders,* 136.

48. Lowrie to Arny, September 30, 1873, *AIC-PHS,* and Lowrie to Commissioner of Indian Affairs, April 22, 1873, *AP.*

49. Lowrie to Commissioner of Indian Affairs, April 22, 1873, *AP.*

50. Gould to Dudley, August 31, 1873, *LR, NM Supt.*

51. Hall to Lowrie, March 10, April 29, June 21, and August 29, 1873, *AIC-PHS.*

CHAPTER FOUR

1. McNitt, *Indian Traders,* 145. Keam's application for a license to trade at Fort Defiance was supplemented by a $5,000 bond secured by Lehman Spiegelberg, a prominent New Mexico businessman, and Herman Ilfeldt, a government contractor.

2. W. F. M. Arny's biography is Lawrence R. Murphy, *Frontier Crusader: William F. M. Arny* (Tucson: University of Arizona Press, 1972). (hereafter cited as Murphy, *Arny*). Arny and Keam's relationship is covered in McNitt, *Indian Traders,* 154–65.

3. Murphy, *Arny,* 19.

4. Hall to Smith, August 4, 1873, *LR, NM Supt.*

5. Arny to Smith, August 16, 1873, *LR, NM Supt.* The Presbyterian physician at Fort Defiance characterized Arny as a "liar and a cheat" and claimed that Arny told him he got his position through political connections, not because of his Presbyterian membership. See J. Menaul to Lowrie, December 2, 1873, *AIC-PHS.*

6. Murphy, *Arny* 150, 197.

7. McNitt, *Indian Traders,* 149–51; and Murphy, *Arny,* 225–27.

8. Arny to Smith, April 8, 1874, *LR, NM Supt.*

9. Arny to Smith, November 11, 1874, *LR, NM Supt.*

10. The photograph of Juanita and Arny and the pictorial blanket is in Amsden, *Navaho Weaving,* 219, pl. 114; and Roessel, *Pictorial History,* 85–86, 152.

11. Quoted in Murphy, *Arny,* 230.

12. Affidavit, William F. M. Arny, September 13, 1875, *AP*.

13. Keam's problems collecting the back pay are in Keam to Smith, July 5, 1873, and Western Union Telegram, August 18, 1873; for Keam's audit see Dudley to Keam, July 28, 1873, and Hall to Dudley, July 28, 1873. For a continuation see Clum to Keam, August 23, 1873, and second comptroller to Keam, November 23, 1874. Keam to Commissioner of Indian Affairs, November 16, 1874. All are in *LR, NM Supt.*

14. Quoted in Murphy, *Arny,* 231.

15. Chiefs to Our Great Father, July 15, 1875, *LR, NM Supt.*

16. Murphy, *Arny,* 234.

17. McNitt, *Indian Traders,* 159–60.

18. Price to Lt. Mahken, AAA General, September 25, 1875, *LR, NM Supt.*

19. Ibid.

20. Ibid.

21. Ibid.

22. Affidavits, W. F. M. Arny, W. W. Owens, and F. J. Tanner, September 13, 1875, *AP.*

23. Ibid.

24. Bernalillo County Court Records, District Court Dockett, Territorial Records of New Mexico, McNitt Collection, New Mexico Records Center and Archives, Santa Fe, New Mexico (hereafter cited as Court Records, *McNitt Collection*).

25. Keam to Lowrie, June 3, and September 7, 1875, *AIC-PHS.* Van Valkenburg, "Interview."

26. McNitt, *Indian Traders,* 161. McNitt cites National Archives, Ledgers of Traders. Why Keam received a license to trade at Hopi is uncertain. Since the location he chose was off any reservation and located on public domain, a license would have been unnecessary. Additionally, Arny would have had some say in approving a license, and based on his past actions, he probably would have denied it. A copy of this license does not appear in the McNitt Collection, nor does it exist in Keam's file in Letters Recieved, Office of Indian Affairs, as do his other licenses. I have not seen the Ledgers of Indian Traders but wonder whether McNitt was not mistaken about Keam's license to trade at Hopi. However, according to Court Records, McNitt Collection, became a citizen of the United States in 1875, a requirement to receive a license.

27. Keam to Lowrie, August 7, and August 9, 1875, *AIC-PHS.*

28. Ibid., September [n.d.], 1875, *AIC-PHS.*

29. Smith to Lowrie, September 2, 1875, *AIC-PHS;* for Presbyterian attitudes, see Coleman, *Presbyterian Missionary Attitudes.*

30. Ibid.

31. Ibid.

32. Keam to Lowrie, September 7, 1875, *AIC-PHS.* The presumption of Lowrie's replies and suggestions are based on the content of letters he received. The secretary's letterpress books are microfilmed in the AIC-PHS Collection, but they are illegible due to their condition and the quality of Lowrie's handwriting.

33. Ibid.

34. Keam to Smith, September 11, 1875, and Smith to Lowrie, September 18, 1875, *AIC-PHS.*

35. Ibid.

36. Ibid.

37. Ibid.

38. Keam to Lowrie, October 21, 1875, *AIC-PHS.*

39. Ibid.

40. Asdáán Libá's belief that Keam was not returning is in Van Valkenburg, "Interview."

41. Ibid.

42. Irvine to Commissioner of Indian Affairs, June 6, and November 14, 1876, *LR, NM Supt.*

43. Keam to Hayes, May 1, 1877, *AP* and *AIC-PHS.*

44. Keam to Lowrie, May 5, 1877, *AIC-PHS.*

45. Ibid.

46. Petition to the Secretary of the Interior, September [n.d.], 1877, *AP.*

47. Ibid.

48. Irvine to Commissioner of Indian Affairs, September 20, 1877, *AP.*

49. Lauderdale to Lowrie, May 20, 1877, *AIC-PHS.*

50. Ibid.

51. Ibid.

52. Commissioner to Secretary of the Interior, September 5, 1877, *AP.*

53. William H. Leckie, *The Buffalo Soldiers: A Narrative of the Negro Cavalry in the West* (Norman: University Oklahoma Press, 1967), 81; Thrapp, *Victorio,* 202.

54. Hatch to Hooker, October 24, 1877, *McNitt Collection.*

55. Quoted in Thrapp, *Victorio,* 202.

56. Ibid.

57. Ibid.

58. 1st Lt. M. B. Hughes to Commanding Officer, Ojo Caliente, November 10, 1877, *McNitt Collection.*

59. Keam to Hatch, January 21, 1878, and Hatch to Keam, February 5, 1878, *McNitt Collection.*

60. Ibid.

61. Keam to Hooker, February 22, 1878, *McNitt Collection.*

62. Keam to Secretary of the Interior, December 12, 1877, and Commissioner of Indian Affairs to Keam, January 4, 1878, *AP.*

63. Ibid.

64. Sherman to Secretary of the Interior, September 9, 1878, in Hayden Biographical Files, Keam Collection.

65. Ibid.

66. Prucha, *The Great Father,* 550.

67. Ibid., 553.

68. Smith to Lowrie, October 17, 1878, *AIC-PHS;* and Smith to Commissioner of Indian Affairs, October 16, 1878, *LR, NM Supt.*

69. Ibid.

70. Ibid.

CHAPTER FIVE

1. Keam to Schurz, Janaury 21, 1879, *LR, NM Supt.*

2. Smith to Lowrie, February 15, 1879, *LR, NM Supt.*

3. Lowrie to Commissioner of Indian Affairs, February 22, 1879, *LR, NM Supt.* The relationship between Keam and Eastman is covered in McNitt, *Indian Traders,* 166–68, 171–76.

4. McNitt, *Indian Traders,* 246–47; Van Valkenburg, "Thomas Keam," 9–12, has Keam in a ranching partnership with Anson Damon. This is unreferenced, and has not been corroborated independently.

5. Sanitary Report, December, 1879, *LR, NM Supt.*

6. Moore, *"Chiefs, Agents, and Soldiers,"* 430–51.

7. McNitt, *Indian Traders,* 172.

8. Eastman to Commissioner of Indian Affairs, January 5, and February 12, 1880, *LR, NM Supt.*

9. Captain John S. Loud, 9th Cavalry, along with five other officers, among them John Pope, supported Keam's appointment in Loud to Assistant Adjutant General, April 27, 1880, *AP;* Secretary of War Alexander Ramsey to Secretary of the Interior, June 19, 1880, *AP;* and Special Order #73, June 23, 1880, *LR, NM Supt.*

10. Special Order #73, June 22, 1880, *LR, NM Supt.*

11. Taylor to Sheldon Jackson, July 23, 1880, *LR, NM Supt.*

12. Bennett to Keam, August 15, 1880, *LR, NM Supt.*

13. Sutherland to Eastman, August 14, 1880, *LR, NM Supt.*

14. The inventory was based on Merritt's 2nd Quarter Inventory amended by Eastman; Eastman to Commissioner, August 26, 1880, *LR, NM Supt.* Among the missing items were half a dozen buckets, 73½ pounds of sugar, 103 pounds of rice, 82 pounds of coffee, 1,281 pounds of corn, 3,250 sewing needles, 46 pounds of indigo dye, 91 yards of linsey, 742 yards of sheeting, 54 yards of gingham, 140 yards of flannel, 419 yards of calico, 25 pounds of nails, 50 pounds of candles, 190 envelopes, and one pair of men's shoes. Eastman's allegations about Merritt are in Eastman to Commissioner, August 26, 1880, *LR, NM Supt.*

15. Bennett to Keam August 15, 1880, *LR, NM Supt.* William Keam died at Fort Wingate, November 30, 1880. Thomas Keam erected a headstone in the churchyard of the Parish Church of Kenwyn, Truro:

In

memory of

GRACE KEAM

widow of

Capt. T. V. Keam,

who departed this life June 21, 1883.

Aged 70 years.

A beloved mother lost to us on earth

at rest in heaven with departed souls.

Also of

WILLIAM HENRY ROGERS,

youngest son of the above

who died November 30, 1880,

Ft. Wingate, New Mexico.

And of

ANN STEPHENS,
Mother of Grace Keam
Erected by her son
Lieut. T. V. Keam,
U.S. Army

I am indebted to Rayma Sharber for her photographs of the Keams' headstones because they provided a partial solution to the mysterious life of William Henry Rogers Keam.

16. I used letters from the Office of Indian Affairs, Letters Received, 1880–present, Record Group 75 and letters from the same source that were in the McNitt Collection. (Hereafter these will be differentiated as LR and LR, *McNitt Collection.)* Captain John S. Loud to Assistant Adjutant General, Department of Missouri, April 27, 1880, unnumbered letter, *McNitt Collection;* Secretary of War Alexander Ramsey to Secretary of the Interior, June 19, 1880, #K959 *McNitt Collection;* Charles Taylor to Sheldon Jackson, July 23, 1880, *LR, NM Supt.;* Thomas Keam to Carl Schurz, September 5, 1880, *AP;* and Hatch to Secretary of Interior, March 14, 1881, *AP.* That there were serious charges against Keam, see Price to Secretary of the Interior, June 15, 1881, *AP.* The charges were never specified.

17. Affidavit of Philip Zoeller in re: Thos. V. Keam. LR, #11725, *McNitt Collection.*

18. Keam to Secretary of the Interior, May 18, 1882, *LR* #10078, Keam's letter for the Navajos is Keam to Secretary of the Interior, May 18, 1882, *LR* #10078, both *McNitt Collection.*

19. Stevens to Keam, June 3, 1882, *LR,* no number, *McNitt Collection.*

20. Ranald S. McKenzie to Commander Headquarters, District of New Mexico, February 10, 1882, and Colonel P. Buell to Assistant Adjutant General, Department of Missouri, March 13, 1882, *LR* #7258, *McNitt Collection.*

21. S. R. Martin, the Department of Justice investigator, to Brewster Cameron, April 7, 1882, *LR* #7256, *McNitt Collection.*

22. Eastman to Ferry, January 24, 1882, *LR* #3817, and Keam to Eastman, spring 1880, *LR* #3817, both *McNitt Collection.*

23. Eastman to Commissioner of Indian Affairs, April 28, 1882, *LR* #8721, *McNitt Collection.*

24. Eastman to Commissioner of Indian Affairs, June 20, 1882, *LR* #11725, *McNitt Collection.*

25. Affidavit of Philip Zoeller in re: Thos. V. Keam, June 20, 1882, *LR* #11725, *McNitt Collection.* McNitt, *Indian Traders,* 177–80, deals with the Merrick-Mitchell issues.

26. Mitchell reported the incident in Mitchell to Eastman, February 27, 1880, *LR, NM Supt.* Robert S. McPherson, *The Northern Navajo Frontier 1860–1900: Expansion through Adversity* (Albuquerque: University of New Mexico Press, 1988), 17–18, 39–50 (hereafter cited as McPherson, *Northern Navajo Frontier),* calls the other miner "Charles Merrick" on p. 17 and "James Merritt" on pp. 41–42. In Mitchell to Eastman, February 27, 1880, *LR, NM Supt.,* Mitchell calls him "Mr. Merritt." In "Indian Imps," March 17, 1880, *Denver Tribune,* he is called "Charles Merrick." These sources, as well as the traders literature (see Introduction, n. 5), are more concerned with the perpetrators of the crime than the victims, and usually refer to them by their last names, except for Richardson, *Navajo Trader,* 167, which refers to Robert Merrick and Herndon Mitchell.

27. Eastman to Commissioner, February 6, and March 20, 1880, *LR, NM Supt.*

28. Affidavit of Philip Zoeller in re: Thos. V. Keam, June 20, 1882, *LR* #11725, *McNitt Collection.*

29. Regarding Merrick and Mitchell's preparations, see McPherson, *Northern Navajo Frontier,* 41–42.

30. Affidavit of Philip Zoeller in re: Thos. V. Keam, *LR* #11725, *McNitt Collection.*

31. Eastman to Commissioner, August 14, 1882, and Affidavits of Philip Zoeller, William Ross, and Jonathan P. Williams, August 14, 1882, *LR* #14834, *McNitt Collection.* Jonathan Williams suffered gold fever, among other things, and what is known of his life is in Yost, *Bread upon the Sands,* 176–83, and *Diamonds in the Desert: The Family History of Bill and Gertie Williams* (Flagstaff, Ariz.: Silver Spruce, 1987), 103–5. Jonathan Williams was her grandfather. William Ross is probably Buckskin Billy Ross, a miner-explorer and ofttimes partner of Williams. See Richardson, *Navajo Trader,* 85, 95.

32. Affidavits of Philip Zoeller, William Ross, and Jonathan P. Williams, August 14, 1882, *LR* #14834, *McNitt Collection.*

33. McNitt, *Indian Traders,* 180-81.

34. Moore, "Chiefs, Agents, and Soldiers," 481-98, clearly defends the thesis that the Navajos were in control of themselves and everyone else with whom they worked.

CHAPTER SIX

1. Although Thomas Keam and others continued to use the name "Keam's Cañon," when the post office was opened in March 1882, the place-name became Keams Canyon. Will C. Barnes, *Arizona Place Names* (Tucson: University of Arizona Press, 1935), 231 (hereafter cited as Barnes, *Arizona Place Names*).

2. 25USC261-266. See also Felix S. Cohen, *Handbook of Federal Indian Law* (Albuquerque: University of New Mexico Press, 1942), 348-49. Thomas Keam was not licensed to trade at Hopi until 1889, seven years after the reservation was created. The $10,000 bond for his license was secured by Victor Mindeleff and I. H. MacDonald, *LR* #19540.

3. Prehistoric trade in the greater American Southwest is examined in Charles C. Di Peso, *Casas Grandes: A Fallen Trading Center of the Gran Chichimeca.* Vol. 3, The *Tardio and Espanoles Periods* (Flagstaff, Ariz.: Northland Press, 1974); Carroll L. Riley, *The Frontier People: The Greater Southwest in the Protohistoric Period,* Occassional Paper, no. 1, Center for Archaeological Investigations (Carbondale: University of Southern Illinois Press, 1982); Carroll L. Riley, *Sixteenth Century Trade in the Greater Southwest,* Mesoamerican Studies, no. 10, University Museum and Art Galleries, (Carbondale: University of Southern Illinois Press, 1976); Carroll L. Riley and Basil C. Hedrick, *Across the Chichimec Sea: Papers in Honor of J. Charles Kelly* (Carbondale: University of Southern Illinois Press, 1978); and David R. Wilcox and W. Bruce Masse, eds., *The Protohistoric Period in the North American Southwest, A.D. 1450-1700,* Anthropological Research Papers, no. 24 (Tempe: Arizona State University, 1981). See also Hall, *Social Change in the Southwest.*

4. Williams Willard Hill, "Navaho Trading and Trading Ritual: A Study of Cultural Dynamics," *Southwestern Journal of Anthropology* 4 (1948): 376-78 (hereafter cited as Hill, "Navaho Trading").

5. Ibid., 382-86; see also Grenville Goodwin, *The Social Organization of the Western Apache* (Tucson: University of Arizona Press, 1969), 72-96.

6. Hill, "Navaho Trading," 383.

7. Ibid., 376–77. See also Hall, *Social Change in the Southwest;* and Jack Forbes, *Apache, Navaho, and Spaniard* (Norman: University of Oklahoma Press, 1960).

8. Richardson, *Navajo Trader* 21, 23.

9. Richardson, "Pioneer Trader to the Navajo," 26–27; James E. Babbitt, "Trading Posts along the Little Colorado," *Plateau* (1986):2–9 (hereafter cited as Babbitt, "Trading Posts along the Little Colorado"); McNitt, *Indian Traders*, 46, 69. See also Klara B. Kelley, "Commercial Networks in the Navajo-Hopi-Zuni Region," (Ph.D. diss., University of New Mexico, 1977) (hereafter cited as Kelley, "Commercial Networks"); John R. Winslowe, "Navajo Traders for Many Moons," *True West* (March-April 1969), 10–14, 63–69 (hereafter cited as Winslowe, "Navajo Traders for Many Moons").

10. The history of trading posts in northeastern Arizona is varied in its completeness and accuracy. In addition to the literature written by or about traders, I have relied on the following for a synthesis for construction and ownership chronology: Babbitt, "Trading Posts along the Little Colorado," 2–9; Mora McManic Brown, "Traders at the Gap," *Desert Magazine* (December 1940), 17–20; Esther Henderson and Chuch Abbott, "Along the Trading Post Trail," *Arizona Highways* (June 1943), 12–19, 41–42; Klara B. Kelley, "Ethnoarchaeology of Navajo Trading Posts," *Kiva* (1985), 19–37 (hereafter cited as Kelley, "Ethnoarchaeology"); Klara B. Kelley, *Navajo Land Use: An Ethnoarchaeological Study* (Orlando: Academic Press, 1986) (hereafter cited as Kelley, *(Navajo Land Use)*); Charles Kelly, "Graveyard of the Gods," *Desert Magazine* (July 1938), 4–6; Maurice Kildare, "Mr. Arbuckle's Coffee," *True West* (May-June 1965), 16–18, 53–54 (herafter cited as Kildare, "Mr. Arbuckle's Coffee"); McNitt, *Indian Traders;* Gladwell "Toney" Richardson, "Bonanza in the Ghost Post," *Desert Magazine* (July 1966), 12–15 (hereafter cited as Richardson, "Bonanza in the Ghost Post"); Richardson, *Navajo Trader;* Richardson, "Pioneer Trader to the Navajo," 26–29; and Winslowe, "Navajo Traders for Many Moons," 10–14, 63–69.

In the first decades of the twentieth century, the Indian trading business became more regulated in part because of the expansion of the reservation. Consequently, many trading posts came under the jurisdiction of the Bureau of Indian Affairs and its agents on the reservation, regardless of the status of the land when the posts were originally built. Additionally, the number of independently owned and operated trading posts was reduced when a handfull of extended families consolidated ownership. They were the Richardsons, descendants of Frederick Smith and George McAdams; the Babbitt brothers, wholesalers from Flagstaff; John Lorenzo Hubbell and his sons, Lorenzo and Roman; and John Wetherill and his relatives. The Richardsons opened or bought out existing posts at Cameron, Tuba City, Rainbow Bridge, Inscription House, Shonto, Kaibito (which they later sold to the Babbitts), and Blue Canyon. Among others, the Babbitts operated posts at Cedar Ridge, Cow Springs, Tonalea, and Tuba City. The Hubbells ran posts at Ganado, Keams Canyon, and Oraibi and eventually took possession of the post at Marble Canyon. The Wetherills ran trading posts at Kayenta; Marsh Pass, where they traded primarily with archaeologists between 1921 and 1923; and Piute Mesa, which was only open during the fall season between 1923 and 1926.

11. Richardson, "Pioneer Trader to the Navajo," 27; Richardson, "Bonanza in the Ghost Post," 13; Kildare, "Mr. Arbuckle's Coffee," 17, photo.

The archaeological evidence associated with abandoned trading posts reflects these architectural characterizations and is covered in Kelley, "Ethnoarchaeology," 19–37. Kelley assembled archaeological records of a number of early twentieth-century trading posts either on or near the eastern boundary of the Navajo Reservation. Mariano's Store, built about 1906, had four rooms, constructed of rock that had been taken from a nearby prehistoric pueblo. Pueblo Alto Trading Post was constructed of sandstone and had a wooden roof. The trading post at Star Lake was a five-room rock building with associated outbuildings and a gas pump. Zeyouma Trading Post, located east of Flagstaff, Arizona, and adjacent to Elden Pueblo, was in operation between 1927 or 1928 and 1933. Its walls were stone, some of which were removed from the walls of Elden Pueblo. It had a poured concrete floor in one room and a wooden floor in the other. The floor joists were set on stones and had no formal foundation. See Roger F. Kelly and Albert E. Ward, "Lessons from Zeyouma Trading Post Near Flagstaff, Arizona," *Historical Archaeology* vi (1972):65–76. Although all of these were temporary posts, their construction and development reflect the same sorts of factors with which more permanent, well-established posts contended.

The archaeological record is supported by the photographic memoir of Elizabeth Compton Hegeman, who lived on the Navajo Reservation between 1925 and 1939. See Hegeman, *Navajo Trading Days*. Her photographs also give some idea of the types of outbuildings and features typical of turn-of-the-century trading posts. At Cedar Ridge, for example, a wool rack was situated on the side of the trading post. These were usually wooden frames, four or five feet tall, on which wool sacks were tied or nailed around the top. As sheared wool was bought, it was stuffed into the sack. At Garcia's Trading Post in Chinle, a twenty- to thirty-foot hitching post doubled as a hitching post and drying rack for cow hides. Net wire fences, and later wooden board fences, were also common around the sides and backs of trading posts, and were used to enclose the trader's house, further delineating boundaries between the trader's world and that of his customers. Charles S. Peterson (1986: 302–61) has described the cultural landscape, fields, and tools at Hubbells Trading Post, the most complex trading post business on the Navajo Reservation ("Homestead and Farm: A History of Farming at Hubbell Trading Post National Historic Site," a report prepared for Southwest Parks and Monuments Association, 1986) (hereafter cited as Peterson, "Homestead and Farm").

12. Herbert Welsh, *Report of a Visit to the Navajo, Pueblo and Hualapais Indians of New Mexico and Arizona* (Philadelphia, Pa.: Indian Rights Association, 1885), 22 (hereafter cited as Welch, *Report of a Visit*).

13. Road-building was the responsibility of the trader. George McAdams laid out and formalized a road connecting the Little Colorado River and his post at Tonalea and the twenty-eight-mile road from Tonalea to Tuba City. Claude Richardson built roads from Tuba City to Kaibito and from Kaibito to The Gap. Hubert, Cecil, and S. I. Richardson spent $10,000 in the mid-1920s blasting a road into Rainbow Lodge. See Richardson, "Bonanza in the Ghost Post," 69.

14. Richardson, *Navajo Trader*, 22–28. Even today, cattle and sheep ranching are often second jobs for traders, especially those with off-reservation posts or those who can lease off-reservation pastures near their posts. See, for example, Roberts, *Stokes Carson*. The relationship between trading and ranching is not covered to any extent in the literature on trading; however, see Charles S. Peterson, "Homestead and Farm," 22–28. See also John G. Bourke, *Snake-Dance of the Moquis* (Tuc-

son: University of Arizona Press, 1984), 83 (hereafter cited as Bourke, *Snake-Dance of the Moquis);* Keam to Herbert Welch, November 24, 1888, Indian Rights Association Papers, Historical Society of Pennsylvania. Keam's ranching enterprise is covered in subsequent chapters.

15. Nequatewa, *Truth of a Hopi,* 130; Alexander M. Stephen, *Hopi Journal of Alexander M. Stephen* (New York, N.Y.: AMS Press, 1969), 1017, 1153. Stephen called Keams Canyon Boñsikya, which means "rush canyon." Stephen may have been referring to Nequatewa's *poongo-sikia.* Lók 'a' *deeshjin,* "reeds extend along black," is from Young and Morgan, *The Navajo Language: A Grammar and Colloquial Dictionary,* rev. ed. (Albuquerque: University of New Mexico, 1980). Raymond E. Lindgren, "A Diary of Kit Carson's Navajo Campaign," *New Mexico Historical Review* 21 (July 1946):235; the inscription is located at the present-day picnic grounds at Lake Maho in Keams Canyon, about twenty-five yards below Keam's original trading post site. McNitt, *Indian Traders,* 46. For on-reservation posts, ownership and staffing can be compiled from Office of Indian Affairs records, as traders and clerks had to be licensed. The history of off-reservation posts is very sketchy, because no licenses were required and records are all but nonexistent.

16. McNitt, *Indian Traders,* 46.

17. Keam's purchases can be found in Fleming to Commissioner of Indian Affairs, November 29, 1882, United States National Archives, Special Files, 1800–1904, file #267, "Charges against Agent Fleming, Moqui Pueblo Agency, 1882–1883."

18. 43USCsec321.

19. McNitt, *Indian Traders,* 186–90, covers Keam's trading post. My description and what follows are based on my surveys of the region, that have been conducted over the last decade, on Keam's maps in *Office of Indian Affairs Record Group 75, Maps,* #1265 "Plan of Trading Post, Shops, Corrals, etc in Keam's Cajon, Arizona," "Topographical Map of Keam's Cañon Showing Position of Springs, Improvements, etc," and "Plan of Residences, Keam's Cañon," December 21, 1886, (hereafter Keam's maps are cited as "Keam maps") and Office of Indian Affairs and Keam to Commissioner, February 11, 1886, *LR* #4589 in *McNitt Collection.* There is nothing left of Keam's original buildings at this location.

20. Schmedding, *Cowboy and Indian Trader,* 322. At Hubbells Trading Post, three butchering racks and the associated butchering pits were excavated in 1973. The racks are made of upright cedar posts. A cross-beam either rested in naturally occurring forks at the top of the posts or was notched into or nailed onto the posts. See Stanley J. Olsen and John Beezley, "Domestic Food Animals From Hubbell Trading Post," *Kiva* (1975):202–203, figs. 1 and 2. Domesticated animals made up at least 98 percent of the faunal remains recovered from the pits (Ibid., 204), and of that, 54 percent were bones of domestic sheep and/or goats, mostly immature animals. Less than 3 percent of the recovered bones were from domestic cows (Ibid., 205). Due to the butchering marks on the bones and the types of bones recovered (complete sheep metapodials, carpals, and tarsals), primary butchering—gutting, skinning, and removing the hind quarters—occured at this location. The absence of sawed bones and skulls indicates that these activities took place somewhere else (Ibid., 205). More than likely, the butchered carcasses were sold, as they are today, in quarters to be further processed and consumed elsewhere.

21. Bourke, *Snake-Dance of the Moquis,* 236, and McNitt, *Indian Traders,* 198.

22. From "Keam maps" and in Keam to Commissioner, February 11, 1886, *LR* #4589 *McNitt Collection.*

23. Ibid.

24. Ibid.

25. Bourke, *Snake-Dance of the Moquis.*

26. From "Keam maps" and in Keam to Commissioner, February 11, 1886, *LR* #4589, *McNitt Collection.*

27. Ibid.

28. Ibid. The map shows a combined flow of water from the springs as 12.000 gallons but does not indicate the rate at which the water flows.

29. There are a number of firsthand accounts of nineteenth- and twentieth-century Indian traders' lives and practices on the Navajo Reservation. I have relied on them, for my understanding of the business. Bill Malone, the trader at Hubbell Trading Post National Historic Site, and Steve Getzwiller, an independent trader, have been more help than they realize. They let me "hang around" and watch their business transactions. Those observations, and their comments, have proved invaluable. The books include Faunce, *Desert Wife;* Fletcher, *The Wetherills of Mesa Verde;* Gillmor and Wetherill, *Traders to the Navajos;* Hannum, *Paint* *the Wind;* Hannum, *Spin a Silver Dollar;* Hegeman, *Navaho Trading Days;* Richardson, *Navajo Trader;* Schmedding, *Cowboy and Indian Trader;* Newcomb, *Navaho Neighbors;* Yost, *Bread upon the Sands;* Yost, *Diamonds in the Desert;* and Roberts, *Stokes Carson.*

30. Roberts, *Stokes Carson,* 100.

31. Quoted in Ruth Underhill, *The Navajos* (Norman: University of Oklahoma Press, 1956), 184.

32. Richardson, *Navajo Trader,* 70, 115.

33. Barnes, *Arizona Place Names,* 231.

34. Quoted in George A. Boyce, *When the Navajos Had Too Many Sheep: The 1940s* (San Francisco, Calif.: The Indian Historian Press, 1974), 38.

35. Welsh, *Report of a Visit,* 24.

36. In an unreferenced article, Babbitt, "Trading Posts along the Little Colorado," 3, identifies this hapless fellow as Leander Smith, a trader at the Wolf Post; however, the story is told in several areas of the reservation about different posts. Perhaps the story of poor Mr. Smith's activities has been adopted by others as an example of an easterner's ignorance.

37. Richardson, *Navajo Trader,* 97–98.

38. Thomas Keam, Application for Appointment as Trader, 1889, *LR* #19540.

39. Bruce Burnham, "The Traders' Influence on the Weaver" in *Wool on a Small-Scale* (Logan: Utah State University Press, 1986), 194.

40. McNitt, *Indian Traders,* 81.

41. For the vagaries of trading, see especially Richardson, *Navajo Trader;* Roberts, *Stokes Carson;* and Schmedding, *Cowboy and Indian Trader.* For an alternative economic interpretation, see Laurence David Weiss, *The Development of Capitalism in the Navajo Nation: A Political-Economic History* Studies in Marxism 15 (Minneapolis, Minn.: MEP Publications, 1984).

42. Burton to Commissioner of Indian Affairs, April 9, 1901, *LR* #20262; and Thomas Keam to Commissioner, April 25, 1901, *LR* #23317.

43. These figures are compiled from Commissioner of Indian Affairs, *Annual Report,* 1872, 1874, 1876, 1877, 1880, 1881, 1883, 1886, 1887, and 1891.

44. Kelley, *Navajo Land Use,* 31.

45. Compiled from Commissioner of Indian Affairs, *Annual Report,* 1886, 1888.

46. Compiled from Commissioner of Indian Affairs, *Annual Report,* 1887 and 1891. Navajo weaving also continued to be an important aspect of Navajo economy and it, too, was tied to the trading post. By the turn of the century, virtually all of the Navajo weaving produced in the San Juan River valley was bought by John Wetherill at his Pueblo Bonito Trading Post, which was owned by the Hyde Exploring Expedition (HEE). The HEE saw that the trade in Navajo weaving was so profitable that it would subsidize traders in exhange for exclusive rights to the rugs produced in their area. In 1899, the HEE opened a store on 23rd Street in New York City to sell its large inventory of rugs. Boyd, "Trading and Weaving," 75–98. In 1901, the Navajo agent S. J. Holsinger reported that the HEE's wagons "are now encountered on every road in the Chaco region, hauling merchandise from the railroad to the interior and returning laden with blankets woven by the Navajos." McNitt, *Indian Traders,* 199–200. The expedition priced its rugs at between \$1.50 to \$5.00 for a 3 × 5 striped rug to \$6.00 to \$20.00 for a larger 5 × 7 fancy rug to \$400.00 for "very fine Bayettas" (Boyd, "Trading and Weaving," 95).

Navajo weavings were also sought after at Lorenzo Hubbell's post at Ganado. By 1900 Hubbell had about three hundred weavers working for him, and by 1902 he had an annual contract to supply the Fred Harvey Houses along the Santa Fe Railroad with Navajo rugs, which netted him between \$20,000 and \$25,000 (Boyd, "Trading and Weaving," 37).

In 1903, J. B. Moore sent out catalogs for Navajo rugs from Crystal Trading Post. His prices were based on size and quality and ranged from 90¢ to \$1.00 per square foot. C. N. Cotton, one-time partner with Hubbell, ran a wholesale business in Gallup, New Mexico, and also sold Navajo rugs from a catalog. His 3 × 5 "Extra Fancy Grade Navajo Blankets" sold for between \$50.00 and \$60.00 each; a 5 × 7 sold for \$120.00 to \$140.00. A "Common Grade Navajo Blanket" useful as a "bath mat or floor covering for porch or summer house or sleeping rooms" sold for between \$20.00 and \$25.00 for a 3 × 5 foot rug and \$60.00 to \$70.00 for a 5 × 8 rug. Garrick Bailey and Roberta Bailey, *A History of the Navajos: The Reservation Years* (Santa Fe, N. Mex.: School of American Research, 1986), 152 (hereafter cited as Baileys, *History of the Navajos*) claim that in 1911 traders paid Navajo weavers a total of about \$675,000 for rugs. In 1913 and 1914 the payment was between \$600,000 and \$700,000. In the 1920s the pay out was about \$400,000.

47. Richard White, *The Roots of Dependency: Subsistence, Environment, and Social Change among the Choctaws, Pawnees, and Navajos* (Lincoln: University of Nebraska Press, 1983), 243–48.

48. Hopi pottery is from the author's work with Hopi pottery collections; Hopi Craftsman Show invoices, 1930–1984; Navajo Craftsman Show invoices, various years, Museum of Northern Arizona; and Laura Graves Allen, *Contemporary Hopi Pottery* (Flagstaff: Museum of Northern Arizona, 1984) (hereafter cited as Allen, *Contemporary Hopi Pottery*).

49. Mrs. White Mountain Smith, "Tom Pavatea," *Desert Magazine* (February 1938):4–6.

50. Peter Whiteley, *Deliberate Acts: Changing Hopi Culture through the Oraibi Split* (Tucson: University of Arizona Press, 1988), 103 (hereafter cited as Whitley, *Deliberate Acts*); Richardson, *Navajo Trader,* 72.

51. F. W. Hodge to Will C. Barnes, June 15, 1932, Hayden Files, Keam Collection.

CHAPTER SEVEN

1. Barnes, *Arizona Place Names,* 231.

2. Keam's relationships with the anthropologists is covered in Mc-Nitt, *Indian Traders,* 190–91. Keam's relations with the Office of Indian Affairs is covered in the next chapter.

3. The establishment of the Bureau of Ethnology is covered in Curtis M. Hinsley Jr., *Savages and Scientists: The Smithsonian Institution and the Development of Anthropology, 1846–1910* (Washington, D.C.: Smithsonian Institution, 1981) (hereafter cited as Hinsley, *Savages and Scientists*). See also Neil Judd, *The Bureau of American Ethnology: A Partial History* (Norman: University of Oklahoma Press, 1968). That the nation's capital was the center of the scientific community, see J. Kirkpatrick Flack, *Desideratum in Washington: The Intellectual Community in the Capital City, 1870–1900* (Cambridge, Mass.: Schenkman Publishing, 1975).

4. James Stevenson, "Illustrated Catalog of the Collections Obtained from the Indians of New Mexico and Arizona in 1879," Bureau of American Ethnology, Annual Report, vol. 2 (1880–1881), 307–42. (hereafter cited as Stevenson, *1879 Illustrated Catalog*).

5. Lewis Henry Morgan, *Ancient Society or, Researches in the Lines of Human Progress from Savagery through Barbarism to Civilization* (Cambridge, Mass.: Belnap Press of Harvard University, 1964).

6. Ibid. The history of anthropology is covered in Hinsley, *Savages and Scientists,* and John O. Brew, *One Hundred Years of Anthropology* (Cambridge, Mass.: Harvard University Press, 1968); Regna Darnell, ed., *Readings in the History of Anthropology* (New York, N.Y.: Harper and Row, 1974); Regna Darnell, "The Development of American Anthropology, 1879–1920: From the Bureau of American Ethnology to Franz Boas," (Ph.D. diss., University of Pennsylvania, 1969); Marvin Harris, *The Rise of Anthropological Theory: A History of the Theories of Culture* (New York, N.Y.: Thomas Y. Crowell Co., 1968); June Helm, ed., *Pioneers in American Anthropology: The Uses of Biography* (Seattle: University of Washington Press, 1966); Joan Mark, *Four Anthropologists: An American Science in its Early Years* (New York, N.Y.: Science History, 1980).

7. Hinsley, *Savages and Scientists,* 150. See also Curtis M. Hinsley Jr., "Anthropology as Science and Politics: The Dilemma of the Bureau of Ethnology, 1879–1904" in *The Uses of Anthropology.* A Special Publication of the American Anthropological Association, vol. 11 (1979): 15–32.

8. Stevenson, *1879 Illustrated Catalog,* 319.

9. The Snake Dance is among the oldest Hopi ceremonies, perhaps predating the Kachina Cult. Rites of the Snake Society alternate with those of the Flute Society. Even though the Snake Dance has fascinated non-Hopis for several generations and is perhaps the best known (but least understood) of the ceremonies, it does not rank higher in importance than other ceremonies in Hopis' minds.

10. John Gregory Bourke's biographer is Joseph C. Porter, *Paper Medicine Man: John Gregory Bourke and His American West* (Norman: University of Oklahoma Press, 1986) (hereafter cited as Porter, *Bourke*). Bourke's life was also covered in Lansing B. Bloom, "Bourke on the Southwest," *New Mexico Historical Review* (1933–1938) 8(1):1–30; 9(1):33–77; 9(2):159–83; 9(3):273–89; 9(4):375–435; 10(1):1–35; 10(4):271–322; 11(1):77–122; 11(2):188–207; 11(3):217–82; 12(1): 41–77; 12(4):337–79; 13(2):192–238. Bourke's and Keam's meeting is covered in McNitt, *Indian Traders,* 168–71.

11. Bourke, *Snake-Dance of the Moquis,* 71.

12. Porter, *Bourke,* 4, 96.

13. Matthews biographical sketch is in Katherine Spencer Halpern, Mary Holt, and Susan Brown McGreevy, *Guide to the Microfilm Edition of* *the Washington Matthews Papers, The Wheelwright Museum of the American Indian, Santa Fe, New Mexico* (Albuquerque: University of New Mexico Press, 1985) (hereafter cited as Halpern, Holt, and McGreevy, *Matthews Papers*).

14. Frank Hamilton Cushing, *Zuni: Selected Writing of Frank Hamilton Cushing* (Lincoln: University of Nebraska Press, 1979), 5.

15. That Cushing should be removed from Zuni is in Sheldon Jackson to Spencer Baird, December 22, 1882, Smithsonian Institution, National Anthropological Archives, Letters Received, 1879–1888; Cushing's run-in with Eastman is in Triloki Nath Pandey, "Anthropologists at Zuni," *Proceedings of the American Philosophical Society* 116 (1972): 324–25. See also Norman J. Bender, ed., *Missionaries, Outlaws, and Indians: Thomas F. Ealy at Lincoln and Zuni, 1878–1881* (Albuquerque: University of New Mexico Press, 1984).

16. Stephen's brief biography is in Alexander M. Stephen, *Hopi Journal of A. M. Stephen,* edited by Elsie Clews Parsons (New York, N.Y.: AMS Press, 1969), xx (hereafter cited as Stephen, *Hopi Journal*). Parsons does not record Stephen's birth year. Edwin L. Wade and Lea McChesney, *America's Great Lost Expedition: The Thomas Keam Collection of Hopi Pottery from the Second Hemenway Expedition, 1890–1894* (Phoenix, Ariz.: Heard Museum, 1980), 10 (hereafter cited as Wade and McChesney, *Lost Expedition*), suggest 1850 as the year of Stephen's birth. Thomas Keam recorded Stephen's age as forty-nine years on the headstone he erected in Keams Canyon in 1894. Parsons says Stephen was educated at the University of Edinburgh; however, Alex Peterson, *Hopi Pottery Symbols: Based on "Pottery of Tusayan, Catalogue of the Keam Collection by Alexander M. Stephen"* (Boulder, Colo.: Johnson Books, 1994), 5, claims there is no record of Stephen attending the university. Be that as it may, Stephen's writings, which are voluminous and almost always published under someone else's name, this being just the most recent example, reveal a man of some education, either formal or self-taught. His correspondence with Jesse Walter Fewkes also reveals a man tormented by the anxieties of the scholar's life, plagued by financial problems, uncooperative informants, and by the frustrations that accompanied his realization that his work benefited the careers of others rather than himself. Fewkes's Hopi work is based exclusively on Stephen's work and manuscripts, and after Stephen's death in 1894, Fewkes did little Hopi writing. See Stephen to Fewkes, numerous letters, July 1891 to March 1894, Smithsonian Institution, National Anthropological Archives, Manuscript and Pamphlet File #4408 (hereafter cited as *SI, NAA, MS* #4408), and Stephen to Washington Matthews, Washington Matthews Papers, The Wheelwright Museum of the American Indian, Santa Fe, New Mexico (hereafter cited as *Matthews Coll.*).

17. Stephen's activities prior to moving to Keams Canyon is in Bourke, *Snake-Dance of the Moquis,* 80.

18. Jesse Green, ed., *Cushing at Zuni: The Correspondence and Journals of Frank Hamilton Cushing, 1879–1884* (Albuquerque: University of New Mexico Press, 1990), 142 (hereafter cited as Green, *Cushing*).

19. Porter, *Bourke,* 98; Bourke, *Snake-Dance of the Moquis,* 104.

20. Bourke, *Snake-Dance of the Moquis,* 89–95. The rock-art panel Bourke refers to is just south of Keam's post. It was carved by one of Carson's men while they were camped in the canyon on August 13, 1863. See Raymond E. Lindgren, "A Diary of Kit Carson's Navaho Campaign, 1863–1864," *New Mexico Historical Review* 21, no. 3 (July 1946): 222–46.

21. Bourke, *Snake-Dance of the Moquis,* 109.

22. Ibid., 111–69; 151.

23. Ibid., 155–56.

24. For literature on the Snake Dance, see W. David Laird, *Hopi Bibliography: Comprehensive and Annotated* (Tucson: University of Arizona Press, 1977). He cites hundreds of references.

25. Bourke, *Snake-Dance of the Moquis,* 224.

26. William Webb and Robert A. Weinstein, *Dwellers at the Source: Photographs of A. C. Vroman, 1895–1904* (Albuquerque: University of New Mexico Press, 1973), 85, see 38, photo 2 (hereafter cited as Webb and Weinstein, *Dwellers at the Source*). See also this volume, 150. Keam also arranged for E. H. Plummer, acting agent for the Navajos, to see the Snake Dance preparations and kiva preparations. See E. H. Plummer, "The Moqui Indian Snake Dance in Arizona," *Frank Leslie's Popular Monthly* (November 1897):500–505. See also Elliott G. McIntire and Sandra R. Gordon, "ten Kate's Account of the Walpi Snake Dance: 1883," *Plateau* 41 (summer 1968):27–33. For an example of the advertising techniques used to encourage tourism to the Snake Dance and Indians of the Southwest in general, see Walter Hough, *The Moki Snake*

Dance (Santa Fe, N. Mex.: Passenger Department of the Santa Fe [Railroad], 1901), and T. C. McLuhan, *Dream Tracks: The Railroad and the American Indian, 1890–1930* (New York, N.Y.: Harry N. Abrams, 1985) (hereafter cited as McLuhan, *Dream Tracks*).

27. Bourke, *Snake-Dance of the Moquis,* 155–56.

28. Thomas V. Keam, "An Indian Snake-Dance," *Chambers's Journal,* 20, no. 994 (January 13, 1883).

29. Ibid.

30. Ibid.

31. Ibid.

32. Laird has worked out the early chronology of Snake Dance literature in *Hopi Bibliography,* 215, 311, 422.

33. Cushing to Baird, January 14, 1882, Smithsonian Institution, National Anthropological Archives, Letters Received 1879–1888 (hereafter cited as *SI, NAA, LR*).

34. Stevenson, *1879 Illustrated Catalog,* 319; James Stevenson, "Illustrated Catalog of the Collection Obtained from the Pueblos of Zuni, New Mexico, and Wolpi *[sic]*, Arizona, in 1881," Bureau of American Anthropology Annual Report, vol. 3 (1881–1882), 519 (hereafter cited Stevenson, *1881 Illustrated Catalog*).

35. John Wesley Powell, "Annual Report of the Director," Bureau of American Ethnology Annual Report, vol. 4 (1882–1883), xxxix–xl (hereafter cited as Powell, "Annual Report").

36. Affidavit of Philip Zoeller in re: Thos. V. Keam, June 20, 1882, Office of Indian Affairs, *LR* #11725, *McNitt Collection.*

37. Stevenson, *1879 Illustrated Catalog,* 319; Stevenson, *1881 Illustrated Catalog,* 519; James Stevenson, "Illustrated Catalog of the Collections Obtained from the Indian of New Mexico in 1880," Bureau of American Ethnology Annual Report, vol. 4, (1880–1881), 423–64; and Powell, "Annual Report," xxxix–xl.

38. There is a long tradition of museum directors and curators employing traders, missionaries, soldiers, and others to collect artifacts for them. See, for example, Douglas Cole, *Captured Heritage: The Scramble for Northwest Coast Artifacts* (Seattle: University of Washington Press, 1985). See also Green, *Cushing,* 305, 311; and Donald Collier and Harry Tschopik Jr., "The Role of Museums in American Anthropology," *American Anthropologist* 56 (1954):768–79.

39. Keam to Baird, September 13, 1884, *SI, NAA, MS* #833.

40. Ibid.

41. Ibid.

42. McChesney was the chief disbursing officer at the United States Geological Survey, and in 1889 he cosigned the bond securing Keam's license to trade.

43. Keam to Baird, September 13, 1884, *SI, NAA,* MS #833.

44. Keam to William H. Holmes, November 7, 1884, *SI, NAA,* MS #833.

45. Ibid.

46. Keam to Holmes, December 13, 1884 *SI, NAA,* MS #833.

47. "Catalog of the Exhibits of the United States Geological Survey and the Bureau of Ethnology at the New Orleans Exposititon," *SI, NAA, LR,* 1879–1888. One of the mummies, that of a child, was excavated by Keam in 1884 from a cist in Canyon del Muerto and subsequently deposited at the United States National Museum. See Cosmos Mindeleff, "Cliff Ruins of Canyon de Chelly, Arizona," Bureau of American Ethnology Annual Report, vol. 16 (1894–1895), 100–101.

48. John W. Powell, "Annual Report of the Director," Bureau of American Ethnology Annual Report, vol. 7 (1885–1886), xxv–xxviii.

49. Keam's relationship with the anthropologists is acknowledged in John Wesley Powell, "Annual Report of the Director," Bureau of American Ethnology Annual Report, vol. 6 (1884–1885), xliv; ibid., 1885–1886, xxix; William H. Holmes, "Pottery of the Ancient Pueblos," Bureau of American Ethnology Annual Report, vol. 4 (1882–1883), 293, 295–97, 321; Garrick Mallery, "Picture-Writing of the American Indians," Bureau of American Ethnology Annual Report, vol. 10 (1888–1889), 50, 604–65, 623; J. Walter Fewkes," The A'losaka Cult of the Hopi Indians," *American Anthropologist* 1 (1899):522, 535; J. Walter Fewkes, "Death of a Celebrated Hopi," *American Anthropologist* 1 (1899): 196; James Mooney, "The Ghost-Dance Religion and the Sioux Outbreak of 1890," Bureau of American Ethnology Annual Report, vol. 14 (1892–1893), 810–15; J. Walter Fewkes, "Two Summers' Work in Pueblo Ruins," Bureau of American Ethnology Annual Report, vol. 22 (1904), 69; and Stewart Culin, "Games of the North American Indians," Bureau of American Ethnology, Annual Report, vol. 24 (1907), 30, 96, 162, 190, 346, 349, 357–58, 363–64, 367, 390, 457, 635, 679, 680, 716, 796, 807.

50. Victor Mindeleff, "A Study of Pueblo Architecture, Tusayan and Cibola," Bureau of American Ethnology Annual Report, vol. 8 (1886–1887), 16–41, 100.

51. John W. Powell, "Annual Report of the Director," Bureau of American Ethnology, Annual Report, vol. 9 (1887–1888), xxxii.

52. John W. Powell, "Introduction," Bureau of American Ethnology Annual Report, vol. 10 (1888–1889), xvii–xviii.

53. Ibid.

54. According the George Wharton James, *Indian Blankets and Their Makers* (Chicago, Ill.: A. C. McClung, 1914), 47, Hubbell or Cotton only bought about three hundred or four hundred striped Navajo blankets in 1884. In 1885 they were beginning to market them and attained some success only after Cotton introduced aniline dyes to the weavers. James claimed this was the beginning of the Navajo rug period. However, Dennis Boyd, "Trading and Weaving," 26, demonstrates that Lorenzo Hubbell's influence on Navajo weaving could not have begun any earlier than 1891. Utley, "The Reservation Trader in Navajo History," 23, concurs. Bailey and Bailey, *A History of the Navajos: The Reservation Years,* 150–51, estimate that the Navajos produced only 2,700 blankets per year as late as 1887. For the development of the trading posts and families mentioned, see Frank McNitt, *Richard Wetherill: Anasazi* (Albuquerque: University of New Mexico Press, 1957), 24, 107. Peter J. McKenna and Scott E. Travis, *Archaeological Investigations at Thunderbird Lodge, Canyon de Chelly, Arizona,* Southwest Cultural Resources Center Professional Papers, no. 20, Branch of Cultural Resources Management, Division of Anthropology (Santa Fe, N. Mex.: National Park Service, 1989), 1. Gillmor and Wetherill, *Traders to the Navajos,* 71, 161.

55. Wade and McChesney, *Lost Expedition,* 7; and Raymond Stewart Brandes, "Frank Hamilton Cushing: Pioneer Americanist," (Ph.D. diss., University of Arizona, 1965), 130 (hereafter cited as Brandes, "Cushing").

56. Brandes, "Cushing," 141.

57. Wade and McChesney, *Lost Expedition,* 8.

58. Hinsley, *Savages and Scientists,* 201.

59. Bill of Sale, April 5, 1892, Hemenway Family Papers, Phillips Library, Peabody Essex Museum, Salem, Massachusetts (hereafter Hemenway Family Papers); Wade and McChesney, *Lost Expedition,* 5.

60. Stephen said they paid him $115 per month, and with that he was still in debt at Keam's post, February 15, 1893. *Washington Matthews Papers.*

61. Bill of Sale, April 5, 1892, Hemenway Family Papers; Wade and McChesney, *Lost Expedition,* 5.

62. Wade and McChesney, *Lost Expedition,* 12, 14.

63. Edwin L. Wade and Lea S. McChesney, *Historic Hopi Ceramics: The Thomas V. Keam Collection of the Peabody Museum of Archaeology and Ethnology, Harvard University* (Cambridge, Mass.: Peabody Museum, 1981), 15 (hereafter cited as Wade and McChesney, *Historic Hopi Ceramics*).

64. See, for example, Allen, *Contemporary Hopi Pottery,* 49.

65. Wade and McChesney, *Historic Hopi Ceramics,* 455.

66. Ibid.

67. For example, Wade and McChesney, *Historic Hopi Ceramics,* see *PM* #43-39-10/43869 C & D, 458.

68. Wade and McChesney, *Historic Hopi Ceramics,* 455. It might be well to point out here, as I did in Allen, *Contemporary Hopi Pottery,* 21–23, that there is some reason to question the accuracy of the story promulgated by Walter Hough, "A Revival of the Ancient Art," *American Anthropologist* 19 (1917):322–23, and repeated by so many others, including Jesse Walter Fewkes, that Nampeyo saw Sikyatki-style designs on potsherds dug up by her husband as he worked for Fewkes excavating Sikyatki ruin. See Wade and McChesney, *Historic Hopi Ceramics,* 455; and Theodore R. Frisbie, "The Influence of J. Walter Fewkes on Nampeyo: Fact or Fiction?" in *The Changing Ways of Southwestern Indians: A Historic Perspective* (Glorieta, N. Mex.: Rio Grande Press, 1973), 231–43.

69. Keam encouraged the reproduction of ancient pieces, and even though Hopi potters responded to his requests, several anthropologists, among them Jesse Walter Fewkes, *Designs on Prehistoric Hopi Pottery* (New York, N.Y.: Dover, 1973), 116 (hereafter cited as Fewkes, *Designs*) and W. H. Holmes, "The Debasement of Pueblo Art," *American Anthropologist* 2 (1899):320, worried that unsuspecting tourists and museum curators would be "taken in" because the reproductions were so good. The changes brought about by commercialization of southwestern Indian arts is covered in many places, among them: Edwin L. Wade, "The History of the Southwest Indian Ethnic Art Market," (Ph.D. diss., University of Washington, 1976); Allen, *Contemporary Hopi Pottery*; Laura Graves Allen, "Navajo Rugs: A Marketing Success,"

Designers West (April 1983):133–38; Nelson H. H. Graburn, ed., *Ethnic and Tourist Arts: Cultural Expressions from the Fourth World* (Berkeley: University of California Press, 1976) (hereafter cited as Graburn, *Ethnic and Tourist Arts*); and Lawrence E. Dawson, Vera-Mae Fredrickson, and Nelson H. H. Graburn, *Traditions in Transition: Culture Contact and Material Change* (Berkeley: Lowie Museum of Anthropology, 1974) (hereafter cited as Dawson, Fredrickson, and Graburn, *Traditions in Transition*). See also Michael B. Stanislawski, "The Ethno-Archaeology of Hopi Pottery Making," *Plateau* 42 (summer 1969):27–33; and Michael B. Stanislawski, Ann Hitchcock, and Barbara B. Stanislawski, "Identification Marks on Hopi and Hopi-Tewa Pottery," *Plateau* 48 (spring 1976):47–66.

70. See, for example, the arguments presented in J. J. Brody, "The Creative Consumer: Survival, Revival, and Invention in Southwest Indian Arts." in Graburn, *Ethnic and Tourist Arts,* 70–84; and Dawson, Fredrickson, and Graburn, *Traditions in Transition,* 45–54, 56–62.

71. See, for example, Allen, *Contemporary Hopi Pottery*, OC1078, OC1079, and E5396, 27.

72. The history and anthropology of world's fairs can be found in Burton Benedict, *The Anthropology of World's Fairs: San Francisco's Panama Pacific International Exposition, 1915* (New York, N.Y.: Scholar's Press, 1983); David F. Burg, *Chicago's White City of 1893* (Lexington: University Press of Kentucky, 1976); Paul Greenhalgh, *Ephemeral Vistas: The Expositions Universelles, Great Exhibitions and World's Fairs, 1851–1939* (Manchester, U.K.: Manchester University Press, 1988); W. H. Holmes, "The World's Fair Congress of Anthropology," *American Anthropologist* (1893):423–34; Badger Reid, *The Great American Fair: The World's Columbian Exposition and American Culture* (Chicago, Ill.: Nelson Hall, 1979); Robert W. Rydell, *All the World's a Fair: Visions of Empire at American International Expositions, 1876–1916* (Chicago: University of Chicago Press, 1984); Benjamin C. Truman, *History of the World's Fair* (Philidelphia, Pa.: H. W. Kelly, 1893); Thomas Wilson, "Anthropology at the Paris Exposition in 1889," *United States National Museum Reports* (1890):641–80. Keam to Commissioner of Indian Affairs, October 22, 1891, Office of Indian Affairs, *LR* #38787, and July 28, 1892, *LR* #28120.

73. Keam to Commissioner of Indian Affairs, May 6, 1898, *LR* #22105; Constant Williams to Commissioner of Indian Affairs, February 21,

1898, *LR* #9856; W. A. Jones to Constant Williams, n.d., *LR* #9856; Keam to Williams, February 17, 1898, *LR* #9856; Keam to Commissioner of Indian Affairs, February 15, 1898, *LR* #9856.

74. Keam to Commissioner of Indian Affairs, May 8, 1900, *LR* #23739; Keam to Commissioner of Indian Affairs, February 12, 1901, *LR* #10393; Keam to Commissioner of Indian Affairs, March 26, 1901, *LR* #17401; Keam to Commissioner of Indian Affairs, April 7, 1901, *LR* #19805; Keam to Commissioner of Indian Affairs, December 19, 1901, *LR* #74527.

75. Keam to Commissioner of Indian Affairs, June 28, 1899, *LR* #31235; Keam to Commissioner of Indian Affairs, June 14, 1899, *LR* #28577; Keam to Slater, July 26, 1899, *LR* #36515; Thompson [for Keam] to Tonner, January 14, 1900, *LR* #3965; Keam to Tonner, May 28, 1900, *LR* #39121.

76. *Accession File* 155, Field Museum of Natural History, Department of Anthropology, Chicago, Illinois, October 1894 (a huge Hopi and Navajo collection); *Accession File* 222, June 1895 (Navajo costumes); *Accession File* 223, July 1895 (Hopi and Navajo material and geological specimens); and *Accession File* 748, April 1901 (four Navajo games) (hereafter Field Museum of Natural History).

77. Smithsonian Institution, *Accession File* 316, 694, 1894. Six Navajo rugs and silver ornaments had been at the Smithsonian Institution since 1884, when he sent this material for the New Orleans exposition (catalog numbers 417, 721–417, 760).

78. Wilma R. Kaemelein, *An Inventory of Southwestern American Indian Specimens in European Museums* (Tucson: University of Arizona Press, 1967), 98–104 (hereafter cited as Kaemelein, *Inventory*). In 1901 the Berlin Museum accessioned about 280 specimens from Keam, including prehistoric pottery and sandals, contemporary tiles, baskets, kachina dolls, and ceremonial materials. The only museum collection Keam ever donated was a small Navajo and Hopi ethnographic collection to the museum in his boyhood home, The Royal Institution of Cornwall (pers. comm. from Les Douch, curator emeritus, January 24, 1986).

79. Kaemelein, *Inventory,* 108, the Leiden Museum cataloged prehistoric stone tools from Keam in 1912; catalog numbers 1830.1–1830.8.

80. Ayer was a significant figure in the Southwest. See Anonymous, "Colonel Edward E. Ayer," *New Mexico Historical Review* 2 (July 1927): 306–7; and John Todd Zimmer, *Catalog of the Edward E. Ayer Ornithological Library,* Field Museum of Natural History, Publication 239, Zoological Series, vol. xvi, November 26 (1926):iii–v (hereafter cited as Zimmer, *Edward E. Ayer*). F. W. Putnam was also a prominent figure in American museums. See Ralph W. Dexter, "The Role of F. W. Putnam in Founding the Field Museum," *Curator* 8 (1970):21–26; and Ralph W. Dexter, "The Role of F. W. Putnam in Developing Anthropology at the American Museum of Natural History," *Curator* 19 (1976):303–10.

81. Phylis Rabinaeu, "North American Anthropology at the Field Museum of Natural History," *American Indian Art* 6 (autumn 1981):31–37, 79.

82. *Accession File* 156, Field Museum of Natural History. See also *Field Columbian Museum Annual Report* (October 1895):50–51.

83. Ibid.

84. Ibid.

85. Keam to Dorsey, March 24, 1900, Field Museum of Natural History.

86. See Zimmer, *Edward E. Ayer,* iii–v; Orton, *Records of California Men,* 122; and Miller, *California Column in New Mexico,* 8, 34.

87. *Accession File* 222, Field Museum of Natural History. See also *Field Columbian Museum Annual Report* (October 1895):50–51.

88. *Accession File* 223, Field Museum of Natural History. See also *Field Columbian Museum Annual Report* (October 1895):50–51; *Field Columbian Museum Annual Report* (October 1899):378.

89. *Accession File* 748, Field Museum of Natural History.

90. *Accession File* 223; Field Museum of Natural History. See also *Field Columbian Museum Annual Report* (October 1895):50–51; Keam to Ayer, June 12, 1895. Keam to Skiff, October 27, 1897; and Keam to Dr. O. C. Farrington, April 9, 1904, all in Field Museum of Natural History.

91. Dorsey to Keam, January 20, 1899, Field Museum of Natural History.

92. Stewart Culin, *Games of the North American Indians* (originally published as an Annual Report for the Bureau of American Ethnology [1902–1903] (New York: Dover, 1975), 96, 162, 190, 346, 349, 357, 358, 363, 367, 390, 391, 635, 680, 716, 796, 807.

93. For the development of kachina dolls, see Frederick J. Dockstader, *The Kachina and the White Man: The Influences of White Culture on the Hopi*

Kachina Cult (Albuquerque: University of New Mexico Press, 1985); and Robert Breunig and Michael Lomatuway'ma, "Kachina Dolls," *Plateau* 54 (1983):3–32.

94. Green, *Cushing,* 140.

95. Keam to Matthews, May 5, 1897, *Washington Matthews Papers.* The publication was clearly Matthews, *Navaho Legends,* Memoirs of the American Folklore Society, no. 5 (Boston, Mass.: Houghton Mifflin, 1897). In Stephen's correspondence with Jesse Walter Fewkes, 1891–1894, *SI, NAA,* MS #4408(4), he constantly complains about his informants, obstructionist elders, and his difficulty in translating the arcane Hopi ceremonial language into English. See also Stephen, *Hopi Journal, of A. M. Stephen* (New York: AMS Press, 1969), 146. "Müsh' ñinovi made claim to the two wooden figurines (Alawi'saka, A'losaka) taken from the Hao' o shrine in the cliff just under the ruin Awa' tovi, on its east side, by T. V. K. [Thomas Varker Keam], in 1881"; and J. Walter Fewkes, "The A'losaka Cult of the Hopi Indians," *American Anthropologist* 1 (1899):522–44.

96. Fewkes, *Designs on Prehistoric Hopi Pottery,* 116, and Wade and McChesney, *Lost Expedition,* 6.

97. Green, *Cushing,* 305; 311.

98. Green, *Cushing,* 312–14. In Bourke to Cushing, November 25, 1882, and in Green, *Cushing,* 250–51, Bourke implies some sort of questionable relationship between Keam and James Stevenson of the Bureau of American Ethnology. However, Green's conclusion in Green, *Cushing,* 402–3, n. 30, that Stevenson was selling collections to Keam is backward. Keam had access to all of the Hopi crafts he wanted and had no reason to buy them from Stevenson, whose access was limited. More than likely Keam was giving Stevenson some sort of kickback on collections Stevenson bought for the bureau.

99. According to Webb and Weinstein, *Dwellers at the Source,* Vroman saw his first Snake Dance in 1895. From 1897 to 1904 he was at Hopi either for the Snake Dance or the Flute Ceremony. His photos of the Snake Dance also capture the tourists at the dance. See photos #67, 93; #68, 94; #71, 96; and #77, 100.

100. Whiteley, *Deliberate Acts,* 84.

101. For Voth's publications and his work with Dorsey, see Laird, *Hopi Bibliography.*

102. Among the thousands of photographs of the Snake Dance showing the invasion of tourists to the area, there are at least two very early motion films of the dance: Thomas Edison's 1898 "Snake Dance at Oraibi" (Webb and Weinstein, *Dwellers at the Source,* 20), and William E. Kopplin [advertising executive for the Santa Fe Railroad], "Walpi," 1912 (McLuhan, *Dream Tracks,* 131–42). The Wetherills at Oljato, the Days at Canyon de Chelly, and Lorenzo Hubbell at Ganado and Oraibi also conducted tours of the Snake Dance.

CHAPTER EIGHT

1. Among the Hopi, identity is defined primarily by one's village of birth. Secondarily, identity is to one's mesa. Consequently, those Hopi who live in Oraibi are referred to (by themselves as well as others in the nineteenth and twentieth centuries) as "Oraibis."

2. Thomas Donaldson, *Moqui Pueblo Indians of Arizona and Pueblo Indians of New Mexico: Extra Census Bulletin* (Washington, D.C.: U.S. Census Printing Office, 1893), 25–36 (hereafter cited as Donaldson, *Moqui Pueblo Indians*). This is also covered in Harry C. James, *Pages from Hopi History* (Tucson: University of Arizona Press, 1974), 85–116 (hereafter cited as James, *Hopi History*).

3. Donaldson, *Moqui Pueblo Indians,* 33–34. See also Raymond E. Lindgren, "A Dairy of Kit Carson's Navajo Campaign," *New Mexico Historical Review* 21 (July 1946):226–46.

4. Wallace Stegner, *Beyond the Hundredth Meridian: John Wesley Powell and the Second Opening of the West* (Lincoln: University of Nebraska Press, 1982), 133–36. See also Don D. Fowler and Catherine S. Fowler, "John Wesley Powell, Anthropologist," *Utah Historical Quarterly* 37 (spring 1969):152–72.

5. Charles S. Peterson, "The Hopis and the Mormons, 1858–1873," *Utah Historical Quarterly* 39 (spring 1971):180–81. See also Ira Judd, "Tuba City: Mormon Settlement," *Arizoniana* (spring 1969):37–42; James H. McClintock, *Mormon Settlement in Arizona* (Tucson: Univerity of Arizona, 1985).

6. Donaldson, *Moqui Pueblo Indians,* 36.

7. Ibid.

8. Commissioner of Indian Affairs, *Annual Report,* 1880, 3; and Donaldson, *Moqui Pueblo Indians,* 36.

9. Sheldon Jackson to Commissioner of Indian Affairs, April 24, 1880, *LR*.

10. Stephen C. McCluskey, "Evangelists, Educators, and Ethnographers and the Establishment of the Hopi Reservation," *Journal of Arizona History* 21 (winter 1980):369 (hereafter cited as McCluskey, "Establishment of the Hopi Reservation").

11. Ibid., 369–72. McCluskey also notes that in 1880 the administration of the Presbyterian missions was divided between the Presbyterian Foreign Missions Board, which would still control the appointment of agents for the Indians for which it was responsible, and the Presbyterian Home Missions Board, which was more responsive to those non-Indian Presbyterians living on the frontier (366–67).

12. Ibid., 372, 378.

13. Keam was not licensed to trade at Hopi until 1889, seven years after the reservation was created. Application for Appointment, Trader, July 29, 1889, *LR* #19540.

14. McCluskey, "Establishment of the Hopi Reservation," 380; Volney H. Jones, "The Establishment of the Hopi Reservation and Some Later Developments Concerning Hopi Lands," *Plateau* 23 (October 1950): 22. There was no treaty with the Hopis, as treaties had been discontinued in 1871; instead President Chester A. Arthur signed an executive order creating the Hopi Reserveation on December 16, 1882:

> It is hereby ordered that the tract of country in the Territory of Arizona, lying and being within the following-described boundaries, viz., beginning on the one hundred and tenth degree of longitude west from Greenwich, at a point 36° 30″ north, thence due west to the one hundred and eleventh degree of longitude west, thence due south to a point of longitude 35° 30″ north, thence due east to the one hundred and tenth degree of longitude, and thence due north to the place of beginning be, and the same is hereby, withdrawn from settlement and sale, and set apart for the use and occupancy of the Moqui and such other Indians as the Secretary of the Interior may see fit to settle thereon.

That the Hopi reservation has been described as a protective measure against encroaching non-Hopis is apparently not quite correct, because neither Sullivan nor Fleming mention encroaching Navajos or

Mormons or the need to set aside a reservation for the Hopis in their annual reports to the commissioner. The language of the executive order is precise, although the clause setting aside the land for the Hopis "and such other Indians" has created much discussion and furor since December 16, 1882. Moencopi, the Hopi village to the west, was not incorporated into the executive order reservation.

15. McCluskey, "Establishment of the Hopi Reservation," 382.

16. Fleming to Commissioner, February 1, 1883, *Special Files.*

17. Fleming to Commissioner, February 1, 1883, *Special Files;* Fleming to Commissioner, February 14, 1883, *Special Files.*

18. Keam's Fair View Post as well as the ranches of Anson Damon and Samuel Day in the Cienega Amarilla, near present-day St. Michaels, Arizona, were jeopardized when the Navajo Reservation was extended by executive order in 1880. Keam sold his post to Walter Fales, while Damon and Day waited for government action. Others, like the Barth brothers of St. Johns, Arizona, "parleyed their lands and water claims, which could have been no more than squatter's rights . . . into payments estimated at $19,000 from the Mormons when they settled there after 1879." Peterson, "Homestead and Farm," 19. Keam's possessory rights to Keams Canyon came to him because he occupied the land. In 1886, the 50th Congress appropriated $10,000 to the secretary of interior to pay off settlers' claims to land that became part of the Navajo Reservation in 1886. "Payment to Settlers on Lands Included in the Navajo Reservation," 50th Cong. sess. 1, ch. 503, 1888.

19. Fleming to Commissioner, February 14, 1883, *Special Files.*

20. Martin to Oury, January 31, 1883, *Special Files.*

21. Blake to Langdon, April 5, 1883, and Langdon to Secretary of Interior, May 1, 1883, *Special Files.* Like the agents before him, Fleming blamed disgruntled former agency employees for this problem. He identified the authors as E. S. Merritt and Jeremiah Sullivan, the former agency teacher and physician, respectively. According to Fleming, neither Merritt nor Sullivan knew anything about the circumstances of the construction and payment for the building, and neither of them had any real knowledge regarding the sale of the building to Keam. He reported that when he got to the agency, Taylor was living in one house and constructing another, both built by the Home Mission Board.

22. Fleming to Commissioner of Indian Affairs, July 6, 1883, *Special*

Files; Commissioner of Indian Affairs, *Annual Report,* 5; Bourke, *Snake-Dance of the Moquis,* 95; and Green, *Cushing,* 313, Alexander Stephen tells Cushing that "since you were here we have transmuted the parson's dwelling."

23. Prucha, *Great Father,* 610. See also ibid., 609–736.

24. Keam to Secretary of the Interior Teller, June 5, 1884, *LR* #11520, *McNitt Collection.* This letter concludes "with kind regards to yourself and family." This is covered in McNitt, *Indian Traders,* 181–85. See also Bowman to Commissioner, July 3, 1884, *LR* #12891; Bowman to Commissioner, July 12, 1884, *LR* #13544; Story of Tug-i-yezzy, July 12, 1884, *LR* #14012; Bowman to Commissioner, August 8, 1884, *LR* #15296; Secretary of War to Secretary of Interior, September 19, 1884, *LR* #18284; and Lt H. P. Kingsbyry to Post Adjutant Fort Wingate, September 1, 1884, *LR* #18284, all *McNitt Collection.* Based on his information, Keam determined the approximate location of the Walcott's murder to have been about forty-five miles north of Keams Canyon, and McNally's to have been thirty to thirty-five miles northwest of Walcott's death site. He reported this to Burton in Bowman to Commissioner, August 8, 1884, *LR* #15296, *McNitt Collection.*

25. Keam to Marshall, May 31, 1884, *LR,* #11520 *McNitt Collection.*

26. Keam to Teller, June 5, 1884, *LR,* #11520 *McNitt Collection.*

27. Secretary of the Interior to Commissioner, June 17, 1884, *LR* #11520, *McNitt Collection.*

28. Keam to Teller, June 5, 1884, *LR* #11520 *McNitt Collection.*

29. Elmer Ellis, *Henry Moore Teller: Defender of the West* (Caldwell, Idaho: Caxton Printers, 1941), 102, 105–106, 140. Before entering politics, Henry Moore Teller practiced law in Colorado, where he specialized in mining issues.

30. The federal government had recognized the importance of education in dealing with the American Indians since the early days of the republic, and even though provisions for schools and teachers were standard items in treaties, the government had proved inconsistent in its dedication and funding. Following the Civil War, however, Indian education became part of a larger reform movement, which was seen as integral to the ultimate goal of Christianizing and "civilizing" the American Indians. In 1877, Secretary of the Interior Carl Schurz devised a comprehensive Indian education program, and from then on education was of primary concern to the Office of Indian Affairs. See, for example, Prucha, *The Great Father,* 687–715.

31. Keam to Teller, June 5, 1884, *LR* #11520. Keam's actions with regard to the school are covered in McNitt, *Indian Traders,* 194–95.

32. Ibid., and Appropriations in Teller to Senate Appropriations Committee, April 29, 1884, *Special Files.*

33. Commissioner of Indian Affairs, *Annual Report,* 1884, 136–37.

34. Ibid.

35. Bowman to Commissioner, December 27, 1884, *LR* #18899, and Keam to Bowman, September 19, 1884, *LR* #18899, *McNitt Collection.*

36. Bowman to Commissioner, May 10, 1885, *LR* #11195, *McNitt Collection.*

37. Keam to Bowman, May 18, 1885, *LR* #11195, *McNitt Collection.*

38. Commissioner of Indian Affairs, *Annual Report* 1885, 410.

39. Keam to Commissioner, October 9, 1885, *LR* #29840, *McNitt Collection.*

40. Ibid.

41. Commissioner to Keam, December 18, 1885, Office of Indian Affairs, Letter Sent, no number, *McNitt Collection.*

42. Keam to Commissioner, October 9, 1885, and January 2, 1886, *LR* #1622, *McNitt Collection.*

43. Keam to Commissioner, January 2, 1886, *LR* #1622, *McNitt Collection.*

44. Ibid.

45. Ibid.

46. Ibid.

47. Keam to Commissioner, January 2, 1886, *LR* #1622 and #1623. The petition is written in Alexander Stephen's handwriting and "signed" with the clan symbols of twenty village elders.

48. Keam to Commissioner, March 4, 1886, *LR* #7443.

49. Keam to Commissioner, April 16, 1886, *LR* #10370; May 6, 1886, *LR* #12936; July 22, 1886, *LR* #20264; Keam to H. C. Yarrow, August 6, 1886, *LR* #21975; Keam to Commissioner, August 12, 1886, *LR* #22118; October 7, 1886, *LR* #27546; November 11, 1886, *LR* #30772. Keam accepts the deal: Commissioner to Keam, April 26, 1887, *LR* #11079; Keam to Commissioner, May 12, 1887, *LR* #13143; and telegram from Keam to Commissioner, May 16, 1887, *LR* #12656.

50. According to Stephen, *Hopi Journal of A. M. Stephen,* 191, n. 1, only a dozen students remained at the school two weeks after it opened and Keam was on his way to First Mesa to see what the problems were.

51. Keam to Riley, October 6, 1887, *LR* #27568.

52. Ibid.

53. William T. Hagan, *The Indian Rights Association: The Herbert Welsh Years, 1882–1904* (Tucson: University of Arizona Press, 1985), 11–19 (hereafter cited as Hagan, *The Indian Rights Association*). The Indian Rights Association, founded in 1882, was just one of a number of associations founded during the nineteenth century to deal with the "Indian problem." These organizations, such as the National Indian Association (1877–1951) and the Lake Mohonk Conference of the Friends of the Indian (1883–1929), were united in that they were basically reform organizations concerned with civil service reforms, increased funding for Indian education, and passage and implementation of the Dawes Act providing land in severalty for the Indians. See Hagan, *The Indian Rights Association;* Francis Paul Prucha, *Americanizing the American Indians: Writings by the "Friends of the Indian," 1880–1900* (Cambridge, Mass.: Harvard University Press, 1973); and Francis Paul Prucha, *American Indian Policy in Crisis: Christian Reformers and the Indian, 1865–1900* (Norman: University of Oklahoma Press, 1976) (hereafter cited as Prucha, *American Indian Policy*); Robert Winston Mardock, *The Reformers and the American Indian* (Columbia: University of Missouri Press, 1971); (hereafter cited as Mardock, *Reformers*); and Armand S. La Potin, ed. *Native American Voluntary Organizations* (New York, N.Y.: Greenwood Press, 1987) (hereafter cited as La Potin, *Voluntary Organizations*).

54. Welsh, *Report of a Visit,* 31–37.

55. Welsh to Keam, December 4, 1888, *LR* #29814.

56. Welsh to Keam, December 6, 1888, and January 28, 1889, Indian Rights Association Papers, Historical Society of Pennsylvania (hereafter cited as *IRAP*).

57. Welsh to Keam, January 25, 1889, *IRAP.*

58. Keam to Commissioner, November 11, 1886, *LR* #30772, *McNitt Collection;* Mrs. [Matilda Coxe] Stevenson, "An Arizona School Site," *Lend a Hand* (February 1886), 121.

59. Keam to Welsh, March 6, 1889, and January 31, 1889, *IRAP.*

60. Keam to Commissioner, May 10, 1888, *LR* #7206; Keam to Welsh, November 24, 1888, *IRAP;* and Welsh to Commissioner, December 4, 1888, *LR* #29814 with note: "comm says——make recommendation for appropriation for purchase of Keams Cañon, much as was done last year."

61. Keam to Commissioner, July 7, 1889, *LR* #17854; and "Deed to US for property known as Keams Cañon, Arizona," July 13, 1889, *LR* #18665. The details in Bailey, "Thomas Varker Keam," that Keam sold his trading post at Fort Defiance for a school and that he received $1,500 for his canyon post are inaccurate in light of this information.

62. Keam to Welsh, March 6, 1889, *IRAP.*

63. "Payment to Settlers on Lands Included in the Navajo Reservation," 50th Congr. session 1, ch. 503, 1888.

64. Peterson, "Homestead and Farm," 15–22.

65. Desert Land Act (19 Stat 377), 1877. The act says that any citizen of requisite age who may be entitled to be a citizen can file on land not to exceed one section of land for 25¢ per acre. His declaration must be filed and water must be conducted to the land within three years. Land does not need to be located on surveyed land. Within three years of filing and proof to register and payment of fees, a patent shall be issued. However, Keam's claim was dismissed. E. Burgess, Registrar U.S. Land Office, Prescott, Arizona, to Keam, August 23, 1887, *LR* #29814. He wrote Keam: "you will have to wait for Government survey, as no provision has been made for Special Survey of Desert Land."

66. This is the present-day location of McGee's and Sons Trading Post, Keams Canyon, Arizona.

67. Keam to Commissioner, February 28, 1890, *LR* #7781.

68. Application for Appointment, Trader, July 29, 1889, *LR* #19540.

69. Keam to Commissioner, July 31, 1890, *LR* #24197.

70. The following reconstruction shows the extent of Keam's cattle-raising operation. Between 1889 and 1901, Keam delivered beef to the Hopi and Navajo Agencies in the following amounts:

Year		Weight (lbs) (beef unless noted)
1889	Hopi Agency	3634
1890	Hopi Agency	5299
1891	Hopi Agency	20,273

1892	Hopi Agency	10,421	
1893	Hopi Agency	23,814	
1894	Hopi Agency	25,060	
1895	Hopi Agency	24,900	
1896	Hopi Agency	32,344	
1897	Hopi Agency	14,912	
	Navajo Agency	9556	
	Hopi Agency	57.5	(mutton)
	Navajo Agency	20,440	(hay)
	Navajo Agency	17,520	(oats)
1898	Hopi Agency	3429	
	Navajo Agency	50,344	
	Navajo Agency	30,000	(hay)
	Navajo Agency	16,000	(oats)
	Navajo Agency	8000	(corn)
1899	Hopi Agency	3674	
	Navajo Agency	22,443	
1900	Hopi Agency	31,248	
1901	Hopi Agency	19,637	

The table above is based on the following: *1889: LR,* #21977, 27312, 27313, 27993, 29605, 31134, 31912, 33582, 35556, 36808, 881; *1890: LR* #10145, 21776, 11891, 16037, 16037, 16719, 17278, 17857, 19390, 34250, 34247, 34246, 34248, 34249; *1891: LR,* #1831, 1803, 2730, 4677, 5567, 6610, 7530, 8497, 9565, 10461, 11321, 11320, 12032, 14093, 14860, 15738, 16893, 18504, 18503, 19255, 19254, 20901, 21963, 22609, 24286, 25416, 26542, 711; *1892: LR,* #27147, 34567, 36058, 41280, 43731, 476; *1893: LR,* #5102, 8832, 12185, 17323, 20791, 24435, 47090, 47089, 592; *1894: LR,* #5560, 5592, 9477, 12792, 17834, 21557, 27486, 40716, 49039, 39160, 1738; *1895: LR,* #6914, 11050, 16076, 20176, 24940, 28330, 33315, 46235, 50804, 976; *1896: LR,* #5506, 10388, 13494, 16123, 22346, 22678, 39172, 42491, 46221, 487; *1897: LR,* #5123, 9306, 13254, 18426, 18426, 22987, 26299, 31101, 49874, 13607, 53648, 4405, 4407, 4406; *1898: LR,* #8851, 12151, 16914, 23022, 28240, 31613, 35024, 35025, 35026, 46369, 54627, 52632, 57189, 1231, 1230; *1899: LR,* #7690, 12952, 22124, 22839, 29611, 31737, 48017, 54409, 54410,

58936, 1322, 1323; *1900: LR,* #7936, 7937, 11976, 11729, 11730, 22510, 27986, 28338, 30350, 49594, 49595, 50758, 50759, 61968, 3001; *1901: LR,* #10381, 14925, 19375, 26036, 31348, 36409.

71. Commissioner of Indian Affairs, *Annual Report,* 1880, 285–86; 1881, 338–39; 1882, 373–74; 1883, 323–24. For contracting in general, see Leonard J. Arrington, *The Changing Economic Structure of the Mountain West, 1850–1900* (Logan: Utah State University Press, 1963); Gerald B. Nash, "Bureaucracy and Reform in the West: Notes on the Influence of a Neglected Interest Group," *Western Historical Quarterly* 2 (1971):295–305; and Frazer, *Forts and Supplies,* 186–89.

72. Like so much of Keam's business, his ranching business is vague. That he was ranching near Dilkon, see Keam to Welsh, November 24, 1880, and July 12, 1888, *IRAP;* he had a one-half interest in "Tobin Ranch" [location unknown] with Lorenzo Hubbell according to Keam to Hubbell, August 19, 1903, in Hubbell Working Papers. The Dilkon ranch was of questionable legality at least to Skes Clansey Begay. See for example, Skes Clansey Begay Affidavit, April 5, 1892, *LR* #13373. Begay, the son of Ganado Mucho, suggests that Keam was in Washington D.C. to "take my place away from me." The area Begay referred to was "about ten miles beyond the reservation line, west from here [Fort Defiance] and south from Keams Canyon, fifty miles south from Keams Canyon." This would place it about where Dilkon is. Begay believed Keam was doing this because "some friends, white men, living near the place told me. They have told me so almost every day when I have seen them, for about a month." The ranching aspect of trading/ranching has not been examined in the literature on traders; however, see Peterson, "Homestead and Farm," 22–28; Bourke, *Snake-Dance of the Moquis,* 67, 70. For many Arizona traders on and near the reservations, ranging cattle was a significantly important aspect of their Indian trade business.

73. Keam's correspondence with Welsh covers the years 1888 to 1896, *IRAP.*

74. Keam to Welsh, October 25, 1888, *IRAP.*

75. Welsh to Keam, November 14, 1888, *IRAP.*

76. Ibid.

77. Ibid.

78. Keam to Welsh, November 24, and December 1, 1888, *IRAP.*

79. Keam to Welsh, December 1, 1888, *IRAP.*

80. Ibid.

81. Keam to Welsh, October 23, 1890, *IRAP.*

82. Keam to Commissioner of Indian Affairs, January 8, 1891, *LR* #1756.

83. Keam to Welsh, December 26, 1894, *LR* #535; and Keam to Welsh, December 26, 1894, *LR* #183.

84. Hopi prophecy told the people to expect the return of the Hopis' benevolent white brother, the *bahana,* who would come to them from the east. Since the arrival of Americans, Hopis have debated whether or not this was the bahana of prophecy. See for example, Nequatewa, *Truth of a Hopi,* 50, and 128–29, n. 31. See also Richard O. Clemmer, *Continuity of Hopi Culture Change* (Ramona, Calif.: Acoma Books, 1978); and Gordon V. Krutz, "The Native's Point of View as an Important Factor in Understading the Dynamics of the Oraibi Split," *Ethnohistory* 20 (1973):79–89.

85. Mrs. Minne Vandever, "An Arizona Letter," *Indians' Friends* (September 1890); James, *Hopi History,* 111; Edmund Nequatewa, *Truth of a Hopi,* 131; Yava, *Big Falling Snow,* 161–64; Peter M. Whiteley, *Deliberate Acts: Changing Hopi Culture through the Oraibia Split* (Tucson: University of Arizona Press, 1988), 72 (hereafter cited as Whiteley, *Deliberate Acts*).

86. Yava, *Big Falling Snow,* 164.

87. Ibid.

88. Ibid. 161–64.

89. Keam to Commissioner, July 24, 1890, *LR* #23269.

90. Ibid.

91. Donaldson, *Moqui Pueblo Indians,* 51.

92. Ibid., 52.

93. Ibid., 54.

94. Ibid., 56.

95. Frederick E. Hoxie, "Redefining Indian Education: Thomas J. Morgan's Program in Disarray," *Arizona and the West* 24 (spring 1982):5–18. See also David Wallace Adams, "Schooling the Hopi: Federal Indian policy Writ Small, 1887–1917," *Pacific Historical Review* 48 (August 1979):335–56.

96. Donaldson, *Moqui Pueblo Indians,* 57.

97. Ibid.

98. Loololma's complaints are in Donaldson, *Moqui Pueblo Indians,* 57–58; Yava, *Big Falling Snow,* 111–13; Nequatewa, *Truth of a Hopi,* 60–68, and 130, n. 41; and Mischa Titiev, "A Historic Figure Writ Small," *Michigan Alumnus Quarterly Review* 62 (August 1956):325–30; but see Whiteley, *Deliberate Acts,* for a more in-depth, and accurate, understanding of the complexity of Loololma's problems at Oraibi. Collins's report on these events in Commissioner of Indian Affairs, *Annual Report,* 1891, 552–53.

99. Donaldson, *Moqui Pueblo Indians,* 57.

100. Ibid., 58.

101. Ibid., 59.

102. Ibid.

103. Ibid., 59–60.

104. Ibid., 59.

105. Ibid., 59–60.

106. Ibid., 59. Enforcement of mandatory attendance policies is still a common topic of conversation among adults of this generation of children. Each has his or her own story of the frightening experience of being torn out of a mother's arms to be taken to Keams Canyon school, or later to boarding schools at Albuquerque, Phoenix, or Riverside, California. For example, see Helen Sekaquaptewa, *Me and Mine: The Life Story of Helen Sekaquaptewa as Told to Louise Udall* (Tucson: University of Arizona Press, 1985), 91–93 (hereafter cited as Sekaquaptewa, *Me and Mine);* and Polingasi Qoyawayma, *No Turning Back: A Hopi Woman's Struggle to Live in Two Worlds* (Albuquerque: University of New Mexico Press, 1964), 17–26 (hereafter cited as Qoyawayma, *No Turning Back).*

107. Donaldson, *Moqui Pueblo Indians,* 60.

108. Whiteley, *Deliberate Acts,* 79.

109. Mischa Titiev, *Old Oraibi: A Study of the Hopi Indians of Third Mesa,* Papers of the Peabody Museum of Archaeology and Ethnology, Harvard University, vol. 22 (Cambridge, Mass.: Peabody Museum, 1944), 77 (hereafter cited as Titiev, *Old Oraibi);* J. Walter Fewkes, "Oraibi in 1890" in "Contributions to Hopi History," Elsie Clews Parsons, ed., *American Anthropologist* 24, (July-September 1922):275–77 (hereafter cited as Fewkes, "Oraibi in 1890"). See also Whiteley, *Deliberate Acts;* Nequatewa, *Truth of a Hopi,* 60–77, and 131–33, n. 47–54; and Yava,

Big Falling Snow, 111–17. See also Fewkes to Hemenway, July 2, 1891, in Wade and McChesney, *Lost Expedition,* 5–6; and "Moqui Disturbances," *The New New York Times,* July 9, 1891; James, *Hopi History,* 117–22.

110. Keam to Welsh, July 17, 1891, *IRAP.*

111. Two companies of soldiers were from the Second Cavalry, Fort Wingate, and two companies were from the Tenth Cavalry at Fort Apache, according to General McCook in Donaldson, *Moqui Pueblo Indians,* 38.

112. Donaldson, *Moqui Pueblo Indians,* 92. The recipient of this report is unknown. It does not appear to have been written to the commissioner, as it was not located in the Office of Indian Affairs Letters Received, nor was it written to Herbert Welsh.

113. Of the nine hostiles, four were released in early 1892; the remaining five, late in 1892. See Whiteley, *Deliberate Acts,* 79.

114. A year and a half later, however, two companies were sent to Oraibi to arrest more "hostiles." These men were imprisoned at Alcatraz Island. The split at Oraibi is also a popular topic of conversation among many older people at Third Mesa. The event has been variously explained. For a traditional American interpretation see Titiev, *Old Oraibi,* and Fewkes, "Oraibi in 1890." But see also the Hopis' accounts of the split, because they suggest entirely different forces at work. Nequatewa, *Truth of a Hopi,* 60–77, and 131–33, n. 47–54; Yava, *Big Falling Snow,* 111–17; Sekaquaptewa, *Me and Mine;* and Qoyawayma, *No Turning Back.* Whiteley's interpretation and analysis in *Deliberate Acts* is based on Hopis' versions of the split, as well as an analysis of the religious and political powers at work. The "official" report is in Commissioner of Indian Affairs, 1895, 96.

115. Stephen, *Hopi Journal,* 491.

116. Like many California Column Volunteer veterans and many traders in northeastern Arizona, Thomas Keam had a long-time interest and investment in mining. As a young man, while employed at the Fort Defiance Agency, Keam was involved in the "diamond fever" sweeping the Southwest in 1872. According to the Santa Fe newspaper, the *New Mexican* (December 3, 1872), one Mr. Buckley, "an agent of the 'Pacific Ruby and Diamond Company' bought stones of a jeweler in Denver as he went back to San Francisco; and when here, he brought back one or more of them and represented them as coming from 'the diamond fields of Arizona.' . . . One stone was shown to a gentleman in this town, which Mr. Buckley called a sapphire. . . . 'Among the [Mr. Buckley's] lot is a ruby found by . . . [Keam] not far from Fort Defiance, for which he has refused one thousand dollars cash.' Mr. Keam refused the offer but let Mr. Buckley have the stone with the understanding that whatever it might prove to be worth, should be sent him. Mr. Keam stated to parties now in this city that it was only a garnet, and gave the parties another, which he said was like the first only smaller . . . [Mr. Keam said;] 'All he knew about diamonds in Arizona was what others said and that he never found any.' Three weeks later, in a letter to the editor, Keam wrote to deny that he had said anything about diamonds in Arizona; of the stone entrusted to Buckley, he said the stones "were supposed to be rubies, and I have not heard it contradicted yet. They were certainly different than any garnets I have ever seen. I do not profess to be a judge of precious stones, but firmly believe, when fairly prospected, the country in this vicinity will produce gems of far greater value than any that have been taken from here yet." (*New Mexican,* December 17, 1872). Both clippings are in Carl Hayden Biographical Files, Arizona Historical Society, Tempe, Arizona. See J. I. Merritt, "Clarence King, Adventerous Geologist," *American West* 19 (July-August 1982): 50–58 for King's experiences during the diamond hoax; and Asbury Harpending, *The Great Diamond Hoax and Other Stirring Incidents in the Life of Asbury Harpending* (Norman: University of Oklahoma Press, 1958). Keam's mining interests are covered in McNitt, *Indian Traders,* 198–99. In early 1883, Keam; Alexander Stephen; Thomas A. McElmell, Keam's friend from Philadelphia; and A. J. Johnson filed on a claim in then Yavapai County, Arizona. The location was described as being "45 miles N.W. from Moen Kopi *[sic],* and about 30 miles S.S.W. from Navajo Mountain," *LR* #38857, August 2, 1900. They worked the mine, whose location was often called and cited on maps as the Keams District, for several years. It is uncertain whether they made any money from it. Stephen's constant complaints about being broke and in debt would suggest that the payoff was slim at best. However, for Keam at least, the hope that mines represented remained alive. Later, Keam had mining interests in the Carizzo Mountains north of Fort Defiance on the Navajo Reservation. Keam to Commissioner, June 6, 1901, *LR*

#31219; and Keam to Commissioner October 11, 1903, *LR* #65919, and October 14, 1903, *LR* #66275.

With the exception of his beef contracting receipts in the archives of the Indian Office, Keam's business records have not been located. It is likely, given the size of his estate and his tendencies, that his business interests were more complex than I have suggested.

CHAPTER NINE

1. See Laird, *Hopi Bibliography.*

2. Peter M. Whiteley, *Deliberate Acts,* 102.

3. Commissioner of Indian Affairs, *Annual Report,* 1902, 153.

4. Whiteley, *Deliberate Acts,* 83–86; and James, *Hopi History,* 147–58.

5. Whiteley, *Deliberate Acts,* 80–81; James, *Hopi History,* 113.

6. James, *Hopi History,* 114.

7. Ibid.

8. Leo Crane, "Memorandum History of the Moqui Indian Reservation and Schools, 1886–1906," Manuscript Collection, MS #135-3-4C, Museum of Northern Arizona, Flagstaff, 16 (hereafter cited as Crane, "Moqui History").

9. Godfrey Sykes, *A Westerly Trend* (Tucson: Arizona Historical Society and the University of Arizona Press, 1984), 229 (hereafter cited as Sykes, *A Westerly Trend*). See also Susan Lowell and Diane Boyer, "Trading Post Honeymoon: The 1895 Diary of Emma Walmisley Sykes," *Journal of Arizona History* (winter 1989):417–44.

10. Yava, *Big Falling Snow,* 122.

11. Sykes, *A Westerly Trend,* 229.

12. Twenty-four United States Statutes 388–91. See D. S. Otis, *The Dawes Act and the Allotment of Indian Lands* (Norman: University of Oklahoma Press, 1973); Wilcomb E. Washburn, *The Assault on Indian Tribalism: The General Alottment Law (Dawes Act) of 1887* (Philadelphia, Pa.: Lippencott, 1975).

13. Prucha. *The Great Father,* 666–71.

14. James, *Hopi History,* 114.

15. Earnest Beaglehole, *Notes on Hopi Economic Life,* Yale University Publications in Anthropology, no. 15 (New Haven: Yale University Press, 1937), 14–18; and Gordon B. Page, "Hopi Land Patterns," *Plateau* 13 (October 1940):29–36.

16. James Mooney, an anthropologist at the Bureau of American Ethnology, visited Hopi in 1893. According to Alexander Stephen, he and Mooney got along quite well. Stephen referred to him as a "bona fide student and close observer." See L. G. Moses, *The Indian Man: A Biography of James Mooney* (Urbana: University of Illinois Press, 1984).

17. Whiteley, *Deliberate Acts,* 81.

18. Phillips to Commissioner, November 6, 1893, *LR* #41495, and November 15, 1893, *LR* #42859.

19. As quoted in Yava, *Big Falling Snow,* 165–66.

20. Keam to Welsh, April 5, 1894, *IRAP.*

21. Welsh to Keam, April 13, 1894, *IRAP.*

22. Keam to Welsh, April 26, 1894, *IRAP.*

23. Welsh to Keam, May 5, 1894, *IRAP.*

24. Commissioner of Indian Affairs, *Annual Report,* 1894, 20. See Hagan, *The Indian Rights Association,* 67–68.

25. Commissioner of Indian Affairs, *Annual Report,* 1894, 100.

26. Whiteley, *Deliberate Acts,* 81.

27. Keam to Welsh, December 24, 1894, *IRAP.*

28. Keam to Commissioner of Indian Affairs, December 3, 1894, *LR* #48373.

29. Commissioner of Indian Affairs, *Annual Report,* 1895, 96.

30. Keam to Commissioner, December 26, 1894, *LR* #183.

31. Keam to Welsh, December 26, 1894, *IRAP.*

32. Keam to Williams, February 25, 1895, *LR* #17454; and Williams to Commissioner, April 15, 1895, *LR* #17454. The plans were not carried forward with haste and the school was finally opened in 1899 after the government paid Williams's widow $250 for the buildings. The relationship between Keam and the Williams family is interesting. It appears that, at this time, Keam and Jonathan Williams were on at least amicable terms. Bill Williams, Jonathan Williams's son, clerked for Keam at the canyon from September 18, 1893, to April 10, 1899, when Keam fired him for accepting pawn, which was a violation of the commissioner's orders. E. H. Plummer to Commissioner, September 18, 1893, *LR* #35851; and Keam to Commissioner, April 10, 1899, *LR* #18083. In 1901, Williams was called upon to attest to Keam's trading practices and morality. In an interview with trader and writer Gladwell "Toney" Richardson, in 1929, Williams did not mention having worked for Keam. Bill Williams's daughter has written about his life and experiences at Keams Canyon, see Yost, *Diamonds in the Desert*, 1–89. For Blue Canyon, see Mildred Hooper and C. R. Hooper, "Blue Canyon: Wonderland in Stone," *Outdoor Arizona* (September 1978):17, 31, 36; and Elizabeth Rigby, "Blue Canyon," Arizona Highways (August 1959): 30–39.

33. Commissioner of Indian Affairs, *Annual Report,* 1899, 383.

34. Whiteley, *Deliberate Acts,* 90–91.

35. Keam to Fewkes, Febraury 22, 1899, *LR* #10160. Fewkes sent Keam's letter on to the commissioner with the note: "Enclosed please find a copy of a letter received today regarding small pox at Moqui." This is hardly the sympathy and forcefulness that Keam expected. Fewkes had left Hopi in the fall of 1898 because of the epidemic. However, other reasons for his leaving are given in Edmund Nequatewa, "Dr. Fewkes and Masauwu: The Birth of a Legend," *Museum of Northern Arizona Notes,* vol. 11 (August 1938):25–27. Apparently Nequatewa had reason to believe that smallpox was not the reason Fewkes left the area.

36. Crane, "Moqui History," 15.

37. This is compiled from Donaldson, *Moqui Pueblo Indians,* and Fewkes, "Oraibi in 1890." See also Victor Mindeleff, "A Study of Pueblo Architecture, Tusayan and Cibola," Bureau of American Ethnology, 8th Annual Report (1886–1887), 3–228.

38. The programs to assimilate the Indians are in Hagan, *The Indian Rights Association;* Prucha, *Americanizing the American Indians;* Prucha, *American Indian Policy in Crisis;* Mardock, *The Reformers and the American Indian;* La Potin, *Native American Voluntary Organizations;* Fritz, *The Movement for Indian Civilization;* and Keller, *American Protestantism.*

39. Springs are in Commissioner of Indian Affairs, *Annual Report,* 1891, 552; and 1892, 652. Wells are in Commissioner of Indian Affairs, *Annual Report,* 1894, 367; and 1895, 359. Dams are in Crane, "Moqui History," 13. Houses are in Commissioner of Indian Affairs, *Annual Report,* 1891, 552; 1892, 652; 1893, 997; and 1895, 367. The model farm is in Commissioner of Indian Affairs, *Annual Report,* 1891, 211.

40. Commissioner of Indian Affairs, *Annual Report,* 1893, 997. Even today, with villages below all mesas, the people who live in them (permanently or semipermanently) still maintain strong religious ties to their village on the mesa. Indeed one's village defines oneself.

41. Commissioner of Indian Affairs, *Annual Report,* 1894, 100.

42. Whitleley, *Deliberate Acts,* 90–91.

43. According to Crane, "Moqui History," 15, the estimated attendance in 1900 was: Keams Canyon, 195; Polacca, 45; Second Mesa School, 84; and Oraibi, 164.

44. Whiteley, *Deliberate Acts,* 90.

45. Prucha, *The Great Father,* 764. Herbert Welsh of the Indian Rights Association regained some of the influence he had lost during the Cleveland Administration, and the Indian Rights Association supported the ideals behind Jones's policies. See Hagan, *The Indian Rights Association,* 190–208.

46. Keam was elected to First Class membership in the Pennsylvania Commandery of the Military Order of the Loyal Legion of the United States, November 12, 1890, insignia number 8232, War Library and Museum of the Military Order of the Loyal Legion of the United States, Philadelphia, Pennsylvania. The Loyal Legion was the first veteran's association founded following the Civil War. It was composed of socially prominent, politically active Republicans. Membership was initially restricted to officers, but not enlisted men (although this was extended some years later.)

47. See Prucha, *The Great Father,* 760–63.

48. Commissioner of Indian Affairs, *Annual Report,* 1900, 5–13; 1901, 1–13; 1902, 1–16.

49. Commissioner of Indian Affairs, *Annual Report,* 1900, 13.

50. Ibid.

51. E. Snyder to Mr. Murphy, July 29, 1897, and Murphy to Commissioner, August 4, 1897, *LR* #32782.

52. Whiteley, *Deliberate Acts,* 91.

53. Keam to Commissioner, November 12, 1899, *LR* #51866.

54. Keam to Commissioner, September 27, 1899, *LR* #46087.

55. Hopi school employees to Commissioner, March 20, 1900, *LR* #17495.

56. Keam to Commissioner, September 27, 1899, *LR* #46087.

57. Keam to Commissioner, February 17, 1901, *LR* #11107.

58. Barnes to Burton, February 14, 1901, in Burton to Commissioner, February 26, 1901, *LR* #15463, and *LR* #28094.

59. Hopi school teachers to Senator W. B. Allison, February 18, 1901,

LR #13211; to William A. Jones, February 18, 1901, *LR* #11918; to Senator M. A. Hanna, February 18, 1901, *LR* #12978; to Representative W. P. Hepburn, February 18, 1901, *LR* #12354; to Vice President of the United States Theodore Roosevelt, February 23, 1901, *LR* #13012; to Senator H. M. Teller, February 18, 1901, *LR* #12885; to M. S. Quay, February 18, 1901, *LR* #11436; and W. E. Meagley to Commissioner, March 3, 1901, *LR* #15648 (hereafter cited as "Teachers' Petitions").

60. Burton and others to Commissioner, February 18, 1901, *LR* #15463.

61. Voorhies to Williams, February 9, 1901, *LR* #11428.

62. Keam to Commissioner, February 19, 1901, *LR* #11428.

63. Williams to Voorhies, February 21, 1901, *LR* #12916.

64. Teachers' Petitions.

65. Ibid.

66. Burton to Commissioner, February 26, 1901, *LR* #15463.

67. Burton to Commissioner, November 7, 1901, Hopi Agency letterpress book, Departmental Letters, August 6, 1901, to March 26, 1902.

68. Ibid.

69. Wright to Commissioner, October 1, 1901, *LR* #56305.

70. Ibid.

71. Ibid.

72. Ibid.

73. Burton to Commissioner, November 30, 1901, Hopi Agency letterpress book, Departmental Letters, August 6, 1901, to March 26, 1902.

74. Keam to Commissioner, October 25, 1900, *LR* #53764.

75. Keam to Commissioner, June 7, 1901, *LR* #30772.

76. Keam to Washington Matthews, August 8, 1896, *Washington Matthews Papers.* Keam said he had been in Philadelphia for an operation. The problem was diagnosed as hydrocele, an infalmation of the scrotum. He was sick again in the spring of 1901, this time with pneumonia. Keam to Matthews, March 31, 1901, *Washington Matthews Papers.*

77. Keam to Hubbell, May 6, 1902, *Hubbell Papers,* Microfilm of Hubbell Correspondence, Hubbell Trading Post, National Historic Site, Ganado, Arizona (hereafter cited as *Hubbell Papers); and* Keam to Culin, May 6, 1902, The Brooklyn Museum Archives, Culin Archival Collection, General Correspondence 2.1 [10]: Keam-Lanman, Brooklyn, New York (hereafter cited as Brooklyn Museum, *Culin Collection).*

78. Commissioner of Indian Affairs, *Annual Report,* 1902, p. 13.

79. Ibid., 14.

80. Educators and reformers hoped that "returned students," those who had been educated in off-reservation schools such as Carlisle Indian School, would serve as examples to their tribes of the benefits of education and the "civilized" life-style. However, they were usually disappointed in the power of returned students to change their families, as they constantly bemoaned the fact that once returned they "reverted" to their old ways, because they were living alone in their civilization. See Wilbert H. Ahern, "The Returned Students: Hampton Institute and Its Indian Alumni, 1873–1893," *Journal of Ethnic Studies* 10 (1983):101–24; Christine Bolt, *American Indian Policy and American Reform: Case Studies of the Campaign to Assimilate the American Indian* (London: Allen and Unwin, 1987).

81. Commissioner of Indian Affairs, *Annual Report,* 1902, 13.

82. Ibid., 14.

83. Whiteley, *Deliberate Acts,* 94.

84. Charles F. Lummis, *Bullying the Moqui* (Prescott, Ariz.: Prescott College Press, 1968). This is a compilation of Lummis's *Out West* magazine articles about the Burton controversy. See also James, *Hopi History,* 123–29.

85. Commissioner of Indian Affairs, *Annual Report,* 1902, 14.

86. Ibid., 14.

87. Ibid.

88. Ibid.

89. Keam to Commissioner, March 27, 1902, *LR* #19096.

90. Keam to Culin, May 6, 1902, Brooklyn Museum, *Culin Collection.*

91. Burton's actions following the short-hair order became even more dictatorial, and he and the teachers at Oraibi Day School perpetuated and exacerbated the factionalization at Oraibi. Because the events had received considerable publicity, especially in Lummis's *Out West* magazine, several teachers were removed and Burton was reprimanded and eventually transferred to another school in 1904.

92. Keam to Matthews, April 16, 1904, *Washington Matthews Papers.*

93. [Bullen?] to Culin, March 23, 1905, Brooklyn Museum, *Culin Collection.*

94. Benjamin F. Miller, M.D. and Claire Brackman Keane, R.N., B.S., *Encyclopedia and Dictionary of Medicine and Nursing* (Philadelphia, Pa.: W. B. Saunders, 1972), 47–48.

95. Keam to Hubbell, May 14, 1902, *Hubbell Papers.* No bill of sale has been recovered from this transaction, so the price paid is unknown. Lorenzo Hubbell Jr. was the operator and putative owner from 1902 to 1918. Van Valkenburg, "Tom Keam," 12, says Keam sold out in 1903.

96. Keam to Hubbell, June 22, 1902, *Hubbell Papers.*

97. James, *Hopi History,* 115.

98. McNitt, *Indian Traders,* 199.

CHAPTER TEN

1. Keam to Culin, September 4, 1902; Keam to Culin, September 13, 1902, Brooklyn Museum, *Culin Collection.*

2. Ibid.

3. Keam to Culin, June 5, 1902, Brooklyn Museum, *Culin Collection.*

4. Keam to Hubbell, May 6, 1902, *Hubbell Papers;* and Keam to Culin, May 5, 1902, Brooklyn Museum, *Culin Collection.*

5. Keam to Hubbell, November 26, 1901, and September 22, 1903, *Hubbell Papers;* and Keam to Commissioner, June 6, 1901, *LR* #31219.

6. Keam to Culin, April 12, 1902; April 17, 1902; August 31, 1903; September 22, 1903; October 4, 1902; October 6, 1903; October 20, 1903; October 29, 1903, December 21, 1903; December 24, 1903; and May 19, 1904, Brooklyn Museum, *Culin Collection.*

7. Keam to Culin, March 18, 1902; April 2, 1902; April 12, 1902; June 15, 1902; August 21, 1902; September 4, 1902; October 22, 1902; September 22, 1903; October 4, 1903; October 20, 1903, Brooklyn Museum, *Culin Collection.* On June 15, 1902, Culin offered Keam $250 for Stephen's papers. Keam declined, saying that the offer was about half what Keam had expected. However, the deal was not finalized, until Keam received $500 more on September 22, 1903. In a letter dated October 22, 1902, Keam told Culin that he intended to go see Stephen's family in Scotland, give them money for the manuscript, and tell them of Culin's plans to publish the material. Keam's contributions to Culin's manuscript on Indian games is discussed in Keam to Culin, April 12, 1902; May 6, 1902; November 9, 1903; and November 28, 1903, Brooklyn Museum, *Culin Collection.* Culin's games manuscript was originally published as an Annual Report for the Bureau of American Ethnology (1902–1903), 29–846. See also Stewart Culin, *Games of the*

North American Indians (New York, N.Y.: Dover, 1975), 96, 162, 190, 346, 349, 357, 358, 363, 367, 390, 391, 635, 680, 716, 796, 807.

8. Keam to Culin, April 2, 1902, and April 17, 1902, Brooklyn Museum, *Culin Collection.*

9. Keam to Hubbell, September 19, 1902; September 30, 1902; October 11, 1902; October 17, 1902, *Hubbell Papers.*

10. Keam to Hubbell, October 17, 1902, and Keam to Culin, October 22, 1902, Brooklyn Museum, *Culin Collection.* Keam sent Culin his address, writing the he could write in care of his cousin F. W. Wing, 27 St. Peter's Square, Ravenscourt Park, London, W. England.

11. Keam to Matthews, April 16, 1904, *Washington Matthews Papers.*

12. Les Douch, curator emeritus, Royal Institute of Cornwall, to author, January 24, 1986.

13. Keam to Culin, December 28, 1902, Note at N[athaniel] B. Bullen, The Parade, Truro, Brookleyn Museum, *Culin Collection.*

14. Les Douch, curator emeritus, Royal Institute of Cornwall, to author, January 24, 1986.

15. Ibid., and *The London Times,* Saturday April 5, 1905. According to her son, Tómas, Asdzáán Libá died in 1939. Van Valkenburg, "Interview."

16. Keam to Hubbell, November 26, 1901, and September 22, 1903, *Hubbell Papers;* and Keam to Commissioner, June 6, 1901, *LR* #31219.

17. Keam to Culin, December 24, 1903, and January 8, 1904, Brooklyn Museum, *Culin Collection.*

18. Keam to Culin, April 12, 1902; April 17, 1902; August 31, 1903; September 22, 1903; October 4, 1902; October 6, 1903; October 20, 1903; October 29, 1903; December 21, 1903; December 24, 1903; May 19, 1904, Brooklyn Museum, *Culin Collection.*

19. Keam to Culin, September 22, 1903, Brooklyn Museum, *Culin Collection.*

20. Keam to Culin, May 19, 1904, Brooklyn Museum, *Culin Collection.*

21. Matthews died April 25, 1905. See Halpern, Holt, and McGreevy, *Guide to the Microfilm Collection of the Washington Matthews Papers,* 8; James Mooney, "In Memoriam: Washington Matthews," *American Anthropologist* 7 (1905):514–23.

22. Stephen died in April 1894. He had been ill throughout the winter, struggling, as he claimed, with Maasauw, or tuberculosis, as Elsie

Clews Parsons believed. Keam removed him from First Mesa to his house at Keams Canyon, where he died. Keam to Fewkes, April 12, 1894, *SI, NAA,* MS #4408(4); and Keam to Herbert Welsh, April 26, 1894, *IRAP.* See also Stephen, *Hopi Journal,* xxi. Keam erected a monument to Stephen, which stands across the highway from the present-day trading post. The carved sandstone marker reads: "In Memory of A. M. Stephen who departed this life Apr 18, 1894. Aged 49 years. A Life Dedicated to science and good deeds."

23. Porter, *Bourke,* 306. On hearing of Bourke's death, Keam wrote Washington Matthews saying that Bourke was a "whole souled man." Keam to Matthews, January 27, 1897, *Washington Matthews Papers.*

24. Green, *Cushing,* 26; H. F. C. Ten Kate, "Frank Hamilton Cushing," *American Anthropologist* 2 (1900):768–71.

25. Keam to Matthews, April 16, 1904, *Washington Matthews Papers.*

26. This is an incomplete, black-edged notecard. Based on the return address (7 the Parade, Truro), the author is probably Bullen to Culin, March 23, 1905, The Brooklyn Museum Archives, Culin Archival Collection, General Correspondence 2.1 [4]: Brown-Crane.

27. *Royal Gazette,* December 1, 1904; Les Douch, Curator Emeritus, Royal Institute of Cornwall, to author, January 24, 1986.

28. *Philadelphia Times,* December 4, 1904.

29. Stewart Culin, "Thomas Varker Keam," *American Anthropologist* 7 (1905):171–72.

30. Ibid.

31. "In Memorium—Thomas Varker Keam," Military Order of the Loyal Legion of the United States, Commandery of the State of Philadelphia, circ. #13, series of 1905. War Library and Museum of the Loyal Legion of the United States, Philadelphia.

32. "Thomas Varker Keam" *Journal of Royal Institution of Cornwall,* 17 (1907):170–71.

BIBLIOGRAPHY

PUBLIC DOCUMENTS

American Indian Correspondence: The Presbyterian Historical Society Collection of Missionaries' Letters, 1833–1893. Philadelphia, Pa.

Bernalillo County Court Records, District Court Dockett, New Mexico Records and Archives Center. Santa Fe, N. Mex.

Brooklyn Museum Archives, Culin Archival Collection, General Correspondence 2.1[10]:Keam-Lanman.

Brooklyn Museum Archives, Culin Archival Collection, General Correspondence 2.1[4]:Brown-Crane.

California Volunteers Collection, California State Archives. Sacramento, Calif.

Field Museum of Natural History Archives and Department of Anthropology Archives. Chicago, Ill.

Carl Hayden Biographical Files, Thomas Keam Collection, Arizona Historical Society, Tempe, Ariz.

Carl Hayden Biographical Files, Van Valkenburg Collection, Arizona Historical Society, Tempe, Ariz.

Hemenway Family Papers. Philips Library, Peabody Museum of Salem. Salem, Mass.

Hubbell Papers, Microfilm of Hubbell Correspondence, Hubbell Trading Post, National Historic Site. Ganado, Ariz.

Indian Rights Association Papers, Historical Society of Pennsylvania. Philadelphia, Pa.

McNitt Collection, New Mexico Records Center and Archives, Santa Fe, N. Mex.

Smithsonian Institution, National Anthropological Archives, Letters Received, 1879–1888. Washington, D.C.

———. National Anthropological Archives, manuscript and pamphlet file 833. Washington, D.C.

———. National Anthropological Archives, manuscript 4408 (4), Correspondence of Alexander Stephen to J. W. Fewkes, 1891–1894. Washington, D.C.

United States National Archives, Department of the Interior, Appointment Papers: New Mexico, Navajo Agency, K-Z, 1872–1903, microcopy M750. Washington, D.C.

———. Letters Received, Office of Indian Affairs, 1849–1880, New Mexico Superintendency, microcopy 234. Washington, D.C.

———. Letters Received, Office of Indian Affairs, 1880–present, Thomas Keam correspondence. Record Group 75. Washington, D.C.

———. Office of Indian Affairs, Commissioner of Indian Affairs, Annual Reports. Washington, D.C.

———. Special Files, 1800–1904, file 267: "Charges against Agent Fleming, Moqui Pueblo Agency, 1882–1883. "Washington, D.C.

———. War Department, Compiled Service Records of Volunteer Union Soldiers Who Served in Organizations from the Territory, microcopy 427. Washington, D.C.

Washington Matthews Papers, Wheelwright Museum of the American Indian. Santa Fe, N. Mex.

UNPUBLISHED WORKS

Boyd, Dennis. "Trading and Weaving: An American-Navajo Symbiosis. "Master's thesis, University of Colorado, 1979.

Brandes, Raymond Stewart. "Frank Hamilton Cushing: Pioneer Americanist." Ph.D. diss., University of Arizona, 1965.

Crane, Leo. "Memorandum History of the Moqui Indian Reservation and Schools, 1886–1906. "Museum of Northern Arizona Manuscript Collection, manuscript 135-3-4C. Flagstaff, Ariz.

Darnell, Regna. "The Development of American Anthropology, 1879–1920: From the Bureau of American Ethnology to Franz Boas." Ph.D. diss., University of Pennsylvania, 1969.

Kelley, Klara B. "Commercial Networks in the Navajo-Hopi-Zuni Region." Ph.D. diss., University of New Mexico, 1977.

Moore, William Haas. "Chiefs, Agents, and Soldiers: Conflict on the Navajo Frontier, 1868–1880." Ph.D. diss., Northern Arizona University, 1988.

Peterson, Charles S. "Homestead and Farm: A History of Farming at the Hubbell Trading Post National Historic Site." A Report Prepared for Southwest Parks and Monuments Association, 1986.

Wade, Edwin Lewis. "The History of the Southwest Indian Ethnic Art Market." Ph.D. diss., University of Washington, 1976.

BOOKS

Adams, William Y. *Shonto: A Study of the Role of the Trader in a Modern Navaho Community.* Bureau of American Ethnology Bulletin 188. Washington, D.C., 1963.

Allen, Laura Graves. *Contemporary Hopi Pottery.* Flagstaff: Museum of Northern Arizona, 1984.

Amsden, Charles Avery. *Navaho Weaving: Its Technic and History.* Glorieta, N. Mex: Rio Grande Press, 1934.

Arrington, Leonard. *The Changing Economic Structure of the Mountain West, 1850–1900.* Logan: Utah State University, 1963.

Bailey, Garrick, and Roberta Bailey. *A History of the Navajos: The Reservation Years.* Santa Fe, N. Mex. School of American Research, 1986.

Bailey, Lynn R. *Bosque Redondo: An American Concentration Camp.* Pasadena, Calif.: Socio-Technical Books, 1970.

————. *Indian Slave Trade in the Southwest: A Study of Slave-Taking and the Traffic in Indian Captives.* Los Angeles, Calif.: Westernlore, 1966.

Barnes, William C. *Arizona Place Names.* University of Arizona Bulletin 6, no. 1. Tucson: University of Arizona, 1935.

Beadle, J. H. *Western Wilds.* Cincinatti, Ohio: Jones Brothers, 1877.

Beaglehole, Ernest. *Notes on Hopi Economic Life.* Yale University Publications in Anthroplogy. no. 15. New Haven: Yale University Press, 1937.

Bender, Norman J., *Missionaries, Outlaws, and Indians: Thomas F. Ealy at Lincoln and Zuni, 1878–1881.* Albuquerque: University of New Mexico Press, 1984.

————. *New Hope for the Indians: The Grant Peace Policy and the Navajos in the 1870s.* Albuquerque: University of New Mexico Press, 1989.

Benedict, Burton. *The Anthropology of the World's Fairs: San Francisco's*

Panama Pacific International Exposition, 1915. New York, N.Y.: Scholar's Press, 1983.

Berry, Claude. *Cornwall.* London: Robert Hale Limited, 1949.

Betjeman, Robert, and A. L. Rouse. *Victorian and Edwardian Cornwall— From Old Photographs.* London: B. T. Batsford, 1974.

Billington, Ray Allen. *Land of Savagery Land of Promise: The European Image of the American Frontier in the Nineteenth Century.* Norman: University of Oklahoma Press, 1981.

Bird, Shelia. *Bygone Truro.* Chichester, Sussex: Phillimore, 1981.

Bolt, Christine. *American Indian Policy and American Reform: Case Studies of the Campaign to Assimilate the American Indian.* London: Allen and Unwin, 1987.

Bourke, John G. *Snake-Dance of the Moqui.* Tucson: University of Arizona Press, 1984.

Boyce, George A. *When the Navajos Had Too Many Sheep: The 1940s.* San Francisco, Calif.: The Indian Historian Press, 1974.

Bradfield, Richard Maitland. *The Changing Patterns of Hopi Agriculture.* Royal Anthrolpological Institute Occassional Paper, no. 30. London: Royal Anthropological Institute, 1971.

Briggs, Asa. *A Social History of England.* New York, NY: Viking, 1983.

Brew, John O. *One Hundred Years of Anthropology.* Cambridge, Mass.: Harvard University Press, 1968.

Brugge, David M. and J. Lee Correll. *The Story of the Navajo Treaties.* Window Rock, Ariz.: Navajo Parks and Recreation, 1971.

Burg, David F. *Chicago's White City of 1893.* Lexington: University Press of Kentucky, 1976.

Clemmer, Richard O. *Continuities of Hopi Culture Change.* Ramona, Calif.: Acoma Books, 1978.

Cohen, Felix S. *Handbook of Federal Indian Law.* Albuquerque: University of New Mexico, 1942.

Cole, Douglas. *Captured Heritage: The Scramble for Northwest Coast Artifacts.* Seattle: University of Washington, 1985.

Coleman, Michael C. *Presbyterian Missionary Attitudes toward American Indians, 1837–1893.* Jackson: University of Mississippi Press, 1985.

Colton, Ray C. *The Civil War in the Western Territories.* Norman: University of Oklahoma Press, 1959.

Conkling, Roscoe P., and Margaret B. Conkling. *The Overland Butterfield Mail, 1857–1869.* 3 vols. Glendale, Calif.: Arthur H. Clark, 1947.

Correll, J. Lee. *Through White Men's Eyes: A Contribution to Navajo History, Chronological Record of the Navajo People from Earliest Times to the Treaty of June 1, 1868.* 6 vols. Window Rock, Ariz.: Navajo Heritage Center, 1979.

Correll, J. Lee, Editha L. Wilson, and David M. Brugge. *Navajo Bibliography with Subject Index.* Rev. ed. 2 vols. Research Report 2. Window Rock, Ariz.: Navajo Tribe, 1969.

————. *Navajo Bibliography with Subject Index.* Rev. ed. 2 vols. Research Report 2, supplement. Window Rock, Ariz. Navajo Tribe, 1973.

Culin, Stewart. *Games of the North American Indian.* New York, N.Y.: Dover, 1975.

Cushing, Frank Hamilton. *Zuni: Selected Writings of Frank Hamilton Cushing.* Edited, with an Introduction, by Jesse Green. Lincoln: University of Nebraska Press, 1979.

Danziger, Edmund Jefferson, Jr. *Indians and Bureaucrats: Administering the Reservation Policy During the Civil War.* Urbana: University of Illinois Press, 1974.

Darnell, Regna, ed. *Readings in the History of Anthropology.* New York, N.Y.: Harper and Row, 1974.

Dawson, Lawrence E., Vera-Mae Fredrickson, and Nelson H. H. Graburn. *Traditions in Transition: Culture Contact and Material Change.* Berkeley, Calif.: Lowie Museum of Anthropology, 1974.

Di Peso, Charles C. *Casas Grandes: A Fallen Trading Center of the Grand Chichimeca,* 8 vols. Edited by Gloria J. Fenner., Flagstaff, Ariz.: Northland Press, 1974.

Dockstader, Frederick J. *The Kachina and the White Man: The Influences of White Culture on the Hopi Kachina Cult.* Albuquerque: University of New Mexico Press, 1985.

Donaldson, Thomas. *Moqui Pueblo Indians of Arizona.* Extra Census Bulletin 11. Washington, D.C.: Census Printing Office, 1893.

Du Maurier, Daphne. *Vanishing Cornwall.* New York, N.Y.: Penguin Books, 1967.

Eggan, Fred. *Social Organization of the Western Pueblos.* Chicago, Ill.: University of Chicago Press, 1950.

Ellis, Elmer. *Henry Moore Teller: Defender of the West.* Caldwell, Idaho: Caxton Printers, 1941.

Ellis, Richard N. *General Pope and United States Indian Policy.* Albuquerque: University of New Mexico Press, 1970.

Faunce, Hilda. *Desert Wife.* New York, NY: Little Brown and Company, 1928. Reprint, Lincoln: University of Nebraska Press, 1981.

Fewkes, J. Walter. *Designs on Prehistoric Hopi Pottery.* New York, N.Y.: Dover, 1973.

Flack, J. Kirkpatrick. *Desideratum in Washington: The Intellectual Community in the Capital City, 1870–1900.* Cambridge, Mass.: Schenkman Publishing, 1975.

Fletcher, Maurine S. *The Wetherills of Mesa Verde: Autobiography of Benjamin Alfred Wetherill.* London: Associated University Presses, 1977.

Forbes, Jack. *Apache, Navaho, and Spaniard.* Norman: University of Oklahoma Press, 1960.

Frazer, Robert W. *Forts and Supplies: The Role of the Army in the Economy of the Southwest, 1846–1861.* Albuquerque: University of New Mexico Press, 1983.

———. *Forts of the West: Military Forts and Presidios and Posts Commonly Called Forts West of the Mississippi River to 1898.* Norman: University of Oklahoma Press, 1965.

Frink, Maurice. *Fort Defiance and the Navajos.* Boulder, Colo.: Pruett Publishing, 1968.

Fritz, Henry E. *The Movement for Indian Civilization, 1860–1890.* Philadelphia: University of Pennsylvania Press, 1963.

Getzwiller, Steve. *The Fine Art of Navajo Weaving.* Tucson, Ariz.: Ray Manley, 1984.

Gillmor, Frances, and Louisa Wade Wetherill. *Traders to the Navajos: The Story of the Wetherills of Kayenta.* Albuquerque: University of New Mexico Press, 1953.

Goodwin, Grenville. *The Social Organization of Western Apache.* Tucson: University of Arizona Press, 1969.

Graburn, Nelson H. H., ed. *Ethnic and Tourist Arts: Cultural Expressions from the Fourth World.* Berkeley: University of California Press, 1976.

Grant, Campbell. *Canyon de Chelly: Its People and Rock Art.* Tucson: University of Arizona Press, 1978.

Green, Jesse, ed. *Cushing at Zuni: The Correspondence and Journals of Frank Hamilton Cushing, 1879–1884.* Albuquerque: University of New Mexico Press, 1990.

Greenhalgh, Paul. *Ephemeral Vistas: The Expositions Universelles, Great Exhibitions and World's Fairs, 1851–1939.* Manchester, U.K.: Manchester University Press, 1988.

Guild, Thelma, and Harvey L. Carter. *Kit Carson: A Pattern for Heroes.* Lincoln: University of Nebraska Press, 1984.

Hack, John T. *The Changing Physical Environment of the Hopi Indians of Arizona.* Papers of the Peabody Museum of American Archaeology and Ethnology, vol. 35. Cambridge, Mass.: Peabody Museum of American Archaeology and Ethnology, 1942.

Hagan, William T. *The Indian Rights Association: The Herbert Welsh Years, 1882–1904.* Tucson: University of Arizona Press, 1985.

Hall, Thomas D. *Social Change in the Southwest, 1350–1880.* Lawrence: University of Kansas Press, 1989.

Halpern, Katherine Spencer, Mary E. Holt, and Susan Brown McGreevy. *Guide to the Microfilm Edition of the Washington Matthews Papers, The Wheelwright Museum of the American Indian, Santa Fe, New Mexico.* Albuquerque: University of New Mexico Press, 1985.

Hannum, Alberta. *Paint the Wind.* New York, N.Y.: Viking, 1958.

———. *Spin a Silver Dollar.* New York, N.Y.: Ballantine, 1944.

Harpending, Asbury. *The Great Diamond Hoax and Other Stirring Incidents in the Life of Asbury Harpending.* Norman: University of Oklahoma Press, 1958.

Harris, Marvin. *The Rise of Anthropological Theory: A History of the Theories of Culture.* New York, N.Y.: Thomas V. Crowell, 1968.

Hegeman, Elizabeth Compton. *Navaho Trading Days.* Albuquerque: University of New Mexico Press, 1963.

Heitman, Francis B. *Historical Register and Dictionary of the United States Army, From its Organization, September 29, 1789, to March 2, 1903.* 2 vols. Urbana: University of Illinois Press, 1965.

Helm, June, ed. *Pioneers in American Anthropology: The Uses of Biography.* Seattle: University of Washington Press, 1966.

Hill, Willard Williams. *Navaho Warfare.* Yale University Publications in Anthropology, no 5. New Haven: Yale University Press, 1936.

Hinsley, Curtis M. *Savages and Scientists: The Smithsonian Institution and the Development of American Anthropology, 1846–1910.* Washington, D.C.: Smithsonian Institution, 1981.

Hoopes, Alban W. *Indian Affairs and Their Administration, with Special Reference to the West, 1849–1860.* New York, N.Y.: Kraus Reprint, 1972.

Horsman, Reginald. *Expansion and American Indian Policy, 1783–1812.* East Lansing: Michigan State University Press, 1967.

Hough, Walter. *The Moki Snake Dance.* Santa Fe, N. Mex.: Passenger Department of the Santa Fe [Railroad], 1901.

Howard, Oliver O. *My Life and Experiences among Our Hostile Indians.* Introduction by Robert M. Utley. New York, N.Y.: DaCapo, 1972.

Hunt, Aurora. *Major General James Henry Carleton, 1814–1873: Western Frontier Dragoon.* Glendale, Calif.: Arthur H. Clark, 1958.

Iverson, Peter. *The Navajos: A Critical Bibliography.* The Newberry Library Center for the History of American Indian Bibliographic Series. Bloomington: Indiana University Press, 1976.

————. *The Navajo Nation.* Albuquerque: University of New Mexico, 1983.

James, George Wharton. *Indian Blankets and Their Makers.* Chicago, IL: A. C. McClung, 1914. Reprint, New York, N.Y.: Dover, 1974.

James, Harry C. *Pages from Hopi History.* Tucson: University of Arizona Press, 1974.

Jenkin, A. K. Hamilton. *Cornwall and Its People.* London: J. M. Dent and Sons, 1945.

Johns, Elizabeth A. H. *Storms Brewed in Other Men's Worlds: The Confrontation of Indians, Spanish, and French in the Southwest, 1540–1795.* College Station: Texas A & M University Press, 1975.

Josephy, Alvin M. Jr. *The Civil War in the West.* New York, N.Y.: Alfred A. Knopf, 1991.

Judd, Neil. *The Bureau of American Ethnology: A Partial History.* Norman: University of Oklahoma Press, 1968.

Kaemelein, Wilma R. *An Inventory of Southwestern American Indian Specimens in European Museums.* Tucson: University of Arizona Press, 1967.

Kappler, Charles J., comp. *Indian Affairs: Laws and Treaties.* 5 vols. New York, N.Y.: AMS Press, 1971.

Kaufman, Alice, and Christopher Selser. *The Navajo Weaving Tradition, 1650 to the Present.* New York, N.Y.: E. P. Dutton, 1985.

Kavena, Juanita Tiger. *Hopi Cookery*. Tucson: University of Arizona Press, 1980.

Kay-Robinson, Denys. *Devon and Cornwall*. New York, N.Y.: Arco Publishing Company, 1977.

Keleher, William A. *Turmoil in New Mexico, 1846–1868*. Santa Fe, N. Mex.: Rydal Press, 1952.

Keller, Robert H. Jr. *American Protestantism and United States Indian Policy, 1869–1882*. Lincoln: University of Nebraska Press, 1983.

Kelley, Klara B. *Navajo Land Use: An Ethnoarchaeological Study*. New York, N.Y.: Academic Press, 1986.

Kelly, Lawrence C. *The Navajo Indians and Federal Indian Policy, 1900–1935*. Tucson: University of Arizona Press, 1968.

———. *Navajo Roundup: Selected Correspondence of Kit Carson's Expedition against the Navajo, 1863–1865*. Boulder, Colo.: Pruett Press, 1970.

Kennedy, Mary Jeanette. *Tales of a Trader's Wife: Life on the Navajo Reservation, 1913–1938*. Albuquerque, N. Mex.: Valliant Co., 1965

———. *The Wind Blows Free*. Albuquerque N. Mex.: Valliant Co., 1970.

Kent, Kate Peck. *Navajo Weaving: Three Centuries of Change*. Santa Fe, N. Mex. School of American Reserach, 1985.

Kluckhohn, Clyde, and Dorothea Leighton. *The Navaho*. Rev. ed. Garden City, N.Y.: Natural History Library, 1962.

Kvasnika, Robert M., and Herman J. Viola, eds. *The Commissioners of Indian Affairs, 1824–1977*. Lincoln: University of Nebraska Press, 1979.

Laird, W. David. *Hopi Bibliography: Comprehensive and Annotated*. Tucson: University of Arizona Press, 1977.

Lamar, Howard. *The Trader on the American Frontier: Myth's Victim*. College Station: Texas A & M University Press, 1977.

La Potin, Armand, ed. *Native American Voluntary Organizations*. New York, N.Y.: Greenwood Press, 1987.

Leckie, William H. *The Buffalo Soldiers: A Narrative of the Negro Cavalry in the West*. Norman: University of Oklahoma Press, 1967.

Link, Martin A., ed. *Navajo: A Century of Progress, 1868–1968*. Window Rock, Ariz.: Navajo Tribe, 1968.

Lummis, Charles F. *Bullying the Moqui*. Edited by Robert Easton and Mackenzie Brown. Prescott, Ariz.: Prescott College Press, 1968.

McClintock, James H. *Mormon Settlement in Arizona*. Tucson: University of Arizona Press, 1985.

McGregor, John C. *Southwestern Archaeology*. Urbana: University of Illinois Press, 1965.

McKenna, Peter J., and Scott E. Travis. *Archaeological Investigations at Thunderbird Lodge, Canyon de Chelly, Arizona*. Southwest Cultural Resources Center Professional Papers, no. 20. Santa Fe, N. Mex.: National Park Service, 1989.

McLuhan, T. C. *Dream Tracks: The Railroad and the American Indian, 1890–1930*. New York, N.Y.: Harry N. Abrams, 1985.

McNitt, Frank. *Richard Wetherill: Anasazi*. Albuquerque: University of New Mexico Press, 1957.

————. *The Indian Traders*. Norman: University of Oklahoma Press, 1962.

————. *Navajo Wars: Military Campaigns, Slave Raids, and Reprisals*. Albuquerque: University of New Mexico Press, 1972.

McPherson, Robert S. *The Northern Navajo Frontier, 1860–1900: Expansion through Adversity*. Albuquerque: University of New Mexico Press, 1988.

Mardock, Robert Winston. *The Reformers and the American Indian*. Columbia: University of Missouri Press, 1971.

Mark, Joan. *Four Anthropologists: An American Science in Its Early Years*. New York, N.Y.: Science History, 1980.

Matthews, Washington. *Navaho Legends*. Memoirs of the American Folklore Society, no. 5. Boston, Mass.: Houghton Mifflin, 1897.

Miller, Benjamin F., M.D., and Claire Brackman Keane, R.N., B.S. *Encyclopedic Dictionary of Medicine and Nursing*. Philadelphia, Pa.: W. B. Saunders, 1972.

Miller, Darlis A. *The California Column in New Mexico*. Albuquerque: University of New Mexico Press, 1982.

Montgomery, Ross Gordon, Watson Smith, and John Otis Brew. *Franciscan Awatovi: The Excavation and Conjectural Reconstruction of a Seventeenth Century Spanish Mission Established at a Hopi Indian Town in Northeastern Arizona*. Papers of the Peabody Museum of American Archaeology and Ethnology, vol. 36. Cambridge, Mass.: Peabody Museum of American Archaeology and Ethnology, 1949.

Moore, William Haas. *Chiefs, Agents, and Soldiers: Conflict on the Navajo*

Frontier, 1868–1882. Albuquerque: University of New Mexico Press, 1994.

Morgan, Lewis Henry. *Ancient Society or Researches in the Lines of Human Progress from Savagery through Barbarism to Civilization*. Cambridge, Mass.: Belknap Press of Harvard University, 1964.

Moses, L. G. *The Indian Man: A Biography of James Mooney*. Urbana: University of Illinois Press, 1984.

Murphy, Lawrence R. *Frontier Crusader: William F. M. Arny*. Tucson: University of Arizona Press, 1972.

Nequatewa, Edmund. *Truth of a Hopi*. Flagstaff, Ariz.: Northland Press, 1967.

Newcomb, Franc Johnson. *Navaho Neighbors*. Norman: University of Oklahoma Press, 1966.

Ogle, Ralph Hedrick. *Federal Control of the Western Apaches, 1846–1886*. Albuquerque: University of New Mexico Press, 1970.

Orton, Brigadier-General Richard H. *Records of California Men in the War of the Rebellion, 1861–1867*. Sacramento, Calif.: State Printing, 1890.

Otis, D. S. *The Dawes Act and the Allotment of Indian Lands*. Norman: University of Oklahoma Press, 1973.

Parman, Donald L. *The Navajos and the New Deal*. New Haven, Yale University Press, 1976.

Pearce, Roy Harvey. *The Savages of America: A Study of the Indian and the Idea of Civilization*. Baltimore, Md.: The Johns Hopkins University Press, 1953.

Perry, Richard J. *Western Apache Heritage: People of the Mountain Corridor*. Austin: University of Texas Press, 1991.

Peterson, Alex. *Hopi Pottery Symbols: Based on "Pottery of Tusayan, Catalogue of the Keam Collection by Alexander M. Stephen."* Boulder, Colo.: Johnson Books, 1994.

Peterson, Charles S. *Take Up Your Mission: Mormon Colonizing along the Little Colorado River, 1870–1900*. Tucson: University of Arizona Press, 1973.

Pettis, George Henry. *The California Column*. Historical Society of New Mexico. Santa Fe, N. Mex.: New Mexican Printing, 1908.

Porter, Joseph C. *Paper Medicine Man: John Gregory Bourke and His American West*. Norman: University of Oklahoma Press, 1986.

Priest, Loring B. *Uncle Sam's Step-Children: The Reformation of United States Indian Policy, 1865–1887.* New York, N.Y.: Octagon Books, 1969.

Prucha, Francis Paul. *American Indian Policy in the Formative Years: The Trade and Intercourse Acts, 1790–1834.* Cambridge, Mass.: Harvard University Press, 1962.

———. *A Guide to the Military Posts of the United States, 1789–1895.* Madison: University of Wisconsin Press, 1964.

———. *Americanizing the American Indians: Writings by "Friends of the Indian," 1880–1900.* Cambridge, Mass.: Harvard University Press, 1973.

———. *American Indian Policy in the Crisis: Christian Reformers and the Indian, 1865–1900.* Norman: University of Oklahoma Press, 1976.

———. *The Churches and the Indian Schools, 1888–1912.* Lincoln: University of Nebraska Press, 1979.

———. *The Great Father: The United States Government and the American Indians.* 2 vols. Lincoln: University of Nebraska Press, 1984.

Qoyawayma, Polingasi. *No Turning Back: A Hopi Indian Woman's Struggle to Live in Two Worlds.* Albuquerque: University of New Mexico Press, 1964.

Quaife, Milo Milton, ed. *Kit Carson's Autobiography.* Lincoln: University of Nebraska Press, 1966.

Richardson, Gladwell. *Navajo Trader.* Edited by Philip Reed Rulon. Tucson: University of Arizona Press, 1986.

Reichard, Gladys A. *Social Life of the Navajo Indians with Some Attention to Minor Ceremonies.* New York, N.Y.: Columbia University Press, 1928. Reprint, New York, N.Y.: AMS Press, 1962.

Reid, Badger. *The Great American Fair: The World's Columbian Exposition and American Culture.* Chicago, Ill.: Nelson Hall, 1979.

Riley, Carroll L. *Sixteenth Century Trade in the Greater Southwest.* Mesoamerican Studies, no. 10, University Museum and Art Galleries. Carbondale: Southern Illinois University Press, 1976.

———. *The Frontier People: The Greater Southwest in the Protohistoric Period.* Occassional Paper, no. 1, Center for Archaeological Investigations. Carbondale: Southern Illinois University, 1982.

Riley, Carroll L., and Basil C. Hedrick. *Across the Chichimec Sea: Papers in Honor of J. Charles Kelly.* Carbondale: Southern Illinois University Press, 1978.

Roberts, Willow. *Stokes Carson: Twentieth Century Trading on the Navajo Reservation*. Albuquerque: University of New Mexico Press, 1987.

Roessel, Robert A. *Pictorial History of the Navajo from 1860 to 1910*. Rough Rock, Ariz.: Rough Rock Demonstration School, 1980.

Roessel, Ruth, ed. *Navajo Stories of the Long Walk Period*. Tsaile, Ariz.: Navajo Community College Press, 1973.

Rydell, Robert W. *All the World's a Fair: Visions of Empire at American International Expositions, 1876–1916*. Chicago, Ill.: University of Chicago Press, 1984.

Sabin, Edwin. *Kit Carson Days, 1809–1869*. 2 vols. New York, N.Y.: Press of the Pioneers, 1935.

Schmeckbier, Lawrence F. *The Office of Indian Affairs: Its History, Activities, and Organization*. Baltimore, Md.: The Johns Hopkins University Press, 1927.

Schmedding, Joseph C. *Cowboy and Indian Trader*. Caldwell, Idaho: Caxton Printers, 1951. Reprint, Albuquerque: University of New Mexico Press, 1974.

Sekaquaptewa, Helen. *Me and Mine: The Life of Helen Sekaquaptewa as Told to Louise Udall*. Tucson: University of Arizona Press, 1985.

Sheehan, Bernard. *Seeds of Extinction: Jeffersonian Philanthropy and the American Indian*. Chapel Hill: University of North Carolina Press, 1973.

Simmons, Marc. *Spanish Government in New Mexico*. Albuquerque: University of New Mexico Press, 1968.

Soulsby, Ian. *A History of Cornwall*. Chichester, Sussex: Phillimore, 1986.

Spicer, Edward H. *Cycles of Conquest: The Legacy of Spain, Mexico, and the United States on the Indians of the Southwest, 1533–1960*. Tucson: University of Arizona Press, 1962.

Stegner, Wallace. *Beyond the Hundredth Meridian: John Welsey Powell and the Second Opening of the West*. Lincoln: University of Nebraska Press, 1982.

Stephen, Alexander M. *Hopi Journal of A. M. Stephen*. Edited by Elsie Clews Parsons. New York, N.Y.: AMS Press, 1969.

Stuart, Paul. *The Indian Office: Growth and Development of an American Institution, 1865–1900*. Ann Arbor, Mich.: UMI Research Press, 1978.

Swift, Roy L. *Three Roads to Chihuahua: The Great Wagon Roads That Opened the Southwest, 1823–1883*. Austin, Tex.: Eakin Press, 1988.

Sykes, Godfrey. *A Westerly Trend*. Tucson: Arizona Historical Society and the University of Arizona Press, 1984.

Taylor, Theodore W. *American Indian Policy*. Mt. Airy, Md.: Lomond Publications, 1983.

―――. *The Bureau of Indian Affairs*. Boulder, Colo.: Westview Press, 1984.

Thompson, Gerald. *The Army and the Navajo*. Tucson: University of Arizona Press, 1976.

Thrapp, Dan L. *Victorio and the Mimbres Apaches*. Norman: University of Oklahoma Press, 1974.

Titiev, Mischa. *Old Oraibi: A Study of the Hopi Indians of Third Mesa*. Papers of the Peabody Museum of American Archaeology and Ethnology, vol. 22. Cambridge, Mass.: Peabody Museum of American Archaeology and Ethnology, 1944.

Trafzer, Clifford. *The Kit Carson Campaign: The Last Great Navajo War*. Norman: University of Oklahoma Press, 1982.

Trennert, Robert A., Jr. *Alternative to Extinction: Federal Indian Policy and the Beginnings of the Reservation System, 1846–1851*. Philadelphia, Pa.: Temple University Press, 1975.

Truman, Benjamin C. *History of the World's Fair*. Philadelphia, Pa.: H. W. Kelly Publishing, 1893. Reprint, New York, N.Y.: Arno, 1976.

Turner, Frederick Jackson. *The Character and Influence of the Indian Trade in Wisconsin: A Study of the Trading Post as an Institution*. Edited, with an Introduction, by Davis Harry Miller and William W. Savage Jr. Norman: University of Oklahoma Press, 1977.

Underhill, Ruth. *The Navajos*. Norman: University of Oklahoma Press, 1956.

Utley, Robert M. *Fort Davis National Historic Site, Texas*. National Park Service Handbook Series, no. 38. Washington, D.C.: National Park Service, 1965.

―――. *Frontiersmen in Blue: The United States Army and the Indian, 1848–1865*. New York, N.Y.: McMillan, 1967.

―――. *Frontier Regulars: The United States Army and the Indian, 1866–1891*. New York, N.Y.: McMillan, 1973.

Wade, Edwin L., and Lea McChesney. *America's Great Lost Expedition: The Thomas Keam Collection of Hopi Pottery from the Second Hemenway Expedition, 1890–1894*. Phoenix, Ariz.: Heard Museum, 1980.

————. *Historic Hopi Ceramics: The Thomas V. Keam Collection of the Peabody Museum of Archaeology and Ethnology, Harvard University.* Cambridge, Mass.: Peabody Museum Press, 1981.

War Department. *The War of the Rebellion: A Compilation of the Official Records of the Union and Confederate Armies, 1861–1865.* 70 vols. in 127 parts, plus general index and atlas. Edited by Captain Robert Scott et. al. Washington, D.C.: Government Printing Office, 1880–1901.

Washburn, Wilcomb E. *The Assault on Indian Tribalism: The General Allotment Law (Dawes Act) of 1887.* Philadelphia, Pa.: Lippincott, 1975.

————. *Red Man's Land / White Man's Law: A Study of the Past and Present Status of the American Indian.* New York, N.Y.: Charles Scribner's Sons, 1971.

Webb, William, and Robert A. Weinstein. *Dwellers at the Source: Southwestern Indian Photographs of A. C. Vroman, 1895–1904.* Albuquerque: University of New Mexico Press, 1973.

Weiss, Laurence David. *The Development of Capitalism in the Navajo Nation: A Political Economic History.* Studies in Marxism, vol. 15. Minneapolis, Minn.: MEP Publications, 1984.

Welsh, Herbert. *Report of a Visit to the Navajo, Pueblo, and Hualapais Indians of New Mexico and Arizona.* Philadelphia, Pa.: Indian Rights Association, 1885.

Wheat, Joe Ben. *Patterns and Sources of Navajo Weaving: Harmsen's Western Americana Collection.* Denver, Colo.: The Printing Establishment, 1977.

White, Richard. *The Roots of Dependency: Subsistence, Environment, and Social Change among the Choctaws, Pawnees, and Navajos.* Lincoln: University of Nebraska Press, 1983.

Whiteley, Peter M. *Delibertate Acts: Changing Hopi Culture through the Oraibi Split.* Tucson: University of Arizona Press, 1988.

Wilcox, David R., and W. Bruce Masse, eds. *The Protohistoric Period in the North American Southwest, A.D. 1450–1700.* Anthropological Research Paper, no. 24. Tempe: Arizona State University, 1981.

Wilson, John P. *Fort Sumner, New Mexico.* Museum of New Mexico Monuments Division. Santa Fe: Museum of New Mexico, 1974.

Yava, Albert. *Big Falling Snow: A Tewa-Hopi Indian's Life and Times and the History and Traditions of His People.* Edited and annotated by Harold Courlander. Albuquerque: University of New Mexico Press, 1978.

Yost, Billie Williams. *Bread upon the Sands.* Caldwell, Idaho: Caxton Printers, 1958.

————. *Diamonds in the Desert: The Family History of Bill and Gertie Williams.* Flagstaff, Ariz.: Silver Spruce Publishing, 1987.

Young, Robert W., and William Morgan. *The Navajo Language: A Grammar and Coloquial Dictionary.* Rev. ed. Albuquerque: University of New Mexico Press, 1980.

Zimmer, John Todd. *Catalog of the Edward E. Ayer Ornithological Library.* Field Museum of Natural History Publication, no. 239. Zoological Series, vol. 16. Chicago, Ill.: Field Museum of Natural History, 1926.

ARTICLES

Anonymous. "In Memorium—Thomas Varker Keam," *Military Order of the Loyal Legion of the United States, Commandery of the State of Pennsylvania,* circular #13 (1905).

————. "Thomas Varker Keam." *Journal of the Royal Institution of Cornwall* 17 (1907):170–71.

————. "Colonel Edward E. Ayer." *New Mexico Historical Review* 2 (July 1927):306–7.

Adams, David Wallace. "Schooling of the Hopi: Federal Indian Policy Writ Small, 1887–1917." *Pacific Historical Review* 48 (August 1979):335–56.

Adams, E. Charles, and Deborah Hull. "Prehistoric and Historic Occupation of the Hopi Mesas." Pp. 11–27 in *Hopi Kachinas: Spirit of Life.* Edited by Dorothy K. Washburn. San Francisco: California Academy of Sciences, 1980.

Ahern, Wilbert H. "The Returned Students: Hampton Institute and its Indian Alumni, 1873–1893." *Journal of Ethnic Studies* 10 (1983):101–24.

Allen, Laura Graves. "Navajo Rugs: A Marketing Success." *Designers West* (April 1983):133–38.

Babbitt, James E. "Trading Posts along the Little Colorado." *Plateau* 57 (1986):2–9.

Bailey, Lynn R. "Thomas Varker Keam, Tusayan Trader." *Arizoniana* 2 (winter 1961):15–19.

Bartlett, Katharine. "Spanish Contacts with the Hopi, 1540–1823." *Museum of Northern Arizona Notes* 6 (June 1934):55–59.

Basso, Keith H. "History of Ethnological Research." In *Handbook of North American Indians.* Edited by Alfonso Ortiz. Vol. 9, *Southwest,* edited by William Sturtevant. Washington, D.C.: Government Printing Office, 1979.

Bloom, Lansing B. "Bourke on the Southwest." *New Mexico Historical Review* (1933–1938) 8:1–30; 9:33–77, 159–83, 273–89, 375–435; 10:1–35, 271–322; 11:77–122, 188–207, 217–82; 12:41–77, 337–79; 13:192–238.

Breunig, Robert G., and Michael Lomatuway'ma. "Hopi: Scenes of Everyday Life." *Plateau* 55 (1983):3–32.

———. "Kachina Dolls." *Plateau* 54 (1983):3–32.

Brew, J. O. "Hopi Prehistory and History to 1850." In *Handbook of North American Indians.* Edited by Alfonso Ortiz. Vol. 9, *Southwest,* edited by William Sturtevant. Washington, D.C.: Government Printing Office, 1979.

Brody, J. J. "The Creative Consumer: Survival, Revival and Invention in Southwest Indian Arts." Pp. 70–84 in *Ethnic and Tourist Arts: Cultural Expressions from the Fourth World,* Edited by Nelson Graburn. Berkeley: University of California Press, 1976.

Brown, Mora McManic. "Traders at the Gap." *Desert Magazine* (December 1940):17–20.

Brugge, David M. "Navajo Prehistory and History to 1850." In *Handbook of North American Indians.* Edited by Alfonso Ortiz. Vol. 9, *Southwest,* edited by William Sturtevant. Washington, D.C.: Government Printing Office, 1979.

Burnham, Bruce. "The Traders' Influence on the Weaver." In *Wool on a Small Scale.* Edited by Lyle G. McNeal. Logan: Utah State University Press, 1986.

Collier, Donald C., and Harry Tschopik Jr. "The Role of Museums in American Anthropology." *American Anthropologist* 56 (1954):768–79.

Culin, Stewart V. "Games of the North American Indians." *Bureau of American Ethnology Annual Report* 24 (1907):1–810.

———"Thomas Varker Keam." *American Anthropologist* 7 (January 1905):171–72.

Dexter, Ralph W. "The Role of F. W. Putnam in Founding the Field Museum." *Curator* 8 (1970):21–26.

————. "The Role of F. W. Putnam in Developing Anthropology at the American Museum of Natural History." *Curator* 19 (1976): 303–10.

Dockstader, Frederick J. "Hopi History, 1850–1940." In *Handbook of North American Indians.* Edited by Alfonso Ortiz. Vol. 9, *Southwest,* edited by William Sturtevant. Washington, D.C.: Government Printing Office, 1979.

Ellis, Richard N. "The Humanitarian Soldiers." *Journal of Arizona History* (summer 1969):53–66.

Fewkes, J. Walter. "Death of a Celebrated Hopi." *American Anthropologist* 1 (1899):196–97.

————. "The A'losaka Cult of the Hopi Indians." *American Anthropologist* 1 (1899):522–44.

————. "Two Summer's Work in Pueblo Ruins." *Bureau of American Ethnology Annual Report* 22 (1904):1–196.

————. "Oraibi in 1890." In "Contributions to Hopi History." Edited by Elsie Clews Parsons. *American Anthropologist* 24 (July-September 1922):253–98.

Finch, L. Boyd. "Arizona in Exile: Confederate Schemes to Recapture the Southwest." *Journal of Arizona History* (spring 1992):57–84.

Foster, James Monroe, Jr. "Fort Bascom, New Mexico." *New Mexico Historical Review* 35 (January 1960):30–62.

Fowler, Don D., and Catherine S. Fowler. "John Wesley Powell, Anthropologist." *Utah Historical Quarterly* 37 (spring 1969):152–72.

Frisbie, Theodore J. "The Influence of J. Walter Fewkes on Nampeyo: Fact or Fiction?" Pp. 231–43 in *The Changing Ways of Southwestern Indians: A Historic Perspective.* Edited by Albert H. Schroeder. Glorieta, N. Mex.: Rio Grande Press, 1973.

Griffith, James Seavey. "Kachinas and Masking." In *Handbook of North American Indians.* Edited by Alfonso Ortiz. Vol. 9, Southwest, edited by William Sturtevant. Washington, D.C: Government Printing Office, 1979.

Gunnerson, Dolores A. "The Southern Athabascans: Their Arrival in the Southwest." *El Palacio* 63 (1956):346–65.

Hargrave, Lyndon Lane. "Oraibi: A Brief History of the Oldest Inhabited Town in the United States." *Museum of Northern Arizona Notes* 4 (January 1932): 1–8.

―――. "Shungopovi." *Museum of Northern Arizona Notes* 2 (April 1930):1–4.

Helm, June. "Bilaterality in the Socio-territorial Organization of the Arctic Drainage Dene." *Ethnohistory* 4 (1965):361–85.

Henderson, Esther, and Church Abbott. "Along the Trading Post Trail." *Arizona Highways* (June 1943):12–19, 41–42.

Hill, Williard Williams. "Navaho Trading and Trading Ritual: A Study of Cultural Dynamics." *Southwestern Journal of Anthropology* 4 (1948): 371–96.

Hinsley, Curtis M. Jr. "Anthropology as Science and Politics: The Dilemmas of the Bureau of American Ethnology, 1879–1904." In *The Uses of Anthropology.* Edited by Walter Goldschmidt. Special publication of the American Anthropologist Association, vol. 11 (1979).

―――. "Ethnographic Charisma and Scientific Routine: Cushing and Fewkes in the American Southwest, 1879–1893." In *Observers Observed: Essays on Ethnographic Field Work.* Edited by George W. Stocking Jr. *History of Anthropology* 1 (1983).

―――. "Zunis and Bramins: Cultural Ambivalence in the Gilded Age." In *Romantic Motives: Essays on Anthropological Sensibility.* Edited by George W. Stocking Jr. *History of Anthropology* 6 (1989).

Hodge, Frederick W. "The Name 'Navajo'." *Masterkey* 23 (1949):78.

Holmes, W. H. "The Debasement of Pueblo Art." *American Anthropologist* 2 (1899):320–21.

―――. "Pottery of the Ancient Pueblos." *Bureau of American Ethnology Annual Report* 14 (1882–1883):257–360.

―――. "A Revival of the Ancient Pottery Art." *American Anthropologist* 19 (1917):322–23.

―――. "The World's Fair Congress of Anthropology." *American Anthropologist* (1893):423–34.

Holterman, Jack. "Mission San Bartolome de Xongopavi." *Plateau* 28 (October 1955):29–36.

―――. "The Mission of San Miguel de Oraibi." *Plateau* 32 (October 1959):39–48.

Hooper, Mildred, and C. R. Hooper. "Blue Canyon: Wonderland in Stone." *Outdoor Arizona* (September 1978):17, 31, 36.

Hough, Walter. "A Revival of the Ancient Art." *American Anthropologist* 19 (1917):322–23.

Hoxie, Frederick E. "Redefining Indian Education: Thomas J. Morgan's Program in Disarray." *Arizona and the West* 24 (spring 1982): 5–18.

Huscher, Betty H., and Harold H. Huscher. "Athanaskan Migration via the Intermontane Region." *American Antiquity* 8 (1942):80–88.

Jones, Volney H. "The Establishment of the Hopi Reservation and Some Later Developments Concerning Hopi Lands." *Plateau* 23 (October 1950):29–36.

Judd, Ira. "Tuba City: Mormon Settlement." *Arizoniana* (Spring 1969): 37–42.

Keam, Thomas Varker. "An Indian Snake-Dance." *Chambers's Journal of Popular Literature, Science and Art* 20 (January 13, 1883):14–16.

Kelley, Klara B. "Ethnoarchaeology of Navajo Trading Posts." *Kiva 51* (fall 1985):19–37.

Kelly, Charles. "Graveyard of the Gods." *Desert Magazine* (July 1938): 4–6.

Kelly, Roger, and Albert E. Ward. "Lessons from Zeyouma Trading Post near Flagstaff, Arizona." *Historical Archaeology* vi (1972):65–76.

Kildare, Maurice. "Mr. Arbuckle's Coffee." *True West* (May-June 1965): 16–18, 53–54.

Kirby, Leo P. "A Civil War Experience in California-Arizona History." *Arizoniana* 2 (spring 1961):20–23.

Krutz, Gordon V. "The Native's Point of View as an Important Factor in Understanding the Dynamics of the Oraibi Split." *Ethnohistory* 20 (1973):79–89.

Lindgren, Raymond E. "A Diary of Kit Carson's Navajo Campaign." *New Mexico Historical Review* 21 (July 1946):226–46.

Lowell, Susan, and Diane Boyer. "Trading Post Honeymoon: The 1895 Diary of Emma Walmisley Sykes." *Journal of Arizona History* 30 (winter 1989):417–44.

McCluskey, Stephen C. "Evangelists, Educators, Ethnographers, and the Establishment of the Hopi Reservation." *Journal of Arizona History* 21 (winter 1980):363–90.

McIntire, Elliott G., and Sandra R. Gordon. "Ten Kate's Account of the Walpi Snake Dance, 1883." *Plateau* 41 (summer 1968):27–33.

Mallery, Garrick. "Picture-Writing of the American Indians." *Bureau of American Ethnology Annual Report* 10 (1888–1889):25–822.

Matthews, Washington. "Navajo Weavers." *Bureau of American Ethnology Annual Report* 3 (1881–1882):371–91.

Merritt, J. I. "Clarence King, Adventerous Geologist." *American West* 19 (July-August 1982):50–58.

Mindeleff, Cosmos. "Cliff Ruins of Canyon de Chelly, Arizona." *Bureau of American Ethnology Annual Report* 16 (1894–1895):79–198.

———. "Navaho Houses." *Bureau of American Ethnology Annual Report* 16 (1895–1896):469–517.

Mindeleff, Victor. "A Study of Pueblo Architecture, Tusayan and Cibola." *Bureau of American Ethnology Annual Report* 8 (1886–1887):3–228.

Mooney, James. "The Ghost-Dance Religion and the Sioux Outbreak of 1890." *Bureau of American Ethnology Annual Report* (1892–1893): 653–1136.

———. "In Memoriam: Washington Matthews." *American Anthropologist* 7 (1905):514–23.

Myers, Lee. "The Enigma of Mangas Coloradas' Death." *New Mexico Historical Review* 41 (October 1966):287–304.

———. "Military Establishments in Southwestern New Mexico: Stepping Stones to Settlement." *New Mexico Historical Review* 43 (January 1968):5–48.

Nash, Gerald B. "Bureaucracy and Reform in the West: Notes on the Influence of a Neglected Interest Group." *Western Historical Quarterly* II (1971):295–305.

Nequatewa, Edmund. "Dr. Fewkes and Masauwu: The Birth of a Legend." *Museum of Northern Arizona Notes* 11 (August 1938):25–27.

Olsen, Stanley J., and John Beezley. "Domestic Food Animals from Hubbell Trading Post." *Kiva* 41 (1975):201–6.

Page, Gordon B. "Hopi Land Patterns." *Plateau* 13 (October 1940): 29–36.

Pandey, Triloki Nath. "Anthropologists at Zuni." *Proceedings of the American Philosophical Society* 16 (1972):321–37.

Peterson, Charles S. "The Hopis and the Mormons, 1858–1873." *Utah Historical Quarterly* 39 (spring 1971):179–94.

Plummer, E. H. "The Moqui Indian Snake Dance in Arizona." *Frank Leslie's Popular Monthly* xliv (November 1897):500–505.

Powell, John Wesley. "Annual Report of the Director." *Bureau of American Ethnology Annual Report* 4 (1882–1883); 6 (1884–1885); 7 (1885–1886); 9 (1887–1888); 10 (1888–1889).

Rabineau, Phyllis. "North American Anthropology at the Field Museum of Natural History." *American Indian Art* 6 (autumn 1981):31–37, 79.

Reeve, Frank D. "Federal Indian Policy in New Mexico, 1858–1880." *New Mexico Historical Review* 13 (1938):146–158.

———. "Navaho-Spanish Diplomacy." *New Mexico Historical Review* 35 (1960):200–235.

———. "The Navaho-Spanish Peace: 1720s–1770s." *New Mexico Historical Review* 34 (1959):9–40.

———. "Navaho-Spanish Wars, 1680–1720." *New Mexico Historical Review* 33 (1959):204–31.

———. "Seventeenth Century Navaho-Spanish Relations." *New Mexico Historical Review* 32 (1957):36–52.

Richardson, Gladwell "Toney." "Bonanza in the Ghost Post." *Desert Magazine* (July 1966):12–15.

———. "Pioneer Trader to the Navajo." *Desert Magazine* (December 1948):26–29.

Rigby, Elizabeth. "Blue Canyon." *Arizona Highways* (August 1959): 30–39.

Rister, C. C. "Harmful Practices of Indian Traders in the Southwest, 1865–1876." *New Mexico Historical Review* 6 (1931):231–48.

Roessel, Robert. "Navajo History, 1850–1923." In *Handbook of North American Indians.* Edited by Alfonso Ortiz. Vol. 10, *Southwest,* edited by William Sturtevant. Washington, D.C.: Government Printing Office, 1983.

Sando, Joe S. "The Pueblo Revolt." In *Handbook of North American Indians.* Edited by Alfonso Ortiz. Vol. 9, Southwest, edited by William Sturtevant. Washington, D.C.: Government Printing Office, 1979.

Schroeder, Albert H. "History of Archaeological Research." In *Handbook of North American Indians.* Edited by Alfonso Ortiz. Vol. 9, Southwest, edited by William Sturtevant. Washington, D.C.: Government Printing Office, 1979.

Simmons, Marc. "History of Pueblo-Spanish Relations to 1821." In *Handbook of North American Indians.* Edited by Alfonso Ortiz. Vol. 9, Southwest, edited by William Sturtevant. Washington, D.C.: Government Printing Office, 1979.

————. "History of Pueblos since 1821." In *Handbook of North American Indians*. Edited by Alfonso Ortiz. Vol. 9, Southwest, edited by William Sturtevant. Washington, D.C.: Government Printing Office, 1979.

Smith, Mrs. White Mountain. "Tom Pavatea." *Desert Magazine* 2 (February 1938):4–6

Stanislawski, Michael B. "The Ethno-Archaeology of Hopi Pottery Making." *Plateau* 42 (summer 1969):27–33.

Stanislawski, Michael B., Ann Hitchcock, and Barbara B. Stanislawski. "Identification Marks on Hopi and Hopi-Tewa Pottery." *Plateau* 48 (spring 1976):46–66.

Stephen, A[lexander] M[cGregor]. "The Navajo." *American Anthropologist* 6 (1893):345–63.

Stevenson, James. "Illustrated Catalog of the Collections Obtained from the Indians of New Mexico and Arizona in 1879." *Bureau of American Ethnology Annual Report* 2 (1880–1881):307–42.

————. "Illustrated Catalog of the Collections Obtained from the Indians of New Mexico and Arizona in 1880." *Bureau of American Ethnology Annual Report* 2 (1880–1881):423–65.

————. "Illustrated Catalog of the Collections Obtained from the Pueblos of Zuni, New Mexico, and Wolpi *[sic]*, Arizona, in 1881" *Bureau of American Ethnology Annual Report* 3 (1881–1882):511–94.

Stevenson, [Matilda Coxe]. "An Arizona School Site." *Lend a Hand* 1 (February 1886):121.

ten Kate, H. F. C. "Frank Hamilton Cushing." *American Anthropologist* 2 (1900):768–71.

Titiev, Mischa. "A Historic Figure Writ Small." *Michigan Alumnus Quarterly Review* 62 (August 1956):325–30.

Utley, Robert M. "The Reservation Trader in Navajo History." *El Palacio* 68 (spring 1961):5–27.

Vandever, Mrs. Minnie. "An Arizona Letter." *Indians' Friends* (September 1890): 4.

Van Valkenburg, Richard. "Tom Keam, Friend of the Moqui." *Desert Magazine* 9 (July 1946):9–12.

Walker, Henry P., ed. "Soldier in the California Column: The Diary of John Teal." *Arizona and the West* 13 (spring 1971):33–82.

Whiting, Alfred W. "Hopi Indian Agriculture: I, Background." *Museum of Northern Arizona Notes* 8 (April 1936):51–53.

Wilson, Thomas. "Anthropology at the Paris Exposition in 1889." *United States National Museum Reports* (1890):641–80.

Winslowe, John R. "Navajo Traders for Many Moons." *True West* (March-April 1969):63–69.

INDEX